The Class of '75

The Class of '75

*Reflections on the Last Quarter of the 20th Century
by Harvard Graduates*

Introduction by
George E. Vaillant

THE NEW PRESS

NEW YORK
LONDON

Compilation © 2003 by The New Press
Introduction © 2003 by George E. Vaillant
"1975" photographs courtesy of Lincoln Studio, Inc. The photographs originally appeared in the yearbook of the Harvard and Radcliffe Class of 1975, published by Harvard Yearbook Publications, Inc.
All rights reserved.
No part of this book may be reproduced, in any form, without written permission from the publisher.

Published in the United States by The New Press, New York, 2003
Distributed by W. W. Norton & Company, Inc., New York

ISBN 1-56584-798-9
CIP available

The New Press was established in 1990 as a not-for-profit alternative to the large, commercial publishing houses currently dominating the book publishing industry. The New Press operates in the public interest rather than for private gain, and is committed to publishing, in innovative ways, works of educational, cultural, and community value that are often deemed insufficiently profitable.

The New Press
38 Greene Street, 4th floor
New York, NY 10013
www.thenewpress.com

In the United Kingdom:
6 Salem Road
London W2 4BU

Book design by Figaro

Printed in the United States of America

10 9 8 7 6 5 4 3 2 1

Introduction

Americans graduating from college in 1975 were sandwiched between two very different generations. Chronologically they were nestled between the moral fervor and liberal ideals of the baby-boomers, who gave them their values, and the self-absorption of the Reagan/Clinton "Me Generation," who provided a climate of unrivaled economic opportunity — a dichotomy exhibited throughout the reflections in this book. The class's years in college, 1971 to 1975, coincided with the resolution of the pitched battles of the 1960s between "Greatest Generation" parents and their "Woodstock Generation" children, with almost every battle decided in favor of the latter's agenda.

Consider:

- In 1971 eighteen-year-olds received the right to vote, and, in the aftermath of the Greenwich Village "Stonewall Riots," the Gay Liberation movement came of age.

- In 1972, the Dow — at 11,000 when this Twenty-fifth Reunion Report first went to press — passed 1,000 for the first time. Thus, the first twenty-five years of paid work for the Class of 1975 coincided with the greatest bull market in the history of America.

- In 1973, the *Roe v. Wade* decision legalized a woman's right to choose, and the last U.S. troops left Vietnam.

- In 1974, Richard Nixon, the man the Woodstock generation loved to hate, was impeached.

- In 1975, Saigon fell, and the Rockefeller Panel formally denounced certain operations of the CIA as illegal.

- Finally, during 1976, the year after they graduated, a parochial but symbolically significant event occurred: The first woman was admitted as a member of the Harvard Club of Boston.

As a member of Harvard's docile and pedestrian Eisenhower-generation Class of 1955, I read with interest the eclectic and adventuresome (to me, anyway) biographies of the Class of 1975 — the last of the baby-boomers, whose adult lives have embraced the last quarter of the twentieth century. Over twenty-five years, they grew up and, for the most part, settled down. But any conformity they display at midlife seems different in kind from my generation's renowned complacency. Where they do end up in traditional careers or stereotypical suburban marriages, these choices seem to be both intentional and informed, incorporating and taking off from the voices of '60s rebellion unknown to me and my peers. Readers must decide for themselves if the experiences of the Harvard Class of 1975 inform their own. And, of course, we must all remember that this book represents a self-selected subset of one class, at one institution, with none of the controls or reporting standards a more scientific study would employ. Yet I believe these reflections provide a fascinating snapshot of a generation that marked the beginning of a sea change in American social history.

Everywhere, the bohemian adolescent freshmen, epitomized in their 1971 photos by long straggly hair, had by 2000 evolved into the sleek, fat-cat look of middle-aged parents of unruly adolescent kittens. As one classmate puts it, "I am bemused at the respectability of my current life in contrast to my offbeat upbringing and confused young adulthood." A former rock-band organizer notes that he has found "a new obsession — golf." One self-described "hippie chick"

evolved into a busy internist after conforming to the rigors of a neu-
rosurgical residency. A man pondering his past writes, "I now spend
more time on the soccer field than at the bridge table. Brahms and
Chopin are better represented in my music library than the Grateful
Dead. My piano gets frequent attention while my guitar gathers dust.
The cupboards now hold porcini mushrooms and truffle oil rather
than Kraft macaroni and cheese." Sometimes, of course, the change
is only skin-deep. As one woman puts it, "Like many Americans, I
reinvented myself to become what I wanted to be. [But] the Catholic
schoolgirl from the Bronx I once was keeps poking out."

On other fronts — notably with respect to changing attitudes about
the role of women in society — the Class of '75's trajectory over the
subsequent decades was one of unmitigated progress. Many 1975
women recall not being fully welcomed by Harvard as freshmen;
then–Radcliffe President Matina Horner had to fight the president of
Harvard, for example, for the right of these women to use the
Harvard athletic facilities. And, surprisingly, the latent sexism that
affected their college years still distorts truth in their Twenty-fifth
Reunion Report, whose introduction states that men outnumbered
women in the class by a ratio of four to one; by my count the ratio
was already down to three to one. This is the class of women, however, who tackled the motherhood/career dilemma head-on for the
first time. While many left promising professional work for a number
of years of pure parenting, at least one articulate woman feels free to
write: "My value system wasn't calibrated for full-time homework
help and lunch-bag packing."

Twenty-five years out of college, the men are more ecstatic about
their marriages than the women. (As sociologist Jesse Bernard cau-
tioned us many years ago, "In every marriage there are two marriages, and his is usually better than hers.") In the 1975 class report,
men are more likely to speak of "a loving wife" while women refer
to "loving families." The 1975 men focus unreservedly on their mar-
ital bliss; the 1975 women are more likely to comment on strengths
and weaknesses, tempering their acknowledgment of loving mar-

riages with comments like "not that it was easy," or noting "tough times and good times." Women speak of "nurturing" their husbands as well as their children, while a not-atypical husband exults in being nurtured: "My greatest joy is without question: my family, my wife (and best friend, seer, advisor)."

Nevertheless, the Harvard husbands in this volume seem kinder and gentler than in past generations. There are still some reports that focus on boastful achievement either of the fathers or of their children. There are still some reports that reveal worldviews that are not yet comfortable that the laws of competition become increasingly less important as one grows toward grandparenthood. But many of the men, and perhaps just as many of the women, speak of their children as Cornelia, the Roman senator's wife, spoke of her children to colleagues who boasted of diamonds and rubies: "These," said Cornelia, and so say many men and women in this report, "are my jewels." As one man writes, "My collegiate aspirations of being a Renaissance man are long forgotten as family and profession require nearly all my attention (coaching, baseball, basketball, attending school functions)."

In terms of careers, I found it hard to distinguish whether the men or the women had achieved more. However, it was very clear that by the time the Class of 1975 were between forty-five and fifty years old, both the men and the women were likely, in one woman's words, to have "stepped off the Fortune 500 escalator." Almost 50% of all those who reported being in finance, business, and commerce were now presidents of their own companies. Some of the companies were pretty small, but with time, class members found it more satisfying to be responsible for their own payrolls than to serve as someone else's better-paid lieutenant.

By the year 2000, contented generativity had taken the place of the thirty-year-old's blind ambition. As one man writes, "We're not rich, trendy or connected, but we're happy." Another man writes, "I have a loving family, a fun job, a home in the most beautiful place on earth, and a daughter who seems destined to exceed her parents in every possible dimension. This must be the definition of happiness." Another summarizes: "At the 10th reunion I was single, living in a high-rise, downtown apartment building and driving an Alfa Romeo GTV 6/2.5. We currently live in an old Victorian home on the North side of Chicago, and I drive a Chevy sedan with a child seat full of crumbs. I am much happier." A classmate notes: "I find myself more interested in helping the kids' school or developing a winning soccer strategy than I do in working on the next business deal."

Some class members are already making the transition from being parental caregivers to grandparental caretakers and keepers of the meaning. (One woman at fifty already had fourteen step-grandchildren!) They are becoming more interested in conserving the world around them than just attending to the progress of their own families. (At age nineteen, class members protested for Greenpeace and the Sierra Club; with advancing maturity they stopped hectoring other people about how to spend their money and began to use their own savings to support land trusts and to conserve forests.)

By the twenty-fifth reunion, a few class members were already chronically physically ill and coming to terms with Erikson's final stage of adult development: integrity — the developmental task that renders old-age infirmities bearable. A victim of Guillain-Barré syndrome reports, "Through meditation on inspirational passages from the saints and scriptures of many faiths, I have come to a sense that it may in this lifetime be possible to deepen my trust in truth while developing a truly loving appreciation of other people's traditions and avatars, and to come to cherish the well-being of others as I learn ever so gradually to detach from my own."

My interest in class reports and in post-collegiate life trajectories goes beyond the purely personal. The year the Class of '75 arrived at college, I had just become director of Harvard's Grant Study of Adult Development — a study of the World War II, Greatest Generation Harvard classes of 1940 through 1944. Originally funded by W. T. Grant, the department store magnate, the study had begun when the men were college sophomores, and it reflected a multidisciplinary effort to understand mental and physical health rather then illness. Since 1940, the men have been studied by biennial questionnaires and occasional interviews. The men's class reports, published every five years, have been scrutinized. Arguably, the Grant Study represents the longest study of adult physical and psychological development in the world.

When the Class of '75 arrived at college in 1971, the Grant Study members had only recently finished celebrating their own twenty-fifth reunions. (Many were uncles and fathers of the Class of 1975.) I am thus in a position to offer up some specific comparisons between the Class of '75 and that of a generation or two earlier. At their twenty-fifth reunion, the Class of 1975 reported more yoga and more home schooling but much less golf and bridge than did the 1940s classes that I had been studying. Unlike the Greatest Generation classes (or my own 1955 class), virtually nobody from 1975 became a psychoanalyst or career military officer. Although marijuana remained illegal, its popularity during this class's college years may have been the reason why, for the first and last time in Harvard history, alcohol abuse was not a significant student health problem. No one from the Class of 1975 reports having worked for the CIA, a common admission on the part of Yale graduates, for example, from the 1950s.

As is clear from their reunion-book pictures, approaching their fifties, members of the Class of 1975 now wear their hair much shorter and wear many more neckties than they ever wore in 1975. On the other hand, looking at my own twenty-fifth-reunion book, I noted that my class (who in 1951 had to wear ties even to breakfast) wore far longer hair at our twenty-fifth reunion (and more neck beads) than we ever wore in 1955. Almost fifty members of the Class of 1975 report supporting themselves with careers in the arts: writing, music, painting, etc. — a higher proportion than a generation earlier. And, of course, many graduates became involved in professions unknown in the 1940s, most notably careers using computers

and the Internet. (The Class of 1975 has at least two retired computer millionaires now "blissfully unemployed." Another classmate
relates, "I joined an obscure public Internet start-up as its general
counsel. E-bay's obscurity didn't last very long.")

Changing secular fashions, especially smoking reduction, exercise
gyms, and seat belts, have left these fifty-year-old graduates healthier than their predecessors. Excluding World War II combat deaths,
10% of the Class of 1940 were dead by their twenty-fifth reunion; so
were 5% of the Class of 1955. Yet only 2% of the men in the Class
of 1975 and 1% of the women had died before their twenty-fifth
reunion (this in spite of the fact that the AIDS epidemic had caught
their generation unawares). Relatively more members of the Class of
1975 have elected to live in Vermont and fewer to live in New York
City than did Harvard graduates two to three decades before.

Compared to students a generation or two before, many more of
the Class of 1975 dropped out of college for at least a year; and,
unfortunately for the accuracy of this introduction, only half of the
Class of 1975 returned their twenty-five-year biographies (previous
Harvard classes had been far more conscientious). Compared to the
average of three children per graduate in the earlier classes, Class of
1975 respondents have not yet quite reproduced themselves; they
have conceived an average of only 1.8 children per class member.
Some of this may be due to women's careers, but some is also due
to improved birth control and changing attitudes toward population
growth. (When my classmates got married, the sale of diaphragms
was still illegal in Massachusetts.)

In 1951, my class had rioted—and been arrested—in order to
elect Pogo (the lovable, if imaginary, swamp possum in Walt Kelly's
comic strip by the same name) president of the United States. Twenty
years later, Harvard undergraduates protested for peace in a real war,
and justice for real minorities. In my class, the men had happily studied in the women's library at Radcliffe, with no thought or concern
about the fact that women were forbidden to study in the men's
library in Harvard Yard. In the Class of 1942, a prescient sophomore

who was concerned with air pollution and contaminated water was viewed as somewhat paranoid and certainly as an outlier. In contrast, many members of the Class of 1975 have been concerned with the environment for all of their adult lives — in either their vocations or their avocations.

This volume of reports reflects other important cultural changes. The adolescent tumult of the older brothers, sisters, and cousins of the Class of 1975 — the college students who had so upset their World War II–veteran fathers by rioting for peace, equality, and loud music — had taught everyone a lesson. By the time the Class of 1975 came of age, their parents were prepared to learn from, instead of battle with, their adolescent children.

The Class of 1975 had already tried in high school the recreational drugs that earlier Harvard classes had not tried until college (and about which the earlier classes demanded college courses). Perhaps it was no accident that by 1975 these same undergraduate courses had evolved into courses on human relationships (for which recreational drugs had once served as such a poor substitute). Perhaps also as a result of the struggles of the previous decade, the Class of 1975 seemed far more interpersonally aware and a more willing-to-hug-each-other generation than my Harvard class or those classes that preceded us. The humanity of the Class of 1975 comes through repeatedly in these biographies.

These class reports also reveal a far less arguable change in American Society — the unshackling of women's careers. While Harvard was still learning with regard to ethnic diversity in 1975, women of that class dramatically illustrate a cultural change in a world that for millennia had wasted the brains of 50% of its population. In the 1980s, I continued to study the growth and development of men for whom a Harvard degree, the GI Bill, and the prosperity of the 1950s had provided every opportunity for growth. However, by then I also had two daughters. What was their adult development going to be like? How wonderful if I could find models for them of achieving women from my parents' generation — an era that, ironically, facilitated careers for women by allowing them to have servants at home. (I knew that my own generation—the inspiration for Betty Friedan's *The Feminine Mystique*—was not going to be much help.) Two potential models had been the mothers (Anne Lindbergh and Barnard dean Millicent Macintosh) of school friends. Each had achieved national reputations while enjoying stable marriages to interesting husbands, and each raised five successful children. Perhaps such women could serve as guides for my generation's daughters, only slightly younger than the Class of 1975.

In 1986, to find such a cohort, my wife and I traveled to Stanford to study as grandmothers the California women whom Lewis Terman had studied as gifted schoolchildren in 1922. These women all had IQs over 140 (tested intelligence well above the modern Harvard mean). In high school the Terman women had been stunning leaders who wished to grow up to be astronomers, physicians, historians, and novelists. They mostly had gone to Stanford and Berkeley, for annual tuition then was still under $100. The tragedy that these women's biographies revealed was that when they were in their late forties, ready for their twenty-fifth reunions, brilliant careers with children were virtually unknown. For example, only thirty gifted women (out of a total of 600 women in Terman's cohort) gained professional achievements comparable to the average achieved by women in the Class of 1975. Collectively, these thirty women gave birth to a total of only seven children (0.2 children per woman). Many of these thirty had remained single or suffered broken marriages. As grandmothers, these women were exciting to interview. None of them blamed society for having given them short shrift. But even in an era that potentially allowed a professional mother to hire housekeepers and nannies, either the careers or the families of these gifted women were stillborn. (Fifty percent of Terman's gifted women had worked full time for most of their lives, but their mean salary—reflecting their job opportunities—was the same as that enjoyed by the inner-city men from Boston whose lives I also studied. The latter men, chosen as controls for Sheldon and

Eleanor Glueck's landmark studies of juvenile delinquency, had mean IQs of 95 and less than eleven grades of education. But they were as well paid as educated women.)

By contrast, most of the women respondents in the Class of 1975 have enjoyed children and distinguished careers. I was thrilled to read biography after biography of women who have had the careers that I had wanted the Terman Study women to have had, careers that I would be proud for my daughters (college classes of 1989 and 1999) to enjoy. Consider what four decades of progress had won. For example, one Terman woman who wished to become a lawyer like her father was told in college that even if she graduated from law school, she would never be allowed to serve as more than a glorified legal assistant. She was probably wise to have listened. In contrast, a law school–bound 1975 Harvard woman reports being advised in college to bag her engagement and focus on her career. Instead, she married in her sophomore year, and is now a partner in a major law firm. Her husband is supportive, and her children have turned out fine.

I don't mean that it has been easy for the women in the Class of 1975 to maintain children, husbands, and careers. Most have had to work longer and harder than their husbands do. Nevertheless, their achievements have been stunning, and their marriages have survived. I have known enough of the class personally to know that their biographies are probably accurate. Their husbands have not only learned to care about parenting but also not infrequently how to help, rather than to sabotage their wives' careers. At least two Class of 1975 men report being contented fulltime househusbands. Others are financially supported by their wives. Still others accepted their role as the "insignificant others" in their wives' brilliant careers. One husband writes that he cooperated by "Holding our children while we listened to their mother [a world class musician] practice the cello."

The acknowledgment of happy marriages comes across more clearly in this report than in the previous twenty-fifth-reunion reports with which I am familiar. One man writes, "Though I must be among the least accomplished of my classmates, I count myself one of the most blessed from my marriage and all that it has brought me." A woman writes, "I firmly believe that the filament of love, duty and friendship that radiate outward from a good marriage, long in place, provide the human ecosystem with an invisible but very precious resilience." One man, twenty-five years after college graduation, writes, "The seminal and best decision I made since graduation was to marry [my wife]. We met when she was in the 8th grade." Another man, married to a Harvard classmate, writes, "I hope that not all happy families are the same. I adore those with whom I share my life."

In these pages one finds a CEO who, as she multitasks while answering her class report, reveals that her husband is running her a bubble bath. Another achieving woman observes that a happy marriage — and the class collectively enjoys a huge number — is something of a status symbol, in the face of the prior dreadful baby-boomer divorce rate. The Class of 1940 had a higher divorce rate than the class of 1975; and their baby-boomer children, marrying during the 1960s, had a higher rate still. In addition, the frequent intraclass 1975 marriages fared far better than the almost-as-frequent Harvard-Radcliffe marriages in my Class of 1955.

The caveat, of course, is that the marriages of the 50% of the class who didn't return their questionnaires may have been less rosy. However, one advantage of studying three Harvard classes in depth for fifty years is that I know a great deal about the lives of men who do not write biographies for their class reports. Such men are less sociable and more disagreeable. They are less practical and live more in fantasy. But, surprisingly, they are not more likely to be depressed or abuse alcohol, and their marriages are only modestly less stable. Nevertheless, the careers and marriages of the women who failed to respond were almost certainly less successful than the ones depicted in this volume.

In addition, the effort that goes into making modern marriages work may be far greater than it was before. For example, one devoted husband commuted from Europe to his two offices, one in Washington, D.C., and one in Australia, so he could spend most of his time with his Harvard wife, who was the U.S. ambassador to the Netherlands. Another devoted Harvard wife elected to retire from her successful banking career in order to follow her husband to London. There she now mows fifteen acres of lawn, makes bread from wheat that she has ground herself, and serves as vice president of the Harvard Club of London.

The class of 1975 and I go way back. In fact, we were freshmen together in 1971: members of the class were the first Harvard undergraduates that I, as a first-year professor playing hooky from the medical school, ever taught. My subject matter was adult development. The aftermath of outrage over the Vietnam War and the killings at Kent State made 1971 life at colleges all across the country tumultuous, particularly for incoming freshman. At Harvard, upperclassmen and women occupied the Harvard administration offices and smashed the windows of Holyoke Health Center. In the basement of the Health Center (where the Grant Study was based) I watched steel bars put up to protect the Harvard telephone exchange from the rebelling students. Later, while still undergraduates, two members of the Class of 1975, now distinguished medical researchers in their own right, helped me write papers on alcohol research. A quarter of a century later, another class member, as a glass-ceiling-smashing editor-in-chief of a major publishing house, accepted my last book on the Grant Study, *Aging Well*, for publication.

I have been reading Harvard twenty-fifth-anniversary class reports from cover to cover since my father's 1922 class report came out in 1947. What strikes me from reading the 1975 biographies is how many of these people I would like to have known and how glad I am that I have known at least a few of them.

George E. Vaillant

Editor's Note

Only class members who gave permission for their reflections and photographs to be included in this volume appear here.

James Bruce Adelson: Since graduation and last Reunion, I've expanded on already established themes. The core is my relationship with Debbie Sheetz (Radcliffe '75), whom I met freshman week, moved in with a month later, married in 1986, and grow with today. Thank you, Harvard, for this single largest contribution to my education!

We have three children: Nathaniel, twelve; Erica, nine; and Jeffrey, four. In parenting, my biggest lesson (not original thinking, I know) is to find pleasure in everyday interactions—conversations while going to school, playing around, driving to soccer games, etc. Our children have grown to where, as parents, you feel the joy and challenge of seeing them blaze off in new directions that you don't know firsthand. The upcoming years will bring more. We've lived in Harvard, Massachusetts, for the last twenty years; children create closer community ties. Right now, we're adding to the house we built in 1983 when we didn't think we'd have children. Home construction crystallizes what's important in your life.

I've spent my entire career in computers, working for several companies that have ranged widely in size, focus, and success. Since 1993, I've been with Lotus (acquired by IBM in 1995), building alliances with other technology companies. Many aspects are stimulating; the biggest professional challenge is believing and seeing that your effort has some positive effect in the world.

I enjoy, albeit less frequently, the same "hobbies" that I'd established by college—hiking, whitewater boating, and skiing. I recently resurrected and attained a goal that I'd set before college—ascent of the Northeast 111, which are 111 peaks in New England and New York over four thousand feet in elevation. At this age, we all pick targets which help us win in our minds, however briefly, the battle against physical and mental aging.

HOME: Harvard, MA **OCCUPATION:** Executive Director, ISV Alliances. Lotus Development (an IBM company) **BIRTHPLACE:** Boston, MA **SECONDARY SCHOOL:** Lincoln-Sudbury Regional High School, Sudbury, MA **YEARS AT COLLEGE:** 1971–75 **DEGREES:** A.B., cum laude, '75; M.S., Massachusetts Inst. of Technology '79 **SPOUSE/PARTNER:** Deborah A. Sheetz, March 1, 1986 (Radcliffe '75) **SPOUSE'S OCCUPATION:** Consultant. BMC Software **CHILDREN:** Nathaniel, 1987; Erica, 1990; Jeffrey, 1995 **HARVARD/RADCLIFFE SIBLINGS:** Lisa Adelson '76; Nancy Adelson Allison, M. Arch. '89

N. Scott Adzick: I am immersed professionally in the field of pediatric surgery. Finished nine years of surgical residency (Massachusetts General Hospital, Boston Children's Hospital) in 1988, followed by seven great years on the faculty at University of California at San Francisco. Moved to Philadelphia four years ago to take the position of surgeon-in-chief at the Children's Hospital of Philadelphia and the C. Everett Koop Professor of Pediatric Surgery at the University of Pennsylvania School of Medicine. My vineyard is the surgical repair of birth defects. I have helped make the fetal surgical repair of life-threatening defects a clinical reality. I enjoy battling with the unsolved problems in pediatric surgery, teaching residents and research fellows, and sometimes making a difference in the youngest patients' lives. To operate and save a child is to save a lifetime. I'll bet that fellow pediatric surgeons and classmates Nick Shorter and Bill Hardin feel the same way.

What is important in my life? Family, health, and work—in that order. Keeping things balanced is a constant challenge. At times I feel like the race car driver Mario Andretti, who said: "If things seem under control, you're just not going fast enough." Sandy and I have been married for seventeen years, and she is an amazing wife, mother, athlete, volunteer, advisor, and my best friend. Our eleven-year-old son will soon beat me in one-on-one basketball and is quite a baseball player. Our family enjoys skiing, traveling, and a yearly summertime trek to Nantucket for rejuvenation.

I am grateful for my Harvard education (seventeen years in the Harvard system has been dubbed "Preparation H"), and the highlight and inspiration were my incredibly talented college, medical school, and residency "classmates" I can't imagine a better life or a luckier guy.

HOME: Haverford, PA OCCUPATION: Pediatric Surgeon. Children's Hospital of Philadelphia BIRTHPLACE: Omaha, NE SECONDARY SCHOOL: Clayton High School, Saint Louis, MO YEARS AT COLLEGE: 1971–75 DEGREES: A.B., cum laude, '75; M.D. '79 SPOUSE/PARTNER: Sandra Ray, June 4, 1983 (Boston Univ. '78) SPOUSE'S OCCUPATION: Pediatric Intensive Care Nurse CHILDREN: Mark Webster, 1988 COLLEGE ACTIVITIES: Basketball; baseball

James Kelly Ahern: Since 1982, I have been living in Ridgefield, Connec-ticut, with my wife, Susy, and our three children. Megan (eighteen) landed very happily at Dartmouth and is a sophomore this year. Jim Jr. (seventeen) is a high school senior and now actively engaged in looking at colleges for next year. He is a very talented guitarist (mostly jazz, blues, and classic rock) and is looking at schools with strong music departments. Katie (fourteen) has just started high school and is giving field hockey a try. Her main extracurricular interests are playing piano and viola. Susy is in the Ph.D. program at Yale for English literature and handed in her dissertation just two weeks ago! Whew! This semester she is teaching two sections of college writing at SUNY, Purchase College as an adjunct professor.

For the past seventeen years, I have been a family physician in our little town. Starting solo, I now have two partners. We really enjoy working together and find practicing family medicine to be fun and rewarding. Work and family take up just about all of my time, though I have enjoyed studying bass guitar over the last two years

HOME: Ridgefield, CT **OCCUPATION:** Physician (family medicine) **BIRTHPLACE:** Libertyville, IL **SECONDARY SCHOOL:** The Hotchkiss School, Lakeville, CT **YEARS AT COLLEGE:** 1971–74 **DEGREES:** A.B., cum laude, '75, ('74); M.D., Univ. of Cincinnati '79 **SPOUSE/PARTNER:** Susan Whitcomb, Dec. 27, 1975 (Wellesley Coll. '75) **SPOUSE'S OCCUPATION:** Adjunct Professor of English Literature. SUNY, Purchase College. **CHILDREN:** Megan, 1980; James Jr., 1982; Caitlin, 1985. **HARVARD/RADCLIFFE SIBLINGS:** Mary Layne Ahern Chlebowski '74 **COLLEGE ACTIVITIES:** Freshman lightweight crew; Hasty Pudding Show, 1973

Thomas Nesbitt Ahlborn: Since June, 1975, I have been blessed with most everything. I have been wonderfully married for nineteen years to Heidi Owen Ahlborn, M.D., who gave up a career in medicine to raise our five very active children.

Following graduation, I spent a memorable year (thanks to Rotary International) at Clare College, Cambridge University, studying history of science. In 1976, I returned to New York City for ten years of medical education and surgical training at the College of Physicians and Surgeons, Columbia University and the Presbyterian Hospital.

I am one of this country's few remaining solo private-practice general surgeons. I enjoy an enviable professional life, i.e., a job caring for people in my community who want to be healthy.

Heidi and I have been supported in our journey by loving families, strong friendships, and a relationship with God and our church.

We have all been granted perfect health (knock wood) and an appreciation for life's frailties.

A lifetime of financial security and the opportunities it provides has come our way. Our family travels frequently in the Unites States and abroad.

We enjoy skiing, golf, ballet, fishing, camping, hiking, Cub Scouts, Brownies, piano, bicycle riding...

My life has been ninety-eight percent hills, two percent valleys.

I hope others have been half as lucky.

HOME: Ridgewood, NJ **OCCUPATION:** Physician **BIRTHPLACE:** Toledo, OH
SECONDARY SCHOOL: New Trier East, Winnetka, IL **YEARS AT COLLEGE:** 1971–75
DEGREES: A.B., magna cum laude, '75; Clare Coll., Cambridge Univ., '76; M.D., Columbia
'80 **SPOUSE/PARTNER:** Heidi Owen, Oct. 18, 1980 (M.D., Columbia '86) **SPOUSE'S
OCCUPATION:** Physician (not currently practicing); Homemaker **CHILDREN:** Andrew,
1983; Katherine, 1985; David, 1988; Scott, 1989; Elizabeth, 1991

William A. Alexander: During the past twenty-five years, my profes-sional life has been a never-ending jazz session. I have been "making it new" every three to five years: medical school, residency training, academic medicine, private practice, and medical management. I have learned that the best manage-ment style is "collective improvisation" and the best leadership style is having the courage to "make it new." During the past twenty-five years my personal life has been a never-ending jam session. It's been about understanding and appreciating life's rhythms. My greatest joy in life is listening to the beat of my personal rhythm section: wife, Alvarita Hanson '75, son, Justin '03, and son, Colin. I love your col-lective rhythm, and I love it when you each solo.

HOME: Atlanta, GA   OCCUPATION: Vice President; Medical Director. CIGNA HealthCare of Georgia   BIRTHPLACE: Nashville, TN   SECONDARY SCHOOL: Virginia Episcopal School, Lynchburg, VA   YEARS AT COLLEGE: 1971–75   DEGREES: A.B., cum laude, '75; M.D., Univ. of Pennsylvania '79   SPOUSE/PARTNER: Avarita L. Hanson, June 14, 1975 (Radcliffe '75) SPOUSE'S OCCUPATION: Self-Employed Attorney (works from home)   CHILDREN: Justin Hanson Alexander, 1981; Colin Hanson Alexander, 1986   HARVARD/RADCLIFFE CHILDREN: Justin Hanson Alexander '03   HARVARD/RADCLIFFE SIBLINGS: Paul G. Alexander '82; M.B.A. '87   COLLEGE ACTIVITIES: Director of jazz department, WHRB, 1972–75; Bureau of Study Counsel, 1971–73; Kuumba Singers, 1972–73; Black Science Students Association, 1971–75; bartender, Harvard Student Agencies, 1972–75

Richard L. Alfred: I entered Harvard in the Class of '74, but graduated in 1975 after a "year off" living in Strasbourg, France. At some point since our graduation, I must have assigned myself to the Class of '75, although I don't remember doing so. The truth is, I consider myself a member of both classes, just as I think of my college years as two distinct halves marked in the middle by my year away.

I have not lived outside the Boston area since graduation and still seem to grav-itate often to Harvard Square. On one of those visits five or six years ago, I was with my two younger children on a beautiful late May afternoon. I found myself on the steps of Matthews South, confronted with the possibility of showing my kids my freshman dorm room. I hadn't been in that room since May 1971, but despite a major renovation of that building, the room felt remarkably unchanged. It was truly a Proustian moment, bringing me back to those days as a freshman, ordering late night take-out from the Hong Kong and staying up most of the night discussing the burning issues of our lives. Things have definitely changed.

I went to Harvard Law School directly from college and graduated in 1978. A week later, I married Lynn Goldsmith, who I had met at a legal services office in Boston while taking a clinical course my second year. Lynn is also a lawyer, but has been at home with our children since our youngest son was born in 1987. We lived in Jamaica Plain and spent most weekends at the two-hundred-year-old farm house that we bought in Wolfeboro, New Hampshire. Ultimately, the burdens of working on that house and tending to our oversized vegetable garden caused us to sell the farm house in 1984. We moved to our current address in Newton a few years later.

We have three boys, Dan, Robbie, and Ben, all of whom are now teenagers. Dan is a freshman at Johns Hopkins; Robbie is a high school junior; and Ben, a seventh grader. Over the years, we have enjoyed many summer vacations hiking in national parks throughout the country and at Lynn's family's beach cottage in Nags Head, North Carolina.

On the professional front, after graduation from law school, I went to work as an associate at a small labor law firm in Boston representing unions. The experience afforded me an opportunity to appear in court regularly and to try arbitration cases all over New England. After three years, though, I decided to move to Hill & Barlow, a mid-sized corporate firm in Boston. Initially, I spent my time working on commercial litigation matters in the firm's trial department. Eventually, I was drawn back to employment and labor cases, albeit on the corporate side. In 1985, I became a partner, and, since 1990, I have chaired the firm's employment and labor law practice. In addition to my "day job," I have been a member of the Newton School Committee since 1992, but after three terms have decided not to run for reelection.

Prioritizing the various aspects of my life has very much been on my mind, especially since last fall (1998) when my father died after a long and difficult illness. Remembering how young and vital he was when I started college and comparing those memories to my own experience this fall as I took my oldest son to school has helped me to focus on the things that are most important in my life. I see this as my challenge for the next five years and beyond, as my other two children prepare to leave home.

HOME: Newton, MA   **OCCUPATION:** Attorney; Member, Hill & Barlow PC (corporate law firm)   **BIRTHPLACE:** Boston, MA   **SECONDARY SCHOOL:** Belmont High School, Belmont, MA   **YEARS AT COLLEGE:** 1970–75   **DEGREES:** A.B., magna cum laude, '75; J.D., '78   **SPOUSE/PARTNER:** Lynn D. Goldsmith, May 28, 1978 (Hollins Coll. '68; J.D., Suffolk Univ. '77; L.L.M., Boston Univ. '94)   **SPOUSE'S OCCUPATION:** Attorney (currently at home with children)   **CHILDREN:** Daniel G., 1981; Robbie T., 1983; Benjamin S., 1987

Frederick Elkins Allen: I worked at *New York* magazine from 1975 to 1983 and left as a senior editor. I joined *American Heritage* as a senior editor in 1985 and have been its managing editor since 1990. I have also been the editor of the quarterly *American Heritage of Invention & Technology* since its founding in 1985. Luck has smiled on me in these and many things, especially my marriage to Erica De Mane.

HOME: New York, NY   **OCCUPATION:** Managing Editor, *American Heritage* magazine; Editor, *American Heritage of Invention & Technology* magazine   **BIRTHPLACE:** New York, NY   **SECONDARY SCHOOL:** Buxton School, Williamstown, MA   **YEARS AT COLLEGE:** 1971–75   **DEGREES:** A.B., magna cum laude, '75   **SPOUSE/PARTNER:** Erica De Mane, June 11, 1988   **SPOUSE'S OCCUPATION:** Author; Chef **HARVARD/RADCLIFFE SIBLINGS:** Henry C. Allen '80   **COLLEGE ACTIVITIES:** Harvard-Radcliffe Orchestra, 1971–75

David Linzee Amory: In our Twentieth Reunion Report, I wrote, "Each day of my life with Sukie, Linzee and John is the best ever." Linzee was eleven years old, John was eight; today, five years later, sixteen and thirteen. Oh my.

I hope not all happy families are the same. I adore those with whom I share my life: Sukie — designer, writer, poet, mother, and my partner in love, life, and work; Linzee — daughter delving into design, sailing, ice hockey, and community service; John — son, artist, drummer, and NHL hopeful; and James the dog, tenor, who loves to walk, wag, whine, sing, and sleep.

All of us will be under one roof for less than two more years, and in trying to make the most of what time we do have, the center of my life is family. I think often about career and accelerating the growth of our architectural practice as "empty nesters," when the kids are out on their own. To their dismay, Sukie and I *want* to spend time with them — meals daily, on the water and the ice, in the classroom (parents' day only), and traveling. "Better to travel well than to arrive."

I spent most of 1976 in youth hostels or under trees, traveling and working in England, Europe, and Egypt. Sukie and I married in 1978 so that she could put me through design school. After a good three years at the Graduate School of Design, Chicago was our home in the eighties, where I cut my teeth as a young architect while Sukie earned her M.B.A. at Northwestern, and, more excitingly, as a new dad with Sukie as the mom. Chicago — what a magnificent city for living and design, I miss it. Our journey back east ten years ago to a new home, new school, new workplace (our own), new friends (and old), and new life has been wonderful, with room for growth and adventure.

Family travel, with Sukie, Linzee, and John, (James stays at his own flea-bag hotel) and most recently with Sukie's parents, has taken us on memorable trips to Nova Scotia and to the gardens, buildings, and never-ending sights and sounds of England, Italy, and France. Challenging at times, but always fresh, often beautiful, and well worth the effort. One day Linzee, thirteen at the time, and John were walking a few steps ahead while Sukie and I were making plans to see just one more church before supper. Linzee quipped to John, "There's a word I'm getting a little sick of hearing—duomo." Oh, my.

HOME: Brookline, MA   **OCCUPATION:** Architect. Amory Architects   **BIRTHPLACE:** Norfolk, VA   **SECONDARY SCHOOL:** Noble & Greenough School, Dedham, MA   **YEARS AT COLLEGE:** 1971–75   **DEGREES:** A.B., cum laude, '75; M.Arch., '80   **SPOUSE/PARTNER:** Susan Shields Taylor (Radcliffe '75)   **SPOUSE'S OCCUPATION:** Business Partner. Amory Architects   **CHILDREN:** Linzee Page, 1983; John Haile, 1986   **COLLEGE ACTIVITIES:** Freshman lightweight crew; Hasty Pudding Theatricals; Drama Club; Lowell House intramural hockey, baseball and crew

---

Susan Shields Taylor Amory: I knew that someday I'd blush to reread my submission to the last Class Report, and now that day has come. Rose-covered cottage? I sound like the worst sort of Martha Stewart acolyte. And yet—it was true then and is true today. I am still content in this small garden, which now holds even more scented, bee-struck roses among a tumble of lavender, perennials and boxwood. You can see an earlier incarnation of my garden on a Smithsonian Website: www.siris.si.edu under archives and manuscripts, archives of American gardens, brooklinema. I am no closer to transforming this passion into a profession. Recently I deflected a compliment on the design for my parents' Virginia garden with the self-deprecating comment, "Well, I'm not really a designer..." My daughter fixed me with a skeptical eye and said, "You have a real self-image problem, Mom." Out of the mouths of babes.

David and I are still married, still work together, still having fun. I can only describe my wonderful life with him in words that will make me blush to reread in the next five years, so I will not attempt it here. Our architecture practice is small but thriving, with a mix of residential, commercial, and institutional work: We recently completed SRO housing for homeless veterans in Roxbury and the new Harvard University Events and Information Center—check it out in Holyoke Center, no longer the dank, piss-soaked wind tunnel it was when we were undergraduates.

We live in the same house but it feels smaller now that we have two adult-sized children in it. Linzee is sixteen; John is thirteen. Both still play hockey with happy disregard for life and limb. Both have David's ease on the water. In July, Linzee sailed as a student crew member on the tall ship H.M.S. *Rose*, from Boston to Nova Scotia and back. Her watch was twelve to four, morning and night, and she spent part of every day in among the topsails. Both Linzee and John rig and sail our skiff, "Zephyr," in the bay where their father grew up sailing. This is just one of many ways that their confidence and self-sufficiency astounds me daily.

My father always held that we should shake up our lives every five to ten years, a principle that he followed throughout his own life with enthusiasm, while we, his family, exhilarated and breathless, flew along on his coattails. As I review my life over the last five years, all the changes seem gentle and incremental, save one: My incomparable father died last month at sixty-seven, lost to the inexorable and swift depredations of Lou Gehrig's disease—a last change that I could happily forego. But the confusion of the last six months held small mercies—an unforgettable journey with my parents, David, Linzee, John, and my nephew, from Paris, through Provence to the Cinque Terra on the Ligurian Sea, to Rome; reading to him during his last days at home before he died in the teeth of Hurricane Floyd. I am left with perhaps his greatest gift to me—a daily example of living, not for the moment, but *in* the moment, with attention, grace, and gratitude for what I still know, five years after the last Class Report, to be my great luck in life and love.

HOME: Brookline, MA   **OCCUPATION:** Business Partner. Amory Architects
BIRTHPLACE: Norfolk, VA   **SECONDARY SCHOOL:** Kenwood School, Chicago, IL
YEARS AT COLLEGE: 1971–75   **DEGREES:** A.B., magna cum laude, '75; M.M., Northwestern Univ. '82   **SPOUSE/PARTNER:** David Linzee Amory, Sept. 9, 1978 (Harvard '75)   **SPOUSE'S OCCUPATION:** Principal Architect. Amory Architects   **CHILDREN:** Linzee Page, 1983; John Haile, 1986   **COLLEGE ACTIVITIES:** Class marshal '75

Carl E. Anderson: After graduation from Harvard, I spent eight months traveling throughout Asia. I completed an M.A. in psychology and an M.D. at Cornell. I pursued postgraduate training in child and adolescent psychiatry at Duke (where I was president of the Harvard Club of the Research Triangle) and Columbia.

Currently, I live in New York City, in Brooklyn Heights. I have a practice in Manhattan and White Plains. A major professional interest is helping people to improve their relationships with family, friends, and their community. I'm also helping people to discover what is important for them in their lives, helping them to achieve their goals and dreams.

An exciting new venture is an Internet business that I've started, in e-commerce. I'm helping people to make money through their own Web-based businesses. I have a related marketing business, which is growing rapidly in Europe and Asia.

I've been blessed with close relationships including my companion, Marianne, who is a child psychologist and partner in my practice, and also my family and friends.

My interests include meeting new people, participating in cultural events in New York, investing, and traveling (throughout Europe, Asia, and the South Pacific). I've been a member of the Harvard Club of New York City and the Lotos Club.

I have an interest in politics, especially in domestic policy relating to children and families. I've served as a policy advisor on a local and state level and plan, at some time, to run for political office.

I was co-producer of an off-off-Broadway musical, *Love Hurts*. I plan to do further work with theater and film production and also some creative writing for theater, concerning family relationships.

HOME: Brooklyn, NY **OCCUPATION:** Child and Adolescent Psychiatrist **BIRTHPLACE:** Minneapolis, MN **SECONDARY SCHOOL:** Alexander Ramsey High School **YEARS AT COLLEGE:** 1971–75 **DEGREES:** A.B., cum laude, '75 **COLLEGE ACTIVITIES:** Cellist, Harvard-Radcliffe Orchestra; treasurer, Adams House Committee; editor, *Adams House Newsletter;* student chairman, Adams House Humanities Tutor Selection Committee; Outing Club

Dale Lynn Anderson: How do you sum up twenty-five years? In that time, I've enjoyed some acute pleasures—pernil, pesto, and bistilla; the family at Noche Buena; Winston, Armik, Feinstein, Mozart, Bach, early music, and jazz; Henry Wiggins, Daniel Martin, Austen, and Shakespeare; baseball and hoops; birding; Lincoln and Jackie Robinson; Sturbridge and Ellis Island; and views of Boston in the sun, Fenway at night, the Delaware in mist, and Monument Valley in color. I've found my vocation in my work and my calling in my family.

In 1976 I married Mercedes Padrino, and we've been happy together ever since. Bless her, she has encouraged, cajoled, pushed, and cuddled me. We have two children—Daniel in 1983 and Charlie in 1987—who are interesting, funny, nice, thoughtful, and a handful. We love them, and we like them.

Senior year, I had no idea what I'd do for a living. Just before graduation, I got a job in publishing and have been doing it ever since. I worked for three small publishers, two in Boston and one in Princeton. I learned a tremendous amount, doing almost every editorial and production task possible. In 1996 I decided to forsake meetings, management headaches, and a regular paycheck. I'm now a full-time freelance writer and editor specializing in history. Mercy freelances too. Surrounded by our books, we spend the day pecking away at our computers, exchanging gossip, factoids, and occasional gripes. It's like studying together, but better—people actually pay us to read and write!

Beyond doing our best to stimulate the economy, we've not addressed big issues in any public way. Instead, we've focused on teaching the kids important values: work hard; care for those you love; respect people who respect others; show humility; keep laughing; and savor the precious and delectable variety of life.

HOME: Newtown, PA **OCCUPATION:** Freelance Writer; Editor **BIRTHPLACE:** Detroit, MI **SECONDARY SCHOOL:** Denby High School, Detroit, MI **YEARS AT COLLEGE:** 1971–75 **DEGREES:** A.B., magna cum laude, '75 **SPOUSE/PARTNER:** Mercedes Barbara Padrino, July 24, 1976 (Radcliffe '75) **SPOUSE'S OCCUPATION:** Freelance Writer; Translator; Editor **CHILDREN:** Daniel Sebastian, 1983; Charles Altomare, 1987 **COLLEGE ACTIVITIES:** Foosball and pinball

Samuel Mather Anderson: Reading through the Twentieth Anniversary Report in 1995, I was struck variously by classmates' wit, honesty, humor, achievement, and struggle. Several individuals whom I barely knew were particularly moving. I wanted to reach out, but neither wrote nor called: procrastination and timidity.

Looking back at myself five years ago, I now feel more weary, yet still fortunate and optimistic. The most important personal blessings are those I derive from my twenty-two-year marriage to a bright, beautiful, thoroughly honest, and endlessly loving woman, and from my twelve-year-old son, who remains full of wonder and promise and goodness. The lines to my graciously aging mother and gentle late father grow even more distinct and precious.

I work very hard at my architectural practice to create enlivening, well-built places and to forge positive working relationships. The most rewarding projects to date have been at the Harvard Art Museums and the Morgan Library.

I send well wishes to you all.

HOME: Leonia, NJ **OCCUPATION:** Architect **BIRTHPLACE:** Oberlin, OH
SECONDARY SCHOOL: Western Reserve Academy, Hudson, OH **YEARS AT COLLEGE:** 1971–75 **DEGREES:** A.B., cum laude, '75; B.Arch., The Cooper Union '82
SPOUSE/PARTNER: Leslie Ayvazian, Nov. 26, 1977 (Univ. of Vermont '70) **SPOUSE'S OCCUPATION:** Playwright; Actress **CHILDREN:** Ivan Stone, 1986
HARVARD/RADCLIFFE SIBLINGS: Philip A. Anderson '70 **COLLEGE ACTIVITIES:** Varsity fencing, 1971–75; Freshman Task Force, 1972–74, chair, 1973–75

Stephen D. Anderson: Aside from my four years at Harvard, and last two years of high school (upstate New York), I've always been on the West Coast: grew up in Berkeley, California, attended grad school (USC) in Los Angeles, and have lived in the Seattle area since 1982. Spent eighteen months as a field biologist in Monteverde, Costa Rica—may retire to that charming country someday. For the past eleven years I've worked with a group of scientists doing basic research in the esoteric field of glycolipid antigens in cell membranes, as related to cellular interactions and cancer development. Have also edited many books on medical topics for a Seattle-based publishing company. My main hobby while in North House was piano playing (pop tunes and standards), and I still enjoy this, but the favorite these days is recreational volleyball. A constant source of joy and amazement is the development of my two sons into talented and distinct personalities. Both are accomplished piano and soccer players. The fifteen-year-old, now starting tenth grade, is 6'4" and the tallest person on either side of his family. We take frequent summer excursions to California. Any classmates passing through Bothell or Seattle are welcome to contact me.

HOME: Bothell, WA   **OCCUPATION:** Scientific Administrator; Editor. Pacific Northwest Research Institute (basic scientific research)   **BIRTHPLACE:** San Francisco, CA
SECONDARY SCHOOL: Cortland Senior High School, Cortland, NY   **YEARS AT COLLEGE:** 1971–75   **DEGREES:** A.B., cum laude, '75; Ph.D., Univ. of Southern California '82   **SPOUSE/PARTNER:** Laurel Jean Wallis, 1982; divorced, 1993 (Western Washington Univ.)   **CHILDREN:** Matthew Wallis Anderson, 1984; Kenneth Galen Anderson, 1986
COLLEGE ACTIVITIES: Freshman crew, 1971

Bernard Raymond Bach, Jr.: No material possessions or professional accolades could surpass the "success" in my personal life. Happily married since 1982 (to the same woman), and blessed with two healthy, beautiful, outgoing, athletic, and bright children, my life is well balanced. My "spare" time is shared with the family. David, fifteen, a high school freshman, and Laura, twelve, keep our family active with their athletic and academic activities. My collegiate aspirations of being a "Renaissance" man are long forgotten—as family and profession require nearly all of my attention (coaching baseball and basketball, attending school functions, etc.). Professionally, my practice is devoted to athletic injuries and I care predominantly for injuries of the knee and shoulder. I am clinically extremely busy but have balanced my professional career with educational and research efforts which have culminated in nearly two hundred publications. Personally, my intercollegiate football injuries have precluded active physical exercise (other than work) but I have developed a passion for fly-fishing. Since our Twentieth Anniversary Report, I have taken up gardening. We have a wonderful English perennial garden. We continue to enjoy collecting antiques, "dude" ranching in Montana, and white-water rafting. The T. B. Quigley Sports Medicine Society (Harvard athletes who are orthopaedic surgeons) keeps me in touch with the College, friends, and indirectly with Cambridge. I am forever grateful to the College for taking a chance with a midwestern jock from a small public high school—I think the investment was a good one.

HOME: River Forest, IL   OCCUPATION: Orthopaedic Surgeon (sports medicine). Midwest Orthopedics   BIRTHPLACE: Ann Arbor, MI   SECONDARY SCHOOL: Northville High School, Northville, MI   YEARS AT COLLEGE: 1971–75   DEGREES: A.B., cum laude, '75; M.D., Univ. of Cincinnati '79   SPOUSE/PARTNER: Elizabeth Ingle, May 8, 1982 (Vanderbilt Univ. '75)   SPOUSE'S OCCUPATION: Homemaker   CHILDREN: David Russel, 1984; Laura Elizabeth, 1987   COLLEGE ACTIVITIES: Freshman intercollegiate football and baseball, 1971–72; varsity football and baseball, 1973–74; class marshal, 1975

Lorenzo Rafael Balderamma: Since 1991 our family has been living in Redlands, California, a town known locally for its Victorian homes and for its elegant public buildings and parks. Redlands is also known for a small private college by the same name. We have enjoyed both the social and cultural events of "town and gown." We are also active at Sacred Heart, our parish church, where we have met people of good will of all ages, including those, like ourselves, who are raising their families.

My wife, Ann, has previously practiced nursing at Downey Community Hospital, specializing in non-invasive cardiovascular testing. Since the birth of our first daughter in 1989, she has been a full-time homemaker.

Our four daughters provide us with much joy and activity. Elizabeth Rose, age ten, and Jackie, age nine, are being educated at the public elementary school; Katherine, age six, is currently being home-schooled. All three older girls are active in Brownies, soccer and music lessons. Our one-year-old, Mary, is learning to talk and can make sounds with the harmonica. A parakeet named Pal wakes us in the morning with his singing, and a beagle named Boston, protects us from things that go bump in the night.

Since graduation from law school, I have been a prosecutor for the San Bernardino County District Attorney's Office. For over seventeen years I have enjoyed a great variety of assignments, including: municipal and superior courts, juvenile court, child support, worker's compensation fraud, and crimes against children. I have also worked in various locales in the desert, mountain, and valley divisions of America's largest county including places with names like Twenty Nine Palms, Needles, Big Bear, Twin Peaks, and Rancho Cucamonga.

I have not seen Harvard since 1981, but I have tried to keep in touch with a few classmates, most notably, Kevin McCarthy, and Mark Bransdorfer, and their families. I have been there in spirit, however, by trying to follow the Red Sox, the Celtics, and the Harvard football team. Over the years our family has put on a number of "college football parties" in the fall. Amidst a great deal of college music, pennants, programs, helmets, and other memorabilia, I have tried to inspire that college spirit that I enjoyed so much at Harvard. Everyone, including a Yale friend, must give a cheer or sing a school song while wearing their school colors. While I am also a Roman Catholic and a devout Subway Alumnus of Notre Dame, Harvard does not take a back seat to any school, as my daughters and I sing for the assemblage "Ten Thousand Men of Harvard" and "Harvardiana."

In my everyday life and work, I believe that Harvard has had as much influence on me as it has had on the Adamses, Roosevelts, and Kennedys. I believe it has broadened my interests in life, as well as my tolerance and appreciation for people of all stations and walks of life. Just as my religion tells me that there are many mansions in my Father's house, so Harvard has taught me that *veritas,* the truth, is found in many books and people.

We look forward to seeing old friends and making new ones at our Reunion. May God bless you all.

HOME: Redlands, CA   **OCCUPATION:** Prosecutor; Deputy District Attorney. San Bernardino County District Attorney   **BIRTHPLACE:** Los Angeles, CA   **SECONDARY SCHOOL:** Servite High School, Anaheim, CA   **YEARS AT COLLEGE:** 1971–75 **DEGREES:** A.B., cum laude, '75; J.D., Western State Univ., '81   **SPOUSE/PARTNER:** Ann Elizabeth Higson, July 1988 (Mount Saint Mary's Coll. '79)   **SPOUSE'S OCCUPATION:** Homemaker (formerly a registered nurse)   **CHILDREN:** Elizabeth Rose, 1989; Jacqueline Theresa, 1990; Katherine Ann, 1993; Mary Victoria Frances, 1998   **COLLEGE ACTIVITIES:** D.U. Club

---

Ralph James Bansiak: Marrying my wife Ellen was the highlight of these past twenty-five years. We have been blessed with a loving relationship and warm, supportive families. Our two sons have kept us focused on what's important in life. As boys, they keep us busy with energetic sports and other activities.

I celebrated my eighteenth anniversary at Arthur Andersen LLP in September 1999. I joined the company as a programmer in 1981 and have worked in systems design, project planning, and customer relations. In 1994, I opened up our customer service help desk and network operations center in Singapore. My wife and boys were able to join me there that summer. That was a wonderful adventure for the four of us, exploring a new country, learning the culture, and hiking with the monkeys on Bukit Timah.

HOME: Palatine, IL   **OCCUPATION:** Customer Service Manager. Arthur Andersen LLP **BIRTHPLACE:** Toledo, OH   **SECONDARY SCHOOL:** Central Catholic High School, Fort Wayne, IN   **YEARS AT COLLEGE:** 1971–75   **DEGREES:** A.B., cum laude, '75; M.A.T., Univ. of Chicago '76; M.Ed., Loyola Univ., '80   **SPOUSE/PARTNER:** Ellen F., June 9, 1979 (Univ. of Notre Dame '76)   **SPOUSE'S OCCUPATION:** Manager (information systems) **CHILDREN:** Michael James, 1987; Thomas Andrew, 1989   **COLLEGE ACTIVITIES:** Ran the Boston Marathon and finished (!); editor, *Leverett House Newsletter;* intramural crew team

William Henry Barrett: Family news: Elizabeth got her B.A. from Rochester in 1998 and now resettles refugees — important and satisfying work — inspired perhaps by her alma mater's motto ("meliora"). Emily is a high school speech and drama star (runner-up in the 1999 state competition). Barbara delights in teaching adults English as a second language. Me? Same old gig. We've traveled some, most memorably for three weeks in Greece and Turkey visiting Christian sites. (Place I most want to see again: Istanbul.) Scouting retirement properties near the Outer Banks as we did last fall "gets me excited, leaves me feelin' confused." (Anyone other than Zube know what song that's from?)

Faith update: We're happily immersed in church work. Barb conducts new member seminars and I'm helping select our next senior pastor — a formidable but exhilarating undertaking. The weekly forum in which I've been debating spiritual issues with men from our former church lives on, now in its nineteenth year. Why did it take me so long to realize that "gospel truth" is more than just a turn of phrase? All that remains is learning how to live what Jesus teaches and how to avoid the obstacles Satan and his staff deliberately place in my path, hoping to cause my downfall. (See Matthew 22:37-40 and 54 F.R.D. 282.) All prayers and suggestions are welcome.

Finally, a word of thanks for the lasting inspirations supplied by faculty members J. B. Jackson, Donald Fleming, Robert Mann, and Tim O'Brien. Thanks also to the oarsmen (and women!) instrumental in creating some memorable and transforming moments — with my frosh boat on the Housatonic the evening before our final race, perfectly balanced at last; with Mather's coed intramural boat, finishing the Head of the Charles in near-darkness, spent but content. Cheers all!

HOME: Olympia Fields, IL   **OCCUPATION:** Partner. Fox and Grove, Chartered (law firm)
BIRTHPLACE: Boston, MA   **SECONDARY SCHOOL:** Germantown Academy, Fort Washington, PA   **YEARS AT COLLEGE:** 1971–75   **DEGREES:** A.B., cum laude, '75; J.D., Loyola Univ. '80   **SPOUSE/PARTNER:** Barbara Anne, Dec. 31, 1981 and May 22, 1982 (North Central Coll. '66)   **SPOUSE'S OCCUPATION:** ESL Instructor. Travelers and Immigrants Aid   **CHILDREN:** Elizabeth Anne, 1976; Emily Holland, 1984   **COLLEGE ACTIVITIES:** Freshman lightweight crew, 1971–72; Mather House crew, 1972–75; Republican Club, 1972–75

Alice Barton: I remember so clearly going to my father's Twenty-fifth Harvard Reunion (Class of '48), and it is daunting, to say the least, to realize I am approaching my own. It has been a wild ride. After graduating, I took a job at Westover School, a girl's boarding school in Middlebury, Connecticut, teaching art history, coaching soccer, and being a dormitory counselor. My first annual salary was a munificent three thousand dollars! It felt great to use all those years of studying to share something with others, and I had the sixties-type notion that if young people were exposed to beauty, it would also make them value the true and the good. During my time at Westover, my future husband, then ex-husband, came down to join me, and we were married in 1977.

After a few years of teaching high school, I felt the yen to pursue my Ph.D. in art history, and was just about to embark on that when I got pregnant with my daughter, Lara. Due to complications early in the pregnancy, I gave up my plans to study and, for the first time in my life, just stopped, prepared for her birth, read Tolstoy and, yes, Pasternak. I am now very grateful that I was shoved off the academic path for a time, as it was a great privilege to be able to stay home and care for my lovely daughter, born in March 1979, and then my son, Seth, born in April 1981. The experience of caring for my children night and day totally changed my priorities, and it was during those years that I first thought about becoming a nurse-midwife. I had appreciated so much the skill and compassion of those who attended the births of my children.

However, in my circuitous way, I started nursing school part-time, realized I came from a different planet from my fellow students, and decided maybe I should take a stab at medical school. I had not taken math or science even in high school, being too much of a hippie chick at the time, and I slid through Harvard with courses barely resembling science. So I had to start by taking algebra and trigonometry. Then my youngest son, Peter, was born in November 1985, just at the time I was separating from my husband. There were some grim years, while I got divorced, reestablished a home for my children, then decided again to try for medical school.

I went to New York Medical College from 1988–1992, one of the few medical schools within commuting distance of my children's school that would accept an aging single mother of three. I actually flourished in medical school, remembering the factors in the clotting cascade by my children's ages! After that, I must have had a little lapse in judgment, and entered a neurosurgery residency. I lasted three years, but it was quite abusive, and I finally decided it wasn't worth the price of never seeing my children awake. I finished my training in internal medicine in 1997, and am now taking care of HIV-infected patients, mostly women, at the Cornell Center for Special Studies, teaching when I can as an instructor at the Cornell Medical School.

My daughter is now flourishing at Wesleyan, and Seth is just applying to colleges (Yale! Brown! — not interested in Harvard because he wants to do a lot of art and music). Peter is just finishing eighth grade. So, we have muddled through, and I am very grateful for the opportunity to use every aspect of my past education and experience in an incredibly demanding and fulfilling job.

HOME: South Nyack, NY   **OCCUPATION:** Instructor in Medicine; Attending Physician. Cornell Medical School   **BIRTHPLACE:** West Longbranch, NJ   **SECONDARY SCHOOL:** Lexington High School, Lexington, MA   **YEARS AT COLLEGE:** 1973–75   **DEGREES:** A.B., cum laude, '75; M.D., New York Medical Coll. '92   **CHILDREN:** Lara H. Wulsin, 1979; Seth Tobias Wulsin, 1981; Peter A. Wulsin, 1985   **HARVARD/RADCLIFFE SIBLINGS:** Margaret Barton '74; Fred Barton '80; Susan Barton '82; Bill Barton '85; Allen Barton '90

Ronald C. Barusch: As some of you know, in the summer of 1999, we returned from our three years of living in Sydney, Australia. We left Virginia with three young children and returned with two teenagers (and an eight-year-old who thinks she should be a teenager!).

After all these years, I still enjoy the practice of law and "doing deals" as a mergers and acquisitions and finance lawyer. The opportunity to work in a new environment was welcome and I return to another challenging project; I am developing a technology practice in northern Virginia and the Washington metropolitan area.

I enjoy my family more than ever. The cross-the-globe moves have been hardest on Cynthia as it seems all the work fell on her no matter what its nature. Now we are all happy to be back in our home and the children are particularly pleased not to have to wear school uniforms. As for Cynthia and me, although we loved Australia and the people, we find it relaxing and comforting to be back in a familiar environment, even if we do have hurricanes.

I look forward to seeing old friends. And as I age, I hope that the time before seeing them next will not add up to twenty-five years. I also hope that I don't look nearly as old as the people who came to their Twenty-fifth Reunion when I lived in Mather House!

HOME: Arlington, VA   **OCCUPATION:** Lawyer; Partner. Skadden, Arps, Slate, Meagher & Flom LLP (law firm)   **BIRTHPLACE:** Oakland, CA   **SECONDARY SCHOOL:** John F. Kennedy High School, Richmond, CA   **YEARS AT COLLEGE:** 1971–74   **DEGREES:** A.B., magna cum laude, '75 ('74); J.D. '78; M.P.P. '78   **SPOUSE/PARTNER:** Cynthia J. Dahlin, May 28, 1977 (Wellesley Coll. '77; M.P.P., Harvard '79)   **CHILDREN:** Margaret C. D., 1985; Christopher C. B., 1986; Julia R. B., 1991   **HARVARD/RADCLIFFE SIBLINGS:** Lawrence R. Barusch, '71; J.D. '75

Rebecca Bascom: The postcard announcing that we stand to have the smallest Twenty-fifth Report in Harvard's history led me to realize that my reticence to summarize twenty-five years in three hundred words is shared. But since I'm curious to read of your lives, it's only fair for me to share some of mine. In the first five years post A.B., I bicycled across the country, found that my first love would not last, felt miserable, stitched a quilt, ran a marathon, sowed some oats, listened with disbelief to someone who told me I'd like research, graduated from medical school, and moved to Baltimore to begin my internship. The next five years I earned my professional stripes, fell in love, became terrified of that fact, gradually settled down, got married, and discovered the deep joy of connectedness.

The next terror was the realization that I wanted to do academic medicine, and wanted to understand why some people couldn't stand common exposures (perfume, tobacco smoke, etc). Back then, I was asked if I'd like to become an expert, and I burst into tears as *yes* and *no* collided in my brain.

As I realized the third of my heart's desires, with the birth of our daughter Anne and son Tom, I finally acknowledged that my mother was not responsible for my (un)happiness (pretty grown up for thirty-five, don't you think?).

These days, I must be in the generative phase. I take great pleasure in asking people (students, fellows, junior faculty, respiratory therapists, colleagues) what "floats their boat" and then in trying to find a place in our organization that lets them do what they love to do and are good at as much as possible. My love of the "big picture" helps me be brilliantly system-minded when I'm not impossibly obtuse. It certainly has not helped me to maintain a neat office.

These days my urges are less urgent. Yoga tapes, leotards, Walkmans, and treadmills attest to the urge to tone my spreading, softening flesh. Herb's running me a bubble bath, calling down to me to finish this report. Our children are watching Friday night TV shows, and we're collectively ignoring the fact that they have not practiced their instruments. My grandmother told me, when I was in college, that the three most important things in life were friends, family, and faith. Those and the fourth f— that her generation was too genteel to discuss.

At Harvard, I walked out of Memorial Chapel at the urging of Mary Daley, who said that there was no place for women in the modern church. In medical school, Fran Storrs counseled a less angry path—saying that to make friends with men would give me a better shot at sharing power. At this twenty-five-year mark, I agree with Fran, but I'm pleased to report that when we say grace before dinner—"God is great, God is good,..." we end more often than not with "A-women."

HOME: Hummelstown, PA   **OCCUPATION:** Professor of Medicine; Chief of Pulmonary, Allergy, and Critical Care Medicine. Penn State College of Medicine   **BIRTHPLACE:** Chicago, IL   **SECONDARY SCHOOL:** South Eugene High School, Eugene, OR   **YEARS AT COLLEGE:** 1971–75 **DEGREES:** A.B., cum laude, '75; M.D., Oregon Health Sciences Univ. '79; M.P.H., Johns Hopkins Univ. '85   **SPOUSE/PARTNER:** T. Herbert Dimmock 3d, Aug. 4, 1983 (Davidson Coll. '74)   **SPOUSE'S OCCUPATION:** Music Director. Handel Choir of Baltimore   **CHILDREN:** Anne Elizabeth Fenton, 1988; Thomas Herbert 4th, 1989 **COLLEGE ACTIVITIES:** American Field Service; lightweight crew, fall 1974; Sweetbriar Junior Year Abroad, Paris, 1973–74; Jordan K cooperative; Harvard Band, 1971–73

Prudence Baxter: I first entered Harvard—or was it Radcliffe?—in the fall of 1968, dropped out seven weeks later (having lived for real the nightmare we've all had about facing an examination in a course we didn't know we were enrolled in), went west and got a part as an extra (dance hall girl) in a Hollywood western, attended riots at Berkeley in 1969, then returned to Cambridge, where time passed and I did various things until returning, again as a new freshman, in 1971, as a member of the class of 1975. I never felt I was a member of this class, mostly lived off-campus (except for a strange year as a freshman in Leverett the first year they had women), and somehow became pre-med, stayed an extra year after graduation to complete requirements, then off to medical school at Case Western Reserve University in Cleveland. Since then, a psychiatry residency back in Cambridge, and a career as a forensic psychiatrist. Have had occasional moments of existential awareness of how unusual it is to be, for example, sitting and talking to a man about how he thought about, planned, and then ultimately shot to death his annoying son. I've become an expert on violence assessment, worked on a death penalty appeal case (the guy is now out), and on battered-woman murder cases. But mostly, I deal with mentally ill and substance abusing people who come to the courts on low level charges (trespassing at Harvard is a frequent offense).

Got married late, have no kids of my own; my Episcopal-priest-turned-psychologist husband has two grown sons to whom I am unable to refer as "my stepchildren." Live in Cambridge with my husband and sixteen-year-old cat, not far from where I grew up. Our next door neighbor has six chickens that wander about her yard and occasionally ours, which just goes to show Cambridge isn't necessarily the place you thought it to be.

Staring fifty in the face, and right on target wondering about the meaning of it all. I'd like an outdoor job, maybe as a forest ranger, but know nothing about forests, have bad knees, and don't want to be a green-uniformed target of some right wing antigovernment zealot.

Coming full circle, I stood in line in the Coop textbook department this fall, twice as old as everybody else, clutching required reading for the elementary Spanish course I'd signed up for at the Extension School. Made me reflect on how I wasted much of my education, even as it educated me, gave me a career, and made my living possible.

HOME: Cambridge, MA   OCCUPATION: Forensic Psychiatrist; Director. Cambridge Court Clinic   BIRTHPLACE: Fort Belvoir, VA   SECONDARY SCHOOL: Commonwealth School, Boston, MA   YEARS AT COLLEGE: 1968–76   DEGREES: A.B., cum laude, '75; M.D., Case Western Reserve Univ. '80   SPOUSE/PARTNER: David Alan Smith, Sept. 2, 1995 (Alfred Univ. '69)   SPOUSE'S OCCUPATION : Child Psychologist; Clinical Director. Cambridge Youth Guidance Center   CHILDREN: Husband has two grown sons   HARVARD/RADCLIFFE SIBLINGS: Alison Baxter '70   COLLEGE ACTIVITIES: Graduating

---

Neal Nathan Beaton: When I first arrived in Cambridge for freshman year, one of my roommates told me how he and his family had stayed in virtually the same dorm just a few months earlier for his father's Twenty-fifth Reunion. Now my wife and I find ourselves taking our oldest son on college tours and he is going to interviews at many of the same schools to which we had applied, since he similarly will be heading off to college just a few months after our Twenty-fifth Reunion.

The question is: when did we become our parents? I guess the good news is that I do not feel like there has been any such generational shift, but the external indicia certainly point that way.

The last twenty-five years are somewhat of a blur looking back at them. There have been some of the unavoidable trials and tribulations of life, but I have little to complain about since I have a wonderful family and work which I enjoy.

Anyone who knew me at college probably knows my wife, Ann, since we were dating before college and have been married since she graduated from Cornell in 1976. After I graduated from Harvard Law, we decided to live in New York City "temporarily" before moving to the suburbs since I knew I would be working long hours and Ann was going back to graduate school. Over twenty years have passed since then, Ann graduated, I am still working long hours, we bought a co-op (and then the apartment next door as well) and have been raising our three sons (who are quite acclimated to city living) so it looks like it's no longer temporary.

Our sons — Eric, Greg, and Andrew — will be seventeen, fourteen, and eight, by the time you read this, and attend the Dalton School, Hunter College High School, and Rodeph Sholom School, respectively. They have consistently made us proud through academic achievements, Little League feats and many other ways, but, most importantly, just by being good people. We have had a lot of fun watching them grow and mature and have been saying at every stage that this has been a good age for them (and us).

I have been with the same law firm, Gilbert, Segall, and Young, since my second year of law school. We like to think that, although it is a relatively small firm by New York City standards, we do work with the same sophistication as anyone elsewhere in a more humane atmosphere which we more directly control. In the last year alone, I have been the lead counsel on the largest acquisition ever outside Japan by a Japanese corporation (involving operations in over thirty-five countries), on a series of high-tech Internet access equipment company acquisitions, and on a biotech joint venture to develop cancer vaccines, while still having time to work on matters for individual clients such as employment agreements and medical partnerships.

I seem to be traveling more and more with the most common destinations being San Francisco (there are times I think I know my way around Silicon Valley as well as New York), Helsinki, London, and Tokyo. It has not been all work as we have managed to find time in recent months to go to places such as the Savonliina Opera Festival in the hinterlands of Finland (courtesy of a client, Nokia) and to Disney World with the whole family.

HOME: New York, NY   OCCUPATION: Lawyer; Partner. Gilbert, Segall, and Young LLP (law firm)   BIRTHPLACE: New York, NY   SECONDARY SCHOOL: Port Chester High School, Port Chester, NY   YEARS AT COLLEGE: 1971–75   DEGREES: A.B., magna cum laude, '75; J.D. '78   SPOUSE/PARTNER: Ann Renee Rosovsky, June 6, 1976 (Cornell '76; Ph.D., ibid. '84)   SPOUSE'S OCCUPATION: Assistant Professor. Dept. of Biological Sciences, State of New York College of Optometry   CHILDREN: Eric, 1982; Greg, 1986; Andrew, 1992   COLLEGE ACTIVITIES: Business editor, Crimson, 1972–75; Eliot House Committee, An Evening with Champions (skating show for the Jimmy Fund), 1973–75; undergraduate associate, Center for International Affairs, 1974–75

Edward Lawrence "Rick" Bedrick: Remarkable to turn around and look at life twenty-five years later, eh? Since Harvard I have become a physician, did my residency in internal medicine in Philadelphia, have been in practice since 1982, the last seven years as part of a group practice with three friends five minutes from my home (this is a great thing, to be able to work with people you like). My wife, best friend, and source of so many good things in life, is Amy. We were married in 1991 and have a two-year-old wondrous child named Nina, who teaches me a lot, daily, happily.

Since moving to Philadelphia in 1979, many good friends have lived some or much of their lives here including classmates Jon Katz (a native son, now on the West Coast) and my former freshman and sophomore roommate Peter Lynch, who lives twenty-five minutes away in New Jersey and is even taller than he was in college owing to the fact that he now stands up straighter (or am I slouching more?).

I am still reading (I spent much of the last two years working my way through Proust), have discovered opera, play tennis (and went through a jogging phase), took up skiing, sailed a bit, cook a bit, and am quite close to our family in both Boston and Philadelphia. I love being a father. I found happiness, peace, and strength when I found Amy.

At forty-six I have far more confidence than I had at twenty-two, take more risks, am more curious and enjoy life more than I did back in college. In this I am trying hard to grow younger, not older, with time. With a two-year old, do I have a choice?

HOME: Elkins Park, PA   OCCUPATION: Physician (internal medicine). Fox Chase Medical Associates (private group practice)   BIRTHPLACE: Boston, MA   SECONDARY SCHOOL: Rivers School, Weston, MA   YEARS AT COLLEGE: 1971–75   DEGREES: A.B., cum laude, '75; M.D., Boston Univ. '79   SPOUSE/PARTNER: Amy Brantz, May 5, 1991 (Princeton '79; J.D., George Washington Univ. '82)   SPOUSE'S OCCUPATION: Financial Consultant. Merrill Lynch   CHILDREN: Nina Fay, 1997

Mary Marckwald Beekman: Highs and lows of twenty-five years in no particular order (yes, I'm doing this online on October 15):

- Ownership of a thirty-year-old Boston Whaler with a Honda 90 four-stroke engine
- Birth of two wonderful children
- Death of two parents
- Conducting a fabulous performance of J. S. Bach's B-minor Mass, which was even attended and favorably reviewed by a critic (icing on the cake!)
- Performing my master's recital during the great blizzard of 1978
- Having the New England premiere of Arvo Paert's *Passio* snowed out by the "blizzard of the century" in 1993 (Do you think the powers that be are trying to tell me something?)
- Performing the New England premiere of Arvo Paert's *Passio* one week later and having it broadcast on WGBH radio
- Marriage (probably the only thing in both categories)
- Helping my best friend through diagnosis and treatment for breast cancer
- Doing outreach with Musica Sacra by performing at mental institutions and as entertainment during the AIDS walk. In the same category, conceiving of and mounting a fund-raiser for institutions run by and for the homeless in Cambridge, which raised over sixteen thousand dollars for them
- Seeing my older son play Jesus in *Godspell*
- Taking up rollerblading and kayaking when I have never been an athlete
- Having my heart race at 240 beats per minute while being interviewed live on radio because of a heart syndrome—Wolff-Parkinson-White—I had had my entire life but had supposedly terminated with a catheter ablation at New England Medical Center
- Going to Oklahoma City to have a second catheter ablation by the world's foremost specialist in this procedure
- Being able to go all out in my mediocre tennis game now that my heart is fixed
- Achieving sporadic instances of living in the moment

HOME: Belmont, MA   **OCCUPATION:** Choral Conductor; Music Director. Musica Sacra; Belmont Open Sings   **BIRTHPLACE:** New York, NY   **SECONDARY SCHOOL:** The Chapin School, New York, NY   **YEARS AT COLLEGE:** 1971–75   **DEGREES:** A.B., cum laude, '75; M.M., New England Conservatory '78   **SPOUSE/PARTNER:** W. David Warner, Aug. 25, 1984 (Univ. of Texas '64)   **SPOUSE'S OCCUPATION:** Systems Analyst. Abt Associates   **CHILDREN:** W. Andrew, 1986; Robert, 1988   **HARVARD/RADCLIFFE SIBLINGS:** William Bedloe Beekman '71   **COLLEGE ACTIVITIES:** University Choir, 1971–75; Signet Society, 1975; Collegium Musicum, 1971

George Arthur Berman: My original career plans required revision when I realized that major league baseball players were required to hit curveballs and that the demand for sheriffs was limited. While waiting to develop alternate plans, I went to law school and seem to have spent twenty years as a civil litigator. Like many classmates, I have acquired children, a spouse, and a mortgage, which have all grown over the years and have been, in turn, sources of effort, expense, wonder, and, ultimately, satisfaction. I recently found the time, after endless procrastination, to finish my first novel since graduation. I enjoyed the experience so much that I hope to read another before our Fiftieth!

HOME: Winchester, MA   **OCCUPATION:** Attorney; Partner. Posternak Blankstein & Lund   **BIRTHPLACE:** Boston, MA   **SECONDARY SCHOOL:** Newton South High School, Newton, MA   **YEARS AT COLLEGE:** 1971–75   **DEGREES:** A.B., magna cum laude, '75; J.D. '79   **SPOUSE/PARTNER:** Regina Roman, July 29, 1980 (Brown '76; J.D., Harvard '79)   **SPOUSE'S OCCUPATION:** Attorney; Partner. Sugarman, Rogers, Barshak & Cohen   **CHILDREN:** Daniel, 1985; Greg, 1989   **COLLEGE ACTIVITIES:** Phillips Brooks House; Lowell House intramurals

Suzanne Powell Bishopric: A chain of financial positions has led me to the perfect "mommy track" job. I completed my M.B.A. in 1979 and worked with FMC in Chicago and Brazil, where I practiced auditing in Portuguese. I left FMC in 1982 for McDonald's, first as a manager of international finance, where I helped make initial investments in South America and the Far East, and later as director of financial markets responsible for hedging, swaps, and debt issuance. I cooked hamburgers at McDonald's in Tokyo and earned a bachelor's degree in hamburgerology from Hamburger University. While speaking about financial futures and options, I met my husband. I left McDonald's to be with him in New York and accepted an appointment as deputy treasurer of the United Nations in 1991, convinced that the then-controller, Kofi Annan, would be a good boss. Upon succeeding to the position of treasurer in 1996, I began the transformation of the Treasury of the United Nations into an operation which would be respectable in any multinational corporation. The most rewarding project to date has been operating the financial aspects of the Oil-for-Food Program, which has allowed Iraq to purchase over $4 billion worth of humanitarian supplies. Our more routine work includes managing a portfolio in excess of $7 billion and effecting a worldwide payroll. William, now six, knows enough about my job to ask questions. In Baghdad in 1998, while American planes were bombing, I was asked over the telephone, "Mommy, do you still have all of Saddam's money?" Not surprisingly, he collects banknotes and coins from all over the world.

HOME: New York, NY   **OCCUPATION:** Treasurer. United Nations (intergovernmental agency)   **BIRTHPLACE:** South Ruislip, United Kingdom   **SECONDARY SCHOOL:** Riverview High School, Sarasota, FL   **YEARS AT COLLEGE:** 1971–75   **DEGREES:** A.B., cum laude, '75; M.B.A. '79   **SPOUSE/PARTNER:** Michael J. Manning, March 11, 1989   **SPOUSE'S OCCUPATION:** President. Stratton Advisers   **CHILDREN:** William von Scheele, 1993   **COLLEGE ACTIVITIES:** Club Ibero Americano

Timothy S. Black: The fates have been kind and good to me since Harvard. Twenty-five years out, I acknowledge my good fortune.

My family centers my life. Marnie and I have been married for twenty-four years, and we have two wonderful daughters: Abby, age thirteen, and Emily, age nine. Each of us thrives off our life together as a family. Nothing is more important to me.

My work as a judge is exhilarating. As a municipal court judge, I see about fifty criminal defendants daily, each charged with various misdemeanors, ranging from public spitting to petty theft to drunk driving to domestic violence. I also adjudicate money disputes of less than fifteen thousand dollars, all traffic offenses, and all minor misdemeanors (like possession of marijuana). I wear a robe, and people call me "Your Honor."

Before being elected judge in 1993, I worked for a decade as a trial lawyer in a big downtown law firm. Before lawyering, I taught English and coached sports at an independent school while I attended law school at night. My first varsity girls soccer team was 0-13-1 (the tie having occurred on a day I was not present).

Marnie taught school for our first twelve years, then stayed home with Abby and Emily for several years, and now works as a tutor (flexible three-quarter-time). The stability in my life and in our daughters' lives comes largely from Marnie.

I miss my friends from Harvard. I had a lot of really good friends. The absorption of my family life and my station as judge have combined, I suppose, to set upon me a certain quietude.

Harvard is an important part of me, and I look forward a great deal to catching up with a lot of good friends who helped shape me way back when.

HOME: Cincinnati, OH   **OCCUPATION:** Judge. Hamilton County Municipal Court
BIRTHPLACE: Brookline, MA   **SECONDARY SCHOOL:** Deerfield Academy, Deerfield,
MA   **YEARS AT COLLEGE:** 1971–75   **DEGREES:** A.B., cum laude, '75; J.D., Northern
Kentucky Univ. '83   **SPOUSE/PARTNER:** Marnie Chapman, June 26, 1976 (Wellesley
Coll. '76)   **SPOUSE'S OCCUPATION:** Tutor. The Seven Hills School   **CHILDREN:**
Abigail, 1986; Emily, 1990   **COLLEGE ACTIVITIES:** Co-captain, varsity sailing, 1974–75

Ellen Howell Bloedel:

No, I won't come to your Reunion; it's
Not my true class year anyhow; besides,
The yearbook matched my name — it gave me fits —
With someone else's picture. Life derides
One's youthful hopes — though I had few of those,
And in the intervening twenty-five years
Have lost the ones I owned. Though I try to close
The door on painful memories, hot tears
Of dumb self-pity still appear, to mark
Recalled rejection by my so-called peers.
One thing of worth remains, its imprint stark,
From that depressing time: there are no seers;
We're in this world alone, and blind. So, sod
What others think! I'm on my own, thank God.

HOME: Salt Lake City, UT   **BIRTHPLACE:** Ancon, Canal Zone   **SECONDARY SCHOOL:** Concord Academy, Concord, MA   **YEARS AT COLLEGE:** 1971–76   **DEGREES:** A.B., magna cum laude, '75 ('76); J.D., Boston Univ. '79   **HARVARD/RADCLIFFE SIBLINGS:** Carla Bloedel Clark, '72

Micah W. Bloomfield: I remember fighting "city hall" when I was at Harvard. There was a big rally where a resolution ("Harvard out of the Gulf") was being adopted. I tried to amend the resolution, so that it was more fair to Israel. I don't believe the powers on stage followed Robert's Rules of Order any better than the Democratic Party does now (I don't know how well the Republicans do).

Recently, I have tried to bring more democracy to my law firm. Enough said.

On a personal level, my two kids are still young (eight and six) and a great deal of fun to be with. I just bought a bike, which I hadn't used for ages, and have started finding the pleasures of Central Park on Sundays.

Jewish religion plays a big part in my life. I am reading the Talmud in Steinsaltz' translation. My favorite books include *Decline and Fall of the Roman Empire, The Magic Mountain,* and *The Ambassadors.* My favorite movies are *The Third Man* and *Shone.*

Recently, I saw Denis Pelli's article in the *Times* and we got in contact. It's fun to meet old friends, though sometimes my recall isn't as good as it should be.

HOME: New York, NY   OCCUPATION: Tax Lawyer; Partner. Stroock & Stroock & Lavan LLP   BIRTHPLACE: Columbus, OH   SECONDARY SCHOOL: Maimonides School, Brookline, MA   YEARS AT COLLEGE: 1971–75   DEGREES: A.B., cum laude, '75; J.D. '78; LL.M., New York Univ. '85   SPOUSE/PARTNER: Nitza Berger, Dec. 14, 1986   SPOUSE'S OCCUPATION: Teacher. New York City Public Schools   CHILDREN: Morton "Doni," 1991; Ariella, 1993   HARVARD/RADCLIFFE SIBLINGS: Hanna Bloomfield Rubins '76; Samuel Bloomfield '79   COLLEGE ACTIVITIES: Quincy House Cultural Affair (it had some other name) with, among others, Leonard Bernstein and Charles Rosen

Elise A. Bloustein: I went to Cambridge University after graduation. After a year researching sixteenth-century marriage practices, I decided not to do a Ph.D. in social history. I came home, worked briefly in New York and then went to Dallas to live with a boyfriend and work as a waitress. Unable to convince myself to live in Texas, I came back east to Harvard Law School. After graduation, I worked for a federal judge, Milton Pollack, in New York. Then I took a job as a litigator in a big Wall Street law firm called Sullivan & Cromwell, where I stayed, quite happy and working very long hours, for the next nine years. Toward the end of my tenure there, both my parents died, I married Sam Greenhoe, and I became pregnant with our first child, Rachel. I left Sullivan & Cromwell in 1990 and spent a year at home with Rachel while Sam got his M.F.A. from Columbia. Then I went to work for a small firm on a part-time/flex-time basis. I became a partner and had a second child, Eli, in 1994.

Last year, after seven years, I left the firm and began to practice on my own, which I am enjoying a great deal. Sam, Rachel, Eli and I live in a brownstone near a park with our dog, Homer; a turtle, Skipperdee; and several fish. I love being a wife, mother, and sister. My proudest professional accomplishment is having succeeded, with a team of my colleagues, in getting a man off death row in North Carolina. After almost twenty years in legal practice, I greatly enjoy exercising my accumulated advocacy skills on behalf of my clients. In my free moments I do yoga, which I highly recommend to all.

HOME: Brooklyn, NY   **OCCUPATION:** Attorney (sole proprietor)   **BIRTHPLACE:** Ithaca, NY   **SECONDARY SCHOOL:** Cambridge School of Weston, Waltham, MA   **YEARS AT COLLEGE:** 1971–75   **DEGREES:** A.B., magna cum laude, '75; J.D. '80   **SPOUSE/PARTNER:** Sam Greenhoe, July 15, 1989 (Univ. of Vermont, '79)   **SPOUSE'S OCCUPATION:** Writer   **CHILDREN:** Rachel Maria Bloustein Greenhoe, 1990; Eli Joseph Bloustein Greenhoe, 1994

Daniel E. Blustein: I settled in Los Angeles not many years after returning from a Sheldon traveling fellowship in Latin America and Europe. I was teaching school when Melanie and I fell in love, married, and traveled to Hong Kong and China. It's fun being a father, and parenting well. Hannah's early childhood choice was art, but later figure skating became her favorite pursuit. Ava's first serious path is playing the piano. No longer a schoolteacher, I give myself to a support role in the girls' training, and work as a supervisor. We have gone camping, and to the Midwest to see friends and family. Melanie would like someday to show the girls and me the places she knew growing up in Vietnam.

HOME: San Gabriel, CA   **OCCUPATION:** Supervisor. Dept. of Water and Power (City of Los Angeles municipal utility)   **SECONDARY SCHOOL:** Woodlands High School, Greenburgh, NY   **YEARS AT COLLEGE:** 1971–75   **SPOUSE/PARTNER:** Melanie Chan, Dec. 19, 1987   **CHILDREN:** Hannah Chan Blustein, 1989; Ava Chan Blustein, 1993   **HARVARD/RADCLIFFE SIBLINGS:** Bonnie E. Blustein '72   **COLLEGE ACTIVITIES:** Loeb Drama Center, 1971–75; Leverett House soccer and softball teams, 1973–75

Roger E. Bohn: My life since graduating from Harvard in 1976 has had ups and downs. I am paid to do research and think about anything I find interesting. I chose an academic field (management) that is both vibrant and in demand. At various times I've taught at MIT, HBS, Oxford, and UCSD, and done research all over the world. Currently I'm working on a book about the structure and development of technological knowledge. Even my old grad school research, on electricity pricing and deregulation, turned out to be hot fifteen years later.

On the down side, my family has suffered from various chronic ailments that have affected all of us. I never got around to starting a company. I did not get along with the power structure or lack of ethics at HBS. And though I did research in 1993 about the Internet, I didn't invest in Cisco!

Concerns: I suffered through 1980s politics, incredulous that few other Americans saw through the con artistry of Reagan and his Alzheimer's. I am amazed and angry at how conservative, in the literal sense, our generation has become. For example, we are at war with our children's generation, trying to dictate their behavior in minute detail. Congress passes more and more laws saying "thou shalt not." Skateboarding, premarital sex, marijuana, and body-piercing are persecuted vigorously, while analogous "adult" entertainments like SUVs, Viagra, alcohol, and firearms are winked at or even subsidized. Consumerism reigns as the preeminent form of recreation.

On the other hand, the rate of technological progress and the shift from physical to information-based activity are very promising for humanity's long-run future. America is strong enough to survive a few decades of weak political leadership. And the over-riding threat of massive nuclear war has subsided.

HOME: San Diego, CA   **OCCUPATION:** Professor. University of California, San Diego
BIRTHPLACE: Boston, MA   **SECONDARY SCHOOL:** Ossining High School, NY; Croton High School, NY; Phillips Exeter Academy, NH   **YEARS AT COLLEGE:** 1971–76
DEGREES: A.B., summa cum laude, '75 ('76); Ph.D., Massachusetts Inst. of Technology '82
SPOUSE/PARTNER: Elizabeth Coppedge, October 1980 (Tufts Univ. '75)   **SPOUSE'S OCCUPATION:** Freelance Fiction and Technical Writer   **CHILDREN:** Kristen "Tess," 1982; Daniel, 1988   **COLLEGE ACTIVITIES:** Varsity lightweight crew, 1971–73

Daniel J. Borden: I'm lucky enough to have worked in a field for the past fifteen years that combines my artistic interests with my technical expertise. And it's still fun to go to work every day — but even more fun to come home! Our family of six keeps the kettle on the boil always. My wife Sarah does an amazing job keeping the household in sync and organized — I could never do it!

Built a home in Vermont with the help of Rod Sidley (Class of '75), Cincinnati's finest architect.

My kids keep me young.

The only good thing about getting older is that your kids grow up.

Go figure.

HOME: Brookline, MA   **OCCUPATION:** Senior Vice President; Director of Creative Services. Wickersham Hunt Schwantner (advertising)   **BIRTHPLACE:** Boston, MA
SECONDARY SCHOOL: Newton High School, Newton, MA   **YEARS AT COLLEGE:**
1971–78   **DEGREES:** A.B. '75 ('80)   **SPOUSE/PARTNER:** Sarah M. Burrows, Aug. 10, 1986 (Alfred Univ. '78; M.B.A., Simmons Coll. '92)   **SPOUSE'S OCCUPATION:** Director of Student Internships. Simmons College   **CHILDREN:** Julia Avery, 1987; Sophia Vivian, 1991; Jacob Warren, 1991; Charlotte Lucy, 1997

Peter L. Borowitz: As detailed in the Tenth Anniversary Report, my potential military career, cut short by receiving number 275 in the Selective Service Lottery for birth year 1953, was revived in 1982 when, in lieu of becoming a soldier, I married one. Eighteen years later I am glad to report that my romance with Talanat Lapid, sergeant (ret.), Israel Defense Forces, remains the greatest event of the last twenty-five years, along with the arrival of our daughters Dana, thirteen, and Kate, ten.

We have now been happily ensconced in Westchester County, New York, for over fifteen years. Talanat, after her initial focus on working for a local newspaper and attending to the needs of our (then-small) children, has now turned her breathtaking energy towards building a career in psychotherapy. She is a fourth-year candidate for a Psy.D. degree in the clinical psychology program at the Ferkauf Institute of Yeshiva University. (Please let me know if any of you would like to discuss your mid-life crisis with her during Reunion week!)

Dana and Kate are now in the eighth and fifth grades at Hackley School, where, I am proud to say, both are exhibiting their theatrical talent. Last year Dana was the star of the Hackley production of *Guys and Dolls,* playing (in light of the dearth of capable male voices) the Stubby Kaye (or, should I say, David Goldbloom '75) role of Nicely-Nicely Johnson. Kate is about to debut as Hermia in *A Midsummer Night's Dream.* I would like to think that my own interest in theater is responsible for their talent, but it's hard to see how a destructive drama critic could have influenced their far more creative skill.

As for my own activities, I graduated from Harvard Law School in 1978, where I was an editor of the *Harvard Law Review,* and joined the New York firm of Debevoise & Plimpton, where I am a partner specializing in corporate bankruptcies and workouts. My career began where the rubber meets the road (representing Chrysler in connection with a federal loan guarantee bailout) and moved on to the heavens above, including airplanes (representing aircraft financiers of Eastern, TWA, and Continental Airlines), satellites (representing the Khrunichev Space Center in Iridium) and stars (representing Kevin Costner, Jonathan Demme, and Merchant/Ivory in the Orion Pictures bankruptcy). All of this has, of course, made it impossible for me to follow up on my former collegiate role as drama critic for the *Harvard Independent* and *Boston Phoenix;* I have now been reduced to writing highly unfavorable reviews of the antics of corporate finance lawyers in various legal periodicals. See, e.g., Borowitz, "Waiving Subrogation Rights and Conjuring Up Demons in Response to Deprizio," 45 *Business Lawyer* 2151 (August 1990).

HOME: Briarcliff Manor, NY   **OCCUPATION:** Partner. Debevoise & Plimpton (law firm)
BIRTHPLACE: Boston, MA   **SECONDARY SCHOOL:** Shaker Heights High School, Shaker Heights, OH   **YEARS AT COLLEGE:** 1971–75   **DEGREES:** A.B., summa cum laude '74; J.D.

'78   **SPOUSE/PARTNER:** Talanat Lapid, Aug. 7, 1982 (Columbia '84)   **SPOUSE'S OCCUPATION:** Candidate for Psy.D., Ferkauf Institute, Yeshiva University   **CHILDREN:** Dana Arielle, 1986; Kate Alexandra, 1989   **HARVARD/RADCLIFFE SIBLINGS:** Andrew S. Borowitz '80   **COLLEGE ACTIVITIES:** *Harvard Independent,* 1971–75; Premiere Society, 1974–75

Helen Bray-Garretson: My current life as a country psychologist, mother of two teenage daughters, and active volunteer seems to suit me well. It took me a few years of traveling and working in the real world after Harvard to get my professional bearings. Eventually I earned a Ph.D. in clinical psychology at Boston University, with a dissertation about autistic children. I now work as a child psychologist in a variety of settings. In private practice, I listen to children talk about divorced parents; in an outpatient mental health center, I help children work on anxiety, depression, and impulsive behavior; in a residential treatment center, I focus on juveniles who are sexually abusive and sexually aggressive.

In 1977 I married the fellow my father introduced as "Pete, the engineer who went to Harvard" who actually turned out to be Frank, the architect who went to the University of Pennsylvania. We moved from Beverly to the Berkshires in 1984 for a breath of fresh air and a slower pace for raising our daughters. At seventeen, Julia is on her way as a multimedia digital artist and just rolls her eyes when I ask her how to forward an e-mail. My fifteen-year old, Eleanor, has a passion for American legal history that is matched only by her love for playing piano. The girls are a joy to me.

My own do-gooder inclinations have flourished out here. I still care about the life of the spirit, both as an individual and as a member of a community and serve as senior warden of the local Episcopal Church. I volunteer on the board of trustees of several organizations supporting children's music and art experiences and continue to sing a sorry alto in the church choir. For me, the sadness about this Reunion is the awareness that my good friend, Betsy Inskeep Smylie, who died this year of a brain tumor, will be present only in spirit and not in person to enjoy a great Reunion.

HOME: Sheffield, MA   **OCCUPATION:** Psychologist   **BIRTHPLACE:** Fitchburg, MA
YEARS AT COLLEGE: 1970–75   **DEGREES:** A.B., cum laude, '75; Ph.D., Boston Univ. '85
SPOUSE/PARTNER: Frank M. Garretson, July 2, 1977 (Univ. of Virginia '68; M. Arch., Univ. of Pennsylvania '74; M.C.P., ibid. '74)   **SPOUSE'S OCCUPATION:** Architect   **CHILDREN:** Julia, 1982; Eleanor, 1984   **COLLEGE ACTIVITIES:** Christian Fellowship; Gilbert and Sullivan Society; community service projects, Meals on Wheels; research assistant, Graduate School of Education

Howard Arthur Brecher: I went directly from college to the joint J.D.-M.B.A. program at Harvard, and then to a law firm in New York City specializing in tax law. While each of my jobs since has been a lawyer's job, broadening additional responsibilities have helped me appreciate the value not only of our college experience, but of so many things I have read or heard or discussed with others over the years.

I have been with a financial publishing and mutual funds company since 1991, as head of a small legal department and as a corporate officer. The majority of the company is owned by the founder's family, so my work involves a family charitable foundation and personal estate and tax issues as well as corporate law.

Through good luck, I met my wife Ellen here in New York, and we were married in 1987. Thus far our home has remained in Manhattan. But what a different home it has been since April 1998.

At that time, we traveled to Nanjing, China, with a diverse and wonderful group of twelve families — each adopting a child through the same U.S. agency. Our daughter, Emma, now five, has learned English rapidly and is enjoying her school and home in America. We think of her as a gift we have received.

Ellen and I have been able to maintain bonds with a few of my great classmates, and look forward to renewing many friendships at the Reunion.

HOME: New York, NY   OCCUPATION: Lawyer; Vice President; Secretary. Value Line, Inc. (investment advisory firm)   BIRTHPLACE: New York, NY   SECONDARY SCHOOL: Roslyn High School, Roslyn Heights, NY   YEARS AT COLLEGE: 1971–75   DEGREES: A.B., magna cum laude, '75; M.B.A. '79; J.D. '79; LL.M., New York Univ. '84
SPOUSE/PARTNER: Ellen Rusch, Nov. 1, 1987 (Chatham Coll.)   SPOUSE'S OCCUPATION: Mother (formerly broadcast business manager, Young & Rubicam Advertising)   CHILDREN: Emma Meredith Nana, 1994, Jiangsu Province, China; adopted, 1998   COLLEGE ACTIVITIES: Debate Council, 1971–74

Peter Ward Broer: I am growing an electronics and medical business in the heartland, as I try occasionally to keep up with my burgeoning family of three boisterous boys and my community-committed wife, planted on Cleveland's "North Coast."

Between trips to the West Coast and the Far East, I spend time applying creative lighting technology to electronics and medical uses, while helping solve customer problems, manage customary crises, and keep venture capitalists productively engaged. I am adding a data point, direction unclear, to the debate about whether a non-engineer can lead a technical company.

My company, Lumitex, treats jaundice in babies, lights surgical procedures inside the body, and backlights electronics displays in cell phones, handheld instruments, and the like. We produce in Cleveland, Southern California, Taipei, and Shanghai.

Before joining Lumitex in its infancy, I was with McKinsey & Company, where I worked with U.S. and European industrial clients in marketing, strategy, and organization. I returned to my Ohio roots from a well-known West Coast business school intending to polish the rust belt, and ended up on a two-year stint in Europe followed by total immersion in midwestern high-tech.

I also survived checkered careers in Massachusetts politics, political consulting in the Middle East, and journalistic assignments requiring me to jump from an airplane, off a cliff, and into dinner with classmate Paul Rosenberg. Fitting background for an entrepreneur.

Along the way, I met my wife, Vikki, in New York, courted her in California, married her in Des Moines, settled with her in Cleveland and, to add to the general confusion, sprouted our first child in Brussels. Vikki is now leading the charge for needed and controversial changes in our community and the children's Montessori school.

HOME: Bratenahl, OH   **OCCUPATION:** President; CEO. Lumitex (electronics display lighting, surgical lighting, and phototherapy)   **Birthplace:** Toledo, OH   **SECONDARY SCHOOL:** Cranbrook School, Bloomfield Hills, MI   **YEARS AT COLLEGE:** 1971–75 **DEGREES:** A.B., cum laude, '75; M.B.A., Stanford Univ. '84   **SPOUSE/PARTNER:** Victoria Urban, 1985 (Stanford Univ. '82)   **SPOUSE'S OCCUPATION:** Mother; Ruffing Montessori School Chairwoman; Bratenahl Planning and Zoning Chairwoman; Charitable Organizer **CHILDREN:** Will, 1988; Ben, 1990; Sam, 1991   **COLLEGE ACTIVITIES:** Harvard Crimson, 1973–74; WHRB, 1973–74; *Christian Science Monitor*, 1973–74; Orson Welles Restaurant, 1972–74; Harvard Student Agencies, 1971–73

Glenn Arthur Brown: The past twenty-five years have brought many challenges and an ever-present thought that life is wonderful.

I have remained in Philadelphia, the city I moved to after graduation. Have yet to find that perfect woman that is capable of sharing my life and I have found life as a single person to be rewarding.

I have been blessed with many wonderful friends from around the country and enjoy my regular communication with them. I am active in M.B.A. associations as well as dental organizations and look forward to the national meetings.

True to Harvard's spirit of volunteerism, I have been actively engaged in many board activities. Currently, A Better Chance public school program in suburban Philadelphia, a large religiously affiliated social service agency, and the board of the Philadelphia Harvard Club take some of my energy.

I continue to manage a busy dental practice, About Your Smile, and serve on the board of a dental independent practice association, Associated Dental Practices.

Physical activity has become important and I may now be in better physical shape than I was twenty-five years ago.

The biggest surprise to me in my recent life was becoming an evening 1L at Temple University's law school. A choice I certainly did not contemplate as an undergraduate student, but one that I am sincerely enjoying halfway through my first semester. I have not yet determined whether this legal education will impact my current businesses, but I am certain it will have a positive effect upon my life.

I look forward to another wonderful twenty-five years.

HOME: Media, PA   **OCCUPATION:** Dentist; President. About Your Smile, PC (Philadelphia-area dental practice). Board Member and Officer, Associated Dental Practices, LLC (an independent practice association that provides a dental network to managed care organizations and insurance carriers)   **BIRTHPLACE:** Fort Knox, KY   **SECONDARY SCHOOL:** Christian Brothers Academy, Syracuse, NY   **YEARS AT COLLEGE:** 1971–75   **DEGREES:** A.B. '75; M.B.A., Univ. of Pennsylvania '80; D.M.D., ibid. '82

Patricia Church Brown: Over the past twenty-five years I have seen the focus of my life shift from science and career to relationships and faith. When I finished college, all of my ambition focused on my future in the medical sciences. I worked for a year in a lab at Massachusetts General Hospital, then entered medicine at Yale Medical School, graduating in 1980. A year as a surgical intern at Bellevue in New York City was one of those experiences I wouldn't want to trade for anything, but also would never want to live through again. After Bellevue I spent several years in residencies in anatomic pathology, lab medicine, and dermatopathology before finally landing in dermatology at Strong Memorial Hospital in Rochester, New York. I completed my training in 1990, then returned home to the Maryland suburbs where I grew up. I practiced dermatology for a year with a group, then started my own solo practice. Interacting with patients and having time to share their concerns has afforded me satisfaction, however, this direct relationship has become more and more difficult to maintain in the face of proliferating government regulation and increasing control by insurance companies.

Over the past few years I have come to derive increasing satisfaction from my nonwork activities. These have included a pilgrimage to the Holy Land, participation in a book club with lawyers, completing Montgomery County Police Citizen Academy (a thirteen-week course where we learned about public safety behind the scenes), playing with and watching my nieces grow up, and becoming part of a caring church community. When I was in college, I could have fairly been described as atheist or agnostic. Over the past twenty years, however, God and Jesus Christ have become for me a real loving presence. I, who was a student of evolution in college, would now say that process is guided by God. Through my faith I have also come to know a group of caring friends who, while providing support in times of distress, are also eager to share life's joys.

HOME: Bethesda, MD   **OCCUPATION:** Physician (dermatologist)   **BIRTHPLACE:** Washington, DC   **SECONDARY SCHOOL:** Walt Whitman High School, Bethesda, MD **YEARS AT COLLEGE:** 1971–75   **DEGREES:** A.B., magna cum laude, '75; M.D., Yale '80 **HARVARD/RADCLIFFE SIBLINGS:** Andrew Gordon Brown '72   **COLLEGE ACTIVITIES:** Harvard-Radcliffe Freshman Chorus, 1971–72; Radcliffe Choral Society, 1972–73; Adams House Committee, 1972–75

David Judson Browning: Robert Nozick didn't teach us the meaning of life in his course by that name in 1974. Twenty-five years later, I think I could write a better paper for the course, but I suspect it would receive a worse grade since it would spring from experience rather than a mental process.

Family life has been the most fun for me since graduation. I've enjoyed home schooling three children as a supplement to their formal education. I am a closet middle school teacher. Figuring ways to better connect with them occupies lots of treadmill thinking time. The feature, "By the Numbers," in each *Scientific American* is a great resource. Cover up the title, show the map, and ask the crew to guess what is being depicted. Count on twenty minutes of animated discussion.

Clare and I enjoyed eight years of each other's company before we had children. I don't think we resent the present absence of time alone as much as we might had we not had this period. Looking ahead to the time when the kids are gone, I wouldn't rush it, but doubt we'll have any empty-nest syndrome. We like walking and hearing about the other's reading.

Work life always threatens to dominate the rest. Repairing retinal detachments is a great job. People usually see better and are grateful, the pay is good, and there is esteem. It can be a powerful drug pulling one in more and more. I have found a useful antidote to be my attempt to publish in the academic journals while writing from a private-practice setting. The sanity restored by frequent rejection letters is healthy; the delight of the odd acceptance letter, welcome.

HOME: Charlotte, NC   **OCCUPATION:** Ophthalmologist   **BIRTHPLACE:** Shreveport, LA   **SECONDARY SCHOOL:** Huntsville High School, Huntsville, AL   **YEARS AT COLLEGE:** 1971–75   **DEGREES:** A.B., cum laude, '75; Ph.D., Duke Univ. '80; M.D., ibid. '81   **SPOUSE/PARTNER:** Clare Pautler, Dec. 27, 1975   **SPOUSE'S OCCUPATION:** Homemaker   **CHILDREN:** Samuel, 1983; Mark, 1986; Anne, 1988

Sally Browning: Although I haven't become rich or famous in the past twenty-five years, I have been very lucky. Since completing a fellowship in pediatric radiology thirteen years ago, I have been practicing at a large, busy Seattle HMO. Partly by default of my gender, I've also become an experienced "breast imager" and am now the mammography section chief. Medicine has been a satisfying career choice, although working conditions for physicians in the late nineties are less than ideal. My work remains challenging, and my professional colleagues provide support and intellectual stimulation. I feel fortunate to have chosen a career about which I remain passionate.

After fifteen years of marriage, I'm still in love with my husband, who has usually been sympathetic and patient, although not home very often. We have two beautiful, energetic children who help us to keep things in perspective (and on the road even more!). The Northwest has been a wonderful place to live and raise a family. Yes, it's gray and rainy a lot, but the variety of activities, scenery, and climate zones within a few hours of Seattle are remarkable, especially for someone who grew up in New England. We've become skiing fanatics — there's often great snow (and sometimes even sunshine) in the mountains, when the city winter is just plain dreary. Staying in adequate condition to prevent injuring myself has been my sole motivation for not becoming a couch potato.

If I could just find the right balance between family, career, and my other interests before I retire!

HOME: Seattle, WA   **OCCUPATION:** Physician. Dept. of Radiology, Group Health Cooperative   **BIRTHPLACE:** Providence, RI   **SECONDARY SCHOOL:** Abbot Academy, Andover, MA   **YEARS AT COLLEGE:** 1971–76   **DEGREES:** A.B., cum laude, '75 ('76); M.D., Boston Univ. '81   **SPOUSE/PARTNER:** Richard Pelman, June 17, 1984 (Univ. of Washington '73; M.D., ibid. '79)   **SPOUSE'S OCCUPATION:** Physician (urologist). Bellevue Urology Associates   **CHILDREN:** Alexander, 1987; Emma, 1990

Jim Arthur Buck: I left Cambridge in 1975 to enter medical school with high hopes and awareness of my potential and limitations. Harvard came with me in the remembrance of the inspirational people I had met, the experiences shared, and the diverse lessons learned.

I was challenged and enthralled by my medical training and enjoyed it immensely (the only exception being the severely rationed sleep allowed with the call schedules of those days). My residency in Baltimore was a time of growth and preparation, learning and teaching, giving and taking in this smorgasbord of life (and death) experience. It was there that I met my wife, a petite dynamo with whom I could talk about anything effortlessly, and we married in 1983, this marking the completion of her internship as a certified nurse midwife and my first year in private practice.

My bride joined me in my beloved Midwest, and we put down roots and entered the world of rural medical practice. The rewards were many but the challenges were substantial, as we were severely understaffed. Trusting that new partners would someday join us, we started our family in 1986 with our firstborn son, Christopher. We were doting parents, but time demands were ridiculous until finally, in 1990, another doctor came our way. Thus equipped and rejuvenated, our family expanded with the birth of our daughter, Noel Nicole, in 1992.

The dynamic balance of nurturing a family and family practice medicine happily occupies my days and nights now, together with the joy of community involvement and the occasional excitement of a visit or a telephone call from old friends from Harvard days. God bless you all, and thanks for all your help and encouragement along life's path! We hope to see you again soon!

HOME: Fairfield, IA   **OCCUPATION:** Physician; President. Fairfield Clinic, PC
BIRTHPLACE: Duluth, MN   **SECONDARY SCHOOL:** Duluth East High School, Duluth, MN   **YEARS AT COLLEGE:** 1971–75   **DEGREES:** A.B., cum laude, '75; M.D., Univ. of Minnesota '79   **SPOUSE/PARTNER:** Ann Elaine, (Towson State Univ. '76; C.N.M., Columbia '83; M.S., ibid. '83)   **SPOUSE'S OCCUPATION:** Certified Nurse Midwife (on leave from Fairfield Clinic)   **CHILDREN:** Christopher Nelson, 1986; Noel Nicole, 1992 **COLLEGE ACTIVITIES:** Eliot House sports (soccer, cross country, basketball, baseball), 1972–75; Eliot House librarian, 1972–75; Christian Fellowship, 1971–75; Gilbert and Sullivan Society Orchestra, 1971–75; Harvard-Radcliffe bands (marching, jazz, concert), 1971–75; Loeb Theatre stage crew, *Psalm of Two Davids*, 1973; orchestra, *Don Giovanni*, 1974; Harvard-Radcliffe Daycare Center, 1971–72

Bren Luree Buckley: I gave up the recurring dream of going into an exam unprepared about five years out of school and replaced it with my dream about Harvard Reunions! In it we are all young and beautiful!

My greatest joy since college has resulted from marrying a supportive spouse and having two daughters. I have also helped to raise two stepchildren, now in their thirties, and they have brought much happiness as well. My oldest daughter, Kydlan, is now eleven and in fifth grade. This winter she will travel to nine states, performing twenty-six times in *A Christmas Carol* with the Nebraska Theater Caravan. She has participated in drama, dance and music since she was three and this is her first professional production. In the summers she attends Interlochen Arts Camp in northern Michigan, which has turned out to be a wonderful event for our whole family.

My second daughter, Manon, soon to be three, is a fearless gymnast who seems eager to follow in Kydlan's footsteps in the arts. She is beautiful, and hopefully you will meet her at the Reunion.

My husband, Douglas, and I have been engaged in a private law practice for several years here in Omaha. Prior to that we lived in Sioux City, where Doug served as general counsel for IBP, and I worked for a two thousand-acre planned community and also developed a cancer center. In the '80s we lived in Chicago and Birmingham, Michigan, the latter when I worked in real estate development with the Taubman Company. My professional activities have mainly involved real estate development, securities and investments, and new ventures. I am always interested in something new and different to build from the ground up.

I have changed a lot since college. I am not so idealistic and the demands of parenting have exceeded my expectations. While I remain interested in politics, presently I don't feel compelled to make my contribution to the world in that venue. If the opportunity to pursue public office presented itself before our Fiftieth, I might take a different position.

HOME: Omaha, NE   **OCCUPATION:** Attorney; Partner. Duchek & Buckley (law firm) **BIRTHPLACE:** Mitchell, SD   **SECONDARY SCHOOL:** Lincoln Southeast High School, Lincoln, NE   **YEARS AT COLLEGE:** 1971–75   **DEGREES:** A.B., cum laude, '75; J.D., Univ. of Nebraska '78; M.B.A., Univ. of Chicago '85   **SPOUSE/PARTNER:** Douglas F. Duchek, May 1, 1982 (Univ. of Nebraska '69; J.D., ibid. '71)   **SPOUSE'S OCCUPATION:** Attorney; Partner. Duchek & Buckley   **CHILDREN:** Kydlan K., 1988; Manon D., 1996   **STEP-CHILDREN:** Mia Kennedy, 1965 (p. Peter Kennedy); Gregory Duchek, 1969   **COLLEGE ACTIVITIES:** Radcliffe crew, 1973–75; cheerleader, 1974–75; Institute for International Development; Kennedy Institute of Politics; Class Committee

Scott Dale Buckley: What is most remarkable and more than a little inspiring to me about our Twenty-fifth Reunion is that I am still here to celebrate it—or at least to contemplate it. Some of you know that I was diagnosed with kidney disease when I was a freshman, and that I received a transplant in 1974. I suffered the rejection of that kidney in 1985, and after three years of peritoneal dialysis, received a second transplant, nearly eleven years to the day that I write this reflection. In 1993, I had my right hip replaced for the second time; during my recuperation, I felt a bump on the side of my forehead. This "bump" was effectively treated with surgery and radiation. Except for a couple of little metastases, which showed up in my right lung in 1995, I have been cancer free since that time, if you discount those pesky little skin lesions, which I can see clearly since I had my cataracts removed.

What is also remarkable to me is that I have been able to have a good life—a loving marriage and satisfying career—in spite of these illnesses. While I have often wondered how life might have been without a major illness, I spend more time in awe of the fact that I have been able to overcome each setback and continue the pursuit of my goals. For many others in similar circumstances have not had such good results. I suppose what has enabled me to move on is my belief that I should do more with my life than recover from major illnesses—perhaps my myopic inability to know any better has also helped.

My wife, Cherri, and I have been married since 1983, a setback from which, many would argue, she will never recover. Fortunately, Cherri has stayed with me and supported me as I confronted each illness and attendant anxieties. Cherri works as a legal assistant for a law firm in Kansas City, and she loves the intricacies of public and private financing. I have been in a consulting firm since 1987. My focus is on the development and efficient management of health care services. I hope that Medicare will not go bankrupt before I need it again.

HOME: Kansas City, MO   **OCCUPATION:** Executive Director. Superior Consultant Company, Inc   **BIRTHPLACE:** Boston, MA   **SECONDARY SCHOOL:** Revere High School, Revere, MA   **YEARS AT COLLEGE:** 1971–73; 1974–76   **DEGREES:** A.B., cum laude, '75 ('76); M.S.P.H., Univ. of Missouri '80   **SPOUSE/PARTNER:** Cherri K. (Park Coll. '92)   **SPOUSE'S OCCUPATION:** Legal Assistant. Polsirelli, White, Vardeman and Shelton

Philip H. Bucksbaum:

Biographia (Lattimore translation)
Twenty-five years after Harvard Graduation,
At the midpoint of my life (if I am lucky),
I'm still showing off the stuff I learned in Hum3.

I live in Ann Arbor: Athens on the Huron!
Revel in the football, Art Fair and the music,
While I try to live the life of a professor.

Years have overflowed with family and physics
In New Jersey, Berkeley, Michigan and Paris.
Learned to say, "Excusez moi de vous déranger."

Caroline (or Chaia, when she feels Israeli)
Is my little girl who brings me flowers. Now she
Likes to paint and swim and tease the cat (named Jackson).

And Roberta, wife and mom and law school teacher,
Leverett Arts alumna, actress, lawyer, scientist,
Thinks of articles on copyrights and patents.

Pipkin, Ramsey, Pound, Purcell, these were my college
Heroes. Physicists of stature and compassion.
Now I fill their journals with my own creations.

Twenty-five years after Finley's sonorous lectures,
Midnight food at Hazens, sherry at the master's,
Now I raise my glass: "A toast to thee, fair Harvard."

HOME: Ann Arbor, MI   **OCCUPATION:** Otto Laporte Professor of Physics. Physics Dept., University of Michigan   **BIRTHPLACE:** Grinnell, IA   **SECONDARY SCHOOL:** Washington High School, Cedar Rapids, IA   **YEARS AT COLLEGE:** 1971–75   **DEGREES:** A.B., magna cum laude, '75; M.A., Univ. of California, Berkeley '78; Ph.D., ibid. '80   **SPOUSE/PARTNER:** Roberta Jean Morris, June 1985 (Brown '71; J.D. Harvard '75; Ph.D., Columbia '85)   **SPOUSE'S OCCUPATION:** Attorney. Gifford Krass; Adjunct Associate Lecturer. Univ. of Michigan School of Law   **CHILDREN:** Caroline, 1992

Edward Jonas Budreika: Worked as research assistant at Children's Hospital Medical Center, Boston, 1976–79, in neuroscience tissue culture and protein biochemistry. Then joined the U.S. Navy to fly and see the world. Was an officer (lieutenant); completed Aviation Officer Candidate School (AOCS) and served on USS Enterprise CVN-65, a nuclear aircraft carrier. Operational test director, 1983–87, at Naval Air Station North Island, San Diego. Served 1979–87, honorable discharge, secret clearance. Worked in various sales positions and became an NASD Registered Representative (Series 22,63,6 securities licensed broker, 1992; a California insurance licensed agent, 1996; an LLC venture capitalist, 1998; and a consultant for exclusive high-yield banking programs catering to the wealthy, 1999 to present).

Owned my own distribution technologies business 1984–1999 (LIDA Enterprises).

Found my niche in business ownership in Internet Tridigital Commerce, 1999.

Private franchising converging three key components: e-commerce, member benefits, independent business ownership (IBO).

Family, including five-year-old Veronika, who is bilingual English/Lithuanian. She attends Lithuanian school in Los Angeles on Saturdays.

Homeowner in beautiful Sorrento Valley, San Diego, California, since May 1995.

Have two Yorkshire Terriers, fraternal twin brothers, Precious and Brother, since 1991.

HOME: San Diego, CA   OCCUPATION: President. INDIGO International (Internet tridigital commerce)   BIRTHPLACE: Boston, MA   SECONDARY SCHOOL: Boston Technical High, Dorchester, MA   YEARS AT COLLEGE: 1971–76   DEGREES: A.B. '75 ('76)   SPOUSE/PARTNER: Angela Irene Michiulis, Nov. 30, 1985 (California State Univ., Northridge '85)   SPOUSE'S OCCUPATION: Vice President. INDIGO International   CHILDREN: Veronika, 1994   COLLEGE ACTIVITIES: Violin, Harvard-Radcliffe Orchestra, 1971–72; secretary, Neo-Lithuanian Organization, 1970–76

Terry Mark Burke: Rabbi Abraham Heschel said at the end of his life, "Tell them to live their lives as if they were creating a work of art."

I traveled in Europe after graduation, living illegally in Paris and trying to write. I worked at the Pangloss Bookshop in Cambridge, selling and cataloguing used scholarly books. I went to Harvard Divinity School and received a master of divinity degree. For part of my training I was a student minister at the Charles Street A.M.E. Church in Roxbury. I was ordained a Unitarian Universalist minister in 1982.

Since January of 1983, I have served as the minister of the First Church in Jamaica Plain, Unitarian Universalist, an urban neighborhood church in a diverse part of Boston. Parish ministry is a generalist vocation; I do many different things and see human experience in an enormous range of pain and joy. At First Church, I am fortunate to work with my wife Ellen, the church music director.

As a parish minister, I have traveled to El Salvador and Nicaragua, studied iconography, and been my denomination's observer at the National Council of Churches Board. I have seen loved ones die and my children born (birth and death look very much alike). I have been happily married to Ellen McGuire, musician and quilter, for seventeen years. Our three children are an endless challenge and joy. They are thriving in the Boston public schools. Willis, twelve, loves music and science; we're reading *Moby Dick* together. Amelia, eight, will probably sing on Broadway, and recently broke her arm being adventurous. Lucyanna, six, loves gymnastics, and asks me questions like, "Why am I me?"

I have been fortunate to have wonderful friends and teachers, especially Carl Scovel of King's Chapel in Boston. My father's death this year has been a profound loss for me; I begin to understand the wisdom of the nineteenth century St. Seraphim of Sarov, who addressed everyone as "My Treasure!" and "My Precious!"

As Thomas Merton discovered at the corner of Fourth and Walnut in Louisville, with people around him appearing to shine like the sun, "Thank God I am a human being, thank God that I am a human being like others."

HOME: Roslindale, MA   OCCUPATION: Minister. First Church in Jamaica Plain, Unitarian Universalist   BIRTHPLACE: Flint, MI   SECONDARY SCHOOL: Bentley High School, Burton, MI   YEARS AT COLLEGE: 1971–75   DEGREES: A.B., cum laude, '75; M.Div. '82   SPOUSE/PARTNER: Ellen Tuthill McGuire, Oct. 3, 1982 (Smith Coll. '75; M.M., New England Conservatory '78)   SPOUSE'S OCCUPATION: Church Musician. First Church in Jamaica Plain   CHILDREN: Willis Tuthill, 1988; Amelia Catherine Ashmead, 1992; Lucyanna Virginia, 1994   COLLEGE ACTIVITIES: Friendships

Wendy Barbara Jackson Burton: I am always bemused by predictions that our children will have to adapt to six or seven career changes in their lifetime — it seems to have already happened to me.

Since graduation, I have been a newspaper reporter in a northern Canadian mining town and a capital city, a union negotiator, a freelance editor, a conference organizer, a nonprofit administrator, and a partner (read: general manager, story editor, script writer, grant officer, and marketing director) with my husband in a television production business. And that's just the work I got paid for.

As a volunteer, I helped launch a national professional association for journalists and served as its first woman president. After years of activism in public education, I chaired a conference that produced some results. My latest project: editor-in-chief of a book profiling our town at the turn of the millennium, a fundraiser for the local community foundation.

All this began with my marriage to Rob Burton, whose sense of adventure was a needed antidote to my cautious nature. We went to Canada for jobs and ended up, among other things, starting a television network: YTV, Canada's first cable TV channel for kids. A few years ago, after an absorbing shareholder battle, we sold our interests and moved to Oakville, a picturesque suburb of Toronto. That move, plus a 1995 car accident, persuaded us to take some time off to consider new directions. During this period, I completed several manuscripts for children's books that I am now peddling.

Other activities have revolved around our children. Their enthusiasms have become ours — everything from hockey to youth center politics. As a family, we have traveled to Cape Cod, Florida, California, and Hawaii. We've shared laughs training a Siamese cat to fetch and an Airedale Terrier to roll over. We've endured trips to the emergency room, arguments about curfews, and three home renovations.

As I sought balance in my own life, I resumed playing the piano, developed a needlepoint habit, and learned to love perennials.

I've now lived in Canada longer than I lived in the U.S., and my world view reflects it. I miss America's "frontier spirit," but I like living in Canada's very civil society.

HOME: Oakville, ON, Canada   **OCCUPATION:** Writer (self-employed)   **BIRTHPLACE:** Los Angeles, CA   **SECONDARY SCHOOL:** Watertown High School, Watertown, NY   **YEARS AT COLLEGE:** 1971–75   **DEGREES:** A.B., cum laude, '75   **SPOUSE/PARTNER:** Rob Burton, Sept. 6, 1975 (Univ. of New Mexico; M.S., Columbia '71)   **SPOUSE'S OCCUPATION:** President. Appletree Television Productions (works from home)   **CHILDREN:** Rachel, 1979; Sarah, 1982; Robert, 1991   **COLLEGE ACTIVITIES:** *Harvard Independent,* 1972; upperclass advisor, Thayer North, 1972–73; *Harvard Crimson,* 1972–75, executive editor, 1974

Robert L. Campbell: Those of us who entered graduate school in the mid to late 1970s didn't know it then, but we were the first to embark on our academic apprenticeships after the "Big crunch" (circa 1970, when exponential growth in academic jobs came to an end). My interests have always pointed me toward teaching and writing, but there were times during my grad school years when the prospect of making a career out of such activities looked entirely hopeless.

After five years with a three-initial corporation, I returned to academia in 1991 and have managed to make a go of it. I have the good fortune to work in an academic department where collegiality hasn't been forgotten, feuding is unknown, and the work of a theoretical psychologist is accorded legitimacy. Heidi, Kyla, and I have the good fortune to live amidst natural beauty in a small town that, thanks to the Internet and the economic growth of upstate South Carolina, is no longer isolated.

The tax exacted from everyone who works in an academic institution is having to contend with overweening administrative bureaucracy. The proportion of revenues diverted into administration has been steadily growing in American universities, though the trend is less advanced than in public K–12 systems. Many of my colleagues complain constantly about boneheaded or duplicitous actions by administrators, but few are yet willing to push for a review of priorities within the university, for meaningful public reports of the university's expenditures, or for administrative downsizing.

I'm far enough into middle age to have seen victories recorded in other struggles that once seemed hopeless. The Kantian orthodoxy of Lawrence Kohlberg no longer prevents other moral conceptions from being taken seriously by moral development researchers. After years of patronizing neglect, critics have come to take Sun Ra's rich musical legacy seriously. It is finally becoming possible for Ayn Rand's literary and philosophical efforts to be treated the way that William Faulkner's or Friedrich Nietzsche's might be — as objects of serious study, instead of hysterical adulation or antischolarly dismissal.

The cause of administrative accountability in higher education has much farther to go. We are still a long way from finding and implementing a better scheme of management to replace the priestly guild or the state agency. By our Fiftieth Reunion, maybe I will be able to report some successes.

HOME: Clemson, SC   **OCCUPATION:** Professor of Psychology. Clemson University
BIRTHPLACE: Dubuque, IA   **SECONDARY SCHOOL:** The Kinkaid School, Houston, TX
YEARS AT COLLEGE: 1971–74   **DEGREES:** A.B., cum laude, '75 ('74); Ph.D., Univ. of Texas,
Austin '86   **SPOUSE/PARTNER:** Jolie-Marie Lachance, 1983, divorced, 1985; Heidi M.
Friedberg, 1991 (William Patterson Coll. '79)   **SPOUSE'S OCCUPATION:** Secretary. Firecom
Ltd.   **CHILDREN:** Kyla Alexandra, 1993   **COLLEGE ACTIVITIES:** WHRB, 1972–73; *Ergo*
newspaper, 1971–74

Mark Stephen Campisano: The last five years have been very good to me. As far as work is concerned, I'm still with McKinsey. I was promoted to the position of general tax counsel, where I'm responsible for all of the tax matters that arise in a firm that has seven hundred partners who practice in forty countries. At home, I'm very happily married, and my wife, Kim, just gave birth to a son, Jonathan, in August 1999. We also have a five-year-old boy, Nicholas, and I have a fourteen-year-old daughter, Eleanor, from a previous marriage. So lately, I haven't suffered through any of those patches of rough pavement that I wrote about in our Twentieth Reunion Report.

That very fact—five smooth years—got me to thinking. Or maybe it was Jonathan's birth, or my own forty-sixth birthday in the same month. But I'd like to share my thoughts with you.

For most of us, most of our life is behind us now. We've buried our fathers and mothers, or we soon will. We're at or near the peak of our careers—which means that we'll soon see our influence declining, and our positions unwinding. Our children will soon be able to outrun us—if they can't already—and soon after that, they'll have to care for us as we had to care for them. If we're fortunate, we'll enjoy long lives. But our Reunion Reports will begin to fill up with obituaries, like the one for my roommate Charlie Overfelt. And finally, Harvard will stop reporting on the Class of 1975 altogether. At the age of ninety, Justice Holmes observed that "Death plucks my ear and says: Live!—I am coming." That's just as true for us.

It begs the question, though. "Live," to be sure—but *for what?* Most of us have spent the last twenty-five years concentrating on achievement; on making a mark in our chosen field of work. Should we continue to live for achievement? I don't think so. Who will remember our achievements, even fifty years after we're dead? Who will reread our briefs, recall our diagnoses, reminisce about our business plans? My old boss, Justice Brennan, had a great career, but even now, his ripples in the pond are fading, and others are washing them away. Eventually, even Mozart will go the way of Ozymandias, and be utterly forgotten. If our achievements aren't truly lasting, then they can't be what we should be living for.

Well then, how about family? I don't want to be a spoilsport, but I don't think that family is worth living for, either. We can invest decades in a relationship, and it still may turn out badly. Even if our children love us dearly, they may be unwise, or unlucky, and so fritter away everything that we give them. To our grandchildren, we'll be peripheral figures—and to our great-grandchildren, we'll be strangers in odd clothes. Everything we do for our families will eventually be passed on to strangers.

Maybe we should just live for the moment? That doesn't work for me, and I doubt it works for you either. Most of us want to believe that our lives have some larger purpose. And even if we don't hold such a belief, I find it hard to imagine truly enjoying any pleasurable experience—great music, or a deep friendship—if we believe, at that same moment, that the experience "really" means nothing beyond the sensation that it's creating in our brain. It seems to me that experiences are only truly pleasurable to the extent that they connect us to something outside or beyond ourselves—so that if we don't believe in anything outside or beyond ourselves, we can't truly enjoy anything that we do.

All of these thoughts were written down a long time ago—and more eloquently—by the author of *Ecclesiastes*. He said that life under the sun—without reference to God—is meaningless. Twenty years ago, I was driven to that conclusion, and so I decided to place my life in the hands of the God of the Old and New Testaments. In other words, I became a Christian.

Becoming a Christian didn't transform my life into a string of uninterrupted successes and pleasures. In our Twentieth Reunion Report, I recounted a painful divorce, and losing custody of my daughter. But becoming a Christian did give me something to live for. Now I can view my achievements—such as they are—as good stewardship of the gifts that God has given me. And I can look forward to God's approval of that good stewardship when I meet Him face to face. As for family, now I can view my children as another great gift—my clearest opportunity to spread the Kingdom of God on earth. And even the pleasures of the moment taste sweeter—now that I know who they come from. I can recognize them as merely a foretaste of the pleasure of meeting Him.

If you're at all interested in what I've said, I invite you to e-mail me. I'd love to start a dialogue, and hope to see you at our Twenty-fifth Reunion.

HOME: Pelham, NY   **OCCUPATION:** General Tax Counsel. McKinsey & Company, Inc. (management consulting)   **BIRTHPLACE:** Norwood, MA   **SECONDARY SCHOOL:** Xaverian Brothers High School, Westwood, MA   **YEARS AT COLLEGE:** 1971–75 **DEGREES:** A.B., magna cum laude, '75; M. Litt., Oxford Univ. '78; J.D., Yale '80 **SPOUSE/PARTNER:** Kimberly Earline, Jan. 11, 1992 (Univ. of California, Davis '89) **CHILDREN:** Eleanor, 1985; Nicholas, 1994; Jonathan, 1999   **COLLEGE ACTIVITIES:** Squash, junior varsity, 1974–75; Phi Beta Kappa, 1974–75

Richard Joseph Cantwell: Happily married to the same wonderful woman (Cathy) for twenty-three years, blessed with three fantastic boys (Bri, seventeen; Steve, fifteen; and A. J., twelve), living in my dream home in the town where I grew up (Wellesley) and traveling the world for Gillette the last fifteen years would suggest a certain predictability to my life. Nothing could be farther from the truth.

Marketing, by definition, deals with changes in consumer behavior and has provided me with a career full of exceptional challenges and good fortune. However, the roller coaster ride of parenting is unquestionably the most fulfilling yet scariest experience of my lifetime. Sharing the ride with Cathy has been a source of constant reassurance.

Along the way, I discovered ten years of coaching youth baseball, basketball, and soccer was the perfect way to share a growing-up experience with my three sons, stay connected to their world, and give something back to the community. With my schedule, family vacations became the important time to reconnect. We adopted a ranch in Colorado as our "getaway" spot, built a cottage by the ocean in Rhode Island, and shared family adventures like whitewater rafting in Idaho to create lasting memories of shared experiences. Now, our eldest is heading off to college (Harvard 2004???) and one can only imagine how that will change his life and ours.

My liberal arts studies at Harvard gave me an indelible window into consumer behavior through which I have enjoyed the marketing of great brand names like Tylenol, Braun, and Gillette. In the process, I've been fortunate to introduce many new products, make commercials that have aired around the world, and, in 1995, I was chosen as one of the top one hundred marketers of the year.

The realities of global commerce have made me realize how small the world really is and how interconnected we all are. For this reason, I'm especially proud of what I have been able to give my family and the love they have returned in exchange.

HOME: Wellesley, MA   **OCCUPATION:** Director, Global Marketing Services. The Gillette Company   **BIRTHPLACE:** Syracuse, NY   **SECONDARY SCHOOL:** Wellesley Senior High School, Wellesley, MA   **YEARS AT COLLEGE:** 1971–75   **DEGREES:** A.B., cum laude, '75; M.B.A., Dartmouth '81   **SPOUSE/PARTNER:** Catherine Rose Fontaine, Aug. 7, 1976 (Colby Sawyer Coll. '73)   **SPOUSE'S OCCUPATION:** Homemaker; Real Estate Agent. Hunneman Coldwell Banker   **CHILDREN:** Brian, 1981; Stephen, 1983; Andrew, 1987

Anders E. Carlsson: Like many of us, I liked Boston enough that I stuck around — for five years of graduate school in physics. After that, I was really ready for a change, spent three years in Ithaca, New York, doing a post-doc, and ended up in Saint Louis (which seems infinite by comparison with Ithaca). Here I teach physics and research biological physics at Washington University. I live, with my wife and two children, in a big old house that takes more of my time than I really care to give to it.

I'm also the pianist for the Unlikely Blues Band.

HOME: Saint Louis, MO **OCCUPATION:** Professor of Physics. Dept. of Physics, Washington University **BIRTHPLACE:** Västervik, Sweden **SECONDARY SCHOOL:** Redwood High School, Larkspur, CA **YEARS AT COLLEGE:** 1971–75 **DEGREES:** A.B., summa cum laude, '75; Ph.D. '81 **SPOUSE/PARTNER:** Christiane, Aug. 11, 1988 **SPOUSE'S OCCUPATION:** Language Professional and Instructor (self-employed) **CHILDREN:** Nils, 1991; Anna, 1992 **COLLEGE ACTIVITIES:** Ping-Pong Club, 1972–74

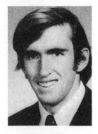

Richard Marshall Cashin: Who I married and what I do have carried me through a joyous twenty-five years. I met Lisa my first day at Harvard and took nine years, several of which were spent a half a world away writing a letter a day, to convince her to marry me. She's fun, smart, fit, dependable, and a pleasure to be with ninety percent of the time. We have two excellent kids that reflect her best qualities and of whom I'm overly proud.

Not since Babylon has there been an economic boom like this with inflation below three percent and business values up to fifteen percent per year for twenty years. I've had the same job, secretary, boss, and phone number for twenty years, and each year it seems to get more interesting, varied, and profitable. We partner with management in the purchase of businesses that make everything from semiconductors to sofa sleepers to cooling towers. The people are energetic, hard working, optimistic, and therefore, generally successful.

The people we met at Harvard have remained our closest friends. I do sports and invest with Harvard friends, we arrange elaborate trips, have spent almost every New Year's at the Smiths' and have dinner at the Weinbergs' every year before the Head of the Charles. Harry Parker remains hugely important to my family. I can't imagine how anyone could have enjoyed being part of the Harvard community more than I.

HOME: New York, NY   **OCCUPATION:** President. Citicorp Venture Capital (private equity investments)   **BIRTHPLACE:** Washington, DC   **SECONDARY SCHOOL:** Phillips Academy, Andover, MA   **YEARS AT COLLEGE:** 1971–75   **DEGREES:** A.B., magna cum laude, '75; M.B.A. '80   **SPOUSE/PARTNER:** Elizabeth "Lisa" Smith, Sept. 6, 1980 (Radcliffe '75)   **SPOUSE'S OCCUPATION:** Consultant to Credit Committee. Local Initiatives Support Corp   **CHILDREN:** Frances B., 1985; Henry B., 1989   **HARVARD/RADCLIFFE SIBLINGS:** Anne Cashin Goldenheim, Ed.M. '74   **COLLEGE ACTIVITIES:** Varsity squash; rowing, three years

Shu Yan Chan: The nice thing about the Twentieth Reunion was linking up with Barbara Backman Treacy '75 from South House and then being able to write a recommendation for her oldest daughter, Erin '01, for admission to Harvard. Talk about fast-forward!

Harvard ties remain important in our family; my wife, Anne Troy '82, and I met via the Harvard Club of Chicago, where I've been a member of the board of directors for fifteen years and involved on the Schools Committee and local club activities. Anne is a past president of the Radcliffe Club and recently a Radcliffe College Alumni Association regional director, so we've been back to Cambridge a few times lately.

Currently, our two-and-one-half-year-old daughter, Kay, is in preschool and is the focus of much of the home life. At the Tenth Reunion, I was single, living in a highrise downtown Chicago apartment building and driving an Alfa Romeo GTV6/2.5. We currently live in an old Victorian home on the north side of Chicago, and I drive a Chevy sedan with a child seat full of crumbs. I'm much happier.

After twenty-five years, I'm just glad to be here. I hope to be able to say the same thing at the Fiftieth.

HOME: Chicago, IL   **OCCUPATION:** President; Managing Broker. Chan Enterprises, Inc. (commercial real estate services)   **BIRTHPLACE:** Hong Kong   **SECONDARY SCHOOL:** Senn High School, Chicago, IL   **YEARS AT COLLEGE:** 1971–75   **DEGREES:** A.B., cum laude, '75   **SPOUSE/PARTNER:** Anne Barbara Troy, May 25, 1991 (Harvard '82) **SPOUSE'S OCCUPATION:** Marketing Research Analyst. Everyday Learning, Inc., Chicago, IL   **CHILDREN:** Katherine, 1997

Paul F. Charnetzki: I try to integrate my work (serving as an expert witness in litigation), my family (wife and three kids) and community service (elected to my local school board). Since Harvard I have had to switch from the Red Sox to the White Sox (still without the distraction of world championships). I have retained my love of country music and as the Haggard song goes, "I've only me to blame cus Momma tried."

HOME: Wilmette, IL   **OCCUPATION:** Partner. Arthur Andersen (litigation support) **BIRTHPLACE:** Valley City, ND   **SECONDARY SCHOOL:** St. George's School, Newport, RI   **YEARS AT COLLEGE:** 1971–75   **DEGREES:** A.B., magna cum laude, '75; M.S.I.A., Carnegie-Mellon Univ.   **SPOUSE/PARTNER:** Anne K. Leary, May 28, 1977 (Harvard '76) **CHILDREN:** Elena, 1984; Paul, 1986; Meara, 1988

Pamela Sue Chassin: Twenty-five years ago...I graduated from Harvard knowing that I would be a full-time, dedicated surgeon and a devoted mother of at least eight children.

Twenty years ago...I realized that surgery and family might not be an ideal combination and moved into public health.

Fifteen years ago...after marrying my true soul mate, our first child was born and my thoughts on being able to balance family and career were forever changed. After our second child was born, I did not return to work for years, enjoying the luxury of full-time mothering and part-time volunteering.

Ten years ago...we moved to rural northwestern Connecticut and learned that life in the country isn't about slowing down, but it is about: being surrounded by incredible beauty, living in a community of caring neighbors, being able to do all of your errands in fifteen minutes (with no lines), driving a lot, having as many dogs and cats as you want, and allowing your children to remain children just a little longer.

Five years ago...I started a business of writing and producing medical minutes for radio, satisfying my professional interests, while letting me choose my own schedule and, most importantly, still allowing me to attend soccer games and school performances. I also jumped into e-commerce early, creating an on-line store, and have dabbled in Web site design, for nonprofit organizations and small businesses.

Life is very rich and full; I feel very lucky.

HOME: Lakeville, CT   **OCCUPATION:** President. HMS Productions, Inc. (health education and health promotion for consumers, via medical minutes for radio broadcast); co-owner. www.begifted.com (on-line store)   **BIRTHPLACE:** New York, NY   **SECONDARY SCHOOL:** Manhasset High School, Manhasset, NY   **YEARS AT COLLEGE:** 1971–75   **DEGREES:** A.B., magna cum laude, '75; M.D., New York Univ. '79; M.P.H., Univ. of North Carolina, Chapel Hill '81   **SPOUSE/PARTNER:** Jared Bruce Zelman, May 29, 1983 (Univ. of California, Riverside)   **SPOUSE'S OCCUPATION:** Physician; Director of Emergency Services. Sharon Hospital   **CHILDREN:** Allison, 1984; Joanna, 1986   **HARVARD/RADCLIFFE SIBLINGS:** Mark Chassin '68, M.D. '73, M.P.P. '73; Richard Chassin '80   **COLLEGE ACTIVITIES:** WHRB; junior varsity baseball manager; Room 13; Undergraduate Admissions Council

Dale Jerome Cherry: I have been involved in the municipal bond brokerage industry for the entire twenty-five years since graduation. During this time, I have worked for nine different firms due to mergers, acquisitions, and the highly transient nature of my field. For four of these years, two partners and I started, ran, and ultimately sold our own "regional boutique" municipal brokerage company.

In my nonworking hours, I have become an accomplished magician, performing in a variety of settings ranging from street fairs to formal dinner parties. I have given free shows for indigent audiences and competed for prizes against other magicians.

But my greatest accomplishment is in the human domain as a husband, parent, and friend. Sue, my wife of twenty-four years, and I have stressed spontaneity and creativity in raising our two daughters. As a result, our girls not only achieve scholastically, but also dance, draw, play music, write, and most important, think, question, and dream.

Sue and I have striven to continue growing by traveling, patronizing the arts, thinking, analyzing, meeting new people, and looking for the all-too-rare "kindred spirit." We have vowed to avoid bitterness, cynicism, and unnecessary conflict and have done our best to help each other stick to this pledge.

With my priorities more in order than ever before, I start the next twenty-five years aspiring to leave a positive mark on all who are part of my life now and in the future.

HOME: Evanston, IL   OCCUPATION: Managing Director. Loop Capital Markets (municipal bond sales)   BIRTHPLACE: Cleveland, OH   SECONDARY SCHOOL: Shaker Heights High School, Shaker Heights, OH   YEARS AT COLLEGE: 1971–74   DEGREES: A.B., cum laude, '75 ('74); M.B.A., Univ. of Chicago '79   SPOUSE/PARTNER: Susan Spaeth, Aug. 9, 1975 (Northwestern Univ. '76)   SPOUSE'S OCCUPATION: Poet (works from home)   CHILDREN: Alison Leigh, 1982; Erica Michelle, 1987   COLLEGE ACTIVITIES: Marching band

Paul Chessin: What a long, strange trip it's been.

Undoubtedly, the most important things in my life, and which I would write about, would be my wife and children. Alas, without such and still single I am. So, please indulge me as I share my life's previous twenty-five years.

From college to law school (J.D. '79) to New York City to make my mark as a young master of the universe in a Park Avenue law firm. Ha! After three and a half years of enduring the grind of city life and tedium of corporate law practice, I set out for the (hopefully) wide-open plains and opportunities of Colorado.

Actually, I escaped the city barely one step ahead of a vicious New York Landlords' Association mob after my hide. It seems they were unhappy with me when my request to have my landlord fix a broken soap dish escalated into a legal World War III. (See *New York Law Journal,* Nov. 30, 1983, p. 1; *Wall Street Journal,* Jan. 23, 1984, p. 1.)

Safely arriving in Denver, I resumed the practice of corporate/commercial litigation. My timing was impeccable; Denver soon plummeted into the Savings and Loan/Real Estate bust of the mid-1980s. Many a law firm fell victim, and I was fortunate to be associated with several of them.

After pinballing around Denver's law firms (out of the five I worked for, three no longer exist), I eventually figured out I wasn't having much fun. So, I decided to take some time off from my career. I became a professional ski bum.

What I thought would be a brief hiatus while I recharged my legal batteries turned into a half dozen or so years as a professional ski patroller with a major Colorado resort. During this time (and as I had done with New York's landlords some years before), I successfully endeared myself to the resort's management, usually through means litigious. One of my greater achievements was unionizing the ski patrol (a byproduct of which was a fifteen-page National Labor Relations Board decision finding that the resort had committed a number of unfair labor practices).

To keep me busy when not on the slopes (or tweaking management), I became a firefighter with a local mountain-town volunteer fire department. There is something exhilarating in racing down the highway in a fifteen-ton fire truck with lights blazing and sirens blaring. However, the real joy is in easing the fear and pain of a child who's hurt and scared and doesn't know why, and watching the child's shocked stare slowly melt into a shy smile.

It was in discovering this real joy that I learned what it was I wanted to do when I grew up. I determined to re-direct my legal career to helping the community and perhaps alleviate the suffering of those in need.

My job search consumed several reams of my résumé. Who would want to hire a lawyer turned ski bum? Ultimately, I successfully prevailed upon a

Colorado Court of Appeals judge willing to take a chance and hire me as her law clerk. The Honorable Sandra I. Rothenberg graciously took me under her wing and provided my legal career the jump-start it so badly needed.

Because of Judge Rothenberg, I soon was offered a position with the Colorado Attorney General's office. It is there that I am now experiencing what for me is the real joy in the practice of law. I am an assistant attorney general in the Consumer Protection Section, protecting the vulnerable and unsuspecting from scammers, schemers, and rip-off artists, and having an absolute blast doing it.

But if I can somehow conquer the politics, I think I'd like to follow in Judge Rothenberg's footsteps and be a judge myself.

There you have it. Twenty-five years in three hundred words (give or take a few hundred).

HOME: Denver, CO   **OCCUPATION:** Assistant Attorney General. Colorado Attorney General's Office   **BIRTHPLACE:** New York, NY   **SECONDARY SCHOOL:** Great Neck South Senior High School, Great Neck, NY   **YEARS AT COLLEGE:** 1971–76   **DEGREES:** A.B., magna cum laude '75 ('76); J.D. '79   **COLLEGE ACTIVITIES:** Lightweight crew, 1971–76; Hasty Pudding Theatricals, 1972–76

Charles John Chester: Still having fun after all these years.

HOME: Metairie, LA   **OCCUPATION:** M.D. (psychiatrist, addictionologist, psychoanalyst). De Paul/Tulane Behavioral Health Center   **BIRTHPLACE:** Chicago, IL **SECONDARY SCHOOL:** Campion Jesuit, Prairie Du Chien, WI   **YEARS AT COLLEGE:** 1971–75   **DEGREES:** A.B., cum laude, '75; M.D., Dartmouth '78   **SPOUSE/PARTNER:** Luckier "in love" than marriage   **CHILDREN:** Matthew, 1985; Camille, 1991 (died, 1991); Zachary, 1993; Lilia Noelle, 1995   **COLLEGE ACTIVITIES:** Freshman lightweight crew, 1971–72; Winthrop House crew team, 1973–75; bartender, Harvard Student Agencies, 1972–75

Bruce B. Chien: You never know what life holds in store for you. After disillusionment in academic medicine (part of the Reagan National Institutes of Health era), I've been practicing in Peoria, Illinois, where most of my energy goes into family, chronic pain management, and (yes) aviation. Amazing how life expands to fill all available time. I've become a flight instructor and teaching that art really gets the juices going.

HOME: Peoria, IL   **OCCUPATION:** Physician   **BIRTHPLACE:** Wyandotte, MI
SECONDARY SCHOOL: New Trier East, Winnetka, IL   **YEARS AT COLLEGE:** 1973–75
DEGREES: A.B., magna cum laude, '75; M.D, Univ. of Chicago '79   **SPOUSE/PARTNER:**
Susan A. Levine, Nov. 19, 1978 (Alfred Univ. '75)   **SPOUSE'S OCCUPATION:** Mom
CHILDREN: Sarah, 1988; Abby, 1990   **HARVARD/RADCLIFFE SIBLINGS:** Agnes Chien
'70   **COLLEGE ACTIVITIES:** Harvard Band; teaching assistant for Dr. George Wald,
1974–75

Daniel T. Chiles: Harvard's junior-year vocational survey revealed that I was unsuited for every profession, so my brother and I began a manufacturing and marketing company called Heatway which is now the second largest radiant floor company in North America.

Call me if your feet are cold.

All day long I do creative stuff: computer animation, shoot and edit videos, build marketing campaigns, write business plans, negotiate financing, and develop new products. I hold seven U.S. patents for radiant products, an aerial display and a fastener called Cliptie.

Last summer we took three adults and six teenage boys on a mountain bike trip down the Continental Divide from Roosville, Montana to Red Mountain south of Butte. We made a video about it, so call me if you want a copy.

In September, I designed and helped organize volunteers to build an eighty-foot bridge which we donated to the local YMCA camp. I'm also a fireworks professional, having obtained my pyrotechnics degree for Class B explosives.

Married with four great kids: Margy has a degree in engineering physics, but she left her career to raise the family. Philip is in college and Amelia is in first grade, so I span the X, Y and soon-to-come Z generation gaps. Thomas and David are in high school and we spend a lot of time together bike riding, fishing and hangin' out.

Biggest moral lapse: Deer hunting. I figure it's hypocritical to eat any meat unless I'm willing to do the dirty work with my own hands.

Self abuse: Managing political campaigns for county and city officials. Win some, lose some.

Looking back: I was cold, lonely, and broke at Harvard; sort of like *Trainspotting* in crimson. It was tough to get in and tough to get out. It was tough love before that term existed.

HOME: Springfield, MO   OCCUPATION: Vice President. Heatway (manufacturing and marketing)   BIRTHPLACE: Springfield, MO   SECONDARY SCHOOL: Glendale High School, Springfield, MO   YEARS AT COLLEGE: 1971–75   DEGREES: A.B., cum laude, '75   SPOUSE/PARTNER: Margy, 1980 (Southwest Missouri State Univ. '80)   SPOUSE'S OCCUPATION: Household CEO   CHILDREN: Philip, 1980; Thomas, 1982; David, 1985; Amelia, 1992   HARVARD/RADCLIFFE SIBLINGS: Jim Chiles '77

William Jonathan Claff: Twenty-five years later and I still have one more expository writing composition to complete: "An Account of My Life since Graduation." On a scale that starts with "What I Did Last Summer" and ends with "Write your Own Obituary" this topic could be on the heavy side. O.K., don't panic; first define the audience; that would be myself, the only person certain to read this, my wife, family, and classmates who were friends and acquaintances. Also, the style should be informal; touching on activities, accomplishments, family, travel, avocations, and concerns. Is this an account or a postdoctoral dissertation on life? The answer is in the mind of the beholder.

The single visible thread that runs through my entire adult life is the computer. The invisible thread is a passion for mathematics, logic, and the sciences in general; the computer simply being a tool with which to explore these subjects. My quest for precision was sometimes mistaken for perfection. To strive for perfection is fun; to be perfect would be a drag.

My vocation, avocation, and accomplishments lie primarily in the computer field. My life's work probably has had little redeeming social value, but I both enjoy my work and am good at it which is more than many can say. Computer programming is an art form requiring a highly creative process. In any field when you create a thing of beauty the self-satisfaction and recognition of others is deeply rewarding. If accomplishment were measured by a lasting impact on others then my long tenure in a variety of roles with the Boston Computer Society would be my major accomplishment. Together with my nationally syndicated radio show, I enjoyed teaching and learning about computers and the computer industry during the explosive early years.

I've also enjoyed traveling; in Europe, and more recently in the Caribbean. I can spend all day snorkeling and photographing coral, sponges, and fish.

HOME: Wellesley, MA   OCCUPATION: Computer Programmer   **SECONDARY SCHOOL:** Newton High School, Newton, MA   **YEARS AT COLLEGE:** 1971–76   **DEGREES:** A.B. '75; S.M. '76   **SPOUSE/PARTNER:** Janet Ruth Strazdes, Oct. 1, 1999 (Boston State Coll. '79; M.E., Univ. of Massachusetts '90)   **SPOUSE'S OCCUPATION:** Computer Network Specialist

---

Cheryl Clark: After graduating in 1975, I wandered from Harvard to MIT and back to Harvard again without knowing what career lay ahead of me. I studied linguistics, speech perception, neurolinguistics, psycholinguistics, and cognitive science, and wound up taking a job in high technology almost by accident after completing graduate school. Today I work as a linguist in a company that specializes in speech recognition. I have a wonderful husband who grew up in New York within twenty miles of my hometown, but who I didn't meet until 1990 while we were both working at Wang Laboratories in Lowell, Massachusetts. Highlights of my post-Harvard life include trips that I have taken to Paris and the south of France and acquiring and updating (while still preserving) the 1870s house that we currently live in only twenty minutes away from Harvard Yard. It feels as though I've been on an odyssey, but there is something about this part of New England that holds me with a strong force. This last decade has been one of particular enrichment. Since the beginning of 1990, I have met the man that I have since married, watched two children develop from preteens to college students at the brink of adulthood, and added three hobbies that keep me in touch with nature (gardening), romance (ballroom dancing), and critical thinking (my book club).

HOME: Arlington, MA   OCCUPATION: Principal Software Linguist. Lernout & Hauspie Speech Products   **BIRTHPLACE:** New York, NY   **SECONDARY SCHOOL:** Hempstead High School, Hempstead, NY   **YEARS AT COLLEGE:** 1971–75   **DEGREES:** A.B., cum laude, '75; Ph.D. '83   **SPOUSE/PARTNER:** Danny E. Brundage, May 14, 1994 (Cornell '74; M.S., ibid. '75)   **SPOUSE'S OCCUPATION:** Senior Consultant. Cisco Systems   **STEP-CHILDREN:** Dana Brundage; Danny Brundage, Jr.

John K. Clarke: I've got it made. I have a terrific wife, Melanie (married for twenty-one-plus years), four wonderful and healthy daughters, a career that I love and am proud of, and a home and a community that we love and greatly enjoy. We count our blessings and are grateful for our good fortune.

Career-wise, immediately after Harvard I spent five years with the General Electric Company in various sales, marketing and business development jobs and then two years at Wharton for my M.B.A. For the last eighteen years I have been making venture capital investments, principally in health care–related businesses. I am the managing general partner of Cardinal Health Partners and DSV Partners. We manage the funds out of two offices, Princeton, New Jersey and Irvine, California. It's been lots of work and lots of fun. Aside from sharing some of the economic success that the industry has enjoyed, I am regularly amazed by the innovative spirit and entrepreneurial passion of the managers and technologists we deal with. The opportunity to work with such talented and motivated people is a great part of what makes my work so rewarding.

My wife, Melanie, has made the more important half of my life rich beyond my deserving. Her energy, commitment, and skill at managing our family are a wonder indeed. Education, music, sports, food, entertainment: making the simple things in life special is one of life's true joys for us.

Our daughters, Julia, Noelle, Ellen, and Isabelle are constant reminders of the myriad blessings of hope, love, energy, enthusiasm, and wonder that this world holds for us. We are deeply grateful for their health and happiness and for our own.

HOME: Princeton, New Jersey   **OCCUPATION:** Managing General Partner. Cardinal Health Partners (venture capital investment)   **BIRTHPLACE:** Elmhurst, IL
SECONDARY SCHOOL: North Haven High School, North Haven, CT   **YEARS AT COLLEGE:** 1971–76   **DEGREES:** A.B. '75 ('76); M.B.A., Univ. of Pennsylvania '82
SPOUSE/PARTNER: Melanie Cognetta, June 24, 1978 (Wellesley Coll. '76)   **SPOUSE'S OCCUPATION:** Homemaker; Musician; Violinist. Princeton Chamber Symphony
CHILDREN: Julia Kennedy Clarke, 1984; Noelle Cognetta Clarke, 1986; Ellen St. Clair Clarke, 1989; Isabelle Raphaella Clarke, 1992   **COLLEGE ACTIVITIES:** Varsity football; varsity track

Bruce H. Cohen: Life after Harvard has been a journey — a fun journey through the evolution of technology of the past twenty-five years. From Cambridge, I went to Baltimore — the land of Orioles, hard-shell crabs, and Johns Hopkins Medical School. Betsy Heller (Wellesley '76, Harvard M.B.A. '78) and I married in 1978. She moved to Baltimore to work at the Black and Decker Manufacturing Company.

In 1980 we moved to Saint Louis — the land of Cardinals, toasted ravioli, and Washington University Medical Center. I continued my medical training in ophthalmology at Barnes Hospital/Washington University Medical Center. I have practiced ophthalmology in Saint Louis since that time with special interests in cataract surgery, diseases of the retina, and refractive surgery. I have the challenges of running a medical practice in the era of the increasing influence of managed care. My spare time is spent between mastering a lousy golf swing, tennis, photography, orchids, skiing, cooking, computers, and a few other distractions.

Betsy joined Ralston Purina Company in 1980. She has survived the acquisition of two major companies, and the sale or spin-off of at least nine companies and still works for Ralston Purina Company, where she has risen to the rank of vice president. She oversees the e-commerce and Internet activities of Ralston Purina.

We have two wonderful sons, Greg, fifteen, and Scott, twelve. They continue to devour the newest offerings from Nintendo 64, and can't imagine what it was like to grow up without VCRs, microwaves, computers, the Internet, and wireless phones. Who can imagine life now without computers, fax machines, e-mail, personal organizers, and the rest of the tools of the connected era?

In recent years we have enjoyed travel to Maine, Florida, California, Colorado, Maryland, the Caribbean, Chicago, Boston, New Orleans, and Philadelphia. I periodically see Paul Sternberg and Dave Browning at ophthalmology meetings. We are looking forward to the return to Cambridge to see the Harvard friends that we have not seen in so long.

HOME: Saint Louis, MO   OCCUPATION: Physician. Ophthalmologist Associated Eye Surgeons, Ltd   BIRTHPLACE: Washington, DC   SECONDARY SCHOOL: Bethesda-Chevy Chase High School, Bethesda, MD   YEARS AT COLLEGE: 1972–76   DEGREES: A.B., magna cum laude, '75 ('76); M.D., Johns Hopkins Univ. '80   SPOUSE/PARTNER: Elizabeth Heller, June 17, 1978 (Wellesley Coll. '76; M.B.A., Harvard '78)   SPOUSE'S OCCUPATION: Vice President. Ralston Purina Co.   CHILDREN: Gregory P., 1985; Scott A., 1988   COLLEGE ACTIVITIES: Freshman crew

Haldan Neal Cohn: Twenty-five years after my graduation from fair Harvard, Phyllis and I are professors of astronomy at Indiana University and well-established Bloomingtonians. Since my Twentieth Anniversary Report, we have been blessed with the birth of a second daughter, Amy, now three years old. Her elder sister, Alison, is now nearly fourteen. Our current parenting experience thus encompasses activities at both nursery and middle school. Alison continues her extracurricular interests in ballet and choir, and Amy has joined her this year in taking ballet and music classes. Alison's bat mitzvah was a major family event of the past year. In addition to Alison's fine demonstration of Hebrew scholarship, Phyllis and I read Torah in public for the first time. It was rewarding for all of us. Alison also placed third in the 1999 Indiana state competition of the National Geography Bee. Amy enjoys reading, drawing, imaginative play, and playground activities, not to mention videos and computer games. Phyllis and I continue to use the WIYN (Wisconsin-Indiana-Yale-National Optical Astronomy Observatories) telescope and the Hubble Space Telescope to study globular star clusters within the Milky Way Galaxy. Our collaborative programs have also been awarded time on the recently launched Chandra X-ray Observatory. We teach astronomy courses from the freshman to the graduate level and now frequently meet our former students around town. Parenting, teaching, and research activities take all of our time and then some. It's been a pretty good quarter century, all in all.

HOME: Bloomington, IN   OCCUPATION: Professor of Astronomy. Dept. of Astronomy, Indiana University   BIRTHPLACE: Redwood City, CA   SECONDARY SCHOOL: Smithtown Central High School, Saint James, NY   YEARS AT COLLEGE: 1971–75   DEGREES: A.B., summa cum laude, '75; M.A., Princeton '77; Ph.D., ibid. '79 SPOUSE/PARTNER: Phyllis M. Lugger, Jan. 14, 1979 (Harvard '76; A.M., ibid. '81; Ph.D., ibid. '82)   SPOUSE'S OCCUPATION: Professor of Astronomy. Indiana University CHILDREN: Alison S., 1985; Amy J., 1996   HARVARD/RADCLIFFE SIBLINGS: Evan R. Cohn '82   COLLEGE ACTIVITIES: Outing Club, 1972–75

Stephen Norfleet Cohn: Good fortune has followed me down the paths I have taken. Upon finishing my Ph.D. in geophysics — to me, the physics of scenery — I rationalized that the earth and what we know about it evolve slowly, but that a new opportunity facing me, computer networking, offered rich challenges and would satisfy my ever-present urge to build and discover. I returned to Cambridge from Pasadena to join the ARRPANET project at Bolt, Beranek and Newman, just in time to help convert the Net to today's protocols, evolve it from the experiment it was to a worldwide operational infrastructure, and push the envelope in areas of networking and security. The television industry's recent lament about declining viewership associated with the rise of the Web would have made this all worthwhile even if I hadn't enjoyed so much fun along the way. Now, lured to electronic commerce, I build high-performance teams in lively and personal Internet start-ups.

A decade ago I met and married Nancy. We've built a wonderful, albeit rather masculine, family. In the current phase, organizing play dates, coaching soccer, and leading the boys to new experiences fill our time. I have learned that balancing work and family is hard, parenting even harder. I have been lucky to remain close to my parents and especially enjoyed working with my father to build the house where Nancy, the boys, and I now live.

HOME: Winchester, MA   OCCUPATION: President, Engineering. SoftLock.com (Internet electronic commerce start-up)   BIRTHPLACE: Boston, MA   SECONDARY SCHOOL: Commonwealth School, Boston, MA   YEARS AT COLLEGE: 1971–75 DEGREES: A.B., cum laude, '75; M.S., California Inst. of Technology '78; Ph.D., ibid. '83 SPOUSE/PARTNER: Nancy Elizabeth Isaac, Sept. 9, 1989 (Middlebury Coll. '78; Sc.D., Harvard '89)   SPOUSE'S OCCUPATION: Public Health Researcher   CHILDREN: Chase Alexandre, 1991; Dylan Andrew, 1993

James Anderson Comer: I have been very fortunate during the past twenty-five years and very much look forward to the next twenty-five years.

I have spent many of these past years attending graduate schools in Georgia. I obtained an M.S. in wildlife biology in 1985 which led me to work on wildlife diseases at the Southeastern Cooperative Wildlife Disease Study, Athens, Georgia. The disease work led me to get a Ph.D. in veterinary parasitology in 1991. These degrees were obtained at the University of Georgia's School of Forest Resources and College of Veterinary Medicine.

I then decided to work in public health on zoonotic diseases (diseases which are transmissible from animals to man, such as Rocky Mountain spotted fever) and got an M.P.H. in epidemiology from Emory University. I have been associated with the Viral and Rickettsial Zoonoses Branch, Centers for Disease Control and Prevention (CDC), Atlanta, since 1995. I have been working on emerging tick-borne diseases and rickettsial diseases of minorities. A highlight was an African trip to Kikwit, which is in what was then Zaire, on the field team from CDC which responded to the large outbreak of Ebola hemorrhagic fever virus which occurred there in 1995.

I have two beautiful daughters, Andrea (fourteen) and Catharine (twelve) who both live in Macon. Andrea has just started at Middlesex School ('03), so I will be in the New England area more often during the next four years. At six feet, Andrea plays basketball and is a power-hitting first base woman in softball. Catharine is at Stratford Academy in Macon, where she plays trombone in the marching band. She also enjoys horseback riding. My parents are healthy, not yet retired, and live in Macon. They have as full a schedule and travel now more than ever.

I still enjoy playing guitars regularly, mostly within the confines of my living room. I have a fine collection of Dobros, including a right-handed model (mine are all left-handed). I have just purchased a home in the Atlanta area, and I am in the process of building a series of brick and stone patios and walkways to improve my view of and access to the CSX freight trains which regularly pass by about thirty yards behind my house (which is why I decided on this house).

As I look back over the last twenty-five years, I realize how fortunate I have been to have enjoyed my good health, my family's good health, an interesting career thus far, a beautiful wife (for awhile), and two fine and beautiful daughters. I can only hope that the next twenty-five years will hold in store more of the same joys and happiness such as I have experienced since I was passing the time away playing guitars and occasionally studying on the banks of the Charles all those years ago.

HOME: Decatur, GA   OCCUPATION: Epidemiologist. Viral and Rickettsial Zoonoses Branch, Centers for Disease Control and Prevention   BIRTHPLACE: Macon, GA SECONDARY SCHOOL: Middlesex School, Concord, MA   YEARS AT COLLEGE: 1971–77   DEGREES: A.B., cum laude, '75 ('77); M.S., Univ. of Georgia '85; Ph.D., ibid. '91; M.P.H., Emory Univ. '98   CHILDREN: Mary A., 1985; Catharine D., 1987

Jan Leslie Connery: Not long after graduating with my degree in chemistry, I stumbled across a job in the (then) fledgling field of science communications, and it was exactly where I belonged. Two years later, I was hired as a communications specialist by an environmental consulting firm. Within a few months there, I met my soul mate and life partner, Reinier.

When that company went bankrupt in the early 1980s, I had an opportunity to help build a small new company from the ashes of the bankrupt firm. Now, sixteen years later, that "new" company is flourishing, with over 360 employees in five offices. My job as a vice president and senior manager there, constantly evolving, has never grown old. I enjoy working creatively with interesting colleagues and clients, and I hope that what we do may help, at least in some modest way, to make the world a better place.

In the early 1980s, I discovered my true passion in life: acting. For the next ten years, I performed a wide variety of roles at many different theaters in the greater Boston area. Acting was interrupted in 1990 with the birth of my first child, Jacob, followed by his brother Lucas in 1994. Inspired by our newfound domesticity, Reinier and I finally decided, three years ago, that it was time to grow up and buy a house. We have settled in Lexington, Massachusetts, and love it here. We are frequently visited by relatives and friends from near and far, many of whom, like us, also grew up in different countries around the world.

I am grateful that my company has allowed me to balance work and motherhood, and with each passing year, am ever more drawn to family, cherishing the time I spend with my two wonderful sons.

HOME: Lexington, MA   **OCCUPATION:** Vice President. Eastern Research Group, Inc. (environmental consulting)   **BIRTHPLACE:** New Rochelle, NY   **SECONDARY SCHOOL:** Henrietta Barnett School, London, England (1966–68); Housatonic Valley Regional High School, Falls Village, CT (1968–1970)   **YEARS AT COLLEGE:** 1971–75   **DEGREES:** A.B., magna cum laude, '75   **SPOUSE/PARTNER:** Reinier Albert Laurin Courant (Delft Inst. of Technology, the Netherlands '59)   **SPOUSE'S OCCUPATION:** Vice President. Mitkem Corporation, RI   **CHILDREN:** Jacob Laurin Connery Courant, 1990; A. Lucas Newell Courant, 1994   **COLLEGE ACTIVITIES:** Photographer, *Harvard Independent,* 1972–73; Choreographer, Harvard Loeb Experimental Theater, 1975

Ronald Meyer Constine: At Harvard, every year seemed distinctly different. Goals were concrete and recognizable. Now, nearly a quarter century has passed, and the years are merging together.

Contacts that I thought would last a lifetime were quickly lost, although the memories of Harvard and its unique personalities has never been far from my thought process. Perhaps, the Reunion will be the impetus to renew old relationships, or a reminder that one can never truly go home again.

After graduating from college and medical school, I married a lovely woman I met in London, with whom I have shared my life for over nineteen years. We are blessed with two wonderful children who have given our lives much direction.

Both Joanne and I have battled health-related problems, and this has unquestionably shaped our lives and several critical decisions. I elected to bypass a fellowship after orthopedic residency, and we ultimately migrated to a small community on the west coast of Florida. While objectively we live in a desirable location, I long for the civility of the true West Coast in California which I forever will consider home. My brother recently reminded me of one of my old personal statements. "I am an economic prisoner in a cultural void." I frequently remember being told while facing serious illness in residency to seek in life "equanimity." I still am.

Although I am witnessing the demise of the private practice of medicine, I have been fortunate in being a part of a successful five-person practice. Now with the new frontier, medicine is not challenging as it once was, but rather tedious and stressful. I believe I have one last chapter left to write in my career.

For the near future, while my son attends Peddie School with aspirations of attending Harvard and my daughter continues in a local public school gifted program, I will stay in a holding pattern. My wife continues to work part-time as an occupational therapist.

Reflections are never easy, but a necessary part of moving forward.

HOME: Port Charlotte, FL   **OCCUPATION:** Physician (orthopedic surgeon)
BIRTHPLACE: San Francisco, CA   **SECONDARY SCHOOL:** George Washington High School, San Francisco, CA   **YEARS AT COLLEGE:** 1971–75   **DEGREES:** A.B., summa cum laude, '75; M.D., Stanford Univ. '79   **SPOUSE/PARTNER:** Joanne Gainer, June 26, 1980 (Univ. of Indiana '75)   **SPOUSE'S OCCUPATION:** Occupational Therapist
CHILDREN: Sean Elliot, 1983; Kara Meyer, 1991   **COLLEGE ACTIVITIES:** Karate Club, 1971–75

James Francis Conway III: I can't believe it. I have been out of Harvard longer than I was old when I graduated. It does not seem possible that it was that long ago.

Over the past twenty-five years life has been good to me. I have a wonderful wife, Susan, and two great, very active children, Jimmy (eleven) and Michelle (nine). My professional life has also been good and rewarding as I have been at the same business for the past seventeen years weathering its ups and downs; thankfully more ups than downs.

I am very much looking forward to getting back on campus for our Twenty-fifth Reunion, but will do so with a touch of sadness. Those days were lots of fun in the early seventies and even though we will attempt to recapture and relive them, it just won't be the same; given our ages that is probably just as well. Can't wait to see everyone, have lots of fun, and share a Harvard weekend with family and friends.

HOME: Andover, MA   **OCCUPATION:** President; CEO. Courier Corp. (book manufacturing)   **BIRTHPLACE:** Lowell, MA   **SECONDARY SCHOOL:** Lowell High School, 1970; Choate, 1971   **YEARS AT COLLEGE:** 1971–75   **DEGREES:** A.B., cum laude, '75; M.B.A., Xavier Univ. '79   **SPOUSE/PARTNER:** Susan Merriam, Oct. 27, 1979 (Lasell Coll.; Univ. of Kentucky '78)   **CHILDREN:** James 4th, 1988; Michelle, 1990   **COLLEGE ACTIVITIES:** Hockey and golf, 1971–75; Pi Eta Club, 1973–75; Spee Club, 1973–75

Ann Dietrich Cooling: The last twenty-five years have quickly gone
by. With a daughter now at Harvard, it seems like it was not very long ago
that I was there, too. I have spent the majority of these years married to Jim
and raising four children. I have moved around in various jobs to fit in with
my "kid" schedule, some related to my degree in VES and others just to keep
me involved with people. I am very active in a large hospital organization
in Kansas City, Health Midwest, and serve on that board plus one of their
hospital boards along with several auxiliary boards. I have chaired their
mental health facility for two years and their nursing school board for the
last several years, which I find to be extremely rewarding.

I am very involved in the American Field Service (AFS) board at my children's school and am responsible for finding our host families each year. We
have an AFS daughter from Colombia who is very much an ongoing part of
our lives, plus surrogate daughters from England and France, too. I also
serve on the long-range planning board, the arts council board, and have
participated in our large fund-raising event at school for the last fifteen
years. My passion is my classical guitar, something I began in Cambridge
years ago and now continue at the music conservatory here; my garden;
reading (as much as I can); and my family.

I have maintained many contacts from the classes of '73, '74 and '75 —
particularly my roommate, Lisa Thiem Cullivan, on a regular basis. I feel
that I haven't truly found my calling yet, but my kids are happy, healthy,
and doing well, so maybe time for me will come later. I would love to hear
from any classmates via e-mail at any time.

HOME: Kansas City, MO   **OCCUPATION:** Art Dealer (for two artists, from galleries in
my home); Part-time Accounting and Retail Sales   **BIRTHPLACE:** Kansas City, MO
SECONDARY SCHOOL: The Barstow School, Kansas City, MO   **YEARS AT COLLEGE:**
1971–75   **DEGREES:** A.B., cum laude, '75   **SPOUSE/PARTNER:** James E. Cooling, July 1,
1978 (Univ. of Missouri '65; J.D., Univ. of Notre Dame '68)   **SPOUSE'S OCCUPATION:**
Attorney   **CHILDREN:** Sara E., 1980; Lisa C., 1981; Catherine G., 1984; James W. J., 1987
HARVARD/RADCLIFFE CHILDREN: Sara E. '02   **HARVARD/RADCLIFFE SIBLINGS:**
Meredith G. Steinhaus '73   **COLLEGE ACTIVITIES:** House manager, Hasty Pudding Club,
1975; various Eliot House activities including Jimmy Fund events

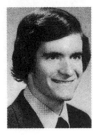

Dennis Paul Corbett: How do I take the measure of the past twenty-five years? There are numerical ways:

- Twenty-four years as a resident of greater Washington, D.C., beginning as transient Georgetown law student and, year by year, establishing community roots.
- Twenty-three years as the husband of Alice, who has shared each evolutionary step of the ride in a loving, complementary way
- Twenty-one years as a communications attorney in two successive private law firms, tackling the professional challenges of counseling clients in a field that manages to constantly reinvent itself
- Eleven years as the father of Ben, learning the parental ropes while marveling at the breadth of his interests and strengths
- And six years as the father of Sam, watching the family bond and life-enjoyment quotient grow for all of us through his gregarious spirit and unflaggingly positive nature.

These years can also be gauged by the enduring images and lessons learned along the way.

- Time seems to be incredibly elastic. If I think about the 1975 graduation ceremony at Quincy House, it seems like a very long time ago. But when, through the kindness of my father's physician in 1996, I was alerted in time to be at his bedside when he passed away, it seemed like a mere nanosecond had elapsed between his death and that of my mother some nineteen years earlier. In a similar way, I feel very much like the same person I was as an undergrad, until I step back and reflectively consider the inexorable, incremental changes wrought by time—some physical but most attitudinal.
- Life is not linear. While Alice and I pursued diverse career paths (hers as a gifted fine artist), we found ourselves on a difficult infertility detour. That road led, however, directly to the wonders of adoption. There is a beautiful symmetry to adoption, in that everyone involved needs each other in the most elemental and fundamental of ways, creating the deepest of family bonds. I have derived particular pleasure from watching my boys develop from infancy without any of my chromosomal limitations.
- While I have spent a lot of time honing and applying my legal skills for the clientele's benefit, and I hope I've made some lasting contributions in the First Amendment area, the time I've put in recently as a trustee of Lowell School (pre-K through grade six) and a trustee of our adoption agency has a different set of rewards—playing a small part both in helping the school relocate to a terrific new campus and in assisting the agency create an endowment for its future.

- Sports provide diversion, with the competitive fires still burning on the tennis court and golf course. They also furnish plenty of parental opportunities. Because Ben likes golf, we can go out together in what I have come to view as one of the magical transformations of my life — from weekend afternoon absentee to devoted parent focused on strengthening the bond with his son. I am also fortunate to coach both Ben's and Sam's soccer teams on Saturdays in spring and fall. Having never played the "beautiful game" myself, I have become very fond of it and all that it teaches about the relationship between individual skill development and team performance.

- Harvard teaches diversity better than it does any academic subject, and I have gradually come to conclude that it knows what it's doing. On a global scale, fear of and ignorance about diversity continuously lead to cataclysmic results. On a personal level, embracing diversity is one of life's most satisfying and liberating experiences.

HOME: Chevy Chase, MD   **OCCUPATION:** Member. Leventhal, Senter & Lerman PLLC (law firm)   **BIRTHPLACE:** Cincinnati, OH   **SECONDARY SCHOOL:** Saint Xavier High School, Cincinnati, OH   **YEARS AT COLLEGE:** 1971–75   **DEGREES:** A.B., magna cum laude, '75; J.D., Georgetown Univ. '79   **SPOUSE/PARTNER:** Alice Agatston, June 26, 1977 (Smith Coll. '75)   **SPOUSE'S OCCUPATION:** Artist (works from home) **CHILDREN:** Benjamin Paul, 1988; Samuel Howard, 1994   **COLLEGE ACTIVITIES:** Editor, *Harvard Crimson,* 1973–75; freshman tennis and squash

Steven James Corning: Are we not all struck with disbelief that twenty-five years have passed like an eye blink? Actually, twenty-four years for me. In the fashion of the day, I took a year off during the 1973–74 academic year and worked for PBS in Washington, D.C. After graduation in 1976, fueled by the broadcasting experience, I merrily trekked off to Los Angeles to chase the film business. Great fun. Modest results.

I returned to Montana in 1979, formed my own company, and have worked in various aspects of real estate development since then — retail, resort, and health care facility development. Great fun. Great results.

The best deal ever, though, has been my marriage to Jennifer Brevik. We continue to amuse, love, and enjoy two great kids. Summers on Flathead Lake, winters skiing at Red Lodge and Big Sky often evoke that sense of Montana as the last best place. And because it is also an emerging place, much still seems possible.

HOME: Billings, MT   **OCCUPATION:** President. The Corning Companies (real estate development)   **BIRTHPLACE:** Billings, MT   **SECONDARY SCHOOL:** Billings Senior High School, Billings, MT   **YEARS AT COLLEGE:** 1971–73; 1974–76   **DEGREES:** A.B., cum laude, '75 ('76)   **SPOUSE/PARTNER:** Jennifer Brevik, Aug. 4, 1984 (Montana State Univ., Billings '83)   **SPOUSE'S OCCUPATION:** Television News Producer; Homemaker   **CHILDREN:** Joseph Harry Corning, 1988; Lillian Brevik Corning, 1991   **COLLEGE ACTIVITIES:** Producer, Moliere's *Tartuffe, Adams House,* spring 1975; producer, *Miss Lonelyhearts,* Loeb Experimental Theater, fall 1975; producer, *Ibsen's Ghosts,* Loeb mainstage, spring 1976

Terry Lee Cowman: For about a dozen years following graduation, I tried to figure out who the heck I was and what I wanted to be when I grew up.

With the birth of my first son, I knew I was meant to be husband and father.

By the time my second son was born, I realized that the role of "friend" was also vital to me, in addition to that of husband and father, and that it is up to me to write the scripts for these roles.

HOME: Manchester, MA   **OCCUPATION:** Vice President. Centerpoint, a division of Oxford Global Resources, Inc. (Centerpoint is the direct staffing division of this international staffing and project consulting company)   **BIRTHPLACE:** Reno, NV

SECONDARY SCHOOL: Sparks High School, Sparks, NV   YEARS AT COLLEGE: 1971–75
DEGREES: A.B., cum laude, '75   SPOUSE/PARTNER: Anne DeLaittre, Feb. 17, 1979 (Tufts
Univ. '79)   SPOUSE'S OCCUPATION: Artist; Homemaker (works from home)
CHILDREN: Ross Wilder, 1987; Scott Davis, 1992   COLLEGE ACTIVITIES: Lightweight
crew, 1971–72; Mather House crew, 1972–75

Michael S. Crane: After graduating from law school I practiced business law in Columbus for about twelve years with two different firms. In
1989 I joined my family's plastics business as general counsel and later
moved into general management after attending Harvard Business School's
Program for Management Development.

My wife and I met while I was attending law school at Ohio State and
she was an undergrad. We have two wonderful boys of whom we are
extremely proud; Danny is fifteen and a sophomore, and David is twelve
and a sixth grader. Both attend their father's alma mater, Columbus
Academy, which went co-ed in 1990 (for which they are grateful). Among
other volunteer activities, Paige especially enjoys serving on the school's
board. In addition to playing golf, I keep busy outside the office following
my sons' activities and keeping up with my wife's desire to travel.

Being at the business school for three months in 1991 was a pleasure
(although everyone in the Square seemed incredibly young), and I look forward to returning to Cambridge for our Reunion.

HOME: Columbus, OH   OCCUPATION: President. Crane Plastics, LLC (manufacturer of
vinyl siding)   BIRTHPLACE: Columbus, OH   SECONDARY SCHOOL: Columbus
Academy, Columbus, OH   YEARS AT COLLEGE: 1971–75   DEGREES: A.B., cum laude,
'75; J.D., Ohio State Univ. '78   SPOUSE/PARTNER: Paige Doucette, March 1, 1980 (Ohio
State Univ. '82)   SPOUSE'S OCCUPATION: Housewife; Volunteer   CHILDREN: Danny,
1984; David, 1987

David Lamont Creighton: Since 1976 I have been leading a very full and varied life, marked by a number of significant twists and turns in the career field. After graduation I helped start an importing business specializing in South American handicrafts, and in 1978, I went to school in Vermont and trained as a luthier. I returned to Boston, where I tried to manage a dual career as a guitarmaker and musician, which was a very enjoyable way to starve. After the Three Mile Island debacle, I entered the environmental fray, eventually heading up a successful state-wide initiative effort in Massachusetts to limit the growth of nuclear power plants and radioactive waste dumps. In 1983 I married Mary Jean Moore, a charming and tenacious activist and technical editor, and we moved to California, where I got my master in public policy at Berkeley. In 1985 I became the program director of TecNica, a nonprofit organization that placed technical volunteers in Nicaragua and southern Africa. During this period I traveled frequently to Central America and worked closely with the Nicaraguan government to counter the terrible consequences of the Contra war. I felt fortunate to work with many Nicaraguans who were trying to bring positive changes to their country, but it was sad to watch the economic and social deterioration resulting from the war. In 1989 I decided to take a break from the stress of international development work, so I went to work as a financial manager for the City of Fairfield in California. Freed from the burden of having to fundraise my paycheck, I found more time to enjoy with my son Robert (born 1986) and participate in normal family life. I also was able to devote more time to my Buddhist practice, leading eventually to my ordination in 1994. I now divide my time between work, teaching meditation, playing cello with the Berkeley Community Chorus and Orchestra, and enjoying my wonderful family.

HOME: Richmond, CA   **OCCUPATION:** Financial Services Manager. Finance Dept., City of Fairfield   **BIRTHPLACE:** Portland, ME   **SECONDARY SCHOOL:** Bethlehem Central High School, Delmar, NY   **YEARS AT COLLEGE:** 1972–76   **DEGREES:** A.B., cum laude, '75 ('76); M.P.P., Univ. of California, Berkeley '85   **SPOUSE/PARTNER:** Mary Jean Moore, June 12, 1983 (Emory Univ. '74)   **SPOUSE'S OCCUPATION:** Elementary School Teacher   **CHILDREN:** Robert Lamont, 1986   **HARVARD/RADCLIFFE SIBLINGS:** Andrew Creighton '81   **COLLEGE ACTIVITIES:** Harvard-Radcliffe Orchestra

William Humphrey Creighton: Spent the first year after Harvard traveling. Then worked for the New York State Division for Youth for two years, met my future wife and finally sold out and went to Stanford for an M.B.A. A marriage, three children and twenty years at IBM later, finds us living in Tokyo. Have had fun the whole time, although finding the right balance between work and family is a challenge. Look back with appreciation at all that I got out of Harvard.

HOME: Ridgefield, CT   **OCCUPATION:** Vice President, Finance. IBM Asia Pacific
BIRTHPLACE: Worcester, MA   **SECONDARY SCHOOL:** East Longmeadow High School, East Longmeadow, MA   **YEARS AT COLLEGE:** 1970–75   **DEGREES:** A.B., magna cum laude, '75; M.B.A., Stanford Univ. '80   **SPOUSE/PARTNER:** Dale A. Hinchcliff
SPOUSE'S OCCUPATION: Homemaker. '80   **CHILDREN:** Jason, 1970 (sp. Michele Magnotta); Cole, 1981; Travis, 1985

Sarah Crichton: So I'm checking out this extremely cute guy on the F-train. He's like the boys I used to know in school—lanky but strong. His jeans are scuffed; his work boots are wrapped in duct tape. He's bent over his Kundera novel, but he must sense I'm studying him because he glances up and shoots me a smile. (Oh, my heart.) Brushing his hair from his eyes, he says: "Want a seat, Ma'am?"

Whoa. When did I become a grown-up? How did I get here? I'm reeling. There's a twenty-five-year-old at the local coffeehouse who makes great lattes and likes to talk to me about what he calls "Old Music," which is to say Mink DeVille, Johnny Thunders, Television—music from the eighties, when I was already married and living in a loft on the Bowery. I told him The Modern Lovers played at a freshman mixer at Currier House (before he was born! I wore a kilt! wrong choice!), and he gave me one of those creeped-out looks, the kind guys get when it occurs to them their mothers have had sex. I wanted to shake him. Hey, I wanted to say, I'm not that damn old!

The truth is, I'm less a ma'am than your basic New York, Armani-armored "execumom." My daughter Eliza, my joy, my light, is nine and a-half and splendid; red-haired, freckly, a singing, dancing, poetry-writing

math whiz of a girl. I'm publisher of Little, Brown, a venerable publishing house (hey, we *made* Louisa May Alcott) that is now a relatively small but choice sliver of the Time-Warner empire.

Twenty-five years ago, I didn't have a clue what I wanted to do. Of course, back then women weren't considered for any of the jobs I've wound up holding. The world changed just in time for me, and I like to think I helped goose those changes along.

I started out as a writer, and I married a fellow writer — a sweet and talented guy from a cotton town in Alabama. We've now been married almost twenty-two years, and he's still writing. But I quickly grew hungry for a steady paycheck and went to work for *Seventeen* magazine. From there I made the leap to *Newsweek,* winding up as one of "The Wallendas," which is what the top editors are called.

Life at a weekly is not for everyone. The hours are brutal and if you're not an adrenaline junkie to begin with, you become one or get chewed up. Me, I adored it for most of the eight years I was there. But then I was hit with one of those periods when everybody dies, and your internal gyroscope is thrown out of whack and you wonder if you'll ever regain your balance.

I craved a new chapter in my life, but what? I was already in my forties. I was sick of magazines, but I'm the money-maker in my family — I couldn't just walk away. Then one night, in classic New York fashion, I popped into a restaurant, ran into an old friend — kiss, kiss, yammer, yammer — long story short, he wound up offering me this, the top post at a top publishing house.

It's a great job, but I can't pretend it's been easy. I'm still deep, deep in a pressure cooker, just a different one. Someday I'll discover a gentler, less-pressured existence. Of course, by the time I do, with my luck, I'll be a lonely widow and my daughter will have moved away years before. It will be time for our Fiftieth Reunion. And, I suspect, I will still be taken aback and a bit crushed if one of those cute young men calls me ma'am.

HOME: Brooklyn, NY   **OCCUPATION:** Publisher. Little, Brown and Company (book publishing)   **BIRTHPLACE:** New York, NY   **SECONDARY SCHOOL:** The Dalton School, New York, NY   **YEARS AT COLLEGE:** 1971–76   **DEGREES:** A.B., cum laude, '75 ('76)   **SPOUSE/PARTNER:** Guy Martin, Sept. 16, 1978 (Haverford Coll. '74)   **SPOUSE'S OCCUPATION:** Journalist; Writer   **CHILDREN:** Eliza Grace, 1990; Susannah Rob, 1995 (died, 1995)   **COLLEGE ACTIVITIES:** *Harvard Crimson*

Michael Francis Cronin: Over the last twenty-five years I have been challenged with learning opportunities while working with smart, creative, and energetic people. As president of Harvard Student Agencies (HSA), I headed straight to Harvard Business School, where I fostered my entrepreneurial urges by operating the student-managed food concession. After graduation, I embarked on my "odyssey" in moving from my hometown Boston to California to begin my career in the venture capital business. I spent two years working for an entrepreneur before joining Security Pacific Capital. I was selected to open up the firm's Boston office in 1985. In 1990, during the nadir of the venture capital industry, I started my own company, Weston Presidio Capital, where I have been ever since. To date, I have made over one hundred investments and have had an inside seat to the dramatic changes that have occurred in our economy over the last twenty-five years. The costs of this view have been occasionally high in terms of time and money, but in all cases the most inspiring view has been observing the entrepreneurial spirit.

Throughout this entire journey, I have benefited from the support and companionship of my wife, Marian, and, over time, our three children. We now have the joy and pleasure of living a part of our lives through their exploits.

My charitable endeavors include the usual Harvard stuff as well as local educational institutions and other interests related to entrepreneurism in the inner city. Most important has been my ongoing involvement with Harvard Student Agencies as an alumni director. We have been able to purchase and renovate the "old Elsie's building" as HSA's permanent home thus ensuring that current and future generations of students will continue to have the opportunity to earn tuition money and gain management experience.

HOME: Weston, MA   OCCUPATION: Managing Partner. Weston Presidio Capital (venture capital investments)   BIRTHPLACE: Boston, MA   SECONDARY SCHOOL: Don Bosco Technical High School, Boston, MA   YEARS AT COLLEGE: 1971–75 DEGREES: A.B., cum laude, '75; M.B.A. '77   SPOUSE/PARTNER: Marian Anne Miller, June 14, 1980 (Trinity Coll. '72)   CHILDREN: Christopher V., 1985; Justin G., 1987; Courtney A., 1988   COLLEGE ACTIVITIES: Harvard Student Agencies, Inc.: laundry manager, 1972–74, director, 1972–75, and president, 1974–75

June V. Cross: Here it is twenty-five years later and I'm just figuring out what I want to be when I grow up! Personally, I've settled down with Waldron Ricks, a jazz musician and trumpeter who has shared my life these last ten years. Although we are childless, our union continues to deepen and reveal new portals for exploration that reverberate in my professional work.

I found the courage, almost ten years ago, to get out of the network rat race and to join the team at PBS's *FRONTLINE* documentary series (Mike Sullivan '68 is executive producer). It is much more fulfilling work. I have been encouraged to exercise my own creative voice, and that in turn has begun a transformative journey that I could have scarcely imagined when I left CBS News.

As I write these words I'm taking a break from my twenty-six-year television career; I'm also finishing my first book, based on a documentary I did for *FRONTLINE* back in 1996 called "Secret Daughter" (and yes, for all those who saw it and want to know: my mother and I remain on close terms). Last year I was a DuBois Institute Fellow. It was gratifying to see the progress the Afro-American Studies Department has made since our trying college days. I did much of the first draft work on the book as a DuBois Fellow and continue my association with the institute (and the libraries! Oh, silent place to work!) this year.

The writer's life agrees with me. While I love the pace, drive, and teamwork of broadcast journalism, my time and my thoughts are now finally my own, at the direction of my own heart's yearning. I hope to recharge that passion that led me to journalism: namely, the desire to tell people's stories in a way that illumines and enlightens. If anyone buys the book I will have to choose between the written and the spoken word!

It's a source of amazement that my life has been determined as much by the decisions I refused to make as by those I made. Standing on the cusp of my second half century, I sense that the years ahead will be even more interesting, with more chances to make a difference, than those now behind me.

I look forward to seeing those of you who make the journey to Cambridge this summer.

HOME: Auburndale, MA   OCCUPATION: TV Producer; Writer; Senior Producer. *Frontline* (documentary series on PBS)   BIRTHPLACE: New York, NY   SECONDARY SCHOOL: Atlantic City High School   YEARS AT COLLEGE: 1971–75   DEGREES: A.B., cum laude, '75   SPOUSE/PARTNER: Waldron Mardi Ricks, Feb. 14, 1990 (New England Conservatory '00)   SPOUSE'S OCCUPATION: Jazz Musician   COLLEGE ACTIVITIES: Radcliffe Union of Students; Black C.A.S.T.; *Harvard Crimson*

Steven T. Dagdigian: I am most grateful to Harvard for allowing me to meet my wife. We've been together for these twenty-five years and now have two wonderful kids, Lilly (thirteen) and Jake (eight). My professional life has revolved around teaching and coaching, mostly at the secondary level. I am now in my sixth year at St. Sebastian's School in Needham, where I grew up. My other stops were at the Peddie School (New Jersey), Clarkson College (New York) and Choate Rosemary Hall (Connecticut). It is great to be back in the Boston area and coaching hockey in the Independent School League is terrific and highly competitive. I also get to be the chauffeur (and occasional coach) for Lilly and Jake's teams as they are also enjoying hockey.

HOME: Dedham, MA   OCCUPATION: Teacher; Coach. St. Sebastian's School
BIRTHPLACE: Needham, MA   SECONDARY SCHOOL: Needham High School   YEARS
AT COLLEGE: 1971–75   SPOUSE/PARTNER: Barbara Baker Matson '75   SPOUSE'S
OCCUPATION: Writer; Editor. *The Boston Globe*   CHILDREN: Lilly Matson Dagdigian,
1986; Jake Matson Dagdigian, 1991   COLLEGE ACTIVITIES: Varsity hockey

---

Thomas Lamont Daniels: The United States has become a much more crowded, yet sprawling place over the last twenty-five years. Since working on a farm in Vermont during summers between Harvard, I have been interested in land use issues. I studied agricultural economics in England and Oregon, and then plunged into the academic world, teaching rural and small town land use planning at Iowa State and Kansas State Universities. Then for nine years, I managed the nationally recognized farmland preservation program in Lancaster County, Pennsylvania. This was a wonderful and rewarding experience; I helped preserve over sixteen thousand acres of some of America's finest farmland in a culturally rich community.

In the fall of 1998, I became a professor of planning at the State University of New York at Albany. I teach courses on regional planning, land conservation, and local economic development.

I have published many articles and a number of books, including: *Holding Our Ground: Protecting America's Farms and Farmland* (Island Press, 1997), *The Small Town Planning Handbook* (Planners Press, 1995), and *When City and Country Collide: Managing Growth in the Metropolitan Fringe* (Island Press, 1999). *When City and Country Collide* was used as a text in a graduate planning course at Harvard in 1999.

I maintain an active schedule speaking and consulting on land conservation throughout the United States. It is heartening to see people striving to take control of the future direction of their communities.

I have been fortunate that my wife, Kathy, shares my passion for the land and professional interests. We also love to travel, and have been to Australia and to Europe a number of times. We are "soccer parents," like many of our generation. Our two boys keep us on the go and younger than our years.

HOME: Delmar, NY   OCCUPATION: Professor. Dept. of Geography and Planning, State University of New York   BIRTHPLACE: Burlington, VT   SECONDARY SCHOOL: Phillips Exeter Academy   YEARS AT COLLEGE: 1971–76   DEGREES: A.B., cum laude '75 ('76); M.S., Univ. of Newcastle (United Kingdom) '77; Ph.D., Oregon State Univ. '84 SPOUSE/PARTNER: Katherine Handwerg, May 19, 1984 (Univ. of California, Berkeley '75) SPOUSE'S OCCUPATION: Land Use Planner   CHILDREN: Ethan H., 1985; Jason E., 1989 HARVARD/RADCLIFFE SIBLINGS: Robert Hoyt Daniels '69; J.D. '72   COLLEGE ACTIVITIES: Freshman tennis team, 1972

Debra-Lynn Genduso Day-Salvatore: Ballet taught me discipline; I found determination.

Harvard taught me how to think; I found creativity.

My first husband taught me independence and self-sufficiency; I found courage.

Graduate school taught me resilience and resourcefulness; I found the true meaning of integrity.

Medical school, residency, and fellowship taught me the inequities of life; I found a cause.

My father's death taught me that I am my own person; I found affirmation.

My job taught me to stand up and fight for what I believe in; I found a voice.

My patients taught me that perfection comes in many sizes, shapes, and packages; I found love.

My husband Jerry (a.k.a. Francis) taught me selfless love; I found the pot of gold.

HOME: Princeton, NJ   OCCUPATION: Medical Geneticist; Chief, Division of Clinical Genetics; Director, Institute for Reproductive and Perinatal Genetics. University of Medicine and Dentistry of New Jersey, Robert Wood Johnson Medical School and St. Peter's University Hospital   BIRTHPLACE: Hoboken, NJ   SECONDARY SCHOOL: Dwight School, Englewood, NJ   YEARS AT COLLEGE: 1971–75   DEGREES: A.B. '75; M.S., New York Univ. '79; Ph.D., Case Western Reserve Univ. '82; M.D., ibid. '86 SPOUSE/PARTNER: Francis P. Salvatore, Sr., Dec. 24, 1988 (Univ. of Miami '44; M.D., MCP Hahnemann Univ. '48)   SPOUSE'S OCCUPATION: Gynecologist   STEPCHILDREN: Six STEP-GRANDCHILDREN: Fourteen

Paul Charles Demakis: While I could not have predicted the specific steps my career has taken, the general direction — law and politics — was foreseeable during my years at Harvard.

I graduated from Harvard Law School in 1978. After graduation, I moved into the Back Bay neighborhood in Boston. I live in a small condominium one block from the Public Garden. I am single.

I was a litigator in two Boston firms for nearly five years. But private practice did not interest me as much as public policy. When Michael Dukakis returned for his second term as governor in 1983, I joined his administration, first as general counsel in the Executive Office of Transportation and Construction and then as tax counsel for the Appellate Tax Board, an agency charged with adjudicating all appeals of state and local tax assessments. In 1986, Governor Dukakis appointed me to be one of the five members of the board, a position I served in for seven years.

Having been politically active since moving into the Back Bay, I decided to run for state representative in 1994. In the most expensive race for a House seat in Massachusetts history, I won the Democratic primary in a four-candidate field by 123 votes. I won the general election with sixty-two percent of the vote. I was reelected in 1996 and 1998.

I composed the incidental music to *Man of Crete,* a series of biographical sketches about Nikos Kazantzakis, which was professionally produced at the Charles Playhouse in Boston in 1981. Unfortunately, however, my career has since left me with too little time to pursue my musical interests.

Another regret during the past twenty-five years has been my failure to stay in touch with my Harvard classmates. I am looking forward to renewing friendships at the Reunion.

HOME: Boston, MA **OCCUPATION:** State Representative. Commonwealth of Massachusetts **BIRTHPLACE:** Lynn, MA **SECONDARY SCHOOL:** Deerfield Academy, Deerfield, MA **YEARS AT COLLEGE:** 1971–75 **DEGREES:** A.B., cum laude, '75; J.D. '78 **COLLEGE ACTIVITIES:** Staff writer, *Harvard Political Review,* 1973–75; Young Democrats, 1973–75

Linda Marie DeMelis: I married Ted Wobber '75 in 1977. We visited California on vacation (my first trip) in 1978, and couldn't figure out why we would want to live anywhere else. Six months later, we sold our Boston-area house and moved to California. It sounds like a sick joke now, but in 1979 one of the reasons we moved out here was the more relaxed lifestyle. Over the past twenty years, many of the things we moved to California to escape — the intense competitiveness, the crowds, the traffic — seem to have followed us across the country. The weather's still good, though.

Our daughter Victoria (Tory), now a teenager, has been the center of our lives for the past fifteen years. Tory is personable, athletic and socially popular — all the things that her bookworm, sedentary parents never were. She seems to be enjoying her high school years — a great gift. The bittersweet moment when she goes off to college on her own seems all too close now.

In 1991, I shocked my family and friends by going to law school. I surprised myself by doing well, and now work at Venture Law Group, a Menlo Park firm that specializes in representing start-up technology companies. Going back to school with, and now working with, men and women half a generation younger than myself has been an exhilarating experience for me.

It's been a long strange trip from the south Bronx to Sand Hill Road. I have so much more than I ever would have thought possible growing up — a happy marriage, a wonderful daughter, a good job, a nice house, enough money. Other times, though, I reflect on what I have left behind. Like many Americans, I reinvented myself to become what I wanted to be, but the Catholic-school girl from the Bronx I once was keeps poking out sometimes.

I'm looking forward to the Reunion, and reestablishing contact with at least one piece of my earlier life.

HOME: Menlo Park, CA   **OCCUPATION:** Attorney. Venture Law Group   **BIRTHPLACE:** Mount Vernon, NY   **SECONDARY SCHOOL:** Evander Childs High School, Bronx, NY **YEARS AT COLLEGE:** 1971–75   **DEGREES:** A.B., magna cum laude, '75; J.D., Univ. of California, San Francisco '94   **SPOUSE/PARTNER:** Edward P. Wobber, Sept. 24, 1977 (Harvard '75)   **SPOUSE'S OCCUPATION:** Computer Programmer. Compaq Computer Corp   **CHILDREN:** Victoria "Tory" Wobber, 1983

Kevin John Denny: I hope it isn't just me with a faulty perception of time's passage. Only "yesterday," I met my wife (Susan) in medical school in New York and convinced her against her better judgment to relocate to San Francisco, where we took our residencies in ophthalmology (mine) and radiology (hers). After adopting two boys (Matthew and Peter), we settled in Mill Valley just north of the Golden Gate Bridge, a stunningly beautiful commute most days.

Life has been a blur of coaching Little League, building a practice, juggling two demanding careers, participating in a coed book group, responding to the AIDS epidemic, watching my boys develop their musical talents, having a lawyer on my speed dial (home construction defects), dealing with my wife's breast cancer, completing centuries on my road bike, performing eye surgery in remote Guatemala, finding comfort in friends, and adding a dog (Stella) to the family mix.

I imagine my classmates have experienced a similar measure of life's vicissitudes. I look forward to hearing your stories at the Reunion.

HOME: Mill Valley, CA   **OCCUPATION:** Ophthalmologist (in clinical practice)
BIRTHPLACE: Milwaukee, WI   **SECONDARY SCHOOL:** Marquette University High School, Milwaukee, WI   **YEARS AT COLLEGE:** 1971–75   **DEGREES:** A.B., cum laude, '75; M.D., New York Univ. '80   **SPOUSE/PARTNER:** Susan Randel, Sept. 4, 1983 (Sarah Lawrence Coll. '73)   **SPOUSE'S OCCUPATION:** Radiologist (in clinical practice)
CHILDREN: Matthew R., 1987; Peter J., 1988   **COLLEGE ACTIVITIES:** Photographer, *Harvard Crimson;* intramural sports

---

Michael Kent Dewberry: My thirteen-year-old son Julian and I reside in the leafy suburb of South Pasadena, and I commute daily to Century City where I litigate. Music remains central in my life, notwithstanding the fact that I'm required to practice law to make my mortgage payments. I'm releasing a CD of original songs on October 30.

All things considered, life is good. My boy is wonderful, and after twenty-one years in this sprawling city I've gotten to know everyone in the circus. I'm blessed with a terrific circle of friends, and would love to hear from my classmates.

HOME: South Pasadena, CA   **OCCUPATION:** Attorney. Billet & Kaplan   **BIRTHPLACE:** Memphis, TN   **SECONDARY SCHOOL:** Cate School, Carpinteria, CA   **YEARS AT COLLEGE:** 1971–78   **DEGREES:** A.B., '75 ('78); J.D., Univ. of Southern California '81   **SPOUSE/PARTNER:** Divorced   **CHILDREN:** Julian Rowe, 1986

John Russell Dewey: At the time of this writing, the Red Sox and Yankees are battling for the 1999 American League Championship Series. Memories of triumph, joy, hope, and challenge flood back from October 1975 as the Red Sox faced the Cincinnati Reds.

Over the past twenty-five years these same themes have emerged. I have weathered sixteen years at American Airlines, worked in every major division of the company, survived three "downsizings," and continue to travel. Travel has been the constant as I have visited over eighty-five countries on all seven continents. My pace has slowed over the past five years, yet the love of exploration persists with an enduring appreciation of family and friends who have generously assisted in my journeys.

In a world of rapid change driven by technology, I am increasingly drawn to places and times of quiet and reflection. I have adhered to a peripatetic lifestyle since graduation, yet I do foresee someday a pacing of these "restless feet" with a partner, and maybe a family.

With the decade of the 1990s achieving economic globalization, I have a great concern with the attendant cultural homogenization and decline. Corporate growth has its place as long as it continues to propel innovation and an opportunity to rethink social norms and develop more progressive lifestyles balancing family, work, environment, and community. I am both hopeful and concerned as we launch into the next millennium.

Twenty-five years ago at Class Day, Dick Gregory shared his concern with us about "sugar pushers." His concern was well-founded. Although sugar was classified as a "controlled substance" in 1962, the consumption per capita in the United States continues to increase. This is an example of how much education is still needed. And yet, the tools of the Internet and advanced communication are standing by to assist. I am hopeful we will continue to progress, but the challenge is to elevate the content of our communications.

I look forward to seeing many friends in a few months and wish everyone well.

HOME: Irving, TX   **OCCUPATION:** Senior Analyst. Marketing. American Airlines (transportation)   **BIRTHPLACE:** Boston, MA   **SECONDARY SCHOOL:** Noble and Greenough School, Dedham, MA   **YEARS AT COLLEGE:** 1971–76   **DEGREES:** A.B., cum laude, '75 ('76); M.B.A., Univ. of California, Los Angeles   **COLLEGE ACTIVITIES:** Spee Club; Outing Club; Hasty Pudding; Lowell House Social Committee '83

James Howard DeWitt: First of all, to those who noticed I didn't graduate with the Class of '75, thanks for missing me. I did graduate the following year although certainly not the better prepared or focused person I'd promised my parents I'd be when arguing that I needed to take a year off. Following graduation I did what any sensible twenty-one-year-old armed with a liberal arts degree did — applied to graduate school. Thinking that I might like to be a documentary filmmaker I was accepted and on my way to a graduate degree in communications when a film editor friend suggested that a better way to become a filmmaker might be to learn a trade which she offered to teach me in four hours. Four hours to become a filmmaker sounded a lot better than three years to become an M.F.A., so I took her up on her offer and a week later I was working for Mark VII Productions and Jack Webb of Dragnet fame. This led to an unremarkable five-year career in film editing and writing — everything from documentaries to adult films. (For details, my official filmographer is Robert Whiting Egan '75 — my one and only fan!) Ultimately I landed in the tool business which supplies metal cutting tools and accessories to machine shops in Southern California. Most of my energy and passion goes into my role as father and husband. I've been married to my wife Lynne for ten happy years. Lynne is a music contractor and special events planner who manages to run a very successful business and have an enormous amount of fun doing it. I am also madly in love with two daughters, Katie, fifteen, and Liza, eight. They are each exceptional young women — smart, funny, athletic, stylishly hip and extraordinarily beautiful. It is an unending source of joy to participate in their busy lives. Watching them grow into thoughtful, energetic, independent human beings has been far and away the most remarkable experience of my adult life.

HOME: Pacific Palisades, CA   **OCCUPATION:** President. Marshall Tool & Supply (industrial distribution)   **BIRTHPLACE:** New York, NY   **SECONDARY SCHOOL:** Beverly Hills High School, Beverly Hills, CA   **YEARS AT COLLEGE:** 1971–76   **DEGREES:** A.B., cum laude, '75 ('76)   **SPOUSE/PARTNER:** Lynne Gordon (Washington Univ. '76) **SPOUSE'S OCCUPATION:** Music Contractor. Lynne Gordon Entertainment **CHILDREN:** Katie June DeWitt, 1984; Liza Bloom Gordon DeWitt, 1991   **COLLEGE ACTIVITIES:** Phillips Brooks House; Outing Club; intramural basketball

Martha Ourieff Diamond: Is it possible that twenty-five years have passed? Life since college has certainly been full, intense, and very gratifying. I left Radcliffe after my sophomore year and transferred to Stanford. I have reflected often on my experience at Harvard, and while it was clearly mixed, and I did not stay, I know that I have never again met such a collection of people as I knew in those two years. I was much happier at Stanford, for a variety of reasons, and studied, lived, and worked in the Bay Area for several years before heading off to graduate school in Michigan. Graduate school in Ann Arbor was, for me, what college is for many others — a rich collage of learning, friendships, growth, and fun. I began my professional life there, I met my husband there, I met my dearest, lifelong friend there, I had my first child there, and I went through psychoanalysis there.

I also never quite got used to midwestern winters, so, about ten years ago, when I was three months pregnant with our twins, we returned to California and settled in San Diego. We now live in a comfortable suburb north of the city, my boys are terrific at thirteen, ten, and ten, Dave is on the faculty at CSPP and in psychoanalytic training, and I have a thriving half-time clinical practice. All is well and I am content. What my chronology does not include, however, is that these ten years have also been marked by incredible trauma, grief, and challenge. My twins, conceived following secondary infertility, were born three months prematurely. We were new in town, in new jobs, with a three-year old. The overwhelming experience of the emergency birth, the Neonatal Intensive Care Unit and the pain and uncertainty of our children's health touched us permanently, and in ways we are still discovering. While we turned out to be very lucky, and ultimately spared some of the most serious sequelae, we were not unscathed: our son Henry was left with a significant hearing loss and ADD, which combine to make communication, learning, and social functioning a constant challenge. To his credit, he is an incredible person, bright, compassionate, and determined to succeed. His brothers have thrived in the context of the family challenges and we feel truly proud. It has only been in the recent past, however, that we have been able to go beyond just coping, to relax, enjoy, and begin to turn our traumatic experiences into something truly positive and meaningful.

Two years ago, Dave and I, along with a colleague, founded the Center for Reproductive Psychology, a group committed to understanding what we call the reproductive story, that internal array of expectations, dreams and hopes that we all carry with us from childhood, about what it will be like to be (or not be) parents. When things go wrong in the process, when the story changes, and things do not go as planned, the experience of loss can be traumatic and overwhelming. In our work, we focus on the education and treatment of people who have experienced a wide range of such reproductive traumas, including infertility, miscarriage, prematurity, etc. We have an active study group, as well as a clinic, we speak frequently at conferences and hospitals and we are working on a book. It has been exciting, stimulating, and ultimately healing, as we have slowly worked through the trauma and grief of our own experience and turned it into something enriching. Life now feels — well, like life, and it continues to flow and unfold in constantly refreshing ways. To my old friends from those early days at Radcliffe, thank you for being part of the fabric of my life, for I have carried you with me throughout these twenty-five years in unspoken but meaningful ways. I wish you all the best.

HOME: San Diego, CA   **OCCUPATION:** Clinical Psychologist (in clinical practice); Co-founder and Director. Center for Reproductive Psychology   **BIRTHPLACE:** Chicago, IL **SECONDARY SCHOOL:** Pacific Palisades High School, Los Angeles, CA   **YEARS AT COLLEGE:** 1971–73   **DEGREES:** B.A., Stanford Univ. '75; M.A., Univ. of Michigan '80; Ph.D., ibid. '83   **SPOUSE/PARTNER:** David J. Diamond, Aug. 14, 1981 (Yale '75; Ph.D., Univ. of Michigan '83)   **SPOUSE'S OCCUPATION:** Clinical Psychologist; Co-founder. Center for Reproductive Psychology; Assistant Professor. California School of Professional Psychology   **CHILDREN:** Jeffrey, 1985; Henry and Benjamin, 1989 (twins)

Mark Joseph DiCamillo: After Harvard, I attended Cornell business school, then moved west to the San Francisco Bay Area, where I've remained ever since. Although there have been lots of changes in my life since graduation (e.g., adjustment to the "Left Coast," giving up on the Yankees and Bills and becoming a die-hard Giants and Niners fan, the addition of five strokes to my golf game), there has been a fair amount of stability as well (e.g., been with the same public opinion research firm since graduate school, married to the same woman for eighteen years, lived in the same house in Mill Valley for sixteen years). The longer we've been here, the more it seems we'll remain. My job as director of California's best known public opinion poll, the Field Poll, has locked me into a long-term relationship with this state that I could not have foreseen twenty-five years ago. Plus, there's the weather, good friends, the Sausalito ferry, downtown San Francisco, and the Olympic Club. Sure beats the life I remember while growing up in Niagara Falls.

HOME: Mill Valley, CA   **OCCUPATION:** Director. The Field Institute/Field Research Corporation (public opinion research)   **BIRTHPLACE:** Niagara Falls, NY   **SECONDARY SCHOOL:** Lewiston-Porter Central School, Youngstown, NY   **YEARS AT COLLEGE:** 1971–75   **DEGREES:** A.B., cum laude, '75; M.B.A., Cornell, '78   **SPOUSE/PARTNER:** Leslie Hughes, April 25, 1981 (Univ. of Buffalo)   **CHILDREN:** Jessica Hughes DiCamillo, 1983   **HARVARD/RADCLIFFE SIBLINGS:** Gary Thomas DiCamillo, M.B.A. '75 **COLLEGE ACTIVITIES:** Golf team, 1971–75; Hasty Pudding Society, 1973–75; Harvard Student Agencies, 1971–75; *Harvard Independent,* 1975

Jane Dickson: In retrospect, my yo-yoing between Harvard and art schools, the Ecole des Beaux Arts, Paris, 1970–71, Harvard 1971–73, the Boston Museum School, 1973–75, Harvard, 1975–76, actually does make sense. I have needed both technical and intellectual skills to create the "iconic fictions on the order of Hopper" *(New York Times)* "...gritty in both subject and substance" *(Los Angeles Times)* for which I am known.

I moved to New York City in 1977, and have been exhibiting my work nationally and internationally ever since. The artist's life has turned out to be more complicated than I could have imagined (so has the world). I paint to examine that confusion, overlaying synthetic materials, with traditional expectations of life and of art, to reach distilled moments of tension where the viewers are left to pick through their own beliefs.

My paintings and prints are in the permanent collections of MoMA, New York City; the Metropolitan Museum of Art, New York City; the Chicago Art Institute; the Whitney Museum; the Library of Congress; the San Francisco Museum of Art; and the Victoria & Albert Museum, London, among others.

I met my husband, filmmaker Charlie Ahearn, in 1978. We married in 1983. Our son, Joseph Sigmund, was born in 1986, and our daughter, Eve Gretchen, was born in 1989. We live in Manhattan.

HOME: New York, NY   OCCUPATION: Artist   YEARS AT COLLEGE: 1971–76
DEGREES: A.B., magna cum laude, '75 ('76)   SPOUSE/PARTNER: Charles Ahearn
CHILDREN: Joseph Sigmund, 1986, Eve Gretchen, 1989

Jeffrey Dielle: My career in information technology at Hewlett-Packard has been a major life focus over the past quarter century. Professionally, I have advanced from junior MVS systems programmer to senior information technology architect and have acquired considerable experience dealing with information security issues in a complex technical and business environment.

For the past decade, I have lived in Sonoma County, about fifty miles north of San Francisco, and I have enjoyed the slower pace and tighter community that thrives here. I have become quite active in a small Reconstructionist synagogue and am greatly enriched by reconnecting to my ethnic and spiritual roots.

At the end of October 1999 I will leave the security of Hewlett-Packard, print up some business cards with the title "Internet Consultant" and take a long vacation. I hope to spend the next quarter century focusing on ongoing and new interpersonal relationships, seeing more of the world, reading some of the great books that I missed in college, exploring new possibilities, and generally enjoying life. All communiqués from fellow travelers are welcome.

HOME: Rohnert Park, CA   OCCUPATION: Internet Consultant   BIRTHPLACE: Palo Alto, CA   SECONDARY SCHOOL: Palo Alto High School, Palo Alto, CA   YEARS AT COLLEGE: 1971–75   DEGREES: A.B., cum laude, '75; J.D., Peninsula Univ. '85 SPOUSE/PARTNER: Kelly Ann Brown, 1984, divorced 1994 (California State Univ., Stanislaus '81; M.A. '84)   COLLEGE ACTIVITIES: Harvard-Radcliffe Hillel, 1971–75; South House Committee, 1973–75

James Kaye Doane: I like to think that for the past twenty-five years I have been preparing to do what I am supposed to do in the next quarter century, whatever that may be. A few weeks after graduation from Harvard I found myself working at a Tokyo magazine polishing my Japanese and my journalism skills. Unpolished and poor, I soon left for the promise of lucre offered at a Japanese trading company. A Japanese salary man I was not destined to be. My Japanese mother was not surprised. Back to the States and law school I went, like many of my classmates. A court clerkship was followed by a stint at a Seattle law firm learning how to replevy trailer homes. Back to Japan I went, this time to a Japanese law firm to learn about more substantial commercial matters — financing for fixing the Panama Canal, that sort of thing. I rode the Japanese economic bubble back to Seattle, where Japanese were buying up the land, and I was a lawyer, shrugging, but doing the deals. The bubble burst, but in good times and bad

times, lawyers find work, and my work has kept me travelling to Japan, meeting with Japanese clients or advising Americans with aspirations of doing business there. At midlife, like many parents, I find the days crowded with one more soccer game to attend, one more carpool to drive, one more dentist appointment where crooked teeth may mean braces. My wife makes me see as a child, bravely introducing me to new places, new perspectives, and fuzzy logic — a needed respite from all that "thinking like a lawyer" at the office. Hope to see you at the Reunion.

HOME: Mercer Island, WA   **OCCUPATION:** Partner. Preston, Gates & Ellis LLP (law firm) **BIRTHPLACE:** Oklahoma, OK   **SECONDARY SCHOOL:** Sammamish High School, Bellevue, WA   **YEARS AT COLLEGE:** 1971–75   **DEGREES:** A.B., cum laude, '75; J.D., Univ. of Pennsylvania '80   **SPOUSE/PARTNER:** Yumi Toma, 1995 (Sophia Univ.)   **SPOUSE'S OCCUPATION:** Museum Volunteer   **CHILDREN:** Two   **COLLEGE ACTIVITIES:** Rugby Club, 1971–75

Frederick Porter Dodd: After taking two and a half years off on the way to my degree, I finished at Harvard in February of 1978 and moved to Washington, D.C. Judy Pappo and I married in 1980 and enjoyed four years together in the Washington area before I dragged us off to Pittsburgh for business school and then to New York City for a job with a no-longer-in-existence bank (Chemical). Jessica was born in New York in 1985 and we returned to Boston in 1987 in search of a more manageable life than we found in New York. I've worked in the treasury department at BankBoston since moving back to New England, work that has been satisfying, enlightening, and frustrating. So, all these years after leaving Harvard, I'm now comfortably settled into nearby Lexington, Massachusetts, and commuting through Harvard Square daily on my way to work as an asset/liability manager at Fleet Bank.

Looking back from today, things that bring a smile include:

- enjoying nineteen years of marriage with Judy;
- watching Jessica grow into a delightful teenager;
- thinking of Jessica reading from the Torah last year at her Bat Mitzvah;
- finding ways to keep singing;
- and surviving all these years in the banking industry.

Some things I regret, include:

- surviving all these years in the banking industry;
- and not keeping up with my friends.

I look forward to catching up and reminiscing.

HOME: Lexington, MA   **OCCUPATION:** Asset and Liability Management. Fleet Bank
BIRTHPLACE: Ponca City, OK   **SECONDARY SCHOOL:** St. Christophers School,
Richmond, VA   **YEARS AT COLLEGE:** 1971–75   **DEGREES:** A.B. '75 ('78); M.B.A.,
Carnegie Mellon Univ. '84   **SPOUSE/PARTNER:** Judith L. Pappo, Oct. 12, 1980.
CHILDREN: Jessica, 1985   **COLLEGE ACTIVITIES:** Krokodiloes, 1971–76

Thomas Andrew Dodds: I am bemused by the respectability of my
current life in contrast to my own offbeat upbringing and confused young
adulthood. Born into a family of long-time pacifists and social activists who
lost their bearings in the sixties, my early time at Harvard remains the most
painful period of my life: parents and siblings who were in turmoil and me
being an achiever who was too stunned to remain focused on anything. It is
not surprising that it took me more than nine years to get through Harvard,
with side trips to communes, a variety of very odd jobs, and several quest-
like journeys. A late epiphany to try medical school, a bizarre choice given
my then-lack of interest in science, spurred me to finish Harvard.

Luckily, my career choice has turned out well and has served as an
anchor. I am temperamentally suited for medicine, especially my specialty
of rehabilitation. I still see it as a calling, despite its problems. I find that, in
my forties, I am comfortable with my perspective on work; I take it, but not
myself or my career, seriously. Rather than ambition, my biggest motivator
is fear of boredom. My varied work and personal activities seem to hold that
fear in check.

The greatest turmoil of the past several years has involved my divorce
and its resulting disruptions. My ex-wife, also a physician, wanted to leave
Dartmouth Medical School, where we both had faculty appointments, and
last year we agreed to move together to Salt Lake City, so as to continue joint
custody of our two sons. The move, while not my idea, has worked out well.
My kids can walk between our respective homes. Half of the time, I am a
harried, single, working parent.

Youthful angst has been replaced by a middle-age awareness that life is
an amazing, fragile, and depleting gift.

HOME: Salt Lake City, UT   **OCCUPATION:** Physician. LDS Hospital, Concord, MA
SECONDARY SCHOOL: Mt. Hermon High School, Mt. Hermon, MA   **YEARS AT
COLLEGE:** 1971-1980   **DEGREES:** A.B., '75 ('80); M.D., Dartmouth '86; M.R.M., '90; Univ.
of Washington; M.P.H., ibid. '92   **SPOUSE/PARTNER:** Divorced, 1998   **CHILDREN:**
Samuel, 1990; Jacob, 1992

Mitchell Lang Dong: Life's been a roller coaster and fortunately, I've been on a roll recently. Business is good, the kids are doing well in school, their soccer teams have been winning and we have been able to spend a lot of time together as a family. But it hasn't always been this good.

Early in my career, I worked hard on my various entrepreneurial ventures in the energy and environmental fields. A few succeeded, a few failed, and a few were O.K. I learned a lot from each start-up and was a little smarter about the next one. Once I married Robin at age thirty-four and we had a family, my outlook and perspective gradually changed. I wanted to spend much more time with my family and sought a business that would allow a flexible lifestyle. I am pleased that running a hedge fund which uses mathematical models for short-term equity trading has allowed me much personal freedom, e.g., I can spend the summers in Italy and coach soccer every day after school. I find myself more interested in helping the kids' school or developing a winning soccer strategy than I do working on the next business deal. Fortunately, I've found some very talented and dedicated junior partners who run my business better than I can.

The next challenges are continuing this great lifestyle and seeing my three daughters through their teenage and early adult years. They are eight, ten, and twelve years old now and we have a lot of family challenges ahead, e.g., dating, doing well in school, getting into a good college, etc. Then Robin and I will have to worry about what to talk about once the kids are gone. Right now we are planning to buy a house in Italy and maybe retire there. Ciao!

HOME: Cambridge, MA   OCCUPATION: President. Chronos Asset Management, Inc. (a hedge fund)   BIRTHPLACE: New York, NY   SECONDARY SCHOOL: Bergenfield High School   YEARS AT COLLEGE: 1971–75   DEGREES: A.B. '75   SPOUSE/PARTNER: Robin LaFoley, Dec. 28, 1986 (Univ. of Massachusetts '73)   SPOUSE'S OCCUPATION: Manager of Children and House   CHILDREN: May Lan, 1987; Cieu Lan, 1989; Dy Lan, 1990
COLLEGE ACTIVITIES: Started an environmental and energy consulting firm with Mary Meyers '76

Thomas Joseph Donovan: When I worked as a porter for the Twenty-fifth Reunion in 1974, I thought little about my own Twenty-fifth. I remember hoping that the Reunion neckties would improve over the polyester numbers doled out then, but I had no vision of how my career would come together or whether I would have any kind of a family. I just assumed that things would work out.

They have. I ended up back in New Hampshire, both for family reasons and for my sense of the importance of place. It was a good choice. I have been married to Stephanie for twenty very good years, and we have two (mostly very good) teenage children. I have had an interesting career as a trial lawyer at the state's largest law firm, with a stint as managing partner. Manchester has been a very good place to raise a family and remain healthy, while affording me the conceit to be a big fish in a small pond.

Looking backward, what surprises me most is the amount of time I have devoted to the nonprofit sector. Maybe Phillips Brooks House has influenced me more than I know. Part of my law practice focuses on nonprofit issues, but I actually look forward to chairing board meetings of nonprofit organizations and foundations. Having been inspired by the work of the Kennedy School's Robert Putnam on the importance of the nonprofit sector, I took a sabbatical from my practice in 1997 to work on the development of nonprofits in Eastern Europe, specifically Hungary and Slovakia. My experience living and working there has led to additional board and consulting work in that region.

I am not certain where my nonprofit activities will lead. To that end, I finally got around to reading Walker Percy's *The Moviegoer* last summer. Like Binx Bolling, I am still searching, and hoping to figure it all out eventually.

HOME: Manchester, NH   **OCCUPATION:** Lawyer. McLane, Graf, Raulerson & Middleton   **BIRTHPLACE:** Concord, NH   **SECONDARY SCHOOL:** Phillips Exeter Academy, Exeter, NH   **YEARS AT COLLEGE:** 1971–75   **DEGREES:** A.B., magna cum laude, '75; J.D., Univ. of Pennsylvania '78   **SPOUSE/PARTNER:** Stephanie K. Williston, Oct. 6, 1979 (Mount Holyoke Coll., '70; Ph.D., Fielding Inst. '00, expected)   **SPOUSE'S OCCUPATION:** Psychologist. Veterans Affairs Research Service, Manchester, NH   **CHILDREN:** Kate, 1982; Patrick, 1985

Brian Eric Drayton: My path since Harvard has twisted and turned — I left to be an editor, but ended up directing a Quaker rest home; followed that by technical writing, then landed at my present spot in 1986, a nonprofit research and development firm focusing on math and science education. The work there has always been challenging and flexible, and it led me back to school and scientific research (plant conservation biology).

Meanwhile, my involvement in Quakerism has led me to significant travel, study, writing, religious work, and some social activism.

All during this time, my home has remained New England, and New England Quakerdom, with doors open to many other worlds.

In science, education, and my religious work, a constant feature has been writing, and the craft of shaping words to carry meaning for education, enlightenment, or simple connection continues to enthrall me.

Life changed forever and for the better when I met Darcy, and our lives have been adventurous and increasingly blessed. Our children are now at an age where they are becoming friends as well as offspring, on top of being among the best of teachers!

I would hope others writing for this Report could agree with me, whether they say it or not: every year I have lived has been better than the one before. I have lost my father, and other dear ones; I have not always succeeded at things I've tried, and have often been my own enemy. Nevertheless, to quote George Fox, "the Lord's power is over all," and despite a deep sense of humanity's folly, I still find the world enchanting and ever deeper in meaning and beauty — including the people in it.

HOME: Lyndeborough, NH   **OCCUPATION:** Project Director; Principal Investigator. TERC (science education research and development)   **BIRTHPLACE:** Bath, ME **SECONDARY SCHOOL:** Cheverus High School, Portland, ME   **YEARS AT COLLEGE:** 1971–75   **DEGREES:** A.B., cum laude, '75; A.M. '78; M.A., Boston Univ. '93; Ph.D., ibid. '99 **SPOUSE/PARTNER:** Darcy, 1975   **SPOUSE'S OCCUPATION:** Teacher. Pine Hill Waldorf School   **CHILDREN:** Micah T., 1979; Abraham G., 1984

Scott Drill: Time has flown way too quickly.

HOME: Edina, MN   **OCCUPATION:** CEO. Insignia Systems, North Plymouth, MN
DEGREES: A.B., cum laude, '75; M.B.A., St. Thomas Coll. '78   **SPOUSE/PARTNER:** Single
CHILDREN: Adam, 1981; Angela, 1986

Judith Singer Droar: I am happy to report that my husband Paul and
I are no longer a couple—we are a threesome since the arrival of our son
Teddy in January 1999. All three are living contentedly, if exhaustedly, in
New Jersey.

I currently work (does one call the breathing space between the morning
"Teddy" shift and the evening "Teddy" shift work or a reprieve?) as a vice
president in pharmaceutical marketing research at a company called Market
Measures, Inc. This has been a recent transition after working for pharmaceutical companies for almost two decades. My major intellectual challenges
alternate between speculating on whether Teddy's eyes will remain blue,
whether anyone will be able to afford Harvard tuition in twenty years, and
trying to figure out whether there was something beyond the front page of
today's newspaper I should have read but missed this morning.
(Fortunately, I realized that health clubs are an unnecessary time extrava-
gance for a person confronting the daily physical challenge of running up
and down stairs ten times a day carrying twenty-five pounds of weight.)

In case you are wondering if my sense of the larger world (not to mention my skill for small talk) have dried up—yes, of course they have. But
many people have reassured us that we will become almost normal people
again in a mere decade or so. And, in any case, my goals for the new millennium are to raise a healthy, curious, and caring boy—and I doubt that
anyone out there has a more ambitious set of goals.

HOME: Morristown, NJ   **OCCUPATION:** Vice President of Business Development.
Market Measures, Inc. (marketing research)   **BIRTHPLACE:** Boston, MA   **SECONDARY
SCHOOL:** Newton High School, Newton, MA   **YEARS AT COLLEGE:** 1971–75
DEGREES: A.B., cum laude, '75; M.B.A., Stanford Univ. '80   **SPOUSE/PARTNER:** Paul
Arthur Droar, Aug. 19, 1990 (St. Johns Coll., Cambridge Univ. '68; M.A., ibid. '72; M.B.A.,
Manchester Univ. '72)   **SPOUSE'S OCCUPATION:** Managing Director. Paul A. Droar
Associates   **CHILDREN:** Theodore Alexander, 1999

Robert Patrick Drucker: Graduation seems like yesterday. We talked about the Twenty-fifth Reunion; the fact that it would be the year 2000 was very amusing. We were happy to own handheld calculators, and think about the day we might even have a computer in our house. Y2K was only an algebraic expression.

Much has happened in the past twenty-five years. Following graduation, I headed south to attend Duke University School of Medicine. After four years of medical school, I married classmate Joan Liversidge, '75. Our first year of marriage consisted of Joan living in Virginia finishing medical school at the University of Virginia, while I was an intern in pediatrics back in Boston at Massachusetts General Hospital. Joan joined me in Boston for her residency in internal medicine. We both decided to pursue careers in infectious diseases and headed to Duke for that training. The promise we made to ourselves is that we would spend three years in North Carolina, and then head back to Boston. It is now sixteen years later, and we are still in Durham — with no plans to leave. Eric and Jenny (born in 1985 and 1987 respectively) have visited New England frequently, but North Carolina is home.

I joined the faculty at Duke following my fellowship in pediatric infectious diseases. I have had varied activities in pediatrics, starting in an HIV research laboratory while caring for children with AIDS. I have now moved away from the lab, and divide my time between patient care, administration, and teaching. My primary responsibility is for medical student education in pediatrics, and in training young(er) pediatricians.

Life keeps getting more hectic and interesting. Eric gets his driving permit in a few months and is an avid swimmer, Jenny has become quite the pianist and dreams about Harvard in her future, and Joan is a worldwide traveler. And we only just graduated.

HOME: Durham, NC   OCCUPATION: Director, Pediatric Student Education. Dept. of Pediatrics, Duke University Medical Center   BIRTHPLACE: Cleveland, OH
SECONDARY SCHOOL: York Mills Collegiate Inst., Toronto, ON, Canada   YEARS AT COLLEGE: 1971–75   DEGREES: A.B., cum laude, '75; M.D., Duke Univ. '79
SPOUSE/PARTNER: Joan Liversidge, May 26, 1979 (Radcliffe '75)   SPOUSE'S OCCUPATION: Chief Medical Officer. Trimeris, Inc.   CHILDREN: Eric Victor, 1985; Jennifer Craig, 1987   COLLEGE ACTIVITIES: Manager, football team, 1971–75; manager, basketball team, 1971–75; manager, lacrosse team, 1971–75

Tom Durwood: After graduation, I formed a small press (Ariel Books) with a childhood buddy and spent fifteen enjoyable years in the New York publishing world. We edited and published young adult history, illustrated classics, and original children's books with some very talented authors and artists.

Barb's and my big adventure came in 1991, when the Mexican government decided to auction off the national chain of movie theaters. I volunteered to lead the push into Latin America on behalf of the family business (AMC) and we moved to Cuernavaca, outside Mexico City. My kids went to Mexican schools and became fluent in Spanish, and we all learned a different way of life and business.

We are now happily resettled in San Diego. I have stumbled into tech commerce with a small and growing-too-rapidly digital media firm (m2), and hope to return to publishing, as well.

As clueless as I have been at various moments since graduation, I have certainly found moments to enjoy in every day. This is mostly due to my wife Barb; with her, everything is an adventure. We have two wonderful, smart, funny kids (Ben, fourteen, and Lily, twelve) and parenting them from babies to toddlers to young adults has been the richest experience possible. Our days start early and are very eventful. Today, I drove Ben and a teammate back from their flag football game. We discussed game highlights, the Pippen-Barkley feud, and Greek myths (among other topics). This evening, we almost burned dinner while trying to lure our cat back inside at coyote time. Tonight, I researched the ancient people of Catal-Huyuk, who built their doors in the roof, with Lily, then listened to her practice piano, and now Ben needs me to help construct a model of the human arm. With any luck, tomorrow will be equally full.

HOME: Santa Fe, CA   **OCCUPATION:** Partner. m2 Digital Media   **BIRTHPLACE:** Kansas City, KS   **SECONDARY SCHOOL:** Mount Hermon School   **YEARS AT COLLEGE:** 1971–75   **DEGREES:** A.B. '75; M.B.A., New York Univ. '86   **SPOUSE/PARTNER:** Barbara Frazer, June 6, 1975 (Trinity Coll. '74)   **CHILDREN:** Ben, 1985; Lily, 1987

David Stephen Edgell: Friendship requires an investment of time. Most of us recognize that time is a precious commodity. My preoccupation is finding time to spend with my wife, Vicky, and our three wonderful children, while pursuing a demanding career at the Hospital for Sick Children. We have adjusted to our move from Montreal to Toronto, but have not been able to adequately maintain the relationships we left behind. This is similar to my Harvard experience. Circumstances have made it difficult to share my life with distant friends. This does not diminish our importance to each other. I encourage those of you who would like to get in touch with old acquaintances to do so, recognizing that as we age our availability increases, but the time left to us does not. I approach the coming years with optimism, knowing that I shall be able to give back a little for the many blessings I have received.

HOME: Markham, ON, Canada   OCCUPATION: Perfusionist (technical specialty, cardiatric program)   BIRTHPLACE: Montreal, PQ, Canada   SECONDARY SCHOOL: Westmount High School, Montreal, PQ, Canada   YEARS AT COLLEGE: 1971–75   DEGREES: A.B. '75   SPOUSE/PARTNER: Mary Victoria Boutin, Dec. 28, 1981   CHILDREN: Stephen, 1983; Chelsea, 1987; Jeremy, 1990

Robert Whiting Egan: From the home office in Larchmont, New York: "Bob Egan's Top Ten List of Things That Have Made My Last Twenty-five Years Rock."

10. New York City. "Life is like a cocktail party, on the streets, Big Apple!" After college I traveled the U.S. looking for a place that stayed open twenty-four-hours-a-day, like me. I chose New York City (over Las Vegas) and stayed twenty-four, fun-filled, serendipitous years. Greenwich Village. The publishing "biz." Mudd Club to Harvard Club. Met my wife. Had kids. Had to move to the 'burbs when my record collection got too big. Still work next to the Flatiron building. "Hey, babe, take a walk on the wild side."

9. Larchmont. "I get up every morning...take the 8:15 into the city." My new life. Bugs and leaves. Stores close at 5:00. Yikes! Bikes!

8. Books. "My cucumber's bigger than yours, Mrs. Wermer!" Books and writing have been my life. Book-clerking at Barnes and Noble led to

Radcliffe Publishing Course, then editorial at Pocket Books, later Ariel Books (finding photos for hundreds of those little books you see at the checkout counter). Wrote and college-lectured on *From Here to Fraternity* (*Animal House* in a book). High point: book ridiculed by Phil Donahue on his show (good for sales). Still a book or two left in the old noggin.

7. Rock-and-roll. "You've been to the finest schools, all right, Mr. Lonely, but you know you only used to get juiced in it." LP to CD, the sound-track to my life. Although I keep somewhat current, the dinosaurs still rule: Thank you Lou, Van, Dr. Bob, Mick, Zep, and Bruce. I am not worthy.

6. Movies. "Do ya feel lucky, punk? Well, do ya?" My great escape. For two hours I can be James Bond, then I'm back to being a dad.

5. The news. "I read the news today, oh boy!" Member news junkies anonymous. *Time, Newsweek,* the *New York Times, National Enquirer, Headline News,* etc. And now the Internet. History...*live!*

4. Funny stuff. "Other than *that,* Mrs. Lincoln — how did you enjoy the play?" Broadway shows, gross-out movies, *Mad Magazine,* Rodney, Beavis, Larry Sanders, twenty-five years of *Saturday Night Live!* "Oh, hello, Newman!"

3. Deep thoughts — regrets? "I've had few, but then again, too few to mention." To future graduates: Save time. Get mentors in your field. Pay for information.

2. Friends. "Aqualung, my friend,... you poor old sod, you see it's only me." When I see old Harvard roommates and friends, it's like we're back in the Yard and nothing's changed....*Except we don't recognize each other.*

1. Spouse and spawn and Mom: "Here's a story — of a man named Brady!"...My life now — the Egan bunch. Twenty-four hours/seven days a week, tons-o-fun (although sometimes I'd like to be reading Hobbes rather than *Calvin and Hobbes*). But I digress...

HOME: Larchmont, NY   **OCCUPATION:** Writer. RAW Interactive, Ltd. (multimedia)
BIRTHPLACE: Cambridge, MA   **SECONDARY SCHOOL:** Belmont High School, Belmont, MA   **YEARS AT COLLEGE:** 1971–75   **DEGREES:** A.B. '75
SPOUSE/PARTNER: Louise Betts, 1985 (Northwestern Univ. '77)   **SPOUSE'S OCCUPATION:** Freelance Writer   **CHILDREN:** Emily, 1987; Alice, 1989; Nicholas, 1991

John Alan Emory: The past twenty-five years have been a memorable journey. The '70s ended with me working in Japan for two years, and returning with a young lady who became my wife (at a dual ceremony where my brother married a German girl). We have two sons, seven years apart, the first of whom is widely talented and a remarkable athlete and swimmer (soon to go to Junior Nationals). The younger one finally learned how to talk when he was five (we were worried), but he has now caught up and is becoming a fine swimmer himself.

Sumie and I both worked in technology jobs, me at ever larger companies (via acquisition), she with the World Bank, and we experienced the stresses of securing and managing day care providers and au pairs. I am now in only my third job, a new Washington office of a growing, small hi-tech company with lots of Ph.D.s, where I juggle system and software engineering, hiring, facilities, security, and marketing. Sumie parted with the World Bank to become an entrepreneur, kayaker, Web mistress, and swim team manager.

We are four years into a large new house with a local herd of deer (who eat our shrubs and flowers) and a three-hour lawn to mow. We have two cats, too many fish, and a guinea pig, and there are occasional threats of adding a dog. Sumie and the boys are in tremendous physical shape from swimming, while I have lapsed and gotten lazy and gray. My work has taken me on extended visits to Japan and Taiwan, to Hawaii and the California desert, to London and Spain, and to Long Island. I've gone skiing in Japan, Wyoming, California, Colorado, and Utah, but far too seldom. I've enjoyed hang gliding at Kitty Hawk, and scuba diving in Maui. My violin gathers dust now (after past glories of Bach, Vivaldi, Jackson Browne, and Chuck Berry), as does my tennis racket, but my guitar is still pretty respectable. Life's been good to me so far.

HOME: McLean, VA   **OCCUPATION:** Associate Division Manager. ALPHATECH, Inc. (mathematical algorithms, software engineering, defense contractor)   **BIRTHPLACE:** Alexandria, VA   **SECONDARY SCHOOL:** Phillips Exeter Academy, Exeter, NH   **YEARS AT COLLEGE:** 1971–75   **DEGREES:** A.B., cum laude, '75; M.B.A., Southern Illinois Univ., Edwardsville '85   **SPOUSE/PARTNER:** Sumie Taniuchi, April 10, 1982 (Tokyo Univ. '72)   **SPOUSE'S OCCUPATION:** Entrepreneur; Swim Team Manager; President. Little Pumpkins, Sumie's Smart Solutions (works from home)   **CHILDREN:** Michael, 1983; Daniel, 1990   **HARVARD/RADCLIFFE SIBLINGS:** Katharine Blair Emory '78 ('80)   **COLLEGE ACTIVITIES:** Orchestra; Lowell House Committee; space table

William A. Englund: There's no question that life abroad gives you a keener appreciation of what's wrong and what's right with America, and that's probably doubly true when you're in Moscow, where Kathy and I have spent most of the past decade. We run a sort of mom-and-pop bureau for the *Baltimore Sun*, trying (in twelve hundred words or less) to make sense of a country that manages to be infuriating, surprising, enchanting, and exasperating all at once. We've juggled wars, crises, tuberculosis outbreaks, economic collapses, and environmental disasters while also shuttling our two daughters around to birthday parties, soccer games, and bowling alleys (yes, even in Moscow). Living here can be a trial at times, especially in the gloom of winter, but I wouldn't have traded it for anything. It has meant we've been together far more as a family than we ever would have been back home in Baltimore. The office is across the hall from our apartment and there's a constant flow of interviews and math homework back and forth between them. When guests come for dinner, the conversations seem more immediate and more vital, perhaps because all of us — Russians and foreigners alike — live in a country where human frailties and heroics are so evident. And even at work all is not dreary: We've written about mushroom gathering in the fall, the astonishing improvement in the quality of Russian beer, the stubborn refusal of the theater to wither away in spite of everything, and the extraordinary beauty of Lake Baikal. Also, our boss is forty-five hundred miles away.

Yet being a foreign correspondent principally consists of bearing witness, and it's hard not to wonder at times if that's sufficient. At best we can hope to inspire or dissuade others; a newspaper is a clumsily powerful institution, but its power is all indirect. Choosing to write means choosing not to act. I spent six weeks in the Balkans a year ago, entertaining and horrifying the good people of Baltimore with tales of brutality and death. Could I do more?

HOME: Moscow, Russia   **OCCUPATION:** Moscow Correspondent. *Baltimore Sun*
BIRTHPLACE: Mount Kisco, NY   **SECONDARY SCHOOL:** Pleasantville High School, Pleasantville, NY   **YEARS AT COLLEGE:** 1971–75   **DEGREES:** A.B., cum laude, '75. M.S., Columbia '76   **SPOUSE/PARTNER:** Kathleen J. Lally, Sept. 13, 1980 (Ohio Univ. '67)
SPOUSE'S OCCUPATION: Moscow Correspondent. *Baltimore Sun*   **CHILDREN:** Kathleen, 1982; Molly, 1986   **COLLEGE ACTIVITIES:** Loeb Theater productions: *Offending the Audience, The Alchemist, Prometheus Bound*; House productions: *Arsenic and Old Lace, Tom Thumb, Measure for Measure*; editorial board, *Harvard Crimson*

John Philip Erlick: A synopsis of the past twenty-five years? — Well, here goes:

- I founded one start-up company (wireless broadband telecommunications)
- Lived in two cities (Seattle and Washington, D.C.)
- Worked in three law firms
- Married four couples (but never got married myself: "J. P. the J.P.")
- Traveled to five continents
- Climbed to the summit of six volcanic peaks in the Pacific Northwest
- Served as president of seven nonprofits (founded a psychiatric hospital; am outgoing president of Harvard-Radcliffe Club of western Washington)
- Have stayed in contact with many (more than eight) of my college classmates and roommates
- Have made countless trips back to Cambridge and Boston (many more than nine)
- Attended our Tenth Reunion in 1985

That sums it up — a few of the details omitted (to protect the innocent). Hope to see many of you at the Twenty-fifth!

HOME: Seattle, WA   **OCCUPATION:** Attorney; Principal. Reed McClue (law firm)
BIRTHPLACE: Boston, MA   **SECONDARY SCHOOL:** Boston Latin School, Boston, MA
YEARS AT COLLEGE: 1971–76   **DEGREES:** A.B., cum laude, '75 ('76); J.D., Georgetown Univ. '81

Arthur Ames Faden: I have stayed in the Boston area since graduation. Ellen and I married in 1976 and we are raising our three children (now ages eleven, thirteen, and sixteen) in the small town of Hopkinton (start of the Boston Marathon). We were fairly involved in the building of our home in a somewhat rural area. The town continues to develop at a moderate pace. We are closely tied to the local community (public schools, church, town politics, and meetings). Our family enjoys sports (soccer, swimming, cycling, basketball, tennis) and outdoor activities (skiing, hiking). This past summer, the five of us climbed to the summit of Mt. Washington, in spite of the mountain's effort to turn us back with cold, wind, and low visibility. Hope to see many of you at the Twenty-fifth!

HOME: Hopkinton, MA   **OCCUPATION:** Technical Consultant. Intelligent Network Unit (INU develops services for public switch telephone network), Lucent Technologies   **BIRTHPLACE:** Boston, MA   **SECONDARY SCHOOL:** Framingham North High School, Framingham, MA   **YEARS AT COLLEGE:** 1971–76   **DEGREES:** A.B., cum laude, '75 ('76)   **SPOUSE/PARTNER:** Ellen Fournier, June 20, 1976 (Univ. of Massachusetts '75; M.P.H., Boston Univ. '82)   **SPOUSE'S OCCUPATION:** Full-time Mother; Volunteer; Former Statistician. Framingham Heart Study   **CHILDREN:** Laura, 1983; Ashley, 1985; Andrew, 1988   **COLLEGE ACTIVITIES:** Varsity soccer team, fall, 1971–74

Ellen Bryan Fair: Twenty-five years seems an impossibly long time to have passed so quickly. After graduation I spent two years as a Peace Corps volunteer in Ivory Coast, West Africa, where I worked as a medical technician in a TB control clinic. Then in 1977, I moved to New York and the rough-and-tumble world of magazine publishing. Spent fourteen years at *Esquire,* the last seven as managing editor, then moved on to two years of consulting, two more as managing editor at *Working Woman* magazine, and landed happily in February of 1997 at *Parenting* and Time, Inc. Life outside of work included twelve years of competitive squash (which ended in 1992 when my elbow refused to cooperate any longer), and now includes as much outdoor activity as a New Yorker can muster, which is to say, not enough!

I've remained single more as a result of circumstance than choice, but am happy in my role as cheerleader for the children of friends and family, and have stayed in touch with many friends from both Harvard and Peace Corps days.

Things that haven't improved much in twenty-five years: health care distribution, corporate ethical standards, tolerance of difference in others. Things that have: the economy, everyone's clothes, the New York subway system. Which means there's hope for us yet in the twenty-five years to come.

HOME: New York, NY   **OCCUPATION:** Managing Editor. *Parenting* magazine, The Parenting Group   **BIRTHPLACE:** New York, NY   **SECONDARY SCHOOL:** Putney School, Putney, VT   **YEARS AT COLLEGE:** 1971–75   **DEGREES:** A.B., cum laude, '75   **COLLEGE ACTIVITIES:** *Harvard Crimson,* 1973–75; squash team, 1973

Ada Mei Fan: Maybe Harvard wasn't so bad for me after all. A smaller, more intellectually intense college with more faculty guidance would have suited me better, but then I might have fallen into an affair with a professor there — I didn't at H-R — in which case, I'd have gotten really screwed up (not that one necessarily does [no offense, anyone], but I would have). Harvard did give me an anthropological worldview that has served me well, an abiding sense of cosmology, some fine tutors, a good and lasting friendship with one professor and his wife, terrific roommates (who remain close) and my husband, Peter Warsaw '72 (also from Chappaqua) — and for all that, I'm most grateful. Although P. and I got married too young — September 1975 — we managed to work things out (not that it was easy) and I have no regrets and now we're looking at a twenty-fifth anniversary, with two daughters who are far too wonderful for us (and they think so too). The day after we got married, we went to Brooks School (where we got robbed the next day) and stayed there for a few years, while Peter taught music and played piano and I dropped out of Boston College's law school and then entered Boston University's film school (which I finished eventually) and then we went to graduate school in Rochester, New York, because P. wanted to go to Eastman and so I went to the University of Rochester (which had a lively and warm English department, which I needed). I wrote for a great weekly and we got our doctorates (eventually) and then moved seventeen years ago to Andover to teach at Phillips Academy, where I still agonize over whether I want to be part of the elitist, ivy-covered establishment and where I always try to be writing something or other, most recently an informal faculty attrition study for our Brace Center for Gender Studies and where P. and I teach an elective together called Words and Music and where I'm hoping to finish revising the manuscript I've been working on forever (which at last has some encouragement from a sympathetic agent and maybe someday will see the light of day, not that you're looking forward to it should you still be reading this). Anyway, while my days are usually very hectic — as are yours — it is nonetheless quite luxurious and exhilarating to be teaching tremendously talented and diverse students and hoping we're encouraging them to build a morally, socially and environmentally conscious society (with effective population controls and universal health care) — while we continue to fill our life with music, P. now being joined by violinist Arianna and cellist Marina, who are both happily caught up in the Saturday thrall of New England Conservatory. Our summers continue to be blissful in New Hampshire (in a community called Eastman, started by Dartmouth), where we're still loving the house that Kaffee built (and where P. plays eighteen to thirty-six-plus holes of golf daily [after piano practice], happy to be joined by any old friends who also golf). Skiing is good at the made-over Sunapee, if anyone wants a winter reunion. We try to see my sister's family in Upper Montclair and P.'s mother, also at Eastman, as often as we can and my parents in Honolulu as much as we can afford to. If I could stave off death, disease, and destruction for my family and friends and the rest of the world, I'd be truly happy. Keep up the e-mail, Kaf and Sarah and Vic — and Lisa (wife of Lynn Chang '75).

HOME: Grantham, NH   **OCCUPATION:** Instructor of English. Phillips Academy
BIRTHPLACE: Princeton, NJ   **SECONDARY SCHOOL:** Horace Greeley High School, Chappaqua, NY   **YEARS AT COLLEGE:** 1971–75   **DEGREES:** A.B., cum laude, '75; M.S., Boston Univ. '79; M.A., Univ. of Rochester '81; Ph.D., ibid. '88   **SPOUSE/PARTNER:** Peter Canton Warsaw, Sept. 7, 1975 (Harvard '72)   **SPOUSE'S OCCUPATION:** Instructor of Music. Phillips Academy, Andover, MA   **CHILDREN:** Arianna Solange, 1986; Marina Cybele, 1989   **COLLEGE ACTIVITIES:** Phillips Brooks House; field hockey

---

David R. Farneti: Upon graduation, I was hired by Bache Halsey Stuart as a stockbroker. In a few years, I was specializing in the futures markets, and co-authored a computerized trading system that I pitched to the large brokerage houses. In 1982, I felt the need to venture out of the corporate world, so I started my own little manufacturing company with the money that I made in the futures markets. Called the company Crimson Precision. Grew that into a nice-sized fabricating center and sold it in 1996. In 1992, started a distribution company for cleanroom apparel. Trademarked a fabric called tc2500. In 1997, I brought a Korean company into the U.S., and placed their garments at strategic semiconductor locations throughout the country. In 1994, started Crimson Consultants, and, finally, in 1998, have made this a stand-alone corporation.

Along this journey, sired three wonderful children, experienced the pure joy of fatherhood, and survived a very traumatic divorce.

In 1997, met a wonderful woman, and was lucky enough to have her accept my proposal, and we married this June. Also, we are expecting our first child in May.

My hobbies and avocations include martial arts, dog breeding (American bulldog). Bred father to Chance, the bulldog in the movie *Homeward Bound*. I also write articles for various specialty bulldog magazines. And am beginning to start my novel (at long last).

HOME: Fort Crane, NY   **OCCUPATION:** CEO. Crimson Consultants (works with small manufacturing companies in improving their bottom line and directing paradigm shifts, where applicable)   **BIRTHPLACE:** Binghamton, NY   **SECONDARY SCHOOL:** Binghamton North High School, Binghamton, NY   **YEARS AT COLLEGE:** 1971–75
DEGREES: A.B. '75   **SPOUSE/PARTNER:** Suzanne Shadduck, Aug. 11, 1979, divorced, 1993 (Broome Community Coll. '73); Lisa Marie Stevens, June 12, 1999 (Salt Lake Community

Coll. '89)   **SPOUSE'S OCCUPATION:** Consultant. Partylite Gifts   **CHILDREN:** Corinne Marie, 1981; Sara Lynn, 1982; Michael David, 1984   **HARVARD/RADCLIFFE SIBLINGS:** Gary William Farneti '71   **COLLEGE ACTIVITIES:** Involvement with Sigma Alpha Epsilon, 1973–75

David Fasano: Afer twelve years in business, I began teaching high school in 1988. After nine years as a high school teacher, administrator, coach, and counselor, I began working in college administration. I am presently serving on the staff at Georgia Tech.

Having had the opportunity to help others realize their potential, I am eagerly looking forward to the next phase of my career in education and service to the community.

I have been active as a member of the Schools and Scholarship Committee for over fifteen years. Meeting young men and women applying for admission to Harvard-Radcliffe helps me to remain connected to Harvard's tradition of commitment and service.

HOME: Tucker, GA   **OCCUPATION:** College Administrator. Georgia Institute of Technology   **BIRTHPLACE:** Boston, MA   **SECONDARY SCHOOL:** Phillips Exeter Academy, Exeter, NH   **DEGREES:** A.B., '75 ('76); M.A., Wesleyan Univ. '95   **SPOUSE/PARTNER:** Mary, Aug. 18, 1991 (St. Michael's Coll. '81; M.A., New Hampshire Coll. '87)   **SPOUSE'S OCCUPATION:** Banker. Wachovia Bank, Tucker, GA

Joseph M. Feller: After receiving my Ph.D. from Berkeley and then teaching and doing research in elementary particle physics for a couple of years at Columbia University, I decided that I'd rather be a lawyer than a physicist. I graduated from Harvard Law School in 1984, clerked for a judge in San Francisco, worked for the Environmental Protection Agency in Washington, D.C., for two years, and then moved to Arizona, where I have been since 1987. I teach environmental law, natural resources law, water law, and property law. at Arizona State University.

My greatest passions are the mountains, deserts, forests, and canyons of the West—both as places to enjoy and resources to protect. For the last ten years I have been engaged in advocacy and litigation to force the U.S. Forest Service and the Bureau of Land Management to protect public lands and resources from excessive and inappropriate livestock grazing and timber cutting and other abusive land-use practices.

OCCUPATION: Professor of Law. College of Law, Arizona State University
BIRTHPLACE: Washington, DC **SECONDARY SCHOOL:** Berkeley High School,
Berkeley, CA **YEARS AT COLLEGE:** 1971–75 **DEGREES:** A.B., cum laude, '75; Ph.D.,
Univ. of California, Berkeley '79; J.D., Harvard '84 **COLLEGE ACTIVITIES:** WHRB,
1971–75; Outing Club, 1971–75; Mountaineering Club, 1971–75

Linda Buck Fields: After college, I attended Harvard Business
School. I worked as a certified public accountant for Ernst & Whinney, as
an assistant vice president in the Investment Division of State Street Bank,
and as a financial consultant for Merrill Lynch, Pierce, Fenner & Smith.
Also, I attained the designation of certified financial planner. I married in
July of 1978, and I was a dedicated career (never considered being an at-
home mom) person, until...

We had our first child, Lawrence, in October of 1983. I was fascinated
with Lawrence and child development issues. I read everything I could read
and attended lots of seminars. I began to anguish over whether to work outside the home or whether to be home with Lawrence. It was a very difficult
decision, until...

I decided to become an at-home mom in January of 1987. I resigned
three times during my last year. Each time my boss told me to take some
time and think about it. He said being at home would be a waste of my education and experience. The third time I resigned, I announced my decision
to the office, so that I would not change my mind. I, too, wondered whether
I would be happy as an at-home mom, until...

I tried it!! I have never regretted that decision. I have been home since
Lawrence was three. He is fifteen and starting college next year. Lauren is
seven and in second grade. I have enjoyed volunteering and being involved
in various child-oriented activities.

I feel incredibly blessed and satisfied, and I wish all of you the best in
your endeavors.

HOME: Saint Louis, MO **OCCUPATION:** Homemaker **BIRTHPLACE:** Saint Louis, MO
SECONDARY SCHOOL: Northwest High School, Saint Louis, MO **YEARS AT
COLLEGE:** 1971–75 **DEGREES:** A.B., cum laude, '75; M.B.A., Harvard '77
SPOUSE/PARTNER: Larry Eugene Fields, July 15, 1978 (Harvard '76) **SPOUSE'S
OCCUPATION:** Director. Health Department, City of Saint Louis **CHILDREN:**
Lawrence Elliott, 1983; Lauren Elaine, 1992 **COLLEGE ACTIVITIES:** Co-director, vice
president, chair, Programming Committee, Kuumba Singers, 1971–75; class marshal

Ira John Finch: I have been very fortunate. The years since college have delivered neither serious illness nor misadventure to me and my family. I am blessed with a thoughtful and levelheaded wife, a devoted companion with a sense of humor and style. My two sons, although different in demeanor, are both intelligent. I spend much of my free time supplementing their education. We live in a peaceful community of plenty. When it seems too quiet and dull, we consider alternatives, but have yet to find a clearly better spot.

My specialty involves performing imaging-guided, minimally invasive procedures throughout the body. I enjoy this mini-surgery tremendously, and the field changes quickly enough to stay interesting. However, I continue to be dismayed by the deterioration of medical practice in this country. Because almost no one pays directly for medical care, the illusion of doctor-patient autonomy has been shattered to cut costs. I wonder how we will be cared for when we are old and sick. As health care contracts, I have found it less depressing to focus on the daily work and ignore the trends.

I recently told my ten year old, who is enthralled by technology, how we grew up thinking stereo systems and hand-held calculators were astonishing. Computers were hidden in some basement and engaged by typing on something resembling a teletype. A mouse was a small rodent inspecting your dorm room if you left food out. There were no faxes, cell phones, CDs, e-mails.... Maybe the telegraph, telephone, and airplane changed the world as much, but I take those innovations for granted just as my son takes the Internet, digital photography, and DVDs for granted.

The discussion made me realize how poorly most of us foresaw the directions in which technology would drive us. I certainly lacked the wisdom or clairvoyance to anticipate the tremendous power of the computer and financial industries. And I can't help feeling twinges of resentment about how these fields have dwarfed other careers.

So I tell my children to project forward, to anticipate change, when they consider their futures. And I try to follow this advice too, acknowledging, on the eve of the year 2000, that major changes are often unpredictable.

HOME: Danville, CA   OCCUPATION: Chairman, Department of Medical Imaging, and Director, Angiography and Interventional Radiology. John Muir Medical Center; Partner. Bay Imaging Consultants   BIRTHPLACE: New York, NY   SECONDARY SCHOOL: Phillips Exeter Academy, Exeter, NH   YEARS AT COLLEGE: 1971–75   DEGREES: A.B., cum laude, '75; M.D., Boston Univ. '79 SPOUSE/PARTNER: Pamela Short, June 5, 1982 (Harvard '78) SPOUSE'S OCCUPATION: Attorney (self-employed) CHILDREN: Andrew, 1988; William, 1993   COLLEGE ACTIVITIES: Theater; *Harvard Crimson*

Paul James Finnegan: It was twenty-nine years ago during my father's Reunion that I, as an incoming freshman, sat in a dorm reading his Twenty-fifth Anniversary Report. He spoke of the family, his career, and the joy of living on the Atlantic Ocean. We now also enjoy living near a large body of water — Lake Michigan. In that intervening period my life has followed a fairly circuitous route from Cambridge to New York, to Hong Kong, back to Cambridge, on to Chicago and finally to Evanston, Illinois.

On graduation day in 1975, I was fortunate to be offered an opportunity by roommate Hugh Hyde's dad to work in the publishing business in New York. I am forever grateful to the late Mr. Hyde for that introduction to the world of business. As a young graduate from Harvard, it was somewhat humbling to have to solicit clients who might not highly prioritize the purchase of advertising in one's publication. It is that type of experience, above all others, that I hope each of our children endures and potentially benefits from, as I feel I have.

In 1977 I was transferred to Hong Kong to oversee the firm's Far East operations. It was a dynamic time to be there and the constant travel throughout Southeast Asia was exhilarating for a twenty-five-year-old. I was torn three years later between staying for the long term and returning to the U.S. Business school won out.

In the early '80s, growing excitement about the venture capital industry led to my decision to work at First Chicago Venture Capital. It seemed to fit and I have been at it ever since. In 1993, our group at First Chicago, with the support of the bank, went out on our own and formed Madison Dearborn Partners. Since then, our group has grown and benefited from favorable and rising capital markets. My area of focus, communications, can be a challenge to keep pace with, but it has provided fascinating insights into how our lives, and those of our children, are changing dramatically.

My time spent with Northlight Theatre, a regional theatre north of Chicago, and the Metropolitan Chicago Council of Camp Fire Boys and Girls, has provided a pleasant balance to the world of finance. I have come to admire the energy and passion of the volunteers and staffs of these organizations as they seek to better the lives of others.

Mary and I married in June 1986, twenty-four months after our first date, a game of *bocce*. With my travel she has carried the load of caring for our three children: Katherine, twelve; Paul, ten; and Alex, eight. It's been fun reliving our own childhoods but, like many, I am torn about the time I have not been able to spend with them. We hope for their happiness in the amazing world they are entering.

HOME: Evanston, IL   **OCCUPATION:** Managing Director; Co-founder. Madison Dearborn Partners, Inc. (venture capital)   **BIRTHPLACE:** Boston, MA   **SECONDARY SCHOOL:** Phillips Academy Andover, Andover, MA   **YEARS AT COLLEGE:** 1971–75 **DEGREES:** A.B., cum laude, '75; M.B.A. '82   **SPOUSE/PARTNER:** Mary McCally, June 28, 1986 (Indiana Univ. '78)   **SPOUSE'S OCCUPATION:** Housewife   **CHILDREN:** Katherine, 1987; Paul, 1989; Alex, 1991   **COLLEGE ACTIVITIES:** Ski team, 1971–75, co-captain, 1974–75; A.D. Club, 1972–75

Ellen Beth Eisenbraun Fitzgerald: After graduation Michael and I moved to Chapel Hill, North Carolina, for medical school for me and grad school for him. I then completed a four-year residency in Ob-Gyn also at Chapel Hill (UNC). We moved to Tulsa, Oklahoma, where I was in private practice for ten years.

Besides the long hours of a doctor, we raised two daughters. I was a founding member of the Oklahoma NARAL (National Abortion Rights Action League) called Oklahomans for Choice.

Health problems (neck surgery times two) forced me to retire early. We have since moved to Houston, Texas.

I am very involved in our younger daughter Kate's competitive horseback riding. We spend three to four hours a day at our barn for her training in jumping, dressage, and cross-country riding. It is a different life from practicing medicine (which I still miss — but not the all-night part!).

HOME: Sugar Land, TX OCCUPATION: Retired M.D BIRTHPLACE: Madison, WI
SECONDARY SCHOOL: C. E. Donart High School, Stillwater, OK YEARS AT COLLEGE:
1973–75 DEGREES: A.B., cum laude, '75; M.D., Univ. of North Carolina '79
SPOUSE/PARTNER: Michael Paul Fitzgerald, June 8, 1973 (Harvard '75) CHILDREN:
Erinn Michelle, 1978; Kathleen Elyse, 1985 COLLEGE ACTIVITIES: Phi Beta Kappa

---

Michael Paul Fitzgerald: Ellen and I were married as juniors, one of only two couples that were married and both undergraduates. It seemed unfashionable at the time, but our friends from Holworthy and Mather House helped us celebrate an Oklahoma wedding in a style unparalleled in our hometown.

Last June we celebrated our twenty-fifth wedding anniversary with our two daughters, Erinn and Kate, as we traveled throughout Italy. Much like our anniversary trip, the last twenty-five years have been rewarding, challenging at times, but always exciting and often unpredictable.

Ellen and I have coordinated careers in the medical field — she as an Ob-Gyn and myself in several progressive roles in management. The experiences gained at Harvard's highly diverse and intellectually challenging environment gave us a superb preparation. I often reflect "tongue in cheek" that my focus on international relations prepared me best for the health care industry.

As I reflect over the journey of the last twenty-five years, I am struck that, while academic pursuits and careers characterize many of our mutual goals, they are only a "means" and rarely an "end" of themselves.

The greatest rewards come from the joy of sharing discoveries with our families and friends. We look forward to seeing our old friends and learning of their journeys over the last several years.

HOME: Sugar Land, TX   OCCUPATION: Chief Administrative Officer   BIRTHPLACE: Houston, TX   SECONDARY SCHOOL: C. E. Donart High School, Stillwater, OK YEARS AT COLLEGE: 1971–75   DEGREES: A.B., cumlaude, '75; M.H.A., Duke Univ. '78 SPOUSE/PARTNER: Ellen Eisenbraun, June 8, 1973 (Radcliffe '75)   SPOUSE'S OCCUPATION: Retired Physician (Ob-Gyn)   CHILDREN: Erinn Michelle, 1978; Kathleen Elyse, 1985

Anthony Flanders: Outwardly, I am a little fatter and a little wiser than I was in college, but otherwise not much changed. For me and those I love, there is a major difference: I used to be unhappy almost all the time, and now I am happy whenever I stop to think about it. Years of absurdly slow and unpleasant psychotherapy made it possible for me to accept happiness, marrying Carla provided happiness, and adopting Rajani clinched it.

I have been away from Cambridge for stints, but I have always come back here. After twenty-five years, and with Rajani starting kindergarten in the public school system, it is finally beginning to feel like home. As for my job, the key features are that I work a flexible thirty-two hours a week, my commute is five minutes by bicycle, I like my co-workers, and I earn more than I need. All that is missing is fulfillment. But I would far rather be fulfilled at home and empty at work than the other way around.

The highlight of my recent life was last year's trip to India with Carla, Rajani, and my father. We revisited the orphanage where Rajani spent twelve of her first fourteen months, and then spent a few more weeks being tourists. When not traveling, I like to read, write, hike, climb, and most recently, dabble in astronomy. To my pride and chagrin, Rajani now climbs trees as well as I do. I shudder to imagine what she will be like in another five years.

HOME: Cambridge, MA   OCCUPATION: Computer Programmer. Belmont Research, Inc.   BIRTHPLACE: New York, NY   SECONDARY SCHOOL: Bronx High School of Science, Bronx, NY   YEARS AT COLLEGE: 1970–75   DEGREES: A.B., cum laude, '75 SPOUSE/PARTNER: Carla Procaskey, Sept. 14, 1991   SPOUSE'S OCCUPATION: Mother CHILDREN: Rajani Elizabeth, 1994 (adopted, 1995)   HARVARD/RADCLIFFE SIBLINGS: Katharine Flanders Mukherji '73; Tamzen Flanders '77   COLLEGE ACTIVITIES: Mountaineering Club

John Henry Flood III: The seminal and best decision I made since graduation was to marry Marianne Sharkey Flood. We met while she was in the eighth grade and I dare say that not the wealthiest, most celebrated or most successful of our classmates has more than I. Our life is centered around our three children and their activities. John Henry is a sophomore at the Lawrenceville School, where he participates in varsity football, wrestling, and lacrosse. Ashley is a freshman at Westfield High School and her passion is gymnastics. My youngest, Sara, is in seventh grade and her extracurricular activities include boys, lacrosse, and soccer — in that order.

Since graduating from the University of Virginia School of Law, I have been lucky enough to work in areas that I enjoy. I started my legal career in 1978 at Rogers, Hoge & Hills in New York City, where I acquired a background in trademark law and sports endorsement contracts (Arthur Ashe). I left private practice to work as legal counsel to a division of Paramount Pictures in New York City. Starting in 1984, and for the next ten years, I worked at NFL Properties, the centralized marketing company of the NFL, where I moved from the legal side to the business side and eventually became president of the company. After a bumpy ending there, for the past five years I have been managing partner at Flood, Johnston & McShane, PC, in New York City, where I specialize in trademarks and sports and entertainment law. I also own a sports and entertainment marketing concern, Oldiron Sports & Entertainment Company, Inc. Our major clients are the Dallas Cowboys and the Seattle Supersonics. We also represent Charles Woodson (Oakland Raiders), Wally Szczerbiak (Minnesota Timberwolves) and Corey Maggette (Orlando Magic) for their marketing activities. It beats a real job!

I look forward to reuniting with old friends at our Twenty-fifth Reunion and wish everyone well with the opportunities and challenges that the next twenty-five years are sure to provide.

HOME: Westfield, NJ   **OCCUPATION:** Managing Partner. Flood, Johnston & McShane (law firm). President. Oldlron Sports & Entertainment Company, Inc.   **BIRTHPLACE:** Newark, NJ **SECONDARY SCHOOL:** The Lawrenceville School, Lawrenceville, NJ **YEARS AT COLLEGE:** 1971–75   **DEGREES:** A.B., magna cum laude, '75; J.D., Univ. of Virginia '78   **SPOUSE/PARTNER:** Marianne Sharkey, June 12, 1976 (Univ. of New Hampshire '76; M.A., New York Univ. '81; Ph.D., ibid. '87)   **SPOUSE'S OCCUPATION:** President. Healthcare Review Consultants (works from home)   **CHILDREN:** John Henry, 1982; Ashley, 1985; Sara, 1987   **HARVARD/RADCLIFFE SIBLINGS:** Mark James Flood '82 **COLLEGE ACTIVITIES:** Football, 1971–75; lacrosse, 1971–74; Undergraduate Admissions Counseling Service, 1971–75; Owl Club; Hasty Pudding

Janet B. Fogel: Twenty-five years breaks down into nine years in San Francisco and sixteen years back in Boston. Life is hectic but satisfying. I've just left the city of Somerville, where I've been a lawyer for more than ten years and am trying to decide what to do next. Meantime, I feel blessed to have good friends (on both coasts) and a happy and healthy family. We're enjoying watching our kids grow up.

HOME: Auburndale, MA   OCCUPATION: Lawyer   BIRTHPLACE: New York, NY
SECONDARY SCHOOL: Scarsdale High School, Scarsdale, NY   YEARS AT COLLEGE:
1971–75   DEGREES: A.B., cum laude, '75; J.D., Univ. of California, Berkeley '80
SPOUSE/PARTNER: Robert Schiegel, 1982 (Univ. of Wisconsin, Madison '73; Ph.D., Univ.
of California, Berkeley '84)   SPOUSE'S OCCUPATION: Research Director. Millennium
Predictive Medicine   CHILDREN: Dana, 1985; Sarah, 1988   HARVARD/RADCLIFFE
SIBLINGS: James Fogel '72   COLLEGE ACTIVITIES: Philips Brooks House; *Harvard*
magazine

Edward Alan Forman: Twenty-five years ago, I never imagined that I'd be reflecting on my post-Harvard life from California. Life can take interesting turns. In 1975, I was a dedicated East-Coaster who envisioned a life in public policy or law. Now I've been living in the San Francisco Bay Area for over twenty years, and have spent most of my career in leading-edge technology companies. I am currently involved in an Internet infrastructure start-up. It's pretty amusing where a Harvard A.B. in fine arts can take you. I enjoy it when prospective investors think I am an engineer! My Harvard education has enabled me to communicate credibly across disciplines. My travels among start-ups over the last twenty years have been exciting, yet sometimes rocky. I've experienced companies that have thrived, closed down, or been merged into bigger enterprises. Except for my current firm, enCommerce, none still operate under the name it had when I worked there. Makes for an interesting résumé!

On a personal note, my wife Jan and I enjoy the joys and challenges of living with our fifteen-year-old daughter, Leslie, and thirteen-year-old son, Ben. We spend our weekends in the cheering sections at water polo, soccer, and tennis tournaments. We've been fortunate enough to take great trips to Europe, Alaska, and Costa Rica. Last summer we went whitewater rafting down the Middle Fork of the Salmon River in Idaho. Our kids had never

been in true wilderness before. (Not even an outhouse!) In the beautiful canyons, we were able to reflect on how ridiculously fast-paced life in the Silicon Valley has become.

Even though I'm on the other side of the country, Harvard remains close at hand. Recently at our local swim club, I counted eight people in the pool who had lived at Mather House during my four-year tenure.

HOME: Atherton, CA   **OCCUPATION:** Vice President, New Market Development. enCommerce, Inc. (software and services)   **BIRTHPLACE:** Boston, MA   **SECONDARY SCHOOL:** Newton South High School, Newton Center, MA   **YEARS AT COLLEGE:** 1971–75   **DEGREES:** A.B., cumlaude, '75; M.B.A., Stanford Univ. '79   **SPOUSE/PARTNER:** Janet Leslie Swanberg, 1981 (Stanford Univ. '75; M.B.A., ibid. '79)   **SPOUSE'S OCCUPATION:** Marketing Consultant. Swanberg Associates (works from home)   **CHILDREN:** Leslie Swanberg Forman, 1984; Benjamin Swanberg Forman, 1986   **COLLEGE ACTIVITIES:** Photo editor, *Harvard Crimson;* freshman lightweight crew

---

Alan Marc Freedman: After that rainy commencement day in '75, I "...loaded up my truck and I moved to Beverly (Hills, that is...)," to pursue a medical career. The transition from a Beverly Hillbilly to Marcus Welby was challenging, and far different than college. However, to this day, unlike Dr. Welby, I do not jump off the Santa Monica pier, nor do I break down patients' doors to convince them to have surgery. Following UCLA Medical School, and two years of general surgery at M.G.H., I was back in "La-La" land for a UCLA urology residency. Since 1986, I reside and work in Newport Beach, fifty miles south of L.A., and have a busy solo urology practice. Hoag Hospital has had me on its executive committee, as well as chairman of the urology department. I've gotten an M.B.A. at University of California, Irvine, but am yet searching for a "Microsoft"-type vision.

I keep in touch with some other '75ers, including Jay Herman, M.D., and Steve Selinger.

After marrying Marsha in 1992, and dabbling in golf, saxophone, and extensive travel, our son Myles was born in August 1998. He is a real gem, with beautiful copper-red hair, and greenish-hazel eyes; he is active, curious, insightful for his age, and always projecting innocence and joy.

Sitting on my porch at night, looking at the serene sea below, listening to the foghorns, I am brought back in reverie to my youth in Boston and my relinquished Boston accent. I see myself sitting on the steps of Hollis Hall in the Yard, first week of freshman year. As my dormmates and I watch the women walk by, I am euphoric with the possibilities for the future. Myles cries, and I am awakened to the realities of now, and things I never could have projected. Thank you, Harvard, for twenty-five years after. With tribute to Dan Fogelberg, "We drank a toast to innocence, we drank a toast to time; living in our eloquence, another auld lang syne."

HOME: Corona del Mar, CA   **OCCUPATION:** Physician; Urologist (private solo practice)   **BIRTHPLACE:** Boston, MA   **SECONDARY SCHOOL:** Boston Public Latin School, Boston, MA   **YEARS AT COLLEGE:** 1971–75   **DEGREES:** A.B., cum laude, '75; M.D., Univ. of California, Los Angeles '79; M.B.A., Univ. of California, Irvine '91   **SPOUSE/PARTNER:** Marsha Grifka, Sept. 4, 1992 (Princeton '74)   **SPOUSE'S OCCUPATION:** Gerontologist; Full-time Mom   **CHILDREN:** Myles Grant, 1998   **COLLEGE ACTIVITIES:** Hockey team manager, 1971—74; Crimson Key Society, 1973–75; Dorm/House football and hockey; volunteer, Boston Children's Hospital, 1973–75

Barbara Fretwell: Life continues to teach me that we are here to learn to love and connect with our families and the people around us. My best teachers are my husband, children, patients, and friends.

HOME: Okemos, MI   **OCCUPATION:** Physician (internal medicine)   **DEGREES:** A.B., magna cum laude, '75; M.D., State Univ. of New York, Buffalo '79   **SPOUSE/PARTNER:** Peter H. Cooke, Oct. 9, 1982   **CHILDREN:** Thomas, 1983; John, 1987; Mary, 1990

Robert Nogel Frisbie: After graduating from Harvard, I learned that life is too short (or too long, depending on your point of view) to spend time doing things you don't enjoy. Having endured Guillain-Barré syndrome in my late twenties and then cancer in my early forties, I came to understand the uncertainties of this world. I work out of my home and try to spend as much time as possible with my very active wife and my four children. I have been involved in real estate development since my junior year at Harvard, when I purchased my first building in Somerville. After spending some time working on Beacon Hill, I moved down to the Philadelphia area in the early '80s, bought an old stone farmhouse, and began raising kids, horses, sheep, chickens, turkeys, guinea hens, dogs, cats, and large-mouth bass, while attempting to stay abreast of real estate projects in Florida, Pennsylvania, Montana, and Massachusetts. My favorite recreational activity is fly-fishing which, coincidentally, takes me to Florida, Montana, and Nantucket, Massachusetts, on a fairly regular basis. My hope for the next twenty-five years is for my entire family to enjoy good health, to have my business prosper, and to have the really big stripers return to the shoals off Nantucket.

HOME: Fort Washington, PA   OCCUPATION: Real Estate Developer   BIRTHPLACE: New York   SECONDARY SCHOOL: Phillips Academy, Andover, MA   YEARS AT COLLEGE: 1971–75   DEGREES: A.B. '75   SPOUSE/PARTNER: Kristine Bast, Sept. 16, 1979 (Smith Coll. '75)   SPOUSE'S OCCUPATION: Writer   CHILDREN: Frances Weeks Frisbie, 1984; Kristin Bast Frisbie, 1986; Robert Nogel Frisbie, 1989; Richard David Frisbie, 1994   HARVARD/RADCLIFFE SIBLINGS: Richard D. Frisbie '71, J.D. '74; David W. Frisbie, M.B.A. '80   COLLEGE ACTIVITIES: Owl Club; varsity lacrosse

---

Deborah R. Levine Frost: I have terribly mixed emotions simply approaching this Twenty-fifth Reunion. My father, who served as a marshal for his Class, was consumed with preparations for his Twenty-fifth — which coincided with our freshman year. Unfortunately, he was killed on Route 128 three weeks after I arrived at Harvard, which not only set into motion a fairly devastating series of events for my family, but rendered my Harvard experience, in contrast to that of both of my parents and numerous relatives, an extremely miserable one. If there were any bright spots, I suppose they coincided with my serving as music director of WHRB, where, despite much opposition, I helped introduce a modern rock format that still seems to be thriving today. Then-unknown artists such as Blondie, the Talking Heads, the Police, and the Cars held some of their first on-air interviews and received some of their earliest spins anywhere under my jurisdiction. These experiences served me well when following the somewhat rockier road chosen by Pete Seeger and Bonnie Raitt and anyone else who discovered early on that the demands of the muse did not necessarily jibe with those of the university. I did not necessarily plan to become a professional rock critic, but given that I was pretty good at it, and it gave me, while still a teenager, a chance to not only see and hear lots of music and generally fulfill most of my fantasies, but to be published regularly, that's what I did. My work appeared for more than two decades everywhere from *Rolling Stone* to the country's leading dailies. In 1988, I married my songwriting partner of several years, Albert Bouchard, who previously founded the platinum-selling arena rockers, Blue Oyster Cult, and our lives have kept changing, and never in ways we might have otherwise anticipated. Together we have a wonderful son, a band and a small independent record company. The malignant tumor our guitar player was diagnosed with two years ago has put the heavy touring on hold for now, and also forced us to rethink our priorities. While our company is thriving with a variety of interesting new releases, sold primarily via the Internet and mail order, we're both determined to devote this precious time not only to our child, but to our community. Albert recently earned a masters in language and literacy, and has been working in an inner city school with some of New York's most disadvantaged kids. I've been working on numerous area issues, most related to improving traffic and safety conditions. I'm sure my former classmates will be tremendously amused to learn that our spare time, such as it is, has been devoted to a new obsession: golf. As if you needed any other sign that Armageddon is near.

HOME: New York, NY   **YEARS AT COLLEGE:** 1971–72; 1974–77

Andrew Earl Furer: Upon graduation from law school, I clerked for Judge Arnold Raum of the United States Tax Court in Washington, D.C., and then practiced law with the Los Angeles tax law firm Brawerman, Kopple & Lerner until 1982. My wife and I were married in California in 1981. Thereafter, we returned to Washington, D.C., where I served as Associate Tax Legislative Counsel of the U.S. Department of Treasury for a time. Next was a three-and-a-half-year stint as an investment banker with Salomon Brothers in New York. In 1987, I co-founded Castine Partners, an investment partnership affiliated with the Robert Bass Group. During that period, much of my time was devoted to board memberships with several public and private companies.

Retirement came in 1993. The family decided to move to Geneva, Switzerland, and tour Europe, which we did until 1997. Our son Alexander became a fluent French speaker and proficient skier while attending boarding school at the Institute Le Rosey in Switzerland. I fell in love with skiing during our winters in Gstaad, so much so that I have skied almost every winter day since learning to ski in 1993! We returned to the U.S. in 1997 to live at Lake Tahoe. Alexander has been a boarding student at Groton School (Groton, Massachusetts) since 1997, and is currently in the fourth form (tenth grade). Skiing, boating, travel, and a new hobby, showing golden retrievers at conformation dog shows, occupy us now.

HOME: Incline Village, NV   **OCCUPATION:** Investment Banker (retired)   **BIRTHPLACE:** Cincinnati, OH   **SECONDARY SCHOOL:** Fullerton Union High School, Fullerton, CA
YEARS AT COLLEGE: 1971–74   **DEGREES:** A.B., cum laude, '75 ('74); J.D. '77
SPOUSE/PARTNER: Eloisa B., June 28, 1981 (Divine Word Univ. [formerly St. Paul's Univ.], Philippines, '63)   **SPOUSE'S OCCUPATION:** Housewife   **CHILDREN:** Alexander Eric, 1984   **COLLEGE ACTIVITIES:** Harvard-Radcliffe Orchestra

David Gordon Gad-Harf: I seem to be at a turning point in my life, marked by my twenty-fifth anniversary of graduating from Harvard, the beginning of my second decade working and living in Detroit, and, most important, the departure of my son to college.

During the first five years after college, I lived in five different cities, involving several different jobs and a quick dose of graduate education. Looking back on that period, every experience was important and enriching, even if some of them were painful.

Without a doubt, the most satisfying, growing experience since graduation has been parenthood, which I fully shared with my wife, Nancy. I also feel very fortunate to have a career that enables me to work with many diverse types of people and to feel that I'm contributing something to my community.

And now, I am excited about a future that, while unclear, promises to be full of new adventures and opportunities.

HOME: West Bloomfield, MI   OCCUPATION: Executive Director. Jewish Community Council of Metropolitan Detroit (nonprofit advocacy organization)   BIRTHPLACE: Erie, PA   SECONDARY SCHOOL: McDowell High School, Erie, PA   YEARS AT COLLEGE: 1971–75   DEGREES: A.B., magna cumlaude, '75; M.S.P.H., Univ. of North Carolina '81   SPOUSE/PARTNER: Nancy Gad, Nov. 11, 1978 (Skidmore Coll. '70) SPOUSE'S OCCUPATION: Regional Director. American Technion Society   CHILDREN: Joshua, 1980   COLLEGE ACTIVITIES: *Harvard Crimson,* 1972–75

Benjamin Winsor Gale: Was that really twenty-five years? I thought by the time of our Twenty-fifth I would have grown middle-aged and quite stout, like the Tailor of Gloucester. Instead, I feel like I'm still waiting to get old. I have yet to switch to bifocals (squinting still works O.K.); and I enjoy the same kinds of entertainment as my kids, although I can't abide rap and they eschew my Tuvan throat singing. I feel fit enough, but pick-up basketball games have largely been replaced by tennis and by the vicarious pleasure of watching my children compete. I suspect I've lost a half step, especially in dribble-drives to the left. The truth is that I notice the passing of time primarily in the passing of my relatives and loved ones.

My biggest problem these days is perfecting a convincing comb-over — I would appreciate any suggestions. My sister, Emily Gale '81, was touting a vitamin A–based product that she said would even work on Jesse Ventura, but I haven't found support for it on the Internet.

My recommendations for staying young: Stretch your elbow ligaments (Throwing sidearm can cover defects in technique.); preserve your grandparents (Winsor Gale '22 is ninety-nine.); move regularly (I moved to California in '79, have lived in eleven urban neighborhoods since, and now reside in a comfortable, tumbled-down place in Mill Valley among the redwoods.); specialize your skills (Tax law has given me an entrée into many interesting lives.); avoid the corporate grind (Whatever can it be good for?); join a Unitarian church (I joined the Marin County church's choir ten years ago and am now a mainstay of the board.); travel (I return to Annisquam, Massachusetts every year.); give all you can to your clients; love your wife and kids.

HOME: Mill Valley, CA   **OCCUPATION:** Lawyer   **BIRTHPLACE:** Quincy, MA
SECONDARY SCHOOL: Mariemont High School, Mariemont, OH   **YEARS AT COLLEGE:** 1971–75   **DEGREES:** A.B., cum laude, '75; J.D., Univ. of California, San Francisco '82; L.L.M., Golden Gate Univ. '87   **SPOUSE/PARTNER:** Kristina Kukkonen, April 19, 1977 (Univ. of California, Berkeley '83)   **CHILDREN:** William, 1985; Sarah, 1988; Katrina, 1994   **HARVARD/RADCLIFFE SIBLINGS:** Emily Gale '81

Raul Isidro Garcia: Stayed in the Boston area these past twenty-five years doing one thing or another. All's well. Turns out it actually is a wonderful life. In spite of making countless stumbles, it all seems to have worked out for the best. Quite remarkable. As far as remembrance of college days, what are sweetest are thoughts of special friends and the times we shared. Over these many years, I have gained a deeper appreciation of the value of friends and family, my own and my beloved wife's. I feel especially fortunate to have gotten to know better my mother and father. My love for each has grown. Each in their own fashion an admirable person, to whom I owe so much. And my in-laws, all of whom live nearby and form our extended family, are the absolute best. How did I luck out? But, the most important events have been the births of our son, Andrew, on April 7, 1991, and daughter, Elizabeth, on December 14, 1992. They're just extraordinary. A continuing source of joy and pride to us. Whatever it is that I may be contributing to their growing up, it has been humbling to realize that it is really they that are helping me to grow up and to finally (maybe) become an adult. Interesting times.

HOME: Wellesley, MA   **OCCUPATION:** Professor; Chairman. Dept. of Health Policy and Health Services Research, Boston University School of Dental Medicine
BIRTHPLACE: Havana, Cuba   **SECONDARY SCHOOL:** Suffern High School, Suffern, NY
YEARS AT COLLEGE: 1971–75   **DEGREES:** A.B., cum laude, '75; D.M.D. '81; M.O.B. '84
SPOUSE/PARTNER: Linnea Wiberg, Nov. 25, 1989 (M.D., Tufts Univ. '88)   **SPOUSE'S OCCUPATION:** Pathologist   **CHILDREN:** Andrew Jose Raul, 1991; Elizabeth Emma, 1992

William Lewis Gardner: After leaving Madison and the University of Wisconsin, Sari and I returned east to Brookline and grew roots. We connected with our community and found happiness in proximity. From our perch on Corey Hill, the local elementary school, where I taught nineteen years of fourth grade, is a ten-minute walk, while Sari's pediatric practice is a three-minute drop.

At present I am in my second of two years' leave from the Brookline Public Schools. I'll probably graduate to fifth grade next year, but in the meanwhile am attempting to savor my time as a domestic partner. I am full-time father to my three sons, aged sixteen, thirteen, and six. While school is in session, I play amateur carpenter, gardener, painter, and paperer, to stay ahead on a house built at the turn of the *last* century. Although I hate to grocery shop, I like to cook.

So while not moving or shaking I am satisfied with my life at the millennium. I try not to take my luck in marriage, family, and good health for granted. I thank good fortune more than the *World's Greatest University* for my circumstance, yet I am nonetheless grateful to have graduated from Harvard in 1975.

HOME: Brookline, MA   **OCCUPATION:** Domestic Partner; Elementary Teacher. Edward Devotion School   **BIRTHPLACE:** April 17, 1953, Boston, MA   **SECONDARY SCHOOL:** Wellesley High School, Wellesley, MA   **YEARS AT COLLEGE:** 1971–75   **DEGREES:** A.B., cum laude, '75   **SPOUSE/PARTNER:** Sari J. Rotter, Jan. 1, 1978 (Simmons Coll.; M.D., Univ. of Wisconsin)   **SPOUSE'S OCCUPATION:** Pediatrician. Children's Hospital, Boston, MA   **CHILDREN:** Walt, 1983; Sam, 1985; Miles, 1993   **HARVARD/RADCLIFFE SIBLINGS:** Louis E. Gardner '88   **COLLEGE ACTIVITIES:** Dunster Drama Society; Phillips Brooks House; waterpipe table

Paula Balboni George: With aging comes maturity, but also a loss of idealism. As we remember our college years, let us rekindle our youthful spirit, revel in our friends and families, commit to our communities, remain humble in our "accomplishments," forsake materialism, and remember the golden rule.

HOME: Wyomissing, PA **OCCUPATION:** Pediatrician; Mother **BIRTHPLACE:** Pennsylvania **SECONDARY SCHOOL:** Simsbury High School, Simsbury, CT **YEARS AT COLLEGE:** 1971–75 **DEGREES:** A.B., summa cum laude, '75; M.D. '79 **SPOUSE/PARTNER:** David L. George, May 13, 1978 (Princeton '74; M.D., Harvard '78) **SPOUSE'S OCCUPATION:** Physician **CHILDREN:** Michael David, 1983; Daniel Abraham, 1985 **COLLEGE ACTIVITIES:** Varsity field hockey

---

Wayne Llewellyn George: To me your request is a rather tall order. Reflecting on my life since graduation is not something I tend to do; and, as you may have gathered from the past Class Reports, it is certainly not in my nature to write about it. I guess it is kind of an American thing, one of the few that I have not embraced, or at least adopted. At any rate, I shall do my best to catch the spirit, so to speak.

Early on I enjoyed a few adventures, including some fairly exciting encounters with grizzlies on the Arctic tundra, a couple of rapidly descending helicopters, and gale winds while crossing Hecate Strait in search of those elusive abalone.

Canadian law has undergone some major changes in the last twenty-odd years. It makes what I do interesting and important. I have found working as a sole practitioner, as I have for the past decade, allows the combination of freedom and responsibility that seems to suit me best. I have managed to attract a number of good clients with interesting problems; and met with sufficient success to keep me satisfied, both personally and professionally.

I have also had the good fortune of meeting and developing friendships and associations with an unusually large number of rare and exceptional people, most notably my wife, Jean. I have found the challenges and rewards of attempting to keep an appropriate balance between professional and business life and my personal and family life, interesting, challenging, and very rewarding. I particularly enjoy what our children have brought into our lives.

Victoria is an attractive city. People even say it is idyllic. For me it seems to possess a mixture of natural beauty, insular charm, urban amenities, proximity to wilderness and rural areas and neighborly sense of community, that lends to keeping the goals and accomplishments of life in their proper prospective.

HOME: Victoria, BC, Canada   OCCUPATION: Lawyer   BIRTHPLACE: Brooks, AB, Canada   SECONDARY SCHOOL: Bassano High School, Bassano, AB, Canada   YEARS AT COLLEGE: 1971–75   DEGREES: A.B. '75; LL.B., Queen's Univ., Kingston, ON '79 SPOUSE/PARTNER: Jean McKay, July 6, 1985 (Univ. of British Columbia '82) CHILDREN: Paul Bryn, 1990; Ross Evan, 1992   COLLEGE ACTIVITIES: Freshman hockey, 1971; junior varsity hockey, 1972–75; Rugby Club, 1971–75

Frank W. Gerold: It has been an interesting twenty-five years, beginning with my move to Texas in 1976. I attended law school in San Antonio, and began my law practice with the oldest law firm west of the Mississippi.

Trial work has provided insight into jobs, disciplines, places, and technologies that I would not have experienced otherwise.

Family life has been wonderful — now married nineteen years with two teens. Like any parent, I seem to fret more about what life has in store for my kids than anything else. How did our parents survive us?

Like many others, I am a caretaker for my mother, who has Alzheimer's. It is an emotional and trying experience, but it has its moments of great humor and shared enjoyment of accomplishing what to most would be relatively simple tasks. As all of us get older, we will have to confront this illness on a more frequent and personal basis. Do what you can to help.

OCCUPATION: Attorney (private practice)   SECONDARY SCHOOL: The Choate School, Wallingford, CT   YEARS AT COLLEGE: 1971–75   DEGREES: A.B. '75; J.D., St. Mary's Univ. '79   SPOUSE/PARTNER: Janet M. (Southwest Texas State Univ.) SPOUSE'S OCCUPATION: Educator; Homemaker   CHILDREN: Frank J., 1982; Lauren A., 1985   HARVARD/RADCLIFFE SIBLINGS: Thomas F. Gerold '74   COLLEGE ACTIVITIES: Varsity lacrosse; Harvard Drama Society; Winthrop House Drama Society

Roy G. Geronemus: Life since graduation in 1975 has been mostly predictable with some surprises. The past quarter century has been filled with hard work, accomplishment, and a content perspective of this time period.

Following the rigors of medical training at the University of Miami School of Medicine followed by a residency and fellowship training in dermatology and dermatological surgery at the New York University Medical Center, I found myself (much to my surprise) as a New Yorker. I spent the first nine years of my post-training medical career as a full-time academician at the New York University Medical Center, where I established myself as an expert in the field of cutaneous laser surgery and Mohs micrographic surgery for skin cancer. I had the good fortune of becoming involved with the clinical development of many laser systems which are commonly used around the world today, with a particular emphasis on the use of lasers in the treatment of congenital malformations and aging skin. This opportunity to develop and work with their devices has led to the publication of over 125 scientific articles including five books.

In 1993 I left the restricted confines of the academic medical center to establish the Laser and Skin Surgery Center of New York, which is now recognized as one of the world's largest laser centers for the treatment of cutaneous disease. This venture has combined the challenge of clinical practice with an entrepreneurial spirit and the travails of dealing with the revolutionary changes in medicine during the late 1990s. My work in these fields has allowed for an opportunity for national and international travel for the purpose of academic presentations.

On a personal level, Gail and I have had the good fortune to raise two sons, Evan, seventeen, and Greg, thirteen. I have taken great pride in their development and have enjoyed fatherhood immensely.

HOME: New York, NY   **OCCUPATION:** Director. Laser and Skin Surgery of New York
BIRTHPLACE: Hollywood, FL   **SECONDARY SCHOOL:** The Lawrenceville School, NJ
YEARS AT COLLEGE: 1971–75   **DEGREES:** A.B., cum laude, '75; M.D., Univ. of Miami '75
SPOUSE/PARTNER: Gail, 1975 (Boston Univ. '75)   **SPOUSE'S OCCUPATION:**
Occupational Therapist. New York, NY   **CHILDREN:** Evan, 1982; Greg, 1986   **COLLEGE**
ACTIVITIES: Varsity swimming; Winthrop House crew

William Francis Giarla: I determined, after graduation, not to let law school dominate my life. Wisely or not, I almost succeeded in that. However, working in a large law firm was more insistently demanding. When I met my wife, Joanne, I decided I needed to invest time to get to know her. I ended up leaving the firm and going to work for a corporation. After fifteen happy years of marriage, I am convinced that was the right choice for me and for us.

Now, twenty-five years after graduation, I find myself in a wonderful, but unusual, place in life. My wife and I have just had our beautiful second child, Kenny. Jo and I had given up trying to give our eight-year-old daughter, Katie, a sibling when, through the wonders of modern science, we gave birth to a baby who is Katie's fraternal twin! Infant care is new fun for Katie, who is herself a joy, but Jo and I are reliving experiences that were distant memories. We're all thoroughly delighted with Kenny's ready smiles.

Another odd aspect of this time in my life is that, standing at the threshold of Kenny's life, the end of my job is in sight. My colleagues and I work cleaning up the environment at plants our company once operated, and litigating with insurers and others over the costs. We've managed to spend about $250 million, collect about $280 million, and come within a few years of finishing the work. Though I like my work and co-workers, I'm not approaching this development passively. I'm already working on new opportunities.

An all-night, freshman-year discussion with my Harvard roommate initiated an important interest for me: trying to determine the "truth" behind my religion. Even more important are my relationship with Jo, raising and enjoying our kids, playing hoops, and trying to revive the place of the front porch in modern American life.

HOME: Pittsburgh, PA   **OCCUPATION:** Senior Attorney. Three Rivers Management (management of environmental cleanups)   **BIRTHPLACE:** Nahant, MA   **SECONDARY SCHOOL:** Lynn Classical High School, Lynn, MA   **YEARS AT COLLEGE:** 1971–75   **DEGREES:** A.B., cum laude, '75; J.D., Duke Univ. '79   **SPOUSE/PARTNER:** M. Joanne Dixon, Nov. 24, 1984 (Allegheny Coll. '79)   **SPOUSE'S OCCUPATION:** Clinical Psychologist. Allegheny Clinical Associates, Mt. Lebanon, PA   **CHILDREN:** Katherine Dixon Giarla, 1990; Kenneth Dixon Giarla, 1999   **COLLEGE ACTIVITIES:** Assistant librarian at the beautiful old Kirkland House library, 1973–75; Kirkland House intramural football and basketball, 1972–75; Kirkland House intramural athlete of the year, 1974–75; reader for blind graduate student, 1973–75; worker at Rico's Sub Villa and the Subway, 1972–75; almost unrelenting fun with friends, 1971–75 (I also consider it a significant triumph that I found a major, history and literature, that allowed me to spend so much time reading great novels)

Verna Catholine Gibbs: I get up and go to the hospital every day to chip away and challenge the power and privilege that is the white masculine cultural heritage. I just don't get it — why do women allow white men to brainwash us into continuing male entitlement, after we have done everything they can do as well if not better? Rather than walk away, shaking my head in bewilderment, I keep on being the assertive, aggressive, big, bold, black, beautiful woman I was the day I left Radcliffe.

When I graduated, I thought that having my Twenty-fifth Reunion in the year 2000 was auspicious. I had a great life plan. I was going to live in San Francisco and be a physician in an academic medical center and do research in immunology and somehow use all the anthropology I had studied for four years. I might or might not get married, but I was going to have two children. I was going to have a girl who I would name Verna (the fourth) and I was going to have a boy who I was going to name Jonathan (the sixth), which is the name given to all the first born sons (of a son) in my family. I envisioned the family dispute about the genetic relatedness and entitlement of my male child versus my brother's male child.

So that's what I did, but I never realized how quickly the twenty-five years would pass. I didn't quite get it all done.

My daughter, Verna Ada, just finished a fifth-grade project on people's perceptions of time. Everyone she interviewed over forty seemed to be a bit caught up by how fast 2000 had approached. Which means but yet again, there is a *time* problem, which is not to be confused with a *space* or a *money* problem.

In twenty-five years, when I retire, I am going to live in another part of the world and be a physician in a women's health center and perform abortions for all women in need and do research in evidence-based medicine and somehow use all that anthropology I studied what will have been by that time fifty years ago. What else is the fossil record?

HOME: San Francisco, CA   **OCCUPATION:** Associate Professor of Surgery. University of California, San Francisco; Staff Surgeon. San Francisco V.A. Medical Center, Surgical Service   **BIRTHPLACE:** Jersey City, NJ   **SECONDARY SCHOOL:** Elisabeth Irwin High School, New York, NY   **YEARS AT COLLEGE:** 1971–75   **DEGREES:** A.B., cum laude, '75; M.D., Duke Univ. '79   **SPOUSE/PARTNER:** Marco G. Patti, Nov. 30, 1985 (Universita di Catania, Italy)   **SPOUSE'S OCCUPATION:** Assistant Professor of Surgery. University of California, San Francisco   **CHILDREN:** Verna Ada, 1989   **COLLEGE ACTIVITIES:** Radcliffe and Currier House crew

Craig Zachary Gilstein: My most satisfying pleasures are spending vacations at the beach with my family, evenings out with my wife, Sheila, throwing a ball around with Josh and Jeremy, and socializing with friends. I continue to enjoy tennis, golf (I have established a fifteen handicap, which I occasionally play to), and playing chess over the Internet.

I currently manage a business unit at Telcordia Technologies (formerly Bellcore) which develops software systems for telecom service providers. My mathematical training at Harvard and UCLA gets little use, save to make me quick on the financials. The rigorous thinking, of course, is used extensively. For professional diversion, I still read the *American Mathematical Monthly* regularly.

Life's interest includes bumps along the road. In 1997, I suffered what is currently referred to as a "cardiac event." An angioplasty procedure remediated the blockage in my right coronary artery, and I am now stronger and in better shape than I have been since graduate school.

OCCUPATION: Vice President; General Manager. Telcordia Technologies (information systems development) **BIRTHPLACE:** New York, NY **SECONDARY SCHOOL:** Woodward High School, Rockville, MD **YEARS AT COLLEGE:** 1971–75 **DEGREES:** A.B., magna cum laude, '75; Ph.D., Univ. of California, Los Angeles '80 **SPOUSE/PARTNER:** Sheila Franklin (Univ. of Illinois '76) **SPOUSE'S OCCUPATION:** Dance and Movement Therapist (self-employed) **CHILDREN:** Jeremy Frank, 1989; Joshua Randy, 1991 **COLLEGE ACTIVITIES:** Wrestling team; chess team; sportswriter, *Harvard Independent;* intramural soccer; intramural softball

Jean Guyton Gispen: It's a good life. Kees and I swim, boat, mess around in the yard, do various home projects, and travel. Had I known that I would marry a Dutchman who studies German history, I would have structured my course load somewhat differently at Harvard, spending time in the language lab. We visit Kees's mom in The Hague with the kids in tow once a year. My Dutch and my German still have quite a ways to go, but it's fun trying them out.

I'm in private practice as a rheumatologist in a group with five general internists. I work from 7:30 in the morning till the schools let out at 2:45, then turn into a chauffeur and a mom. The paperwork gets done late at night. I'm finishing a five-year stint on the rheumatology advisory committee for the U.S. Pharmacopeia. No articles published, but I've just finished a chapter for a rheumatology textbook.

For exercise, Kees and I swim in the Ole Miss pool while the kids swim with a swim team. Apparently, though, my freestyle has egregious flaws. The kids' coach came up to me last night saying, "Mrs. Gispen. I just can't stand it any more! Your right hand is O.K., but your left hand is entering the water *all wrong!*" Hopefully I'm still coachable, and can correct the error.

The kids are a delight, smarter and stronger than I ever was.

HOME: Oxford, MS   **OCCUPATION:** Rheumatologist   **DEGREES:** A.B., summa cum laude, '75; M.D., Duke Univ. '79   **SPOUSE/PARTNER:** Kees Gispen, July 27, 1985
CHILDREN: Fiona, 1987; Adrienne, 1989

William Riley Glass: I recall how impossibly distant our Twenty-fifth Reunion seemed when a speaker during freshman week reminded us to be ready for a celebration in the year 2000. Though he neglected to point out that it would correspond with the Y2K bug, I feel as little prepared for the one as the other despite what seems like should be ample time to get ready for both! The day-to-day rush continues to pick up steam while my hoped-for perspective of age has yet to develop. Hopefully the Reunion and sharing with classmates will provide the catalyst for that.

I'm at least reasonably settled and content, splitting my time between homes in Cambridge and Provincetown on Cape Cod with a good amount of business-related travel thrown in. I started a software company before it was so popular (and lucrative) to do so, but have kept at it for fifteen years. I have enjoyed the opportunity it has provided to help integrate technology in educational settings along with both the exhilaration and frustration of being my own boss. The opportunities still seem endless, and rapidly expanding, which only accentuates the limits of my own resources and seems to make time slip by even faster.

HOME: Cambridge, MA   OCCUPATION: President. Harvard Associates, Inc.; Terrapin Software (educational software development and publishing)   BIRTHPLACE: Fort Benning, GA   SECONDARY SCHOOL: Bryan Station High School, Lexington, KY   YEARS AT COLLEGE: 1971–75   DEGREES: A.B., cum laude, '75; M.WA. '81   COLLEGE ACTIVITIES: Republican Club; *Harvard Political Review*; Crimson Key Society; AIESEC

Maud Worcester Gleason: What I like best about our household is the way it resembles a hedgerow. It shelters many forms of life. We live on six acres with huge trees and innumerable bushes. There are goats, fish, and sheep; tenants old and young; guests medical and musical; rolling stones coming briefly to moss; children going and coming; three pianos; all kinds of rodents and uninvited inhabitants; topped off by a bachelor peacock who commands the scene from a seat of lordly splendor in the Deodar cedar tree.

This is not the stuff of headlines, but I firmly believe that the filaments of love, duty, and friendship that radiate outward from a good marriage long in place provide the human ecosystem with an invisible but very precious resiliency. In this small way, the gift that we have each other becomes an offering we can make to the world outside.

Though I have colleagues, an intellectual life, a reputation, even a job, I don't have an academic career in the traditional sense. This does mean I will be spared the fate of jaded cynic or department chairman. I think of my classics endeavors as a small business, something like a boutique winery: in teaching and writing, limits on quantity make it easier to focus on quality. Though I don't have the intense need that I had earlier in my life to escape to the past as a realm of transcendence, I take a much keener pleasure in appreciating the peculiarities of my fellow humans in the present. Not working full-time makes it possible to experience work, in large measure, as play. It also makes it possible to study music, stay out of overdrive (which I'm afraid leaves me short-tempered), and experience a level of intimacy with my children that would not be possible otherwise.

Since graduation, the landmark event of my physical existence was coming down with Guillain-Barré syndrome in 1983. All of a sudden, while still in my twenties, I found myself in the situation of the very old, in which the body is no longer a comfortable or even a safe place to be. Since then, as I have continued, doggedly and joyfully, to develop physical strength and learned better how to manage pain, I have had the odd experience of growing younger as I age. One intellectual benefit of all this, which has actually proved helpful in my research, is being forced to conceive of the body as a problematic category once it can no longer be taken for granted as the vehicle of one's will. The spiritual benefits of such an experience are also intriguing: it's like being enrolled willy-nilly in an ascetic apprenticeship. I think my nervous system has always preferred tranquility to stimulation, but illness certainly gave me a push to gain some control over the stormy sea of the mind. In the process, practicing meditation on inspirational passages from the saints and scriptures of many faiths, I have come to sense that it may in this lifetime be possible to deepen my trust in truth while developing to a truly loving appreciation of other people's traditions and avatars, and to come to cherish the well-being of others as I learn, ever so gradually, to detach from my own.

I am so much looking forward to seeing the faces and hearing the stories of many friends, old and new, at the Reunion.

HOME: Los Gatos, CA   **OCCUPATION:** Lecturer in Classics. Stanford University
BIRTHPLACE: New York, NY   **SECONDARY SCHOOL:** The Dalton School, New York, NY   **YEARS AT COLLEGE:** 1971–75   **DEGREES:** A.B., summa cum laude, '75; B.A., Oxford Univ. '77; M.A., ibid. '77; Ph.D., Univ. of California, Berkeley '90
SPOUSE/PARTNER: Frederick O. Holley, Dec. 30, 1978 (Harvard '74)   **SPOUSE'S OCCUPATION:** Anesthesiologist   **CHILDREN:** Elizabeth, 1982; Bobby, 1988

Richard Miles Goldberg: Instinctive, investigative, informal, ichthyologist, iconoclast, idealizer, idiocrat, insured, imbuer, impressionable, immunized, individualistic, intertwined, indefatigable, impeller, interventional, invested, involved, INTJ, ironic, iceman, inexplicable, inexorable.

HOME: Rochester, MN   **OCCUPATION:** Consultant; Associate Professor of Oncology. Mayo Clinic   **BIRTHPLACE:** Utica, NY   **SECONDARY SCHOOL:** New Hartford Central High School, New Hartford, NY   **YEARS AT COLLEGE:** 1971–75   **DEGREES:** A.B., cum laude, '75; M.D., State Univ. of New York, Upstate Medical Center '79
SPOUSE/PARTNER: Lynda, March 13, 1983 (Georgia State Univ. '79; M.B.A., Bloomsburg Univ. '92)   **SPOUSE'S OCCUPATION:** Teacher. Rochester School District   **CHILDREN:** Julia R., 1985; Samuel A., 1988

Wendy F. Goldberg: On occasion, well-intentioned friends have asked me with a polite bewilderment: "How is it that a gal born and bred in Boston—a native of the North raised in the shadow of Bunker Hill, the Boston Marathon, and Fenway Park—has given herself over to the land of magnolias and mockingbirds where Bayards and Quentins swap tales by the hour and the light in August serves as the perfect medium for ghosts?" Cain't rightly say, but for the last twenty-five years I've been deeply immersed in Faulkner's Yoknapatawpha County. While completing my dissertation on Faulkner for Yale and teaching writing and critical thinking in the English department at Stanford, I dabbled in the composition of "faux" for the Annual Faux Faulkner Contest. I found this peculiar marriage of scholarship and screwball comedy irresistible and sustaining. After playing the bridesmaid tirelessly, in the Faux Faulkner Contest and at the wedding of friends, I married my husband, Jerry White, in June of 1993 (O blessed day) and won the Faux Faulkner Contest in 1997. The prize was a trip for two to Oxford, Mississippi in late July. I read my faux at the conference celebrating the one hundredth anniversary of Faulkner's birth and drank Jack Daniels 'round the table where Faulkner composed *Absalom, Absalom!*

My piece (*Dying to Lie Down*) was set in Boston and Cambridge and found Quentin (Sprintin') Compson (at that moment when he is about to plunge into the Charles) suddenly overtaken by and carried along with the inexorable surge of the mighty Boston Marathon. When Quentin shouts defiance at his father, the latter shoots back: "that what they lamed you up at Hahvad—that tarnished temple of too-much-talk where sour-faced summa cum latelys dispense earfuls of errant nonsense to packs of precocious young pups..."

HOME: Mountain View, CA   **OCCUPATION:** Lecturer in English. Stanford University, Department of English   **BIRTHPLACE:** Boston, MA   **SECONDARY SCHOOL:** Newton South High School, Newton, MA   **YEARS AT COLLEGE:** 1971–75   **DEGREES:** A.B., cum laude, '75; M.A., Yale '76; Ph.D., ibid. '96   **SPOUSE/PARTNER:** Jerome David White, June 20, 1993 (New York Univ. '48)   **SPOUSE'S OCCUPATION:** Website Developer (works from home)

David Samuel Goldbloom: Immediately following graduation, I had the good fortune of a two-year sojourn at Oxford courtesy of the Rhodes Trust, where I sustained some Harvard friendships and made many new ones. Nancy and I married following her graduation from Radcliffe and we enjoyed our first year of married life in Oxford before returning to the rigors of medical school back in Canada at McGill. We recently celebrated our twenty-third anniversary and she has been a wonderful constant in my life since graduation. Medical school ultimately propelled me toward psychiatry and following a residency at McGill, I undertook a three-year research fellowship in eating disorders at the University of Toronto, which has been my home ever since. I have grown up professionally within the University Department of Psychiatry, struggling to balance the satisfactions and demands of clinical care, research, and teaching. Our sons, Daniel and Will, provide us with happiness—and challenges—that we could not have anticipated.

My roommates from the Harvard years—particularly Dick Raines, Tyler Miller, Mike Bromwich, and Jim O'Connell—remain important friends who try to get together on an irregular, but always intensely familiar basis. While I strain now to understand essays that I wrote at Harvard on obscure themes in philosophy, politics, or literature—or to recall the content of lectures and reading, I can easily access memories of the people I befriended and the things we did together. The broadening of my world through the people I met and knew at Harvard was a great privilege. As Yeats wrote: "Think where man's glory most begins and ends, and say my glory was I had such friends."

HOME: Toronto, ON, Canada   **OCCUPATION:** Professor of Psychiatry. University of Toronto; Physician-in-Chief. Centre for Addiction and Mental Health   **BIRTHPLACE:** Montreal, PQ, Canada   **SECONDARY SCHOOL:** Lower Canada Coll., Montreal, PQ; Halifax Grammar School, Halifax, NS; Neuchatel Junior Coll., Neuchatel, Switzerland   **YEARS AT COLLEGE:** 1971–75 **DEGREES:** A.B., cum laude, '75; B.A., Univ. of Oxford, '77; M.D., McGill Univ. '81; C.M., ibid. '81; M.A., Univ. of Oxford '83   **SPOUSE/PARTNER:** Nancy Ellen Epstein, June 27, 1976 (Harvard '76; M.D., F.R.C.S.C., McGill Univ.)   **SPOUSE'S OCCUPATION:** Ophthalmologist (private practice)   **CHILDREN:** Daniel, 1985; William, 1987   **COLLEGE ACTIVITIES:** Various theatrical productions: *Blue Denim, The Bull Gets the Matador, Once in a Lifetime, A Thousand Clowns, Guys and Dolls, Mad About Mintz;* the McGovern campaign

---

George Dana Gollin: This is how we have ended up: Melanie, Cordelia, and I live in Champaign, Illinois, where I teach physics at the University of Illinois and do research in elementary particle physics, while Melanie helps run the National Center for Supercomputing Applications, where the first Web browser (Mosaic) was invented. I am a professor; Melanie is a senior associate director. Our daughter, Cordelia, is eleven, strong-willed, decent, messy, extroverted. She is fluent in French thanks to a sabbatical year we spent in Marseille, but more about that later.

The University of Illinois is a fine school, and I feel I understand the role of public universities in our society better than I did when I was younger. Bright students from families with limited horizons come here and discover that the world is a place filled with engaging ideas, books, music. They blossom, and follow paths that were previously closed to them. Perhaps best of all, some of them realize that it is possible to find work that is pleasurable, so that they won't be crippled by forty years at a mind-numbing job.

The amount and diversity of raw talent at the university is astonishing. I worked up a presentation on the physics of dance a few years ago, and spent some time watching the remarkable dance faculty going about their business. I get to meet colleagues in other fields at meetings, during delays on the commuter flights out of Champaign, and at parties hosted by mutual acquaintances. It's a pleasure to run into so much interesting conversation. The town is nicely managed, with good public transport, excellent parks, a fine library, and loads of music, but the area is flat, and nearly devoid of rivers and lakes. It's not a place for a long bicycle ride, since there's nothing to see besides corn and bean fields once you're past the edges of town.

We lived in Cassis, just east of Marseille, during the 1998–99 school year. Melanie and I had visitors' appointments at labs in Marseille, while Cordelia went to the public (elementary) school in Cassis. The year was nearly perfect. Because of the everyday business of schools, play dates, and childcare, we became friends with some of our neighbors, and lived there as members of the community, rather than visitors passing an extended stay. People we met were open, accepting, and curious. Amusing to us: they tended to use their children as spies ("Do the Americans eat hamburgers for dinner?") since Cordelia's buddies got to see how we lived (thanks to sleepovers and dinner invitations) before their parents had a peek at us. We hope to stay in touch with several of the families, and are working on various schemes involving kid exchanges and the like. Everything (positive) that is said about food in France is true, and it was a pleasure to be there during the impeachment of President Clinton. It's an adjustment being back in the United States, where high levels of handgun violence are tolerated and universal health care is absent. I miss the chance to speak French every day.

The work Melanie and I did was interesting for both of us. I began looking into physics to pursue after the current line of research (done in collaboration with a large number of other physicists at an accelerator at Cornell) loses its luster. Day-to-day business at both our labs was conducted in French, and I liked my colleagues and the research we were doing.

And so to the central question: Am I happy? Well, yes and no. You understand.

HOME: Champaign, IL   OCCUPATION: Professor of Physics (research and teaching). Department of Physics, University of Illinois   BIRTHPLACE: New York, NY   SECONDARY SCHOOL: Freeport High School, Freeport, NY   YEARS AT COLLEGE: 1971–75   DEGREES: A.B., magna cum laude, '75; M.A., Princeton '76; Ph.D., ibid. '80   SPOUSE/PARTNER: Melanie Jane Loots, Nov. 25, 1978 (Radcliffe '75)   SPOUSE'S OCCUPATION: Senior Associate Director. National Center for Supercomputing Applications, Beckman Institute, University of Illinois   CHILDREN: Cordelia Rose Loots-Gollin, 1988   COLLEGE ACTIVITIES: Dunster House intramural crew, 1975; stage hand, Bach Society Orchestra

Richard Lee Gooch: I was living in a tent on the beach in Mexico when it occurred to me I was outside the chain of life. An M.B.A. or J.D. was the answer, I thought. Never planning to practice, I began the study of law. On graduation, I moved to San Francisco in 1980 and happily, have been here since. The corporate life has been rewarding, but has, at times, sucked the poetry out of my life. The beauty of San Francisco, the tolerant attitudes of the people, the cultural diversity, the strident organizers, my own political and social activism have all combined to put the poetry right back.

Now, I own a condominium on the beach in Mexico, prefer a bed to a sleeping bag, and would rather do volunteer work for nonprofits than climb more rungs of the corporate ladder. I've always thought I would reach my personal best at age seventy-two. I am enjoying the journey immensely.

HOME: San Francisco, CA   OCCUPATION: Director. Union Pacific Railroad (real estate)
BIRTHPLACE: Santa Fe, NM   SECONDARY SCHOOL: U.S. Capitol Page School, Washington, DC   YEARS AT COLLEGE: 1971–75   DEGREES: A.B. '75; J.D., Univ. of New Mexico '80

Sarah Webster Goodwin: If at twenty-one I had known, had even guessed, that life could be this full, I would have spared myself a lot of anguish. Three healthy children, a husband who still surprises me, work that challenges and satisfies daily, both my parents still well, a secure home: it can't last, and it's an illusion, but one I know enough to be grateful for. I'm an English professor and department chair at Skidmore. My colleagues are brilliant and decent, and my students — let me tell you what teaching is like. It's a Pisgah sight. You're going up a mountain and then you get that view, and it's radiating from their faces. It's addictive. Maybe we're reading Hurston or Heaney or Jorie Graham. I live for that view.

I love my work, and I work hard just about all the time. Never find time to exercise, write letters, read for fun, or go through the piles. But I come to hear the piano going, or the cello or the violin or the flute, a houseful of music, work, kids, Steve. Impossible to say how it all fits, shreds and all, catfights, mess, lost bills, weeds, hamster food, papers, Harry Potter, piles of laundry. Steve plays the flute and owns a sheet music store, having left his job teaching Sanskrit and Greek at Brown five years ago. We know every music teacher and musician in town, and have an insider's view of small retail: Want to hear about it? But I still believe in it.

I can't talk about the children without being grossly sentimental, so I won't. They're a glance from God.

As for the world beyond our (virtual) hearth, there may be time for it later. Trained for complexity, I find politics utterly distasteful, but what else will make things better?

HOME: Saratoga Springs, NY   **OCCUPATION:** Professor; Department Chair. Dept. of English, Skidmore College   **BIRTHPLACE:** Fort Belvoir, VA   **SECONDARY SCHOOL:** Palo Alto High School, Palo Alto, CA   **YEARS AT COLLEGE:** 1971–75   **DEGREES:** A.B., magna cum laude, '75; M.A., Brown '83; Ph.D., ibid. '83   **SPOUSE/PARTNER:** Robert E. "Steve" Goodwin, June 12, 1982 (Ph.D., Brown '85)   **SPOUSE'S OCCUPATION:** Proprietor. Saratoga Music Center   **CHILDREN:** Eva, 1986; Hannah, 1988; Stephan, 1991 **COLLEGE ACTIVITIES:** It was all significant

---

James Dickinson Grant: The direction of my life over the past twenty-five years was set by learning Transcendental Meditation my sophomore year at Harvard. I took a leave from Harvard the following year to become a teacher of Transcendental Meditation, an experience that opened me to a new vision of the potential for human development — the possibility of gaining enlightenment. This expanded understanding of human potential sharpened my interest in education and inspired me to get a doctorate in education.

In the past fifteen years, aside from a year-and-a-half stint on a teaching Fulbright in China, I have been at Maharishi University of Management (formerly Maharishi International University). I have been a faculty member in the education department and served in a number of administrative posts, including, for the last five years as dean of the College of Arts and Sciences. My years at M.U.M. have been greatly fulfilling. I have enjoyed helping to pioneer a new paradigm of holistic education that focuses on development of consciousness and benefited greatly from the company of kindred spirits all devoted to the pursuit of enlightenment.

My life journey has been immeasurably enriched over the past twenty years by my wonderful wife, Ann. She has taught me about the value of self-less giving, and she continuously teaches me by the integrity of her being. Our children Joy (fifteen) and Divindy (twelve) bring us great happiness. Not only are they excellent students and athletes, but they have beautiful hearts. We feel supremely blessed.

As we look to the new millennium, I am very hopeful. We as human beings have a huge untapped potential, and, as this is unfolded through proper education, there will be a flowering of human life in a way that we can now scarcely imagine.

HOME: Fairfield, IA   **OCCUPATION:** Dean; Associate Professor of Education. College of Arts and Sciences, Maharishi University of Management   **BIRTHPLACE:** Washington, DC   **SECONDARY SCHOOL:** Woodrow Wilson High School, Washington, DC   **YEARS AT COLLEGE:** 1971–76   **DEGREES:** A.B., cum laude, '75 ('76); M.S., Maharishi European Research Univ. '80; Ed.M., Harvard '81; Ed.D., ibid. '85   **SPOUSE/PARTNER:** Ann Griffiths, June 16, 1979 (Mills Coll. '70; M.A., Boston Univ. '84; M.A., Maharishi Univ. of Management '99)   **SPOUSE'S OCCUPATION:** Homemaker; Part-Time Librarian. Fairfield Public Library   **CHILDREN:** Joy Meredith, 1984; Divindy Anne, 1987   **HARVARD/RADCLIFFE SIBLINGS:** John Putnam Grant '73   **COLLEGE ACTIVITIES:** International Meditation Society, 1973–76; Crimson Key, 1973–75; crew, 1971–72

Neil Sanford Greenspan: My life now revolves around my wife and two sons, work-related activities (immunology research, teaching, and directing a clinical histocompatibility testing laboratory), and a few personal activities, such as tennis, reading, and listening to music. Time turns out to be, at least for me, the limiting factor in life. Therefore, it is gratifying that whatever knowledge or insight I gained from my time as an undergraduate has been useful to me both professionally and personally. My thanks are due to my late parents, my friends from those years, and even (some of) my professors. Memorable "recent" times include spending ten days in Paris with my wife, my elder son's bar mitzvah weekend, and climbing a very modest peak with a spectacular view of the Bitterroot River Valley outside of Missoula, Montana. Our family's most enjoyable and relaxing time is spent during our annual summer vacation on the beach at Hilton Head Island, South Carolina. My simplest hope is for more time, preferably well spent.

HOME: Shaker Heights, OH   **OCCUPATION:** Professor of Pathology. Case Western Reserve University; Director, Clinical Histocompatibility Laboratory. University Hospitals of Cleveland   **BIRTHPLACE:** Chicago, IL   **SECONDARY SCHOOL:** Niles North School, Skokie, IL   **YEARS AT COLLEGE:** 1971–75   **DEGREES:** A.B., magna cum laude, '75; M.D., Univ. of Pennsylvania '81; Ph.D., ibid. '81   **SPOUSE/PARTNER:** Judith Keene, 1980 (Univ. of Massachusetts '76)   **SPOUSE'S OCCUPATION:** Regional Manager. Keene Advertising, Inc. (works from home)   **CHILDREN:** Aaron Jacob Greenspan, 1983; Simon Keene Greenspan, 1985   **COLLEGE ACTIVITIES:** Intramural tennis and razzledazzle football for South House

J. David Grizzle: When I graduated, I hoped that it would be unnecessary at this time to complete a Twenty-fifth Anniversary Report. I assumed that my achievements would be well known by all of you from simply reading the *New York Times*. That fantasy never became a reality. I am very grateful for the reality I have enjoyed, and I am sure that the fulfillment of my fantasies could not have been more gratifying than what has come to pass.

I have been an officer at Continental Airlines (or one of its many former affiliates) now for fifteen years. I never imagined staying at any job that long. I just didn't feel at liberty to leave, and now I feel quite glad to have stuck around. I am responsible for developing and managing our global alliance and airline investment program. My sons say my job consists of flying to the great cities of the world and having dinner. It's not too inaccurate a description. For a poor kid from Lithonia, Georgia, it's not bad compensation for the years I spent dreaming of all the places I feared I would never visit. Enabling me to have a life that cannot even be imagined by my parents and their relatives is one of the blessings that Harvard afforded me.

Another benefit of Harvard — and the most deeply transforming one — is that it enabled me to meet my wife, Anne Fletcher '77. She and I married after Harvard Law School and we have recently celebrated twenty-one years of (for me, at least) blissful matrimony. She and I share similar energy levels and growing interior lives — traits that I think form a good foundation for a long marriage, and which we both began to initiate and test when we were neighbors at Winthrop House. Anne is the greatest gift I took away with me from Harvard.

Starting this fall, though, I collect another dividend from Harvard. My eldest son (of three) begins his freshman year at Harvard. I admit I have dreamed of this event from before he was born. It is hard not to want to relive my experience though him; even though I realize how completely different our experiences will in fact be if, for no other reason, because of our wildly divergent starting points.

I hope, though, when my son approaches his Twenty-fifth Reunion, he will be as delighted as I am with what Harvard will have afforded him.

HOME: Houston, TX   **OCCUPATION:** Senior Vice President, Corporate Development. Continental Airlines   **BIRTHPLACE:** Lithonia, GA   **SECONDARY SCHOOL:** East Atlanta High School, Atlanta, GA   **YEARS AT COLLEGE:** 1971–75   **DEGREES:** A.B., magna cum laude, '75; J.D. '78   **SPOUSE/PARTNER:** Anne Fletcher, 1978 (Radcliffe '77) **SPOUSE'S OCCUPATION:** Family Therapist   **CHILDREN:** Benjamin D., 1981; Joshua P. F., 1985; Andrew T., 1990   **HARVARD/RADCLIFFE CHILDREN:** Benjamin D. Grizzle '03 **COLLEGE ACTIVITIES:** Committee on Houses and Undergraduate Life, 1973–74; Harvard Band, 1971–74; Yearbook, 1972–75; Winthrop House Committee, 1972–74

Robert Alan Gross: Many ups and downs since graduation, but fortunately, mostly ups. After much training, I reached my goal of being a clinician-researcher-teacher, now on the faculty of the University of Rochester. My clinical work centers on the treatment of those with severe epilepsy, challenging but rewarding work. It is humbling to care for those who face severe illness with dignity and courage, and joyful when they can be helped. I am graced with highly talented, wonderful colleagues. Laboratory research affords the chance to ask fundamental questions about biology and (sometimes!) being able to answer them. It is especially fun when working with others who enjoy asking the same questions. (If only writing grants or getting funding was easier!) Teaching keeps me on my toes, about my fields of interest, and about people.

My greatest fortune is my family. After my first marriage failed during residency, I found, to my delight, that life and love can begin again in one's thirties. My wife Marsha is still my best friend and we greatly enjoy our two sons, Jacob (nine) and Daniel (six). Marsha works as a nurse practitioner in the Cancer Center here, so we have the pleasure of talking about patient care, and (sometimes) working together with a patient. Our sons are (of course, this is Dad writing) smart, sensitive, handsome and a ton of fun. Just seeing their faces as we read about tense moments in Harry Potter's adventures, is, well, the best.

There hardly seems enough time for personal pursuits! I still love listening to live and recorded music and continue to add to my music collection (classical, jazz, blues). Reading a good book is still a pleasure and luxury. Sailing on a friend's boat on Irondequoit Bay renews the spirit. We love visiting the Adirondacks and nearby Canada, or visiting family, but none of it is any better than the simple pleasure of taking family hikes in nearby woods and stopping for birds to eat seeds from your hand.

HOME: Pittsford, NY **OCCUPATION:** Associate Professor of Neurology, Pharmacology, and Physiology. University of Rochester **BIRTHPLACE:** Worcester, MA **SECONDARY SCHOOL:** Doherty Memorial High School, Worcester, MA **YEARS AT COLLEGE:** 1971–75 **DEGREES:** A.B., summa cum laude, '75; M.D., Washington Univ. in Saint Louis '81; Ph.D., ibid. '81 **SPOUSE/PARTNER:** Marsha Deters, April 22, 1989 (Saint Louis Univ., 1983; M.S.N., Univ. of Rochester, 1998) **SPOUSE'S OCCUPATION:** Nurse Practitioner. Strong Memorial Hospital Cancer Center, University of Rochester **CHILDREN:** Jacob Benjamin, 1990; Daniel Joseph, 1993 **COLLEGE ACTIVITIES:** Hasty Pudding, 1972–75

Joel Lawrence Gurin: My life since Harvard has been a series of events that I could never have predicted, and that continue to surprise me. I graduated with a degree in biochemistry and no future plans. A love of writing and a friend at Harvard Press launched me into a career as a science writer and editor. I was a founding editor, and later editor-in-chief, of *American Health* magazine, the first mainstream health magazine of the '80s. I co-authored four books, including *The Dieter's Dilemma* — a scientifically-based antidiet book — and a book on mind/body medicine.

In 1991, I joined *Consumer Reports* as its science editor. I became the top editor of the magazine in 1994, and executive vice president of Consumers Union, the parent organization, in 1997. I now oversee areas as diverse as Website development and labor relations. It's been a constant learning experience, and a rare opportunity. The organization is truly consumer-oriented — with no hidden agendas — and I think we can make an important difference in people's lives.

Somewhere between Cambridge and New York, I lived in San Francisco, where I met my wife Carol, who was then a graduate student in psychology. After twenty-three years together, we have a strong marriage and three great kids. With one in high school, one in middle school, and one in grade school, it's an ongoing tutorial in parenting — always a challenge, but often wonderful.

I feel lucky that things have worked out so well, and fortunate that I've been able to build a somewhat unusual career by doing things I enjoy. I'm also aware of how much I take for granted day to day. I'm trying to slow down, focus a bit less on work, appreciate my family, meditate on the meaning of life, and do more to help deal with the massive problems facing the country and the planet.

HOME: Scarsdale, NY   **OCCUPATION:** Executive Vice President. Consumers Union (publisher of *Consumer Reports* magazine)   **BIRTHPLACE:** Ann Arbor, MI
SECONDARY SCHOOL: Pioneer High School, Ann Arbor, MI   **YEARS AT COLLEGE:** 1971–75   **DEGREES:** A.B., magna cum laude, '75   **SPOUSE/PARTNER:** Carol Duchow, Aug. 22, 1982 (Yale '73)   **SPOUSE'S OCCUPATION:** Clinical Psychologist (currently getting specialty training in neuropsychology)   **CHILDREN:** Alison May, 1983; Joanna Ellyn, 1987; Benjamin Reed, 1992   **COLLEGE ACTIVITIES:** President, Currier House Film

Linda Rae Zane Haan: Looking back on the last twenty-five years, my strongest feeling is one of thankfulness, for on balance, the years have been very good. Rick and I were married a year after graduation and shortly thereafter moved to the suburbs of northern New Jersey, which I've come to love.

Following graduate school, I joined Novartis Pharmaceuticals (formerly Sandoz) in 1980 and spent many years there, holding various managerial positions in the finance, marketing, systems and sales administration areas. However, eventually I became disillusioned with the large corporate setting, and two years ago I decided to move on and left the company. That change was liberating; I have not looked back. Currently self-employed, I am writing and consulting in the field of business communications.

Family is central in my life, and I savor our time together. I have found raising our three children to be the most challenging — yet most rewarding — endeavor of my life. As I teach them, I find I'm constantly learning along the way.

Another important influence in my life is Judaism, which I have rediscovered in recent years. Last year we made a family pilgrimage to Israel, thereby fulfilling a lifelong dream of mine. I've become very active in synagogue life and currently serve as president of my temple. This role provides an opportunity for me to give back for all that has been given to me.

At this point of my life, I feel I can now more keenly appreciate the goodness and beauty to be found all around me. I take great pleasure in activities such as cross-country skiing, cooking, and reading short stories. I'm bent on maintaining my good health. I've been blessed with many good friends who have enhanced my journey. And I'm grateful for the good life that Rick and I have built together.

HOME: Morristown, NJ   **OCCUPATION:** Consultant; Writer. CommuniConcepts (business communications)   **BIRTHPLACE:** Boston, MA   **SECONDARY SCHOOL:** Revere High School, Revere, MA   **YEARS AT COLLEGE:** 1971–75   **DEGREES:** A.B., cum laude, '75; M.B.A., New York Univ. '80   **SPOUSE/PARTNER:** Rick Allan Haan, Aug. 8, 1976 (Harvard '75; M.B.A., Univ. of Michigan '77)   **SPOUSE'S OCCUPATION:** Vice President. CJDS Datatrak   **CHILDREN:** Justin, 1983; Aaron, 1986; Michelle, 1990   **COLLEGE ACTIVITIES:** Big Brothers–Big Sisters Program, Phillips Brooks House

Rick Allan Haan: As I begin to prepare and think about our Twenty-fifth Reunion, I continue to appreciate and value my Harvard education. I have always pointed my interests and career to the technical side, and have worked in computer technology since I left school. Yet, I find that my success in business and in volunteer activities often depends on my liberal arts education.

I have continued my interest in Harvard by being active in the Harvard Club of New Jersey, interviewing applicants for twenty years, serving as the area co-ordinator for our Schools and Scholarships Committee and was elected an officer of the club for four years, including president in 1997–98. I never fail to be amazed at the quality of applicants that apply to Harvard from northern New Jersey.

I studied environmental sciences at Harvard but was never able to make it a career, so I use it in my volunteer activities for my town. I've been on our local Zoning Board of Adjustment for eleven years, sitting as chairman for the last two years. I also am a member of our Open Space Committee, trying to preserve the little bit of open space that remains in our ever-developing part of New Jersey. Yes, Sociology 10 is useful!

But technology continues to drive me, providing the tools and the stresses. I manage a company that develops systems for the advertising industry, and most recently, guided it through the process of being acquired by a two-billion-dollar advertising services company.

My wife of twenty-three years, Linda '75 and I also face the hectic lifestyle of handling three children and their school activities. But we still have time to enjoy the pleasures they bring, as we found in the reaffirming trip that we took last year to Israel.

HOME: Morristown, NJ   OCCUPATION: Vice President. CJDS Datatrak Systems (computer software)   BIRTHPLACE: Grand Rapids, MI   SECONDARY SCHOOL: Eastern High School, Lansing, MI   YEARS AT COLLEGE: 1971–75   DEGREES: A.B., cum laude, '75; M.B.A. Univ. of Michigan '77   SPOUSE/PARTNER: Linda Zane, Aug. 8, 1976 (Radcliffe '75)   SPOUSE'S OCCUPATION: Self-Employed Financial Analyst (business communications)   CHILDREN: Justin Harris, 1983; Aaron Charles, 1986; Michelle Candace, 1990

Roxane Zand Hakimzadeh: How does one summarize in under three hundred words a revolution, a divorce, two children, doctoral work, and arts administration work in the U.K.? Impossible. Therefore I look forward to talking with old friends at the Reunion!

HOME: London, England   **OCCUPATION:** Consultant   **BIRTHPLACE:** Tehran, Iran
SECONDARY SCHOOL: Charters Towers School   **YEARS AT COLLEGE:** 1971–75
DEGREES: A.B., cum laude, '75   **SPOUSE/PARTNER:** Divorced   **CHILDREN:** Vahid,
1981; Karim, 1986   **COLLEGE ACTIVITIES:** Hasty Pudding (make-up girl!), Crimson Key,
House drama

Timothy J. Hackert: So, there I was, cruising through life, minding my own business (commercial real estate law) and not focusing on anything else. Oh, sure, I was married in 1979 and we had three kids, but Darcy stayed home with the kids and I worked. And then, not long ago, I woke up to discover that, in addition to my wife of twenty years, my home was occupied by: a fifteen-year-old daughter who is nearly six feet tall and kills time at school in between cross-country meets, basketball games, and track meets; a twelve-year-old boy scout, runner, Pokémon master and self-proclaimed computer nerd; and a nine-year-old competitive swimmer who is often described as a "high-maintenance" child!

And so, my life has changed. I work less at the office, delegate more, and spend my time differently. I go to games and meets to watch my kids compete and I go to other games and meets to work concessions and otherwise help support the programs. I also teach sixth grade Sunday school and help with Boy Scouts (camping, bike rides, hiking, and other nonstrenuous activities). Beyond this, Darcy and I are developing a hazy picture of life after kids and retirement. We know it will mean a permanent return to our beloved Cape Cod, where we have summered since 1986. Not much else is clear at this point, but we're too busy to plan!

HOME: Centerville, OH   **OCCUPATION:** Attorney. Thompson, Hine & Flory LLP (law
firm)   **BIRTHPLACE:** McCook, NE   **SECONDARY SCHOOL:** Palisade High School,
Palisade, NE   **YEARS AT COLLEGE:** 1971–75   **DEGREES:** A.B., cum laude, '75; J.D., New
York Univ. '79   **SPOUSE/PARTNER:** Darcy K., March 17, 1979 (Wheaton Coll. '77)
SPOUSE'S OCCUPATION: Registrar. St. Paul's Episcopal Church   **CHILDREN:** Emily S.,
1984; Timothy J., Jr., 1986; Lydia D., 1990   **HARVARD/RADCLIFFE SIBLINGS:** Girard M.
Hackert '78 (deceased)   **COLLEGE ACTIVITIES:** Freshman heavyweight crew; junior
varsity lightweight crew; varsity lightweight crew

Thomas Hadley II: My twenty-five years since Harvard are a blur of events that are best highlighted by significant family occasions. I would have little to write about if I had not married Lee Ann in August 1991. What should have been a typical honeymoon cruise to Bermuda turned into our first real adventure together when our captain decided to sail right into Hurricane Bob. For twelve hours, we bounced in thirty-to-fifty-foot seas before the storm finally passed. It was later reported in the Bermuda newspaper that the Nordic Prince, our seaworthy vessel, had pitched to as much as thirty-nine degrees during the worst of it. Anyone caring for more details, see me at the Reunion — I enjoy telling the story.

Having survived the hurricane, we wasted no time in starting a family. Laura joined us just twenty minutes before the fourth of July 1992. And now, the blur of events is marked by birthdays and holidays and special times that only a family can share. Madeline came along in time for Christmas 1994. Sometimes having two children has seemed to accelerate time, and I have not learned how to slow things down. Anyone having the answer to this problem, see me at the Reunion.

As for significant family events, I will only mention one: my parents' fiftieth wedding anniversary. Our whole family, sister Patti and husband, two boys; brother Fred '81 and wife, one boy; joined my parents in Bermuda, where they had honeymooned in 1948. As an anniversary gift, Lee Ann and I had spent three months gathering photos and managed to put together thirteen hundred into a video that we presented to Mom and Dad on June 12, 1998. I think it was the best present anyone could ever give — the memories of fifty years together. I hope Laura and Madeline will do the same for us some day.

If anyone's interested in my professional life — see me at the Reunion. I'll tell you more than you want to know.

HOME: Columbus, OH   OCCUPATION: Senior Vice President. Acordia, Inc. (insurance brokerage)   BIRTHPLACE: Columbus, OH   SECONDARY SCHOOL: The Columbus Academy, Columbus, OH   YEARS AT COLLEGE: 1971–75   DEGREES: A.B., cum laude, '75   SPOUSE/PARTNER: Lee Ann Voeller, Aug. 17, 1991 (Ohio State Univ. '78) CHILDREN: Laura E., 1992; Madeline A., 1994

James E. Harrell, Jr.: After graduation, the reality of work became all too apparent. The ensuing thirteen years were spent learning the trade of cardiothoracic surgery, including three years of medical school at Baylor, a couple of years surgery at Hopkins, chest surgery at Baylor, and a fellowship in pediatric cardiothoracic surgery at the Harley Street Clinic/Hospital for Sick Children in London. After two years in East Bay, California, I took an academic position in Little Rock with the University of Arkansas. Since then, I have become the director of our Cardiac Transplant Program with almost one hundred transplants (mostly children) to date. Although I did a lot of adult surgery the first eight years, our practice at Arkansas Children's has grown to where I do only pediatric chest cases now. In addition, I have been gratified by the teaching experience gained from our residency program, and our clinical research in the areas of extracorporeal membrane oxygenator (ECMO), transplantation, and cardiac valves.

On the personal side, I was married to Beth Waldrup for fifteen years prior to our divorce, and we were blessed with three wonderful children. Fortunately, Beth and I have maintained a good relationship since. Beth is attending a Methodist seminary in Dallas as she prepares to enter the ministry. The kids have been a delight as they have grown. They appear to have some interest in going to the Northeast or the Bay Area for college.

My fiancée, Ms. Marty Lundy, and I are planning to tie the knot soon. Marty is a R.N./transplant coordinator at Children's, and is also an Arkansan.

While in Arkansas, I have developed a love for fly-fishing—our trout water is quite good (*big* browns). The Little Red River is my favorite hangout.

I am looking forward to seeing friends at the Reunion, especially Steve McConnell, Dan White, and Todd Stitzer.

HOME: Little Rock, AR   **OCCUPATION:** Physician (pediatric cardiothoracic surgeon); Associate Professor of Surgery. University of Arkansas for Medical Sciences, Division of Cardiothoracic Surgery   **BIRTHPLACE:** Ft. Benning, GA   **SECONDARY SCHOOL:** Robert E. Peary High School, Montgomery County, MD   **YEARS AT COLLEGE:** 1971–75   **DEGREES:** A.B., cum laude, '75; M.D., Baylor Coll. of Medicine '78   **SPOUSE/PARTNER:** Beth A. Waldrup, April 17, 1982; divorced, April 1997   **CHILDREN:** J. Wells, 1984; Elizabeth Anne, 1986; Lauren Allison, 1987   **COLLEGE ACTIVITIES:** Baseball: freshman, 1972, junior varsity, 1973, varsity 1974–75; saxophone, Harvard Band, 1971–75; publisher, *Harvard Independent;* Fox Club, 1972–75

Emily Stella Harris: I am amazed at how little I knew at graduation about where I was going or how all the pieces would fall together. At this point, it looks familiar, but the path had many turns. I met my husband white water rafting and am pleased to be settled in northern California. We have two boys, a bunch of pets, and enjoy living in an environment where we can be outside so much of the year, are able to bike through town on bike paths, and camp at the beach or in the high Sierras during vacations. My household of boys is no doubt just deserts for my own tomboy existence. My sons have humbled me as a parent and are excellent mentors for my practice and teaching of child and adolescent psychiatry. The biggest challenge by far has been and remains survival in academic medicine. I have been sustained by my commitment to improving mental health services for children and families and to training the next generation of adult and child psychiatrists. I feel pretty lucky that I have been able to define and follow my own path and that I've landed on my feet.

HOME: Davis, CA   OCCUPATION: Associate Professor. Dept. of Psychiatry, University of California, Davis Medical Center   BIRTHPLACE: Washington, DC   SECONDARY SCHOOL: New Rochelle High School, New Rochelle, NY   YEARS AT COLLEGE: 1971–75   DEGREES: A.B., cum laude, '75; M.D., New York Univ. '79   SPOUSE/PARTNER: Robert Canning, June 7, 1987 (Univ. of Delaware '73)   SPOUSE'S OCCUPATION: Psychologist. University of California, Davis Medical Center   CHILDREN: Stephen, 1990; Benjamin, 1994   COLLEGE ACTIVITIES: Gilbert & Sullivan, 1973–75

Thomas A. Harris: Career, family, and community involvement are important commitments in my life. The practice of dentistry is the business of dentistry — it goes well. Pat and I are continuously challenged by our kids. "Ask your Mom" is my response to most issues! My wife, Pat, is my best friend. She has put up with me for twenty-five years of married life! Amazing — where has the time gone?

Through membership on the local board of health, we brought to vote an ordinance that if passed would have eliminated "second-hand smoke" from restaurants and other public places. Finally....I attended a concert at Soldiers Field a couple of years ago — the Stones! Life is good!!!

HOME: Arlington Heights, IL   OCCUPATION: Dentist. Plum Grove Dental Associates   BIRTHPLACE: Berwyn, IL   SECONDARY SCHOOL: Arlington High School, Arlington Heights, IL   YEARS AT COLLEGE: 1971–76   DEGREES: A.B. '75 ('76); DD.S. '82   SPOUSE/PARTNER: Patricia Koch (Southern Methodist Univ. '75)   SPOUSE'S OCCUPATION: Great Wife and Mother   CHILDREN: Brad, 1978; Mandy, 1981; Abby, 1988; Anna, 1989

Kim Neiter Hays: For me, one of the most significant events of the past twenty-five years was becoming an expatriate. I am now permanently settled in Bern with my Swiss husband and Swiss-American son. Despite loving Bern and having a very happy life here, I sometimes regret that I will live out the rest of my days in a foreign language — or two, actually: German and Swiss-German dialect, both of which I use every day, but neither of which I feel truly comfortable in. Also very important to me has been the discovery that motherhood is more fun than anything I have ever done for a living; since Tommy was born seven years ago I have worked only part-time in order to be with him. Looking back over the years since college, I am proud of all the different things I have done, which include being a factory worker in Sweden, helping to run an advocacy group called Action for Children's Television, getting a Ph.D. in sociology, writing a book, teaching sociology at a Swiss university (in German!) and working five years as a gymnasium-level English teacher. All of it has been interesting and worthwhile — but at the age of forty-five I still have nothing I can call a career. Nevertheless, I have so far lived a life that was full of novelty, rich in friendships and close family ties, and astonishingly free from financial and medical worries. So I consider myself lucky and continue to hope that something I can call a life's work will materialize over the next twenty-five years.

HOME: Bern, Switzerland   **OCCUPATION:** English Teacher; Freelance Writer
BIRTHPLACE: Greenwich, CT   **SECONDARY SCHOOL:** West Vancouver Secondary School, BC, Canada   **YEARS AT COLLEGE:** 1971–75   **DEGREES:** A.B., magna cum laude, '75; Ph.D., Univ. of California, Berkeley '90   **SPOUSE/PARTNER:** Peter Stucker, July 30, 1988 (M.A., Univ. of Bern '85)   **SPOUSE'S OCCUPATION:** Management Consultant. Softlab A.G.   **CHILDREN:** Thomas Gabriel, 1993

Blayne R. Heckel: After leaving Harvard, I spent a year at Cambridge University, where I studied physics and was fortunate to have the opportunity to visit many parts of Europe. I returned to Harvard for graduate studies and was soon sent to Grenoble to pursue my dissertation at a neutron research institute. After spending five years at Grenoble, I joined the faculty at the University of Washington Department of Physics and I have been in Seattle for sixteen years.

Shortly after moving to Seattle, I married the girl who sat behind me in high school French class, Mary Hillyer, and we are in the process of raising three wonderful children. Seattle has proven to be a great place to call home, although its remote location puts us far from family and early friends.

I spend my time primarily with my family, making improvements to our home, trying to stay reasonably fit, and working on my research projects at the university. I am fortunate to have a job that doubles as a hobby. One of these days, I might even discover something. The last twenty-five years have been good ones, although too fleeting. I look forward to seeing all of the classmates that I've missed for the last twenty-five years.

HOME: Seattle, WA   OCCUPATION: Professor of Physics   BIRTHPLACE: Milwaukee, WI   SECONDARY SCHOOL: Wauwatosa West High School, Wauwatosa, WI   YEARS AT COLLEGE: 1971–75   DEGREES: A.B., summa cum laude, '75; Ph.D. '81 SPOUSE/PARTNER: Mary J. Hillyer, Feb. 11, 1984 (Univ. of Northern Colorado) CHILDREN: Garret Miles, 1984; Brynn Conway, 1986; Riley Zane, 1988   COLLEGE ACTIVITIES: Track team, 1971–75

David Joel Hellerstein: What I don't have, twenty-five years out: a dumpster in the side yard and a whole-house gut-job renovation underway, a decorator, an SUV, a country club membership, stock options, a seven-figure paycheck. Or a dozen other indicators of New York suburban success, end-of-millennium style. Not that I don't want any of those things (stock options would be nice), but it doesn't seem worth organizing one's life around them, as do so many of our contemporaries. What is this — the sudden rush for gaining and displaying wealth — that everything else is so easily thrown aside? Call me a cynic (or worse) but it seems to me that all the Lexus four-wheel-drive vehicles and chintz swags reveal a certain lack of imagination on our generation's part in dealing with our new-found power and wealth. I thought we were going to change the world!

Enough grumbling, I guess. Here, for the record, are a few details of my own life (though in comparison to reports from earlier years which feel like letters home from summer camp, this seems like somewhat more of a first draft of an obituary!). I'm married to Lisa Perry Hellerstein ('77, M.P.P. '81) who I met one fateful and lucky day in the fall of her freshman year, during orientation at North House. We have been happily married for seventeen years, and have three great kids (Sarah, twelve, Ben, ten, and Jason, six), not to mention a rabbit, two gerbils, a hamster, and a frog. We live in Westchester County (hence the above social commentary) and I work at Beth Israel Medical Center in New York, where I direct the outpatient division in the department of psychiatry. I am actually doing research (after years of swearing that I never would) in the areas of psychopharmacology and the treatment of schizophrenic substance abusers, and after years of struggle have risen to the lofty position of associate professor. To the dismay of critics everywhere I have continued to write essays, fiction, and the like. My books include *Battles of Life and Death* (essays), *Loving Touches* (novel) and *A Family of Doctors* (memoir), as well as the upcoming black comedy e-novel, *Stone Babies* (to be available on www.electronpress.com). I also waste an inordinate amount of time on my Websites, including www.hellerstein.net, and www.becomingadoctor.com, which dispenses advice of dubious value to credulous pre-meds everywhere. Lisa is now in business school on a part-time basis, with the still-idealistic goal of directing a nonprofit organization. We're not rich, trendy, or connected, but we're happy. Overall, even for those of us lacking stock options, life can have its rewards!

HOME: Larchmont, NY   **OCCUPATION:** Psychiatrist; Chief, Outpatient Psychiatry. Beth Israel Medical Center; Associate Professor of Psychiatry. Albert Einstein College of Medicine   **BIRTHPLACE:** Cleveland, OH   **SECONDARY SCHOOL:** Hawken School, Gates Mills, OH   **YEARS AT COLLEGE:** 1971–76   **DEGREES:** A.B., magna cum laude, '75('76); M.D., Stanford Univ. '80   **SPOUSE/PARTNER:** Lisa Perry, Oct. 16, 1983 ('77) **SPOUSE'S OCCUPATION:** Student. New York University, Stern School of Business **CHILDREN:** Sarah Nicole, 1987; Benjamin Perry, 1989; Jason Samuel, 1993   **COLLEGE ACTIVITIES:** Drama critic, *Harvard Independent,* 1973–76

Jennifer Thomas Helmick: After college I worked as a union activist and all-around machinist, learning about people and life in a very different way. I met my husband, a loud-mouthed, lovable Italian, at my place of work. With our marriage I became stepmom to three teenage boys. I had no idea what I was in for. In 1984 our daughter Adrienne was born; now, all of a sudden, she's a beautiful, exuberant teenager. In 1986 I went to graduate school to study occupational safety and health, and then took a science writing position at the firm where I am now a vice president. I have also spent many happy hours volunteering at my daughter's Waldorf school. Our family has been challenged over the past five years by my husband's serious chronic illnesses, but we're all pretty resilient.

As for acquiring wisdom, I feel like Achilles trying to catch the tortoise: with each step in life, I might be a little closer, but I'll never actually get there. For the most part, though, I've reveled in the race.

I am not sending a picture, because I look exactly the way I did in 1975, except for a bit of gray hair and a few more laugh lines.

HOME: Peabody, MA **OCCUPATION:** Vice President. Eastern Research Group, Inc. (environmental consulting) **BIRTHPLACE:** Newcastle, PA **SECONDARY SCHOOL:** Miami-Palmetto High School, Miami, FL **YEARS AT COLLEGE:** 1971–75 **DEGREES:** A.B. '75; M.S., Tufts Univ. '88 **SPOUSE/PARTNER:** Angelo Terenzi, April 4, 1981 **SPOUSE'S OCCUPATION:** Tool and Diemaker. General Electric Company **CHILDREN:** Adrienne, 1984 **COLLEGE ACTIVITIES:** E4A

Mary Sue Henifin: For the past few years my passion has been masters women's rowing on the Delaware River with Swan Creek Rowing Club in Lambertville, New Jersey. A high point was attending the Row As One Camp for masters women at Mt. Holyoke College, coached by former Olympic gold medallist Holly Metcalf. Eight masters women in a boat rowing together feels powerful. I don't know why I didn't discover rowing at Radcliffe (some of my friends at the Women's Center and RUS rowed crew). Rowing has also become a family sport. I'm attempting doubles rowing with my husband (he has a perfectionist surgeon's attitude, which is good when he does surgery, but not for our doubles rowing), and we're not sure if our marriage can survive our efforts. This Labor Day weekend, for the first time, our eight-year-old daughter joined us on the river, rowing my single shell.

When I am not on the Delaware River, I practice law at Buchanan Ingersoll in Princeton, where I am an environmental partner. I still write on science/public policy issues, and recently co-authored *New Jersey*

Brownfields Law, a book on how to redevelop former industrial properties. Trying to put policy into action, I work with community organizations in the City of Trenton, where we live, including the development of a new charter public school in Trenton on the site of the former laundry for Trenton Psychiatric Hospital.

HOME: Trenton, NJ   **OCCUPATION:** Partner. Buchanan Ingersoll PC (law firm)
BIRTHPLACE: Hood River, OR   **SECONDARY SCHOOL:** Woodrow Wilson High School, Portland, OR   **YEARS AT COLLEGE:** 1971–77   **DEGREES:** A.B., cum laude, '75 ('77); M.P.H., Columbia Univ. '81; J.D, Rutgers Univ. '85   **SPOUSE/PARTNER:** Howard W. Hardy III, 1982 (Harvard '76)   **SPOUSE'S OCCUPATION:** Surgeon (private practice)
CHILDREN: Frances Henifin Hardy, 1990   **COLLEGE ACTIVITIES:** Treasurer, Radcliffe Union of Students (RUS), 1975–76; Women's Center Collective, 1975–77

Miles Herter: After twenty-five years, I still don't have the answers, but I'm starting to have a pretty good grasp of the questions. I have somehow reconciled an ever-present desire for peace and simplicity with a penchant for accumulating clutter that comforts me with the knowledge that even though I don't need it today, I've got it if I need it tomorrow. I find that my life is built on dichotomies. I seek to live lightly on the earth, to eat only those foods that will sustain this body and not tear it down while at the same time maintaining peace in a car full of kids whose greatest earthly desire of the moment is a stop at McDonald's. That'll be four happy meals with plenty of dipping sauce, please. Balance...balance!

I adore my wife, Penny, and our kids, Rachel, Steffen, and Fiona, and I can't imagine being on this earth without them. Experiencing the world through the eyes of my family is for me a constant source of joy, wonder, and amusement. I seek the gift of one hundred percent presence in any given moment, with them and in all things, to be totally here and not distracted by that disaster past or this problem looming. But I guess the ultimate telltale is that while I like to think that I've stepped beyond that disorganized college kid of twenty-five years ago, I still had to call and plead for an extension on the deadline for this document. Balance...balance!

HOME: Wenham, MA   **OCCUPATION:** Actor; Teacher   **BIRTHPLACE:** Boston, MA
SECONDARY SCHOOL: St. Paul's School, Concord, NH   **YEARS AT COLLEGE:** 1971–76
DEGREES: A.B., cum laude, '75 ('76)   **SPOUSE/PARTNER:** Penny Fekany, April 19, 1986 (Univ. of North Carolina)   **SPOUSE'S OCCUPATION:** Dancer; Teacher; Mom
CHILDREN: Rachel, 1990; Steffen, 1993; Fiona, 1999   **COLLEGE ACTIVITIES:** Ski team; Dramatic Club

Don Hirsohn: I've been wanting to revisit those Psych/Social Relations days, trying to remember what Erik Eriksen wrote about this stage of life but have been too busy.

I've been wanting to revisit those contemplative days, trying to reawaken old Zen. I gaze deep into the eyes of my three-year-old. Utter mayhem.

Things have changed. I rode pedicab in Waikiki, hitched a latticeworks across the U.S. and Canada, hiked the Appalachian Trail, traveled around the world for three years, helped drag Apple back from the dead, and all the time beating my head against a wall trying to get published. Now I'm doing diapers. I still have no idea what I'm going to do when I grow up and that was last year.

HOME: Napa, CA   OCCUPATION: President. Quintessence Corp. (computer consulting)   BIRTHPLACE: Akron, OH   SECONDARY SCHOOL: Foxboro High School, Foxboro, MA   YEARS AT COLLEGE: 1971–75   DEGREES: A.B., magna cum laude, '75   SPOUSE/PARTNER: Sabine Goor, July 23, 1994 (University Coll., Ireland '82)   SPOUSE'S OCCUPATION: Instructor (Suzuki violin and viola); Concert Violist   CHILDREN: Quinn, 1997   COLLEGE ACTIVITIES: Student director, intramural athletics; football and basketball announcer, WHRB

Charles J. Hitchcock: Despite a couple of patents, I drifted away from my chemistry degree not long after graduation. Its last use was an entry to the world of computers; a friend needed a "Chemish" speaker to interpret for software engineers. Computers later sent me to Harvard's Extension School for the official paper and the organizing theory to back up the practical experience; after twenty years I still get a kick out of building something that works.

I've dabbled in juggling, flying, fencing, hang gliding, change ringing, and skydiving, but music and science fiction have been constant avocations. I've sung with Chorus pro Musica for twenty-three years, on a few obscure recordings, in Carnegie Hall, and various less-expected venues (including an episode of *Spenser for Hire*); I'm still learning music and technique but miss the focus of singers in Collegium Musicum. More of my time goes to the "unmediagenic" type of science fiction conventions populated mostly by voracious readers. I've worked on dozens of these conventions — sometimes by plan and sometimes answering an emergency — as far away as Australia, and chaired three. In planning and intensity conventions are not unlike college theater, except that a convention draws in friends from around the world or gives me a reason to visit someplace interesting *now* instead of "when I get around to it." I've edited four collections for the New England Science Fiction Association, which has developed a successful line of revivals of authors not appreciated by the "marketroids" now in charge of commercial publishing. I didn't plan any of this — I entered publishing by not stepping back quickly enough when a chair asked for volunteers — but I've found some measure of satisfaction in it, and I certainly can't complain of boredom.

HOME: Brighton, MA   **OCCUPATION:** Principle Software Engineer. Parametric Technology Corp. (software for mechanical CAD/CAM/CAE and process management) **BIRTHPLACE:** Washington, DC   **SECONDARY SCHOOL:** Williston Academy, Easthampton, MA   **YEARS AT COLLEGE:** 1971–73; 1974–75   **DEGREES:** A.B. '75 **SPOUSE/PARTNER:** Deborah M. Snyder, April 22, 1994 (Millersville Univ. '80) **SPOUSE'S OCCUPATION:** State Filing Coordinator (insurance)   **COLLEGE ACTIVITIES:** Theater (Harvard Dramatic Club, Leverett, Lowell, Gilbert & Sullivan); Collegium Musicum; WHRB

Susan Mina Rubin Hodara: Upon graduation, I followed my inclination towards animated flimmaking, and, after moving to Manhattan, received an M.F.A. from the film department at Columbia University in 1979. I worked for the Harold Friedman Consortium as a producer of animation and special effects for television commercials until 1982, when I joined a small computer graphics software company. During this period, I published a book entitled *Animation: The Art and the Industry* (Prentice-Hall).

All this offered little personal satisfaction compared with meeting my husband, Paul Hodara, and giving birth to two daughters, Sofie (now age thirteen) and Ariel (age eleven). Becoming a mother rooted me as I'd never felt rooted before, and as a result, in 1987, I began working (part-time, from home) for a parenting newspaper in New York City called *Big Apple Parent*, of which I am now editor-in-chief (also part-time, from home) and for which I write a monthly column on contemporary parenting.

I currently live in Chappaqua, New York, where time is at a premium every day, spent helping the girls with schoolwork far more intense than I remember it; editing; expanding my freelance writing to publications including *Parents* magazine and the *New York Times;* and enjoying pleasures such as reading, seeing friends, and being with family.

If you'd asked me at Harvard to imagine my life twenty-five years later, I couldn't have come up with anything more fulfilling than the life I'm living now. The rewards I receive from raising my daughters, the satisfaction I get from doing my job well, the relief I feel at having significant flexibility in my work life, the moments I steal to appreciate the natural beauty around me, and illusory though it may be, the sense that I've found a place inside and around me where I belong, all fill me with periods of calm and content which perhaps have always been my goal.

HOME: Mt. Kisco, NY   **OCCUPATION:** Editor-in-Chief; Columnist. *Big Apple Parent* (parenting newspaper in New York City)   **BIRTHPLACE:** Washington, DC
SECONDARY SCHOOL: Belmont High School, Belmont, MA   **YEARS AT COLLEGE:** 1971–75   **DEGREES:** A.B., cum laude, '75; M.F.A., Columbia '79   **SPOUSE/PARTNER:** Paul Sterling Hodara, Oct. 9, 1983 (California Inst. of the Arts, '75)   **SPOUSE'S OCCUPATION:** President. Netwave Technologies (computer networking)   **CHILDREN:** Sofie Elana, 1986; Ariel Marissa, 1988   **HARVARD/RADCLIFFE SIBLINGS:** Eric Robert Rubin '77; David Haskell Rubin '80

William Jay Hornbeck II: As a sole practitioner attorney-at-law with three children, I have made and saved less money than I thought I would, but I have had more fun and less stress than I thought I would.

I am active in Gideons (who distribute Bibles). I have coached youth soccer for over ten years. I have been busy raising my three sons. We like to travel to Georgia, where my wife has family and to Michigan, where I have family.

The biggest change from graduation is one of focus. Instead of focusing so much on my accomplishments in life, I am more focused on the great things God has done in my life and other lives. I put less confidence in the flesh and more confidence in Jesus Christ.

As an attorney and as a husband and father, it is natural for me to be anxious about many things. But, I am learning that God does not just sit in heaven with His arms folded, watching what we do. God is actively involved in the world and in our lives. I have discovered the truth of Psalm 34:19: "Many are the afflictions of the righteous; But the Lord delivers him out of them all."

We look forward to the Twenty-fifth Reunion and seeing you all. I'll be there with my wife and three sons (ages sixteen, fourteen, and nine), so I hope there are a lot of other kids and teenagers around or at least patience for mine.

HOME: Saint Petersburg, FL   **OCCUPATION:** Attorney (private practice)   **BIRTHPLACE:** Detroit, MI   **SECONDARY SCHOOL:** Western Michigan Christian High School
YEARS AT COLLEGE: 1971–75   **DEGREES:** A.B., cum laude, '75; J.D., Stetson Univ. '79
SPOUSE/PARTNER: Theresa Elaine Barrett (Gainesville Coll. '76)   **SPOUSE'S OCCUPATION:** Full-Time Mother/Homemaker; Part-Time Legal Assistant   **CHILDREN:** William Jay Hornbeck, 3d, 1982; John Michael Hornbeck, 1984; Joshua Barrett Hornbeck, 1990

Constance Rae Hornig: In the spring of 1975 it seemed to me that almost all of my classmates were heading to graduate school, with a large number of doctors and lawyers. My boyfriend, Neil Coleman, aspired to law or business school. So I matriculated at the University of Chicago Law School for no compelling reason of interest or experience. Consequently I feel very lucky that I enjoy my law practice. My clients are municipal employees responsible for solid-waste management. They work hard; they care about public health and safety; and they are appreciative of any help I can give them. My husband, Ted Humphreville '75, puzzles over my enjoyment of drafting detailed waste collection, materials recycling, and garbage disposal agreements.

In 1978 I began practice as a municipal bond lawyer in Manhattan. Every night from August through New Year's Day I visited a museum, concert, opera or ballet. I took architectural walks. I attended classes in meteorology and geology at the Natural History Museum and Wagner at New York University and medieval philosophy at the New School. I love New York.

As tax laws changed I spent many year-ends working eighty, even one-hundred-hour weeks closing bond deals, but then took magical solo trips through China. I was bit by a Lhasa apso in Tibet and had to evacuate for rabies shots. I traveled to the end of the silk road, in Kasgar. My public van was hit by a military truck on the Burmese Road to Dali. But my three months in China has filled Ted's and my home with monkey masks and other Chinese artifacts — and memories — to enrich the life of our daughter, Mae, who we adopted in China last year.

In 1983 I moved to San Francisco, where my law firm occupied the fiftieth floor of the tall, black, Bank of America skyscraper with panoramic views sweeping from the Bay Bridge across the Golden Gate to Potrero Hills in the south. I could watch the fog roll in beneath me.

I moved to Japan in 1988 when I was awarded a Fulbright Fellowship to study Japanese financing of waste incineration facilities. I was affiliated with the Universities of Tokyo and Kyoto (the Harvard and Yale of Japan). I coordinated visits to incinerators with *matsuri* (festivals) through the country, and immersed myself in *Noh* drama, *kasuri* (ikat) and *shibori* (tie dye) textiles, and temple architecture. Everyone should take a sabbatical each decade.

After returning to practice in New York, I met Ted at the wedding of Mary Myers Kauppila '76 in an Ojai orange grove. I moved to Los Angeles, bought my first car, opened my own law practice, married Ted (at age thirty-eight), bought a craftsman house, planted a fragrant and fruity garden...and adopted Mae. Ted and I have reached age forty-six with toddler Mae, two fox terriers, one orphaned spaniel, and two cat nemeses (black and white).

I no longer travel to Colombia or west Africa or traverse Asia from Bali to Bukhara, but I travel, often with Ted and Mae, across the U.S.A. when I teach solid-waste contracting courses and speak at symposia sponsored by the Solid Waste Association of North America, in which I am an international board member.

My Radcliffe admissions essay ("Describe a valuable learning experience") detailed my favorite books, grades one through twelve. The walls of every room in the house are lined with books, including many Oconomowoc Public Library discards gathered for me by my mother, who was killed in a car crash the week after she retired as a reference librarian there. Now I am enjoying rediscovering those books as I read to Mae, like my mom read to me. The rhythms of life bring comfort and contentment.

HOME: Los Angeles, CA **OCCUPATION:** Lawyer (sole practitioner representing state and local governments in regulatory, financing, and contract procurement matters relating to municipal solid-waste management) **BIRTHPLACE:** Milwaukee, WI **SECONDARY SCHOOL:** Oconomowoc High School, Oconomowoc, WI **YEARS AT COLLEGE:** 1971–75 **DEGREES:** A.B., magna cum laude, '75; J.D., Univ. of Chicago '78 **SPOUSE/PARTNER:** Edward "Ted" Taylor Humphreville, May 17, 1992 (Harvard '75) **SPOUSE'S OCCUPATION:** Tax Accountant; CPA (sole proprietor) **CHILDREN:** Mae Elizabeth, 1992 (adopted 1998 in Jiujiang, China)

Joy Horowitz: How could twenty-five years have passed if I'm still nineteen? Thank God for Harvard (the Adams House dining hall) because that's where I met Brock. Life is short, art is long and love never dies. Girls rule.

HOME: Santa Monica, CA **OCCUPATION:** Writer **DEGREES:** A.B., cum laude, '75; M.S.L., Yale '82 **SPOUSE/PARTNER:** Brock Walsh, Dec. 30, 1977 (Harvard '75) **CHILDREN:** Trevor, 1984; Gus, 1987; Lucy, 1993

Brian David Hotchkiss: As I skid toward the deadline for this life summary, I cannot shake the memory of a pregraduation dinner hosted by a classmate's father, a Harvard alumnus and self-styled Cassandra: "It's all over," he said. "College is the best four years of life. It's all downhill from here." I was appalled to hear this highly regarded surgeon be so unequivocal. Did he know something I didn't? Or didn't wish to know?

My time at Harvard taught me to recognize what I did not know, what I needed and wanted to learn, and best of all how to go about the process of self-education. It demonstrated the importance of standing on my own, facing into the wind when necessary, and following my instincts and passions. I did not come away with two crucial elements: a timetable and foresight.

As I sat in Centenary Theater—sodden, excited, confused—I predicted none of the directions the path I was following would take. Who could guess that I would move to New York in 1978 and flourish there for twelve years? I would have laughed at the idea of my cobbling together a checkered resume with everything from assistant director of a world-class art gallery to general manager of the country's premier gay-men's chorus.

Nor would I have believed that the experience I was about to garner over three years of torturous employment at the Harvard College Library (1975–78) would pave the way for the career I ultimately embraced—making books. Through years of honing my skills in most elements of publishing, particularly its editorial aspects, I returned to Boston in 1990 to be senior editor for art books at Bulfinch Press, the illustrated-book division of Little, Brown.

What would have strained credulity most, however, was that I would actually meet my soul mate. I'm not sure I even believed in such things back then, but in 1987, I met Peter Blaiwas, a brilliant graphic designer in New York. When I was offered the job at Little, Brown, it was Peter's encouragement—and his accompaniment—that made it feasible for our move to Boston. And it is as partners of a different kind that we founded Vernon Press in 1994.

For me, twenty-five years has the apparent duration of both a moment and an epoch. Memories of "college days" are only fleeting and vague. It's too tough to stretch my mind back that far when I need to extend it forward as I move toward what, I am sure, will be the best years of my life.

HOME: Boston, MA   OCCUPATION: Editorial Director. Vernon Press, Inc. (book producer)   SECONDARY SCHOOL: Chateaugay Central High School, Chateaugay, NY   YEARS AT COLLEGE: 1971–75   DEGREES: A.B., cum laude, '75   SPOUSE/PARTNER: Peter Michael Blaiwas, 1987 (Pratt Inst. '79)   SPOUSE'S OCCUPATION: Design and Production Director. Vernon Press, Inc.   COLLEGE ACTIVITIES: South House Film Society, 1973–75

James Richard Hughes: God is gracious.

HOME: Scarborough, ON, Canada   **OCCUPATION:** Vice President. EDS Systemhouse (systems integration)   **BIRTHPLACE:** Lima, OH   **SECONDARY SCHOOL:** Sir John A. Macdonald School, Scarborough, ON, Canada   **YEARS AT COLLEGE:** 1971–75 **DEGREES:** A.B., cum laude, '75; M.A., Univ. of British Columbia '77   **SPOUSE/PARTNER:** Lillian Ruaño, June 7, 1975   **SPOUSE'S OCCUPATION:** Homemaker   **CHILDREN:** Andrew, 1977; Aletha, 1980; Jotham, 1981; Timothy, 1983; Ryan, 1986; Jennifer, 1990 (adopted, 1992)   **COLLEGE ACTIVITIES:** Cross-country, 1971–72; track 1971–72; Gilbert and Sullivan Players, 1972–75

Edward Taylor Humphreville: I went to California in 1981. After

figuring out I didn't want to be a lawyer, I started an accounting/tax practice from scratch. I went to California because I set a goal. The Californians that I met at Harvard seemed to go after things. No goal was impossible. You can be who you want to be here. Don't worry, there is a flip side to that argument. It's a nice day every day and I even like it when it rains. Something different.

I am a director of the Los Angeles branch of the California Society of CPAs. CPAs are actually interesting people. I have been quite involved in the Westside Technology and Users Group of the CSCPA — 150 CPAs meeting monthly at the UCLA Faculty Club talking about technology, it's vision and application. I am very impressed with UCLA graduates.

I am a member of All Saints Episcopal Church in Beverly Hills — a great church. I am also a member of the prayer teams and am enrolled in a four-year course called Education for Ministry out of the University of the South in Sewanee, Tennessee. Among other things this is an in-depth study of the Bible. Last year and so far this year we have studied the Hebrew Scriptures. Right now we are reading the post-exilic writings. It's a fair amount of reading. A lot of interesting people in the class.

I love going to secondhand bookstores and have a comprehensive list of all the Los Angeles stores.

I am married to Constance Hornig '75. She is three days older than I. She is a "garbage lawyer" — doing solid waste contracting. She has helped put in the Oxnard and Sacramento MRFs (material recovery facility) along with a lot of other stuff. I feel like I know every garbage person in California and a lot all through the U.S. She is very involved with SWANA — the Solid Waste Association of North America. We met at the wedding of Mary Myers Kauppila '77, in Ojai. I was her escort. (We didn't know each other at Harvard.) It has been a very happy nine years. There is a God.

We adopted our daughter Mae from China in February 1998. Mae-Mae (little sister in Cantonese) is super. Mae means beautiful. Mei Wah is the plum blossom that blooms in the spring snow (a symbol of perseverance). Mae was left in the Third Cotton Factory of Juijang on May 7, 1997. The Chinese at the orphanage called her "Jumbo." Mae Qua means the United States — the beautiful country.

Constance's mother (Lois Mae Hornig) died in a car accident three years ago. Her dad was very wracked up but has made a recovery.

So I guess every day is a Mae day.

We're having a blast with life and I surely don't miss the Boston winters. My best to all my diverse and talented classmates.

HOME: Los Angeles, CA   **OCCUPATION:** Certified Public Accountant; Tax Accountant (private practice)   **BIRTHPLACE:** New London, CT   **SECONDARY SCHOOL:** Middlesex School, Concord, MA   **YEARS AT COLLEGE:** 1971–76   **DEGREES:** A.B., cum laude, '75 ('76); A.A., Bentley Coll. '79; M.S.T., ibid. '81   **SPOUSE/PARTNER:** Constance Rae Hornig, May 17, 1992 (Harvard '75)   **SPOUSE'S OCCUPATION:** Lawyer (private practice from home)   **CHILDREN:** Mae Elizabeth, 1997 (adopted, 1998 from Juiiang, China) **HARVARD/RADCLIFFE SIBLINGS:** John Evans Humphreville '69, M.B.A. '75; Robert Averill Humphreville '80   **COLLEGE ACTIVITIES:** Squash '75; Christian Fellowship; Fox Club

---

Hugh Musgrave Hyde, Jr.: Hello to my 1975 classmates. I hope our Twenty-fifth Reunion finds you in good spirits and good health.

On a sad note I continue to miss and pray for our classmate Teddy Thorndike, who died in 1987 and my father, Class of 1944, who died in 1994.

To date I've been blessed by a strong family, friends and good health.

My composite career consists of being (1) a patient advocate at a northern New Jersey state psychiatric hospital; (2) a teaching tennis professional; (3) a file clerk at a northern New Jersey law firm.

I've enjoyed considerable travel having lived in New York City, northern California, Chicago, and Hong Kong. Some of my favorite places include Berkeley, California; London; and Cape Cod (Chatham).

Perhaps my experiences of the past twenty-five years could be summed up in the following poem:

What's Important?

What's important?
A friend — someone with whom you can walk and talk
A room with a good light — so you can read late at night

What you think and say, what you do and pray
To meet the test, you do your best
To share, to care, to dare
And when it counts to be there.

HOME: Mendham, NJ   **OCCUPATION:** Staff Advocate (part-time). New Jersey
Protection and Advocacy   **BIRTHPLACE:** Morristown, NJ   **SECONDARY SCHOOL:**
Groton School, Groton, MA   **YEARS AT COLLEGE:** 1971–75   **COLLEGE ACTIVITIES:**
Varsity tennis team, 1974–75

Lawrence Vincent Jackson: Life has had its pressures along with
the ups and downs everyone faces. All-in-all, I've been *very* lucky to have
had a wonderful twenty-five years.

Life after graduation was tough as my dad died within a few months and
divorce was on the horizon. However, the picture started to brighten. I actually had fun at the various jobs I had, while also enjoying the real work of
being a dad and husband. We've moved eleven times since graduation, living in New York, New Jersey, Michigan, Dallas (twice), Atlanta, southern
California and now northern California. Without a doubt, we like the San
Francisco Bay Area the best — the only negative is being three-thousand
miles from our families.

Kim and I have three wonderful kids who basically wear us out! The
upside is that I *do* know Pokémon! Though we enjoy nice vacations (i.e.,
Easter in Maine), the challenge is to insure our kids get exposure to diverse
environments. It's tougher than normal when in the year 2000 your kids are
nearly the only Afro-Americans in the *public school!* Some things just won't
change easily I guess.

I am looking forward to my next phase in life (hopefully in the next four
years) when I retire from the corporate world of options and shareholder
stuff to teach math to inner city kids — and hopefully relate even better (definitely spend more time) with my own!

HOME: Alamo, CA   **OCCUPATION:** Senior Vice President. Safeway, Inc. (retail grocery)
BIRTHPLACE: Washington, DC   **SECONDARY SCHOOL:** St. John's School, Washington,
DC   **YEARS AT COLLEGE:** 1971–75   **DEGREEES:** A.B. '75; M.B.A. '79
SPOUSE/PARTNER: Kimberly Brown (Harvard '86)   **CHILDREN:** Vincent; Elliott;
Madison   **COLLEGE ACTIVITIES:** *Harvard Independent;* basketball; learning, growing,
and having fun!

Randy Jackson: When I left Harvard in 1975 as a crash and burn victim, my immediate prospects were "Paper or plastic?" or "Do you want fries with that?" Fortunately, there were plenty of gullible employers back then who were so impressed with Harvard that they never asked about class rank (or lack thereof). That I have achieved a modicum of success in the corporate world is testament to the fact that it's not what you know, but what people think you know.

HOME: Chicago, IL   **OCCUPATION:** President. Monsanto Consumer Food **BIRTHPLACE:** , Memphis, TN   **SECONDARY SCHOOL:** Booker T. Washington High School, Memphis, TN   **YEARS AT COLLEGE:** 1971–75   **DEGREES:** A.B. '75 ('83) **SPOUSE/PARTNER:** Diane Grigsby, May 27, 1995 (Illinois State Univ. '82; M.P.A., Univ. of Illinois, Springfield '84)   **SPOUSE'S OCCUPATION:** Chief of Staff. Chicago Public Schools   **CHILDREN:** Katherine Zoraida, 1998   **COLLEGE ACTIVITIES:** Kuumba Singers

Kurt Christopher Jacobsen: I have a wife that has both supported my own aspirations and expanded my view of the world in new and unpredictable ways. I am thankful that I have been an active participant in the raising of my two sons, now ages six and nine.

Since my college days, I have been leading classes and support groups in Reevaluation Counseling, which teaches people to take turns listening to each other so that they may think and act more effectively in their lives. This work has been an anchor for me, allowing me to make sense out of the sometimes confusing world of human relationships. The insights that I have gained into the dynamics of racism, sexism, anti-Semitism, and other forms of oppression have been particularly useful.

My work life has been varied. I taught high school math for seven years, then pursued my childhood dream of producing sports on television for another seven years. I spent three years as a stay-at-home dad when my first son was born, then returned to teaching high school math. Now that both children are in school, I have decided to do something new, and am in a two-year program at Bunker Hill Community College to become an echocardiographer, someone who does ultrasound studies on a patient's heart.

My zigzag career path has been shaped by my struggles with the issue of economic class. My father was an uneducated immigrant commercial fisherman, and I became an American success story, landing with a scholarship at Harvard. I was attracted to the siren's song of upward mobility and economic security, but there were so many ways that I felt out of place in that environment. My pursuit of echocardiography is based on my desire to have meaningful work that leaves me feeling more grounded in my class background.

HOME: Milton, MA   **OCCUPATION:** Student. Bunker Hill Community College
BIRTHPLACE: Seattle, WA   **SECONDARY SCHOOL:** Ballard High School, Seattle, WA
YEARS AT COLLEGE: 1971–75   **DEGREES:** A.B., cum laude, '75   **SPOUSE/PARTNER:**
Martha Hinds, Sept.. 17, 1988 (Smith Coll. '80)   **SPOUSE'S OCCUPATION:** Mathematics
Teacher. Milton Academy   **CHILDREN:** Leif, 1990; Erik, 1993

Michael Richard Jacobson: Men react differently to the creeping onset of middle age. Some buy red convertibles. Others have affairs. I changed jobs. After more than seventeen years at the law firm I joined straight out of law school, I succumbed to the prevailing Silicon Valley madness and joined an obscure, prepublic Internet start-up as its general counsel. eBay's obscurity didn't last very long, and now I find myself spending my days confronting an unending stream of unanswerable questions: If a breast pump is a medical device, can it be resold used? What are the intellectual property rights in an online reputation and who owns them? Is there a legal problem in arranging the sale of a Cuban cigar from a Londoner to a Berliner using computer facilities in California? How about a copy of *Mein Kampf?* It has to be one of the most interesting, challenging, and exhausting legal jobs in the country, and I'm having fun, I think.

I have managed to keep stability in the rest of my life. My wife still puts up with me (although not always with our son, who is as strong-minded as his mom). We've lived in the same area for almost twenty years, the same house for five. Although "extracurricular" time has been one casualty of the job change (trying to get a year's worth of work done every two months is time consuming), I still treasure my time with my family and have concluded that almost anything can be dealt with if you retain your sense of humor.

HOME: Palo Alto, CA   **OCCUPATION:** Vice President, Legal Affairs. eBay Inc.
BIRTHPLACE: Boston, MA   **SECONDARY SCHOOL:** Commonwealth School, Boston,
MA   **YEARS AT COLLEGE:** 1971–75   **DEGREES:** A.B., magna cum laude, '75; J.D.,
Stanford Univ. '81   **SPOUSE/PARTNER:** Trine J. Sorensen (Univ. of Washington '75)
SPOUSE'S OCCUPATION: Self-Employed   **CHILDREN:** Matthew, 1990   **COLLEGE
ACTIVITIES:** Manager, heavyweight crew

J. Parker Jameson: Twelve days after graduation, I began a fourteen-month stint working with youth in Liverpool, England, followed by three months bicycling across Europe. At Thanksgiving of 1976, I was back in my hometown of Abilene, Texas, selling men's clothing in a department store and trying to discern what vocation God might have given me. My desire to find a God-given vocation grew out of the most important experience of my time at Harvard-Radcliffe, out of the many experiences there for which I am thankful.

In the fall of 1972, a friend invited me to participate in a retreat hosted by the Harvard-Radcliffe Christian Fellowship. I was and am a life-long Episcopalian, but on that retreat for the first time I heard someone say that each of us could have a personal relationship with Jesus Christ, in addition to the relationship we have with Him through the church. With the prayers and support of my small group, that day I asked for that relationship to become real in my life. That was the beginning of my adult walk in faith, and everything since has been an outgrowth of that relationship.

In the fall of 1977, I entered the Episcopal Seminary in Austin, Texas, on a trial basis, and fell in love with it. One of the joys of my life was later serving for six years as a trustee of my seminary. After four years of study, during which I met and married the daughter of one of my older classmates, I graduated in 1981. Paula and I moved to Amarillo, Texas, where for two years I was half-time assistant at St. Peter's Episcopal Church in Amarillo and half-time priest-in-charge of St. Paul's Episcopal Church in Dumas, Texas. Paula completed a masters in psychology while we were there.

For five years beginning in 1983, I was one of the assistants at a large church, St. Luke's in San Antonio, Texas, primarily responsible for pastoral care, teaching, and liturgy. I did "mass quantities" (no pun intended) of weddings, baptisms, and funerals. Our first child, Sterling, was born memorably in January 1985 during the worst snowstorm to hit San Antonio in a century.

We left San Antonio in 1988 for Alexandria, Louisiana, where for nine years I was rector of St. Timothy's Episcopal Church. Our second child, Marcus, was born on a Sunday morning a month to the day after we arrived there; perhaps needless to say, I missed church that day. The first five years there were good years for the parish, but at the expense of my working myself into burnout and depression. I am thankful for prayer, good therapy, and modern medication, and as I recovered I grew spiritually and emotionally in ways that might not have been possible without suffering. At the same time, the changes in my life were resented by some members of the congregation. After a difficult process of negotiations, I left St. Timothy's in 1997 with a year's severance package.

Paula and I and our boys relocated to Austin, Texas, for a sabbatical year of healing, rest, and discernment about the future. Over and over again, even during the three months of negotiations, we were aware of God's grace at work in our lives. A year after arriving in Austin, the rector of the parish that we were attending invited me to join him as his associate at St. Luke's on the Lake, with a magnificent view of the main basin of Lake Travis and the surrounding Texas Hill Country. The Youth Group here says that "You come for the view, and stay for the family." Certainly St. Luke's is the most spiritually mature congregation in which I have served, a place of healing and genuine warmth.

I am having the best time of my life teaching adult Bible studies, working with the Alpha course (an evangelism program), and sharing in the general preaching, worship leading, visiting, and serving responsibilities. God is "growing me" into greater emotional and spiritual maturity, to finally catch up with my intellectual and academic capacities. I am hoping to begin work on a doctor of ministry degree in the summer of 2000. Sterling is a guitar-playing, soccer-playing, quiet, reserved, and responsible ninth-grader. Marcus is a piano and cornet-playing, articulate, and funny sixth grader. After years of being the stay-at-home parent, Paula is exploring her own vocation as a retreat leader and spiritual director.

In the intervening twenty-five years I have been blessed, richly blessed, in both suffering and joy. My family and I understand ourselves to be enormously blessed. Thanks be to God for all that has been, is, and will be.

HOME: Austin, TX   OCCUPATION: Episcopal Priest; Associate Rector   BIRTHPLACE: Abilene, TX   SECONDARY SCHOOL: Cooper High School, Abilene, TX   YEARS AT COLLEGE: 1971–75   DEGREES: A.B., cum laude, '75; M.Div., Episcopal Theological Seminary of the Southwest '81   SPOUSE/PARTNER: Paula Whitfield, Jan. 17, 1981 (Univ. of Texas, Austin '73; M.A., West Texas State Univ., Canyon '83)   SPOUSE'S OCCUPATION: Homemaker; Retreat Leader (self-employed, works from home)   CHILDREN: Sterling M., 985; Marcus P., 1988   COLLEGE ACTIVITIES: Christian Fellowship, 1972–75; Leverett House Arts Society, 1972–75

Steven Augustine Janicek: The journey has been interesting. After graduating in June 1977 from Stanford, I moved back to Canada to work for J. P. Morgan for twelve years before moving back to New York City in 1990. Both of our children were born here before we returned to Canada in mid-1993. We returned to New York City in 1997 not for the ever-strong U.S. dollar, but for family reasons.

In mid-1995 we discovered that our son, Alex, was autistic. Not only was Alex autistic, but he was also hyperlexic. Our son could not speak, had no interest in any social activities, and barely knew that his parents or sister existed...yet he could spell and read at an eight-year-old level when he was five. This skill may someday help Alex to adjust to society and its expectations of him, but at the same time we have a daughter, Julia, who is dyslexic and has auditory processing problems. Although this has been a tad stressful, we have learned to appreciate every little achievement, to truly practice parental love and patience and understand that being unique is a positive, not a negative.

We learn something new every day from our beautiful, talented children, and Alex, now seven and a half, is beginning to speak. We are exceptionally grateful to all the caring professionals who are creating these miracles for our children. We look forward to the continuing journey.

HOME: Princeton, NJ   **OCCUPATION:** Director. Scotia Capital Markets (U.S.A.) Inc.; Manager. Money Market Sales Force   **BIRTHPLACE:** Petrolia, ON, Canada
SECONDARY SCHOOL: East Lambton Secondary School, Watford, ON, Canada
YEARS AT COLLEGE: 1971–75   **DEGREES:** A.B., cum laude, '75; M.B.A., Stanford Univ. '77
SPOUSE/PARTNER: Susan E. Devereau, 1981, divorced, 1987; Patricia M. Durelle, 1989
SPOUSE'S OCCUPATION: Housewife   **CHILDREN:** Julia Ann, 1990; Alexander Steven,
1992   **COLLEGE ACTIVITIES:** Freshman hockey team, 1971; varsity hockey team, 1972–75

Thomas Russell Jevon: My marriage of the last eleven years and my decision to return to do pre-med after finishing college, and then go on to become a family doctor, have been the defining events since graduation. While this sounds like a pretty conventional odyssey it certainly hasn't felt that way to me; I'm far more positive about life, far less filled with regrets, and far more willing to consider dramatic change in my life than I expected I would be when contemplating life twenty-five years out of college. As is true for many, my wife and children are the central and sustaining part of my life. My work as a family doctor is certainly challenging, sometimes frustrating. Call it maturity, the complacency of the booming economic times, the fact that our children, aged ten, eight, and five, appear to be at a wonderful stage, but I am amazingly happy and fulfilled in comparison to the angst of my college and postcollege years.

HOME: Winchester, MA   **OCCUPATION:** Physician   **BIRTHPLACE:** Salem, MA
SECONDARY SCHOOL: Lincoln-Sudbury Regional High School   **YEARS AT COLLEGE:**
1971–75   **DEGREES:** A.B., cum laude, '75; M.D., Case Western Reserve Univ. '83
SPOUSE/PARTNER: Louise Richardson, June 18, 1988 (Trinity Coll.; A.M., Harvard '84;
Ph.D. '89)   **SPOUSE'S OCCUPATION:** Associate Professor of Government. Center for
European Studies, Harvard University   **CHILDREN:** Ciara, 1989; Fiona, 1991; Rory, 1994

Scott William Johnson: No doubt my visual and environmental studies (art/architecture) major at Harvard was excellent (if a bit unusual) preparation for my career as an investment banker. After a year working in a community redevelopment organization in Brooklyn's Bedford Stuyvesant section, I went to Stanford for an M.B.A. and, as it turned out, to meet my wife, a classmate. We lived in New York's Greenwich Village for three years and then in the suburbs for ten while I worked on financings and mergers at Goldman Sachs, mostly in the energy industry group. My wife Joan worked for some years with a large company until we had our second daughter, at which point she made our two girls her main priority. In 1991 I left Goldman Sachs to move to Houston and co-found a small energy investment banking firm (Weisser Johnson). Despite a few anxious moments, I have gotten a big charge out of working for myself in a small firm. Our four-person Houston office is most congenial, and I think it is fair to say that we all really enjoy our work — helping smaller companies grow by attracting capital and arranging acquisitions.

Houston was a big and welcome change from New York. Much shorter commuting time, less travel, an open and welcoming social ethic, easy movement around town, and great diversity in urban offerings have combined to win an endorsement from the whole family. I have been able to be more involved with my girls, from coaching YMCA soccer teams to attending volleyball matches or just being together more in the evenings. Now that they are in tenth and eleventh grade and beginning to become less available for family events, I am more grateful than ever that I had the time with them that I did.

Joan and I will have been married for twenty-one years at the time of the Reunion. Like many, we have had some ups and downs, but we have learned much about how to love and support each other while also making room for our differences. The more time goes by the stronger becomes my realization that there just is not anything as important to me as her and our two girls. Lesser pleasures include running, tennis, windsurfing, skiing (especially helicopter skiing in Canada), occasional golf, movies, Comets games (women's basketball), and vacation travel.

HOME: Houston, TX   **OCCUPATION:** Principal. Weisser, Johnson & Co. (investment banking — private financing and mergers — for the energy industry)   **BIRTHPLACE:** New York, NY   **SECONDARY SCHOOL:** St. Paul's School, Concord, NH   **YEARS AT COLLEGE:** 1971–75   **DEGREES:** A.B., magna cum laude, '75; M.B.A., Stanford Univ. '78   **SPOUSE/PARTNER:** Joan Rewbridge Ifland, Dec. 31, 1978 (Oberlin Coll '74)   **SPOUSE'S OCCUPATION:** Author; Food Consultant   **CHILDREN:** Claire I, 1983; Camille I., 1984   **COLLEGE ACTIVITIES:** Ski team, 1971–75; Fly Club, 1972–75

David Eugene Johnston: After I left Harvard I entered graduate school in biochemistry at MIT. I soon became restless to change from "pure" science to medicine. I married my girlfriend from college, Sandy, and we moved to Pittsburgh, where I attended medical school. Eventually we moved back to Boston for another thirteen years, where I finished my medical and academic training, and started a career in academic medicine at Tufts University–New England Medical Center. In 1994 we moved to Albuquerque, New Mexico, where I joined the University of New Mexico School of Medicine. I continue to do some laboratory and clinical research in liver physiology and disease, as well as taking care of patients with digestive and liver disorders. Sandy and I find that our children are quite different than we are. They both yearn to get back to the big cities and bright lights back east. Our fifteen-year-old daughter is intensively involved in music and theater, and our twelve-year-old son is an avid athlete who aspires to become a Republican congressman. I've been very busy with my family, medicine, and science since I graduated from college. It seems strange to me that I could have graduated from Harvard a quarter century ago. I consider myself a recent graduate.

HOME: Albuquerque, NM   OCCUPATION: Physician; Associate Professor of Medicine (gastroenterology). University of New Mexico School of Medicine   BIRTHPLACE: Lancaster, PA   SECONDARY SCHOOL: Octorara Area High School, Atglen, PA   YEARS AT COLLEGE: 1971–75   DEGREES: A.B., magna cum laude, '75; M.D., Univ. of Pittsburgh '81   SPOUSE/PARTNER: Sandra Huntington Parkhurst (Simmons Coll. '75)   SPOUSE'S OCCUPATION: Homemaker   CHILDREN: Susan Elizabeth, 1984; Steven Eugene, 1986

Charles Weldon Jones: Twenty-five years is such a long time and yet such a short time. I went to Harvard planning to become a high school biology teacher. Finding that the study of biology was too enticing to stop at the undergraduate level, I pursued a Ph.D. at Harvard, and then continued with a post-doctoral fellowship at Stanford Medical School. While I was successful at research (*Science, Nature, Cell* publications), I decided I didn't want to follow the straight research track. Instead, I followed my heart and ended up at a small Christian liberal arts college in Minnesota. Now I am a professor of biology and have been chair of the biology department for eleven years. I still do some research with students and occasionally publish in the area of molecular biology, but my focus both in my teaching and my research is undergraduate education. With no family here, the college and my church have pretty much become my life. I very much enjoy the challenges of higher education and I have to admit that it tickles me to see what we can accomplish at my college without the resources of a "Harvard." I guess I must be doing something right — in 1995 the Carnegie Foundation named me Minnesota professor of the year, which has been a highlight of my career to date. A significant portion of my spare time is devoted to student activities: supervising student research activities, serving as advisor to our biology honor society, taking students to research symposia and conventions, and hosting activities at my home. While the pace can get stressful, the rewards, as they say, are "bountiful."

Outside of school, I am active in the Methodist church, occasionally teach Sunday school, sing in the choir, etc. I also dabble in genealogy and have spent a part of each of my two past sabbaticals (one at Harvard and the other at the Mayo Clinic) traveling to learn about my past. I also enjoy traveling, having been to China and Norway the past two summers (although I must admit a lot of my traveling is in conjunction with scientific and education meetings).

With no "biological" children, my students (whether they like it or not!) have become my surrogate children. My joys come from their achievements and watching them develop into outstanding young men and women of character. Here's to another twenty-five!

HOME: Arden Hills, MN   **OCCUPATION:** College Professor. Department of Biology, Bethel College   **BIRTHPLACE:** Providence, RI   **SECONDARY SCHOOL:** Fryeburg Academy, Fryeburg, ME   **YEARS AT COLLEGE:** 1971–75   **DEGREES:** A.B., magna cum laude, '75; A.M. Ph.D. '80   **COLLEGE ACTIVITIES:** Christian Fellowship; Undergraduate Admissions Council; Harvard-Radcliffe Chorus

Peter Lawson Jones: Although the years since our commencement have not brought me great material wealth, the experiences of the past quarter century have, nonetheless, greatly enriched my life.

Since graduation I have lived in Washington, D.C., San Francisco, Los Angeles, Columbus, and Cleveland. I have worked for a congresswoman, a winning presidential campaign, a state supreme court justice, as president of a company that secures full-time employment for welfare recipients, and as an attorney with firms both large and small. None of those jobs, however, gave me the sense of fulfillment that I now receive as a member of the Ohio House of Representatives.

My path to the state legislature was hardly without obstructions, though. After being elected twice to the Shaker Heights City Council, I endured a series of electoral setbacks. In 1990, I finished second in a nine-person primary race for state senate. Two years later, I fell one vote short of securing an appointment to that body. In 1994, as one-half of the Democratic gubernatorial team and the first African-American ever to be nominated to run for lieutenant governor in the history of Ohio, my running mate and I lost to a popular Republican incumbent.

Thus, my political future was in jeopardy when I ran for state representative in the 1996 Democratic primary against an opponent who would outspend me four-to-one. Fortunately, I prevailed with over sixty percent of the vote and went on to an easy general election victory. I was reelected in 1998 with nearly eighty percent of the vote. In only my third year in the legislature, I serve as ranking member of the House Finance and Appropriations Committee and play a significant role in determining how the state spends nearly $50 billion on various biennial budgets.

As someone who vowed never to marry or have children, the most fulfilling aspect of my life, however, has surprisingly been... family. This year my wife, Lisa (bright, beautiful, engaging, and long-suffering), and I will celebrate our fifteenth wedding anniversary. By the time you read this, we will have three children, Ryan, Leah and Master or Ms. X. (Yes, I'll be changing diapers at forty-seven!) Both Ryan and Leah are excellent students; Ryan excels at any sport he tries while Leah is destined for Broadway or the silver screen. Most importantly, they're good "kidz." I can't believe I'm bragging about them, something else I pledged never to do.

Well, I've used up my three hundred words. Anyway, I should leave something for us to chat about at the Reunion. See you then.

HOME: Shaker Heights, OH   **OCCUPATION:** State Representative. Attorney; Partner. Roetzel & Andress   **BIRTHPLACE:** Cleveland, OH   **SECONDARY SCHOOL:** Shaker Heights High School, Shaker Heights, OH   **YEARS AT COLLEGE:** 1971–75   **DEGREES:**

A.B., magna cum laude, '75; J.D. '80   **SPOUSE/PARTNER:** Lisa Payne, Oct. 12, 1985
(Eastern Michigan Univ. '80)   **SPOUSE'S OCCUPATION:** Registrar. Shaker Heights Board
of Education   **CHILDREN:** Ryan Charles, 1988; Leah Danielle, 1992   **COLLEGE
ACTIVITIES:** Honors: magna cum laude, government; Rhodes Scholarship nominee;
recipient, Harvard John F. Kennedy Institute of Politics summer fellowship; Harvard
National Scholarship; Paul Revere Frothingham Scholarship and Currier House Senior
Creativity Award; organizations: president, Black C.A.S.T. (African-American student
theater group); academic chairman, Harvard-Radcliffe Association of African and
African-American Students; intramural baseball; special achievement: my full-length
play, *The Family Line,* was produced in the Loeb Experimental Theatre in May 1975

John Bradbury Judkins: I remember my dad's twenty-fifth college
reunion quite clearly and can hardly believe that I am as old as he was then.
(Actually I'm not, chronologically, by a matter of a year and a half, and, mentally, by a matter of decades — a reflection on me rather than him.) Twenty-
five years is quite a time to cover in three hundred words, but here goes. After
graduation I began the process, which is still continuing, of finding the perfect job. It took me two cities, two jobs, three years (and enough time away
from academia to forget how poorly I fared in college) to settle on law school
(and two sets of applications and some additional college coursework to convince law schools that my poor college performance should not be a barrier).
As a lawyer (and this may be part of the problem in my search for the perfect
job), I have practiced: as a legal services attorney (very satisfying in part, very
depressing in part, and entirely demanding, but most notably, as my reason
for leaving, located in cold, wintry, and geographically challenged Chicago);
as a private practice attorney representing tenants under the San Francisco
rent control law (high stress, juggling many clients, and often imminent trials, usually in a good cause); as a federal government attorney for the Social
Security Administration (in a word, boring); and for the last decade as a
municipal attorney, which is mostly varied and interesting and sometimes
personally rewarding. But I'm still thinking about finding work that is more
important, valuable. As I say, the process continues.

   On the home front, a great wife and partner who takes on far more than
her share of the load, and two boys who are, well, boys and brothers, with
all the good and bad that both of those imply, and who share my love of
physical activity, the outdoors, and participation in sports. I have great fun
playing with them and watching them play. We live in a beautiful, wooded,
small, diverse (funk, hippie, old-timers, and more recently arrived yuppies)
town of eight thousand in the hilly (or to those of you in the Plains, moun-

tainous) area just north of San Francisco and tucked under the flank of Mt. Tamalpais (pronounced not anything like it's spelled). We are involved in the boys' sports and in local politics and issues (via the Planning Commission of which I am the chair, the local public schools where my wife devotes much of her "free" time and in other causes). I can honestly say that I love who I live with and where I live (but note that there are far too many people in the San Francisco Bay Area, the traffic is horrible, and the cost of living and housing astronomical and anyone who is thinking of relocating out here should definitely reconsider or, better yet, not move here — think Seattle or some other place, please).

I won't be able to attend the Reunion, but would welcome contact from my roommates (Oakes Ames, Fred Fisher, David Lake) and other friends from the past by email or otherwise.

HOME: Fairfax, VA   **OCCUPATION:** Assistant City Attorney. City of Richmond
BIRTHPLACE: Evanston, IL   **SECONDARY SCHOOL:** Hotchiss School, Lakeville, CT
YEARS AT COLLEGE: 1971–75   **DEGREES:** A.B. '75; J.D., Univ. of California, Berkeley, '81
SPOUSE/PARTNER: Sandra Gartzman, July 5, 1987 (Indiana Univ. '79; J.D., Northwestern Univ. '82)   **SPOUSE'S OCCUPATION:** Senior Administrative Law Judge. San Francisco Rent Stabilization and Arbitration Board   **CHILDREN:** Jonathon, 1989; Benjamin, 1992
COLLEGE ACTIVITIES: Freshman and varsity lacrosse, 1972–74; other activities that might disqualify me from federal office — well, maybe not, given how long ago it was

---

Elliot William Justin: The greatest gift that Harvard provided was the opportunity to study and live with "the best and the brightest," to learn how much and how little that means by measuring myself against others, and to appreciate the weak correlation between intelligence and wisdom, or knowledge and virtue. Who among us starting in 1971 considered that Governor Reagan was right, that the millennium would witness Communism in the garbage can of history, or that the Socialist mystique in which almost all of us participated would evaporate? Who anticipated that "the most progressive and spiritually inclined generation in our nation's history" (as I recall the characterization in a *Crimson* editorial) would pursue and enjoy such unprecedented material success?

With nostalgia, I recall the "salon" for intellectuals in the main reading room of Widener Library. I remember especially the discussions about the rotting effect of relativism on the arts and politics. There, also I began a life-long course of extracurricular reading in the classics and history, a passion that I hope to pass on to my children. An overlooked work that I recommend highly is the *Hestviken Saga,* by Sigrid Undset, an epic that rivals *War and*

Peace in complexity and momentum of narrative, insight into a diversity of characters, and poetically vivid descriptions of nature.

Looking back reminds me, too, that life is brief, true companions rare, and love is sublime. While ambition and character play important roles in determining our lives, luck is decisive. I owe the unanticipated joy of my family to an encounter with a student waitress in Grendel's Den. We dated for six weeks and moved on in the style of that time, ironically because I did not believe in the "unity of souls." But eleven years later, providence brought us together on Houston Street in Manhattan. I have been happy ever since. While I enjoy the practice of emergency medicine, and am the president of Pegasus Emergency Group, the most challenging and satisfying work in my life at present is helping my wife educate our children at home.

Looking forward to our Fiftieth, and with fond regards to Govan, Krstofiak, Walsh, Perkins, Mendes, Zelinsky, Peck, Ward, Weiss, et al.

HOME: Lambertville, NJ   OCCUPATION: President. Pegasus Emergency Group; Director of Emergency Services. Hunterdon Medical Center   BIRTHPLACE: New York, NY   SECONDARY SCHOOL: Woodmere Academy, Woodmere, NY   YEARS AT COLLEGE: 1971–75   DEGREES: A.B., cum laude, '75; M.D., Boston Univ. '79; B.U.S.M., ibid. '79   SPOUSE/PARTNER: Ann Wray, May 1988 (Beloit Coll. '75)   CHILDREN: Grant; Eric; Eleanor   HARVARD/RADCLIFFE SIBLINGS: Mark Justin '71   COLLEGE ACTIVITIES: Initiated the raft race on the Charles with Kevin Ward and Michael Peck from Adams House (and other unofficial hijinks)

Robert James Kaneda: I've lived abroad for most of the time (thirteen years and counting) since graduation, as a Peace Corps volunteer and Foreign Service officer. Stops include Upper Volta (now Burkina Faso), Haiti, France, and Japan. It's nice to be back for a second stay in France, but I miss the adventure some of the other places offered. I sometimes wonder about the wisdom of leading such a nomadic life, but on balance it's been fun and enlightening — new people, new languages, new political regimes, new sights, new sounds, new views of the U.S., new flora, new fauna, new foods, new intestinal tract ailments. All part of the charm.

Harvard seems very distant, and, judging from the alumni publications and so forth, a lot more full of itself than when we were there. A Foreign Service (FS) friend, who also went to undergrad at Harvard, tells an amusing anecdote. While serving at our embassy in Rome, my friend was talking about colleges and such with another FS officer, who was bemoaning the fact that he had not attended an Ivy League school. He said something along the lines of "Gee, just think what I could have become if I had gone to an

Ivy League school," whereupon my friend said "You could be a Foreign Service officer serving in Embassy Rome."

On the personal front, all is solid with my friend Mathilde Kazes, a tolerant and gentle person who is always ready to travel and explore.

HOME: Paris, France   OCCUPATION: Diplomat. United States Department of State   BIRTHPLACE: Los Angeles, LA   SECONDARY SCHOOL: Fairfax High School, Los Angeles, CA   YEARS AT COLLEGE: 1971–75   DEGREES: A.B., cum laude, '75; J.D., Univ. of California '82; M.A., Ecole Nationale d'Administration de France '98   SPOUSE/PARTNER: Mathilde Kazes (Univ. of Paris V, Rene Descartes, Hospital Necker '84)   SPOUSE'S OCCUPATION: Physician

---

Kaffee Kang: To borrow from Jorge Luis Borges's theme in *Remorse*, but to diverge from his conclusion...I have achieved the only thing my parents have ever hoped for me: happiness. In 2000, my husband Joe McGill and I will have been married twenty-two years. Through the years, Joe has taught me a few things about unconditional love and kept me focused on what is truly important in life. We have two wonderful children, Becky and Martha. And for the last eighteen years, parenting has been our most important function and the source of our greatest joys. Becky is a compassionate nurturer and Martha is a voracious thinker. Both girls have developed into individuals we admire and like. My parents are still well and I have a renewed appreciation for their efforts and struggles from China to the U.S. My emotional bond to my roommates from college (Vic, Sarah, and Ada) remains strong and we have resumed our talks, intimate and mundane alike, through e-mail. I own and run my own small architectural firm, specializing in projects in the public sector. And in this professional capacity, I have realized the three career goals I was unaware I was searching for until I stumbled upon them: a degree of self-determination; enjoyment of the day-to-day; and the opportunity to make a small contribution to society. I look forward now to having more time in the future to paint, garden, hold babies, and learn to dance.

HOME: Sudbury, MA   OCCUPATION: President. Kang Associates, Inc. (architectural firm)   BIRTHPLACE: Keelung, Taiwan   SECONDARY SCHOOL: Bronx High School of Science, Bronx, NY   YEARS AT COLLEGE: 1971–75   DEGREES: A.B., magna cum laude, '75; M.Arch., Univ. of Pennsylvania '78   SPOUSE/PARTNER: Joseph Charles McGill, June 24, 1978 (Pennsylvania State Univ. '73; M.S.W., Univ. of Pennsylvania '79)   SPOUSE'S OCCUPATION: Assistant Professor. University of Massachusetts Medical Center, Dept. of Psychiatry   CHILDREN: Rebecca Kang McGill, 1982; Martha Kang McGill, 1985   COLLEGE ACTIVITIES: *Harvard Crimson;* Yearbook

James Fraser Kasting: After leaving Harvard, I studied atmospheric sciences at University of California, San Diego and Michigan. There (in Michigan) I met my wife, Sharon, who was in the business school and also in the graduate dorm where I was the resident assistant. Sharon and I moved out to the Boulder/Denver area after graduation. She worked for a consulting firm, while I did a post-doc at the National Center for Atmospheric Research. While there, I got a call from a planetary science researcher at NASA Ames (out in the San Francisco Bay Area) asking if I would come join their group. So, I did, and we stayed out there for seven years, having two boys in the process. Eventually, I took a teaching job at Penn State, where we have been for the past eleven years. We had one more boy after we got here, so now we have three. I currently do research on planetary atmosphere evolution and on the question of whether there are habitable planets around other stars. I'm on the science working group for a NASA project called Terrestrial Planet Finder that we hope will someday answer that question and perhaps even tell us whether life exists on such planets. In the meantime, I like to run, swim, and play tennis, when I am not hobbled by one injury or another. Being a closet athlete was easier when I was younger. (As you can guess, I am injured as I write this!)

HOME: State College, PA   OCCUPATION: Professor of Geosciences. Pennsylvania State University   BIRTHPLACE: Schenectady, NY   SECONDARY SCHOOL: Westport High School, Louisville, KY   YEARS AT COLLEGE: 1971–75   DEGREES: A.B., summa cum laude, '75; Ph.D., Univ. of Michigan '79   SPOUSE/PARTNER: Sharon (Miami Univ. of Ohio '77)   SPOUSE'S OCCUPATION: Treasurer. State College Presbyterian Church   CHILDREN: Jeffrey, 1983; Patrick, 1985; Mark, 1991   COLLEGE ACTIVITIES: Junior varsity wrestling

Jonathan G. Katz: It took me a decade or more after Harvard to "settle down." Two of those years were spent living in Iran and traveling, but much of that time was also taken up with nondescript jobs in various East Coast cities. In 1985 I returned to school and finally married. As it turns out—as I perhaps knew all along—the academic life suits me. In 1996 I published a great book that everyone should read about a fifteenth-century Sufi dreamer named al-Zawawi who routinely talked with the Prophet Muhammad. Now I'm researching a book about the French "civilizing mission" that takes as its departure the story of a French physician who was murdered in Marrakech in 1907.

Neither study is biography in a strict sense, but they both concern the interplay between an individual's own desires and the external forces beyond his control.

I've witnessed this struggle up close as my two young daughters try to deal with their parents' recent divorce. Sadly, they've discovered that life isn't always what one wants it to be. In the end I know they'll manage. More than I, they take great comfort in the rainy routines of small-town Oregon life. And yet I have to confess that I feel a renewed sense of confidence and adventure. Being unexpectedly "unsettled" once again is, I've discovered, not altogether bad.

HOME: Corvallis, OR **OCCUPATION:** Associate Professor. Dept. of History, Oregon State University **BIRTHPLACE:** Philadelphia, PA **SECONDARY SCHOOL:** Springfield High School, Montgomery County, PA **YEARS AT COLLEGE:** 1971–75 **DEGREES:** A.B., cum laude, '75; Ph.D., Princeton '90 **CHILDREN:** Madeleine, 1989; Suzanne, 1992

Scott Austin Kaufer: After graduation, some *Crimson* friends and I decided to start an "alternative" weekly newspaper, as was then the fashion, and to do it in Minneapolis, Minnesota, where the five of us, in the entirety of our lives, had resided for a combined total of zero days. God bless our Harvard hubris. We descended on Minneapolis in Ryder trucks. Bought a bunch of billboards proclaiming that the city was more interesting than its journalism. Promised that we would change that.

It may not surprise you that our missionary work went unappreciated by the indigenous population we had come to save; *Metropolis* folded after forty-five issues. So I got back in a Ryder truck, heading east this time, for New York City. There I would bury a couple more publications (*New Times, LOOK*), start a softball league (our center fielder was a cop who played with a loaded gun tucked into his waistband), get mugged (by an off-duty security guard), and ache to return home to Los Angeles, finally doing so after four years in Manhattan, a place that I still think is best viewed from a rearview mirror.

I went to work for *California* magazine, and soon became its editor-in-chief. I was twenty-nine. I remember wishing that I was a few years older, so that I could do the job smarter. I was wrong. I was smarter then, dumber now. (Anyone else feel that way? Maybe we can start a support group or something.) The job ended when a new owner wanted to bend some journalistic rules. I quit in protest, which now seems a bit melodramatic, but of course I'm dumber now, so maybe I got it right after all.

I spent the next year reading novels, playing tennis, and lying on beaches in the Yucatan, none of which paid particularly well. So when a softball buddy offered me a job in television, I accepted, and found myself at Warner Brothers as vice president of comedy development. Stayed five years, moving *Murphy Brown, China Beach,* and lots of lesser fare through the network development gauntlets. Quit to become a TV writer/producer — first for other people's shows (*The X-Files, Arliss,* etc.), and lately for myself, writing network pilot scripts.

In 1994, while working on a project that took me briefly to New York, I met an astonishingly beautiful woman named Ainslie Olsheim. One rainy night we talked so long over dinner that the restaurant's staff went home and said we could just let ourselves out. What I remember most about that night is how the depth of her heart and mind took my breath away. Within a week, I knew I wanted to marry her. Within a month, I had.

By Reunion time, Ainslie and I will be approaching our sixth wedding anniversary. She was a TV producer when I met her, but she later received her masters in psychology and now works as a psychotherapist. We live in

Los Angeles, but are increasingly restless there. We often talk about chucking it all and moving—in our latest fantasy, to Kauai. Or maybe to a small town in rural Massachusetts. We love New England, and fly there every year, to see Fenway in its twilight, to walk the streets of Cambridge. And I swear that every gawky and credulous Harvard kid that we pass on Plympton Street strikes me as exactly my age—which is why I find this Twenty-fifth Reunion stuff so disconcerting. Maybe I will have made my peace with it by June. If not, please come visit us in Kauai.

HOME: Los Angeles, CA   **OCCUPATION:** Television Writer; Producer   **BIRTHPLACE:** Los Angeles, CA   **SECONDARY SCHOOL:** Oakwood Secondary School, Los Angeles, CA   **YEARS AT COLLEGE:** 1971–76   **DEGREES:** A.B. '75 ('76)   **SPOUSE/PARTNER:** Ainslie March Olsheim, Sept. 20, 1994 (New York Univ. '89)   **SPOUSE'S OCCUPATION:** Psychotherapist   **COLLEGE ACTIVITIES:** *Harvard Crimson*, 1971–76

James Keefe: We are living well and happily in the San Francisco Bay Area and look forward to seeing old friends at the Reunion.

HOME: Lafayette, CA   **OCCUPATION:** Investor   **YEARS AT COLLEGE:** 1971–75   **DEGREES:** A.B., cum laude, '75; M.A. Stanford Univ. '77; M.B.A., ibid. '77   **SPOUSE/PARTNER:** Lorna Lee, Oct. 27, 1979   **CHILDREN:** Courtney, 1982; Cameron, 1987

John Charles Keller: A few good friends; a heavyweight degree; a handful of excellent classes; life's transition from Wigglesworth to Peabody Terrace — these are twenty-five-plus-year-old enduring memories. With three in college, "now" is predictable and reason for rejoicing! Excellent students, good athletes, and varied interests make parents proud. The rose of my life, mother of our children — others should be so blessed.

HOME: Davis, CA   **OCCUPATION:** Research Specialist (law enforcement)
SECONDARY SCHOOL: Pleasant Hill High School, Pleasant Hill, CA   **YEARS AT COLLEGE:** 1971–75   **DEGREES:** A.B. '75   **SPOUSE/PARTNER:** Catherine Lynn (Sacramento City Coll.)   **SPOUSE'S OCCUPATION:** Sign Language Interpreter (independent contractor)   **CHILDREN:** John Christopher, 1976; Julie, 1978; Lauren, 1981; David, 1984   **COLLEGE ACTIVITIES:** Frosh cross-country, fall 1971; frosh indoor track, winter 1971

Thomas Patrick Kenney: After graduation I spent two years at Notre Dame taking a masters in philosophy. At Harvard I was a major in psychology and social relations. I then taught four years at West Virginia State College. I was not happy and was neither surprised nor disappointed when I was let go.

I then worked with the mentally handicapped at an institution. Next I spent a semester in a theological seminary. Then in 1983, I was in the Washington, D.C. area with thirteen hundred dollars and no prospects. I was that close to being homeless. The stress of this triggered a psychotic episode and in due course I was diagnosed as paranoid schizophrenic. In the meantime I had found a job at Atlantic Research Corporation. That gave me insurance, until in 1986 when I was given disability. That ran out two years later and I got Social Security Disability Income (SSDI). But because I had never made any good money the SSDI was small, but not small enough to qualify for food stamps. However I did get a room in a housing complex or low-income housing as it is called. After ten years I got a HUD voucher and moved to an apartment that, while subsidized by HUD, isn't really in a complex.

Throughout all this, I maintained my interest in philosophy: Aristotle, Aquinas, Maritain, and the late scholastic commentators. My therapist helped me accept that I would never publish or teach. It's my hobby. I never married. I don't include a photo since my medication causes weight gain as a side-effect.

HOME: Naples, FL   **OCCUPATION:** Disabled (due to schizophrenia)   **BIRTHPLACE:** Sistersville, WV   **SECONDARY SCHOOL:** St. Joseph's School, Vienna, WV   **YEARS AT COLLEGE:** 1971–75   **DEGREES:** A.B., cum laude, '75; M.A., Univ. of Notre Dame '77

Daniel Jacob Kligler: "Never a dull moment" is a favorite answer of Israelis when asked to comment on life here, and it is very apt. Nothing is simple. The news is always in your face, and thousands of years of history are in your backyard—sometimes literally. When we dug our swimming pool a couple of years ago, we uncovered Roman columns. (Zippori, the sleepy farm village where we live, was the capital of Galilee and seat of the Sanhedrin eighteen hundred years ago.) When the Antiquities Authority found out, they came and took the columns away and cited me for digging without proper supervision.

Roberta and I moved to Israel in 1979, shortly after finishing graduate school, and we have been here ever since. Our four children were all born here. Our oldest, Eitan, is doing his three years of compulsory army service in an elite infantry unit, including a stint in Lebanon—more news in our face and sleepless nights. Our daughter, Talia, is in her senior year of high school and getting ready for her own army service. Perhaps by the time our younger boys, Netanel and Yosef, reach army age, we will have peace.

My news is that I recently finished law school and will take the Israeli bar exam shortly. Several years ago, after nearly fifteen years in the electronics industry here, I was ready for a change. I accepted an offer from a patent law firm whose client I had been in the past to train with them as a patent agent. The new job turned out far better than I could have expected. There is such a flowering of high-tech industry and invention here, fueled by the enthusiasm of the U.S. capital markets, that patent work for me has been like being a child in a candy shop—and getting paid to taste the goods. I decided to get the law degree in order to fill out my credentials, and I did it somehow while working full-time. It is good to have it behind me.

For the next twenty-five years, I look forward most to seeing our children grow up and, God willing, raising their own families. It would be all right with me, though, if the next quarter century were a bit less interesting than the past one.

HOME: Moshav Zippori, Israel **OCCUPATION:** Patent Attorney (patent agent) **BIRTHPLACE:** New York, NY **SECONDARY SCHOOL:** White Plains High School, White Plains, NY **YEARS AT COLLEGE:** 1972–75 **DEGREES:** A.B., summa cum laude, '75; M.S., Stanford Univ. '76; Ph.D., ibid. '79; LL.B., Univ. of Manchester '99 **SPOUSE/PARTNER:** Roberta Bell, 1973 (Brandeis Univ. '75) **SPOUSE'S OCCUPATION:** Executive Director. Project Oren, Oranim Teachers' Seminary **CHILDREN:** Eitan, 1979; Talia, 1982; Netanel, 1985; Yosef, 1988 **HARVARD/RADCLIFFE SIBLINGS:** Benjamin Eli Kligler '82 **COLLEGE ACTIVITIES:** Hillel Foundation

Mitchell A. Kline: Like many of my classmates, I pursued a law career after college. I seriously considered entering the political arena, as a candidate. However, in 1983, after five years as a prosecutor, and a better look at the dark side of politics, I decided to join my dad in a thriving business.

In 1995 we went out of business, not only because I was not as entrepreneurial as Bill Gates, and I reentered the legal profession. I was selected to serve as an administrative law judge with the Illinois Human Rights Commission, which involved deciding and mediating employment discrimination cases. I found it very satisfying when I was successful in persuading the parties to settle their case. In January of 1999 I became a sole practitioner concentrating in labor, employment, and property tax law as well as mediation.

Periodically, I still think about being a candidate. However, I do not have a desire to take action presently because of the exorbitant amount of time required away from my family and the invasion of privacy.

I have been married eleven years. We have three children: Ari, age nine; Richard, age seven; and Jacqueline, age five. I regret not taking the courses at Harvard on marriage and parenting. Thus, I have been forced to learn about these complex subjects mostly from experience. Although I may not graduate summa cum laude in these areas, I have learned a huge amount. My wife has helped make me a better person as she is a very unselfish person. I enjoyed coaching my two sons in Little League this past summer. They each were very proud of me, for some strange reason, and I loved how they and their teammates responded to my encouragement. My daughter has a beautiful laugh, and I enjoy triggering her laughter.

I am looking forward to spending some time with many of you old people in June.

HOME: Highland Park, IL   **OCCUPATION:** Attorney (private practice labor and employment law)   **BIRTHPLACE:** Harvey, IL   **SECONDARY SCHOOL:** Bloom Township High School, Chicago Heights, IL   **YEARS AT COLLEGE:** 1971–75   **DEGREES:** A.B., cum laude, '75; J.D., Indiana Univ. '78   **SPOUSE/PARTNER:** Cherie Berzon, Oct. 1, 1988 (Univ. of Miami '78)   **SPOUSE'S OCCUPATION:** Employment and Education Consultant. URHIRED X (works from home)   **CHILDREN:** Ari, 1990; Richard, 1992; Jacqueline, 1995 **COLLEGE ACTIVITIES:** Phillips Brooks House; Hillel; intramural sports; elected to a student-faculty committee

Ellen Cooper Klyce: Until I was twenty-five, I was the most secular person I knew. My life was about my own vision and my desire to achieve results as soon as possible. Immediately after graduation, I joined Westinghouse Broadcasting Company in a highly competitive and desirable management trainee position. By the time I was twenty-three I had achieved some corporate recognition and won a few awards and was toying with either Harvard Business School or a Fulbright fellowship to Nigeria as the next glamour stop on my journey. Instead I had a manic episode, and spent several weeks at McLean Hospital. In 1979, with a tempered view of life, I got a great job in the Harvard Development Office, working on the College's capital campaign. In my spare time I would look through Twenty-fifth Reunion Reports for interesting personal revelations. Those three years mattered; I learned some alchemy about raising money. In the summer of 1981, I innocently attended my high school reunion which was crashed by a man who turned out to be the love of my life. It was a sign when he produced a pocketknife and fixed the broken pinball machine at the party after Don Simon's wedding. Karen Gordon Mills was supposed to be my chaperone, but she abandoned me and Brig offered to take me home. Which he did. Since then we've had three children — each fascinating, inspiring, and humbling. For twelve of my eighteen years back in Memphis, I worked at Memphis College of Art, mostly as director of development. Now I have attained the dreaded designation of the unemployed matron: community volunteer. I think I prefer community promoter. Many days I careen through carpools and lists without paying enough attention. But now and then there are moments of wonder. Life is amazing. I actually live with a sense of community and connection. There are many people I cherish and I get to be with them. Every once in a while I think I get it. Mostly I feel grateful.

HOME: Memphis, TN **OCCUPATION:** Friend **BIRTHPLACE:** Memphis, TN
SECONDARY SCHOOL: White Station High School, Memphis, TN **YEARS AT COLLEGE:** 1971–75 **SPOUSE/PARTNER:** Brig Klyce, Jan. 23, 1982 (Princeton '70)
SPOUSE'S OCCUPATION: President. Acorn Enterprises **CHILDREN:** Polly, 1983; Walter, 1988; Rebecca, 1993

Scott Gregory Knudson: At this point, the simple and undramatic seem most reliable, the laughter of children, the comfort of a good marriage, and the loyalty of good friends. In 1988 Elisa and I moved to Minnesota and now have a family of four children. Nothing else has been so demanding nor so rewarding.

HOME: Saint Paul, MN   **OCCUPATION:** Attorney. Briggs & Morgan PA   **BIRTHPLACE:** Minneapolis, MN   **SECONDARY SCHOOL:** Albert Lea Senior High, Albert Lea, MN   **YEARS AT COLLEGE:** 1971–75   **DEGREES:** A.B., cum laude, '75; J.D, Univ. of Minnesota '80   **SPOUSE/PARTNER:** Elisa Pacini, Sept. 5, 1987 (Mount Holyoke Coll. '82)   **SPOUSE'S OCCUPATION:** Homemaker   **CHILDREN:** Peter, 1989; Amelia, 1991; Sonja, 1995; Mari, 1999   **COLLEGE ACTIVITIES:** Outing Club; freshman crew; intramural football, crew, track; Winthrop House Drama and Film Societies; Phillips Brooks House; Small Claims Court and Advisory Services

Martin Koehler: After a riotous period lived in Boston as a rolling stone, I passed enough programs at the University of Massachusetts at Boston and at Boston University to settle down to teaching. I have co-written three books, in the field of psychology. I have two girlfriends, neither live-in. My parents, thank god, are still healthy, though divorced. I listen to WHRB often; I support the Charles River Watershed Association, the Boston Adult Literacy Fund, the City-Wide Friends of the Boston Public Library, the National Geographic Society, the Police Olympics, and the Police Activities League.

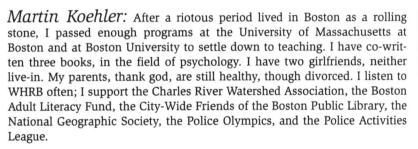

HOME: Cambridge, MA

Gary Kollin: Eleven years ago when I married Connie, life truly first began. Among her other attributes, she opened my eyes to the wonderful world of parenthood when we became foster parents and eventually adopted four of the seventeen children we cared for over the years. Alissa and Jeremy are both seven and are not biologically related; Nicholas is four and his biological brother Joel is three. They are bright, adorable, and wonderful; and that is especially true because they are not biologically related to me.

Since college, I worked as a computer programmer and went to law school at the University of Miami. I have been a state prosecutor, a state public defender, and a private practitioner. In 1993, I argued the case of *Smith v. United States,* 508 U.S. 223 (1993), before the United States Supreme Court. While the thrust of my practice remains in the criminal law arena, I also handle police misconduct cases and won a class action suit against the local sheriff for post-acquittal detention.

Reminiscing on the times back at Harvard, the many hours I spent playing poker in "The Poker Room" in Currier House allow me to now be a raconteur relating stories of times spent going head to head against Bill Gates in poker games. Unfortunately, I was not able to multiply my poker winnings to same degree he did. Perhaps those of us who return for the Twenty-fifth can join together for a game of high-low and discuss the big pots (and other big fish stories) we missed over the years.

HOME: Davie, FL   OCCUPATION: Attorney (private practice)   BIRTHPLACE: Miami Beach, FL   SECONDARY SCHOOL: Miami Beach Senior High School, Miami Beach, FL
YEARS AT COLLEGE: 1971–75   DEGREES: A.B. '75; J.D., Univ. of Miami '79
SPOUSE/PARTNER: Constance Marie Grande, Feb. 4, 1989   SPOUSE'S OCCUPATION: Homemaker Extraordinaire   CHILDREN: Alissa Elizabeth, 1993; Jeremy Sol, 1993; Nicholas Anthony, 1995; Joel Vincent, 1997   COLLEGE ACTIVITIES: Currier House poker team

Duane August Kolterman: During the summer following my graduation from Harvard in 1975, I took a course in tropical botany in southern Florida. In the fall of 1975 I began my graduate studies in Botany in Madison, Wisconsin, where I spent ten very eventful years. Three years after obtaining my Ph.D., I moved to Mayagüez, Puerto Rico, to assume an assistant professorship in the Department of Biology at the University of Puerto Rico, Mayagüez Campus. I began teaching in Spanish in my second year, was promoted to associate professor after my third year, received tenure after my fifth year, and was promoted to professor after my eighth year. I am now almost halfway to retirement, and quite content with my job and life in Puerto Rico. I was associate director of my department for two and a half years, and have participated actively in the Curriculum Committee of the Faculty of Arts and Sciences and the ATLANTEA Project of the University of Puerto Rico, which is devoted to promoting academic collaboration in the Caribbean. I have also done choral singing and participated in the Horticultural Society of Western Puerto Rico. I do not return to the States very often; a trip to attend the XVI International Botanical Congress in Saint Louis this summer was my longest visit since I moved to Puerto Rico. I do, however, travel around the Caribbean, particularly to Cuba and the Dominican Republic. At Harvard, I started out in chemistry, then switched to Latin and Portuguese, and finally finished up in biology; I feel that I have been able to put everything I learned as an undergraduate to good use. The Twenty-fifth will be my first Harvard Class Reunion, and I look forward to reestablishing contact with old friends.

HOME: Mayagüez, PR   OCCUPATION: Professor. Departamento de Biologia, Universidad de Puerto Rico   BIRTHPLACE: Wilmington, DE   SECONDARY SCHOOL: Unionville High School, Unionville, PA   YEARS AT COLLEGE: 1971–75   DEGREES: A.B., cum laude, '75; M.S., Univ. of Wisconsin, Madison '78; Ph.D., ibid., '82

Jeffrey Burnett Kopp: After college, I went to medical school, where I met Susan Pisano, who became my wife in 1985. I trained clinically in internal medicine in Seattle. I came to realize that I was more academically inclined than I had realized, and found a reawakened childhood interest in natural history and science. Susan and I moved to Washington, D.C., to allow me to pursue training in laboratory research, a career change I had never expected. I now work to understand how viruses, both known viruses such as HIV and unknown or unrecognized viruses, damage the kidney, and to devise better treatments for kidney disease. I have a laboratory at the NIH and also see research patients; for me it is the best of both worlds.

We adopted our son Andrew in 1996, after a long wait on our part. He is teaching us, and hopefully we are teaching him, how to love and create a family and appreciate the world as if it were always new. As a family we enjoy hiking and fishing, and spend several weeks a year at a family cabin in the mountains in Gunnison County, Colorado. The cabin is at timberline, with a nearby spring for water and a wood stove for heat and a generator for electricity, and is a wonderful escape. My main exercise is squash, which I have played at least three times weekly for the past fifteen years, with barely perceptible improvement. We have become active in the Episcopal church and as we approach the millennium, I am teaching middle schoolers about the past two millennial turns.

HOME: Bethesda, MD   OCCUPATION: Senior Investigator. National Institutes of Health (medical research)   SECONDARY SCHOOL: Belmont Hill School, Belmont, MA   YEARS AT COLLEGE: 1971–75   DEGREES: A.B., magna cum laude, '75; M. D., Univ. of Pennsylvania '80   SPOUSE/PARTNER: Susan Marie Pisano, July 27, 1985 (Chestnut Hill Coll. '71)   SPOUSE'S OCCUPATION: Communications Director. American Association of Health Plans   CHILDREN: Andrew Emerson, 1996   HARVARD/RADCLIFFE SIBLINGS: Bradford Burnett Kopp '73   COLLEGE ACTIVITIES: Outing Club, 1971–73; Delphic Club, 1973–75; Eliot House crew, 1974–75

Peter Austin Koretsky: Life after graduation has been everything I hoped it would be—fun, meaningful, challenging, rewarding, and with a modicum of sadness and grief. The biggest change for me is that the things I used to take for granted I now treasure—my health and that of my loved ones, love, and the ability to make myself happy and bring happiness to the lives of those around me.

I actually graduated a year behind the Class because I accepted a position at the *Anniston, Alabama Star* in March 1975. They later fired me when they realized I had dropped out of college to work there. After returning to Harvard to graduate I moved to Chicago, where I worked in various capacities in the commodities futures markets. I also worked a variety of jobs in a hospital and took pre-med courses at night.

After medical school I trained at Emory to be a gastroenterologist. I then moved to a quiet beach community in east central Florida, where I joined a small multispecialty group practice. I became chief of medicine at our local hospital and board chairman of the group during a phase of rapid growth.

Presently I spend most of my time working, raising my two young children, and enjoying the unexpected circumstance of being a forty-five-year-old single male. I live on the beach, drive a convertible, run, play chess and the piano, garden, and take care of my kids. Life is great and I'm very happy. I treasure my Harvard education.

HOME: Melbourne Beach, FL   **OCCUPATION:** Physician   **BIRTHPLACE:** Boston, MA
SECONDARY SCHOOL: Brookline High School, Brookline, MA   **YEARS AT COLLEGE:**
1971–76   **DEGREES:** A.B. '75 ('76); M.D., Boston Univ. '83; M.B.A., Florida Inst. of
Technology '99   **CHILDREN:** Alexander James, 1990; Brenna Afton, 1992   **COLLEGE
ACTIVITIES:** Chess Club and team, 1971–75; Democrat's Club, 1973–74; Winthrop House
government, 1973–74

Joseph A. Kovacs: Twenty-five years later: I'm married (fourteen years) with five boys, ages six (twins) to twelve. I'm a physician, graduate of Cornell Medical School and spent seven years in Manhattan after college (seems like ages ago). I've been at the National Institutes of Health for the past seventeen years (hard to believe), since coming to the D.C. area for a two- to three-year stint while I decided what I wanted to do with my life. I've spent that time on AIDS research, primarily clinical studies of immunotherapeutics, but with a basic research laboratory effort studying Pneumocystis carinii (causes pneumonia). My greatest joy is without question my family. Carol, my wife (and best friend/seer/advisor) retired after twenty years in the military/public health Service to take care of our boys after the twins were born. They're a handful (they're boys!) but are our lives. Our free time: chauffeuring for soccer, basketball, etc. We live in Potomac, with a view of horse farms, on a quiet street that's great for kids. We've just started taking family vacations to go skiing or to the beach. I've not kept in touch with many of the Class of '75, but talk to Jeff Ferry, and my medical school roommate, Tom Lee. Doug Dolginow is a neighbor and friend. I remember with fondness Hollis, the roommate club (Adams House) and the *Crimson*. Photography was my pas-

sion then but now is a rarely indulged pastime. I'm a Mac addict, Yankee fan (since '59) and have become a Redskins fan ('82). My primary goal in life: to raise our kids to do well, work hard, know right from wrong, and to be happy (and successful).

HOME: Potomac, MD   **OCCUPATION:** Senior Investigator. Critical Care Medicine Dept., Clinical Center, National Institutes of Health   **SECONDARY SCHOOL:** The Kew-Forest School, Forest Hills, NY   **YEARS AT COLLEGE:** 1971–75   **DEGREES:** A.B., magna cum laude '75; M.D., Cornell '79   **SPOUSE/PARTNER:** Carol A. Karwoski, July 20, 1985 (Univ. of Maryland '76)   **SPOUSE'S OCCUPATION:** Retired Public Health Service Officer; Mother   **CHILDREN:** Joseph, 1987; Stephen, 1990; Michael, 1991; Nicholas and William, 1992 (twins)   **COLLEGE ACTIVITIES:** *Harvard Crimson,* 1971–75

Susan Scheinberg Kristol: The year 2000 will be a busy one for my family. Bill and I will celebrate our twenty-fifth wedding anniversary; Rebecca, our oldest, will graduate from high school and go to college; our daughter Anne will be completing her first year of high school; and our son Joe will celebrate his Bar Mitzvah. Finally, because Bill's activities revolve around national politics, I know that he will be working nonstop and traveling full-time.

After graduating from Harvard, I stayed on to complete my Ph.D. in classical philology. I married Bill Kristol '73, Ph.D. '79, the December after graduation: For a while we both pursued academic careers. I taught Greek and Latin as an assistant professor at the University of Pennsylvania and Brandeis, while Bill taught political theory at Penn and then the Kennedy School at Harvard. It was lots of fun.

In 1985, we moved to Washington, D.C., temporarily — we thought — so that Bill could be a special assistant at the Department of Education while I took a year of leave to study ancient comedy. We found Washington more exciting than we had expected, and we ended up resigning from our academic positions and moving here permanently.

Since that time I have been immersed in the world of the volunteer mom, and have found enormous satisfaction learning to do things I never learned in all my years at Harvard — editing a newsletter, teaching art, planning a breakfast for seven hundred, giving a sermon, organizing a fun fair, and so on. I have been a Junior Great Books leader, a PTA president, and the president of my synagogue sisterhood. Sometimes I think about going back to teaching Latin, but I'm a little reluctant just yet to give up the flexibility of my current schedule for a "steady job."

HOME: McLean, VA   OCCUPATION: Housewife   BIRTHPLACE: New York, NY   SEC-
ONDARY SCHOOL: Scarsdale High School, Scarsdale, NY   YEARS AT COLLEGE:
1971–75   DEGREES: A.B., summa cum laude, '75; Ph.D. '81   SPOUSE/PARTNER: William
Kristol, Dec. 28, 1975 (Harvard '73; Ph.D. '79)   SPOUSE'S OCCUPATION: Editor;
Publisher. *The Weekly Standard*   CHILDREN: Rebecca, 1982; Anne, 1985; Joseph, 1987
COLLEGE ACTIVITIES: Harvard-Radcliffe choruses, 1971–73

Thomas Charles Krystofiak: Much has changed at the last
minute. A software firm I helped found in 1984 was acquired five years ago
by a much larger company. Not only did this not make me a millionaire, the
big boys decided last month that our entire office was expendable, and I am
now without a job. But this is all, as they say, perfect. I have wanted, more
than anything, to spend time as a writer, yet my practical side could not see
how to make that happen. But now, per force, I am free—and I will, for a
time, resist the pull of the commercial world. I am just now home from three
weeks in India, in spiritual pilgrimage in the north. And now I set about to
face the dreams and demons of "my true calling," and will discover what it
is I really have to say.

I have let my hair grow even longer than in 1975, and for much the same
reasons. Midlife crisis? Feels more like midlife crucible. The tests keep getting deeper, the subjects richer and more mysterious.

Diana and I have been married for sixteen years, and we continue to surprise ourselves with our resilience and our obstinacy, our blindness and our
vision, our capacity for growth. Our daughter Anjali is ten, and she is like a
beautiful pearl. We have lived in Fairfield, Iowa, since 1983, a quiet, yet
strangely cosmopolitan farm town that holds one of the world's largest communities of teachers and practitioners of transcendental meditation, the profound and simple value of which continues to endure.

Harvard seems far, far away.

HOME: Fairfield, IA   OCCUPATION: Blissfully Unemployed   BIRTHPLACE: Milwaukee,
WI   SECONDARY SCHOOL: Marquette University High School, Milwaukee, WI
YEARS AT COLLEGE: 1971–75   DEGREES: A.B., magna cum laude, '75; M. A., Cambridge
Univ., '77   SPOUSE/PARTNER: Diana Evrard, Sept. 3, 1983   CHILDREN: Anjali, 1989

Charles Edward Kuntz: Unlike many of my law graduate colleagues from the late 1970s, I'm still in the law business with a private firm. Since 1996, I have been a partner in the Atlanta office of Holland & Knight, a megafirm with nine hundred-plus lawyers in sixteen offices. In recent years I have been practicing commercial real estate law, although I'm fully prepared to resume my career as a loan workout specialist when the inevitable downturn in commercial real estate occurs. I survived my midlife crisis relatively unscathed with the most obvious symptoms being an obsession with weight machines (which at one point had me approaching the dimensions of a human square) and various forms of facial hair (increasingly gray). Kathy retired from her twenty-year career at Union Carbide in 1997 to stay home with our boys and it's the best decision we ever made. Philip and Charlie have prospered under her tutelage and Kathy has spent much rewarding time in various volunteer pursuits, mostly involving church and school. Fortunately, both boys are excellent athletes (Philip is a ranked tennis player and baseball player and Charlie is an accomplished swimmer and diver) which has eased my transition from sports participant to coach and occasionally overzealous sports parent. Meanwhile oldest child Audrey is a senior and is off to college in the fall. Assuming I survive Y2K (I couldn't even get the Class Report Website to work), we'll be at the Twenty-fifth Reunion and hopefully the Fiftieth as well.

HOME: Dunwoody, GA   OCCUPATION: Partner. Holland & Knight LLP (law firm)
BIRTHPLACE: Danbury, CT   SECONDARY SCHOOL: John Jay High School, Cross River, NY   YEARS AT COLLEGE: 1971–75   DEGREES: A.B., cum laude, '75; J.D., Emory Univ. '78 SPOUSE/PARTNER: Katherine Carr (West Virginia Univ. '76)   SPOUSE'S OCCUPATION: Stay-at-Home Mom   CHILDREN: Audrey N. Kuntz, 1982; Philip Carr Kuntz, 1989; Charles Edward Kuntz, Jr., 1991   COLLEGE ACTIVITIES: Freshman football, 1971; Rugby Club, 1973–75

Seth Kupferberg: Soon after graduation I read *The Charterhouse of Parma*, Stendhal's great novel set during the period of reaction that followed the French Revolution. The book's mix of concern and cynicism about political life, near-despair about history and confidence, almost gaiety, about love's power for individuals, remain vivid to me, and time has solved one of the book's mysteries. I was puzzled by one character, the humane, liberal advisor working for a petty despot. Why would he do that? Didn't he know that things would change? The answer now seems obvious. Twenty-five years is a long time to wait for change.

I think we've been living through a disheartening period like the one Stendhal wrote about. I'm not complaining—I've been blessed in my wife, in our wonderful children, and even in my work (I hope to do good work and more writing in the future, too)—but I find it baffling that visions of widening kindness and respectful cooperation should be so enveloped in the orb of greed and money. I've tried to be true to the dreams of our youth, which I'm sure will one day again be fashionable and which in the meantime, Jeanie and I try to pass on to our children. As a lawyer I represent unions, which for all their faults, stand for the promise that people can reason together and that real self-interest includes mutual care. I've argued unsuccessfully in the U.S. Supreme Court and smuggled a slice of cake to a day-care worker unjustly jailed at a demonstration. As a father, I marvel at Samuel's and Sarah's generosity, creativity, and high spirits, love for each other, and at-homeness in the world. I hope they are never stifled or worn down.

HOME: Larchmont, NY   **OCCUPATION:** Lawyer. Sipser, Weinstock, Harper & Dorn, LLP   **BIRTHPLACE:** New York, NY   **SECONDARY SCHOOL:** Forest Hills High School, New York, NY   **YEARS AT COLLEGE:** 1971–75   **DEGREES:** A.B., magna cum laude, '75; J.D. '79   **SPOUSE/PARTNER:** Jean Grumet, June 26, 1983 (City Coll. of New York '73)   **SPOUSE'S OCCUPATION:** Lawyer; Full-Time Mother (currently)   **CHILDREN:** Samuel, 1994; Sarah, 1994   **COLLEGE ACTIVITIES:** *Harvard Crimson*

Philip Ivo Kuttner: Oops! Back in the music world again—but in an ancillary position this time. Writing and editing supertitles for the San Francisco Opera (SFO) is tremendous fun. Where else could I get paid to attend opening nights featuring some of my favorite singers? My greatest accomplishment in the past year has been to restore the use of the word "queen" (banned for fifteen years) in SFO's supertitles.

I am still conducting for North Bay Opera in Fairfield, which gives me great pleasure. Our recent production of *Don Giovanni* surpassed even the brilliant Loeb production I remember so vividly from the 1970s.

As I approach the age of fifty, I am beginning to feel grown-up. It's an unfamiliar feeling, but a gratifying one. At the same time, I am more curious and excited than ever about what the future may bring. After seeing the Berlin Wall fall and apartheid crumble, who knows? We may even live to see universal health care in this country!

HOME: San Francisco, CA   **OCCUPATION:** Supertitle Editor; Assistant Musical Administrator. San Francisco Opera   **BIRTHPLACE:** Washington, DC   **YEARS AT COLLEGE:** 1971–75   **DEGREES:** A.B., cum laude, '75; M.M. Peabody Inst. '78; M.M., San Francisco Conservatory of Music '87

David Alan Laskin: Remembering the waves of pure terror I felt every time I had to write a college paper, I'm amazed that I ended up becoming a professional writer. The best part is that I get to write about pretty much what I choose. Recently, this has included literary biography (I've done two group portraits of American writers — *A Common Life*, about literary friendships, and *Partisans*, about the marriages and politics of the New York intellectuals) and cultural histories of weather (*Braving the Elements* and *Rains All the Time*). A high point: flying into Hurricane Bonnie to do a story for *Smithsonian* magazine on how the Weather Channel gears up for a major "event."

My three daughters — Emily, now a high school freshman, and eleven-year-old, non-identical twins Sarah and Alice — are going great guns, careening through school, loving team sports (where did that come from?), memorizing every hip-hop song that makes the pop charts. High points: watching Emily ski nimbly down a bump run that had just turned my knees to Jell-O; seeing Sarah and Alice finesse a soccer ball down a wet green field on their "select" team; convincing all three girls to take Latin; camping on Mount Rainier on a perfect early September weekend; growing enough lettuce in my very own yard to keep the family in greens from April to August. Kate, my wife and soul mate and comrade-in-arms, pines for our "real" home — New York — but so far, six years in, Seattle is fine by me — even the weather.

Where does Harvard fit in? I think, looking back, that what I really learned there was how to learn. My life as a writer has been a series of liberal educations — natural history (why didn't I take "rocks for jocks"?!), literary history, meteorology, swatches of psychology, and botany. The only difference is that now I get paid for it — though pay is a relative term. Anyway, if I fail to appear at the Twenty-fifth, greetings to all.

HOME: Seattle, WA **OCCUPATION:** Writer **BORN:** New York, N.Y. **SECONDARY SCHOOL:** Senior High, Great Neck, NY **YEARS AT COLLEGE:** 1971–75 **DEGREES:** A.B., magna cum laude, '75; M.A., Oxford Univ. '77 **SPOUSE/PARTNER:** Kate O'Neill, April 17, 1982 (Stanford Univ. '75) **SPOUSE'S OCCUPATION:** Law Professor. Univ. of Washington **CHILDREN:** Emily, 1985; Sarah and Alice, 1987 (twins)

Thomas Henry Lee, Jr.: If, at graduation, someone had told me that I would enter the new millennium surrounded by dark, lovely, and mysterious women, I would have been skeptical. However, that is the way things have worked out. Upstairs, my wife, Soheyla Gharib, is working on geometry problems with my eleven-year-old daughter, Simm. I can hear our, nine-year-old, Sabrina in the next room, reading *Amelia Bedelia* to our six-year-old, Ariana.

Except for lonely times like Super Bowl Sunday, life in this environment suits me fine. Soheyla and I are both children of immigrants who came to the U.S. from Iran and China, respectively, in the late 1940s. During our internal medicine training at Peter Bent Brigham Hospital, we realized we were both from the interface of an old culture and American life. Our three daughters are the only Iranian-Chinese children we have ever seen, and give new meaning to the phrase "hybrid vigor."

My work life was initially focused on research, but today it is more of an all-out scramble just to make the health care system work. I am the chief medical officer of the physician network started by Brigham and Women's and Massachusetts General Hospitals. In this role (and outside of it), I find myself among a minority of physicians who defend managed care. Most of my work is aimed at developing systems, financial and otherwise, that improve care or at least make it more efficient. I need my medical background, of course, but I also find myself calling upon skills I first learned at the *Harvard Crimson* or during long meals at the Adams House dining hall.

Like most others from '75 with whom I remain in touch, I struggle to find the right balance between the work I love and the family I love even more. I may not have it right, but there is no question that the struggle is worthwhile.

HOME: Milton, MA   **OCCUPATION:** Associate Professor of Medicine. Harvard Medical School; Medical Director. Partners Community Health Care, Inc   **BIRTHPLACE:** Schenectady, NY   **SECONDARY SCHOOL:** Nether Providence High School, Wallford, PA   **YEARS AT COLLEGE:** 1971–75   **DEGREES:** A.B., magna cum laude, '75; M.E.P. '87   **SPOUSE/PARTNER:** Soheyla Dana Gharib, 1986 (Case Western Reserve Univ. '75)   **SPOUSE'S OCCUPATION:** Medical Director. Women's Health Center, Brigham and Women's Hospital, Boston, MA   **CHILDREN:** Simm, 1987; Sabrina, 1989; Ariana, 1993   **HARVARD/RADCLIFFE SIBLINGS:** William Frank Lee '72; Richard Theodore Lee '79   **COLLEGE ACTIVITIES:** *Harvard Crimson*, 1972–75

Royal Willis Leith: A year out of college and halfway through a two-year secular degree at Harvard Divinity School, I persuaded Mary Joan Winn to marry me. We met at the beginning of freshman week, when I was a junior and she was a freshman, and we have been together ever since. Though I must be among the least accomplished of my classmates, I count myself one of the most blessed for my marriage and all that it has brought me.

A little graduate school sufficed to convince me that I did not desire a lot more. So I abandoned ambitions of a doctorate in English and returned to an earlier and more modest goal: teaching high school. In this too I made a fortunate decision. Although I have often chafed at the workload, the pathetic compensation, and the obscurity, I believe that I am doing what I do best, in a profession that gives me daily opportunities to serve others.

I began teaching at Governor Dummer Academy, where I somehow figured out how to teach without the aid of formal mentors or any supervision. My first year was the most difficult of my life, but I discovered that I had a tremendous capacity for hard work, a capacity that I wish I had discovered earlier.

Mary Joan meanwhile began a doctorate program in Harvard's Near Eastern Languages and Civilizations program. Because of her long commute I sought employment closer to Boston and ended up at Buckingham Browne & Nichols, where I am now in my twenty-first year on the English faculty.

Long summer vacations and considerable professional autonomy have enabled me to broaden my interests in several rewarding areas. Among the most notable: accompanying Mary Joan on two Harvard-affiliated archaeological excavations in Jordan; advising BB&N's student newspaper for fourteen years and raising it from very little to national prominence; developing an interest in American nineteenth-century art history and becoming an expert in a small corner in the field, lecturing in Florence and London and writing one monograph and several articles; learning to play the bassoon; and teaching an innovative art history course based primarily in museums and other off-campus sites.

Though I welcomed early marriage, I shied away from early parenthood, but today I find much of my greatest joy in our two children, Billy and Tom. They have been playing cello and violin, respectively, for several years, and the significant role that parents play in guiding young musicians has been one of the most profound teaching experiences of my life. Most important, Billy and Tom have lively minds and kind hearts.

I remember well a moment early in freshman year when my good friend Michael announced his revelation that our Twenty-fifth Reunion would occur in the year 2000. Having spent almost all of the intervening years in Cambridge, I feel in some respects that I have never left Harvard. Though I will be otherwise occupied during Reunion week, I look back upon college years as some of my best, and I am grateful to the friends who helped make them so.

HOME: Cambridge, MA   OCCUPATION: English and Art History Teacher. Buckingham,
Browne & Nichols School   BIRTHPLACE: Boston, MA   SECONDARY SCHOOL: Noble
and Greenough School, Dedham, MA   YEARS AT COLLEGE: 1971–75   DEGREES: A.B.,
cum laude, '75; M.T.S. '77   SPOUSE/PARTNER: Mary Joan Winn, Sept. 4, 1976 (Harvard
'77, A.M. '83, Ph.D '90)   SPOUSE'S OCCUPATION: Professor of Religion. Stonehill
College   CHILDREN: William Winn Leith, 1991; Thomas Bell Leith, 1993   COLLEGE
ACTIVITIES: Harvard University Choir, 1971–77

Brad Edward Leithauser: What I liked best about our Tenth Reunion
was seeing how wrong I'd been about everyone. We'll never again know as
much as we knew at twenty-two, thank goodness — an age when the future
paths of friends and classmates look fixed and legible. At the Tenth, it was
cheering to see that some Class ne'er-do-well had done so well he'd made
mega-zillions; that the straitlaced, necktie-loving kid who'd lived down the
hall, so clearly bound for Wall Street, had become a beachcomber.

It seems my own path has been pretty predictable, though. I wrote
steadily in college, and I'm writing steadily today. I've published nine books
in all: four novels, four collections of poetry, and a selection of essays. My
wife, Mary Jo Salter ('76), has also been filling a bookshelf: four collections
of poetry and a children's book.

Like most freelancers, I've bounced around. I was *Time* magazine's theater critic for a year, and served for a semester in the University of Iceland's
English Department. We've also lived in Japan, Italy, England, and France.
Travel has been facilitated by grants — including a Guggenheim Fellowship
and a MacArthur Award.

We have two daughters, Emily (sixteen) and Hilary (eleven). To my great
dismay, the Commonwealth of Massachusetts recently deemed Emily road-
worthy. She's been given her learner's permit, and I've spent hours circling
the parking lots of Mount Holyoke College — where, when I'm not nervously
giving driver's education instruction, I teach English.

I've mostly devoted the last few years to what I hope won't prove to be a
titanic folly: a novel-in-verse about an imaginary turn-of-the-century lepi-
dopterist (butterflies). Though I don't quite see how it will be turned into a
TV miniseries, working on it has been (as my eleven-year-old would say)
"funner" than anything.

HOME: Amherst, MA   OCCUPATION: Emily Dickinson Lecturer in the Humanities.
English Dept., Mount Holyoke College   BIRTHPLACE: Detroit, MI   SECONDARY
SCHOOL: Cranbrook School for Boys, Bloomfield Hills, MI   YEARS AT COLLEGE:
1971–75   DEGREES: A.B., magna cum laude, '75; J.D. '80   SPOUSE/PARTNER: Mary Jo
Salter, Aug. 2, 1980 (Harvard '76)   SPOUSE'S OCCUPATION: Emily Dickinson Lecturer in
the Humanities. Mount Holyoke College   CHILDREN: Emily, 1983; Hilary, 1988

Sara Margery Lewis: Still turning 'round the wheel of life. Since 1991, I have been on the faculty at Tufts University (a wonderful institution), where I teach biostatistics and evolutionary ecology, mentor undergraduate and graduate students, and have an inordinate fondness for doing research on the sex lives of seahorses and beetles. I feel extremely lucky that I continue to find amazement in my daily work, and rejoice in those tiny glimpses into the sacred depths that living underwater and nights with fireflies have given me. I share the delights of love and family (and *Deep Space Nine*) with Thomas, two great kids, Ben and Zack, and Iguaçu the Wonder Pup. Wandering around Cambridge I find myself haunting our old stomping grounds, although nothing will ever be able to replace Elsie's Reubens. I'm looking forward to meeting friends old and new at the Y2K Reunion.

HOME: Lincoln, MA   **OCCUPATION:** Associate Professor. Dept. of Biology, Tufts University   **BIRTHPLACE:** New Haven, CT   **SECONDARY SCHOOL:** Amity Regional Senior High, Woodbridge, CT   **YEARS AT COLLEGE:** 1971–76   **DEGREES:** A.B., magna cum laude '75 ('76); Ph.D., Duke Univ. '84   **SPOUSE/PARTNER:** Thomas Michel, 1984 (Harvard '77; M.D., Duke Univ. '84; Ph.D., ibid. '84)   **SPOUSE'S OCCUPATION:** Cardiologist. Brigham and Women's Hospital   **CHILDREN:** Benjamin Lewis Michel, 1988; Zachary Elias Michel, 1991

Paul Kimberley Ling: I am pleased that Joy and I are entering our twenty-fourth year of marriage. Apparently we were lucky in love. Our daughter, Alla, will be seventeen years old and entering her senior year of high school. Alla is our pride and joy. She is "deaf" (don't call her hearing-impaired) and proud of it. She is bright enough to apply to Harvard College.

I love being a clinical psychologist. My specialty is working with post-traumatic stress disorder and utilizing clinical hypnosis. A great deal of my daily work is with good old-fashioned, psychoanalytic psychotherapy. To have survived as a private-practice shrink is no small accomplishment.

My passion has been fighting the HMO and managed care movement in health and mental health. I am a leader in several grassroots organizations including the Ad Hoc Committee to Defend Health Care. I have gotten quite good at political organizing and in working with the media. Whether it is CBS's *60 Minutes* or the *Boston Globe*, I have had a hand in bringing managed care abuses to the public's attention. The eventual collapse of the HMO, corporate for-profit system is our goal. I vow to devote my skills, devotion, and energy to bringing down this corrupt and evil system.

I feel that I have two spiritual fathers: the historical Buddha and Genghis Khan. With the passage of time there seems to be more of a synthesis in my soul.
HOME: Sharon, MA   **OCCUPATION:** Clinical Psychologist (sole proprietor in private practice)   **BIRTHPLACE:** Oceanside   **SECONDARY SCHOOL:** Lynbrook Senior High School, Lynbrook, NY   **YEARS AT COLLEGE:** 1971–75   **DEGREES:** A.B., cum laude, '75 **DEGREES:** '75; Ph.D., Boston Univ. '81   **SPOUSE/PARTNER:** T. Joy DePiero, 1976 (Boston Univ.; M.D., ibid. '75)   **SPOUSE'S OCCUPATION:** Staff Neurologist. Health South Braintree Hospital; Instructor. Boston University School of Medicine   **CHILDREN:** Alexandra Elise, 1983   **COLLEGE ACTIVITIES:** The people, both teachers and peers, helped shape my values and attitudes. I would cite no one activity

---

Thomas M. Lock: We've been in Buffalo for ten years now. The parents are busy trying to do more and more with less in the "new health care environment." I'm involved in clinical research on treatments for Attention Deficit Hyperactivity Disorder and providing care for children with disabilities. Kathleen is a pediatric rheumatologist and immunologist. Sarah is a freshman in high school and would rather be figure skating than anything else. Andrew plays soccer any time that he can and goes to SUNY, Buffalo, for an advanced math program. Adam is in third grade and he and his friends frequently cross the border to engage young Canadians in their national game. Did you know that Canadian immigration has a special designation for "hockey"?

I can't tell you what all this has to do with Harvard right now. Maybe I'll figure it out some time after the kids are grown up.

HOME: Williamsville, NY   **OCCUPATION:** Associate Professor of Clinical Pediatrics. School of Medicine and Biomedical Sciences, State University of New York, Buffalo, Robert Warner Rehabilitation Center, Children's Hospital of Buffalo   **BIRTHPLACE:** Long Branch, NJ   **SECONDARY SCHOOL:** Guilderland Central High School, Guilderland Center, NY   **YEARS AT COLLEGE:** 1971–75   **DEGREES:** A.B., cum laude, '75; M.D., Univ. of Wisconsin, Madison '79   **SPOUSE/PARTNER:** Kathleen M. O'Neil (Wellesley Coll. '74; M.D., Tufts Univ. '78)   **SPOUSE'S OCCUPATION:** Associate Professor of Clinical Pediatrics. School of Medicine and Biomedical Sciences, State University of New York at Buffalo, Children's Hospital of Buffalo   **CHILDREN:** Sarah, 1985; Andrew, 1987; Adam, 1991   **COLLEGE ACTIVITIES:** Heavyweight crew, 1971–75

Peter John Lynch: Looking back on the last twenty-five years of my life, I realize that, for the most part, everything has gone according to plan — not always mine — but someone's.

I look back on my days at Harvard fondly. I now know I really should have gone to "The Game" (at least once), attended the Bernstein lectures, made more friends. But I did do some wonderful things, not the least of which was to graduate. I sincerely thank "Mother Harvard" for all the doors she has opened for me.

I always thought I would push my children — two smart, beautiful, real young ladies — to go to Harvard to have the same opportunities I have. But, after five years of homeschooling, I see who they are. They want careers and lives. They can go to whatever college that will make their dreams come true.

All in all, I'm happy. I'm happy I married the woman I did, in a leap of faith, almost twenty years ago. I am happy and proud to be the father of my daughters.

I'm not so happy that my parents died just as I was becoming a man. And that they never got to meet my family.

I'm happy that I have a trade that I do well. I'm not so happy that it keeps me away from what I really want to do for long hours. But, it pays the bills, and, at its best, it makes me think.

Twenty-five years is a long time, and yet I didn't see it go. I'll try to watch more closely this time.

HOME: Merchantville, NJ   OCCUPATION: Attorney. Christie, Pabarue, Mortensen & Young   BIRTHPLACE: Braintree, MA   SECONDARY SCHOOL: St. John's Prep, Danvers, MA   YEARS AT COLLEGE: 1971–75   DEGREES: A.B., magna cum laude, '75; M.Phil., University Coll., London '77; J.D., Univ. of Pennsylvania '80   SPOUSE/PARTNER: Susan Mauer, Feb. 15, 1981 (Rider Coll. '77)   SPOUSE'S OCCUPATION: Currently homeschooling our daughters   CHILDREN: Elizabeth Rita, 1984; Katherine Eleanor, 1986   HARVARD/RADCLIFFE SIBLINGS: Dennis J. Lynch '63

Richard Hausman Lyon: After sitting down last September to write about the past twenty-five years, I did what still comes naturally when I'm faced with a tough Harvard assignment: I asked for an extension. After all, my wife Valerie and I were expecting our first child (my first ever, in fact) within weeks, and I couldn't see putting these reflections on paper before such an event. What I hadn't imagined, though, was that a few days later, in a scene I liken to *ER* on LSD, I'd be delivering our baby Sarah myself, on the floor of the freight elevator in our Manhattan apartment building, at 5:55 in the morning, with our six-year-old Sam, my stepson, watching the entire show. It continues, in less frantic but equally thrilling form, with each passing day.

Even beyond our baby's spectacular debut, it's fair to say that my life has changed more dramatically in the past year or so than in any of the previous twenty-four: I've gotten married, finally, gaining a wonderful partner in Val and also a terrific son in the transaction; my home has been transformed from a spacious apartment for one into an increasingly cramped *shtetl* for four; I'm getting ready to move out of the city I've lived in since college and buy a house in the suburbs; and after thinking about it for a long, long time, I'm just now finishing up what I hope will be my first album as a recording artist, a collection of solo piano pieces.

Lyon Music, now almost five years old, continues to expand in new and unexpected directions. In addition to the TV themes and commercial tracks we've done for folks like MCI, Volvo, Chase Bank, and ABC News (thanks, Tom), we also produce spots for many of today's top recording artists, including Backstreet Boys, Will Smith, and Britney Spears. As a composer myself, I've had the great fortune of sitting in a movie theater and hearing a big orchestra playing my music on a soundtrack, and also of hearing some of my Harvard-era heroes like Taj Mahal and Richie Havens sing my songs. Meanwhile, I haven't let my career dilute my passion for Democratic politics, and for the fourth time since 1988, I'll take a week off this summer to help run the Democratic Convention speech writing SWAT team with classmate John Gillespie.

My relationships from Harvard have shaped and deeply enriched my life: among them the two best men at my wedding; my songwriting partner; my bass player and favorite arranger; my Adams House girlfriend, whom I still call on her birthday; the pals who helped my company get on its feet; and the others who've occasionally helped me get back on mine. I look forward with delight to seeing all of you in June.

HOME: New York, NY **OCCUPATION:** Composer. Lyon Music, Inc. **BIRTHPLACE:** Washington, DC **SECONDARY SCHOOL:** Western School, Washington, DC **YEARS AT COLLEGE:** 1971–76 **DEGREES:** A.B. '75 **SPOUSE/PARTNER:** Valerie Kardon, 1998 (Univ. of Pennsylvania '82) **SPOUSE'S OCCUPATION:** Physician (family practice) **CHILDREN:** Sarah Marjorie, 1999 **STEPCHILDREN:** Samuel Kardon Ravetz, 1993 **HARVARD/RADCLIFFE SIBLINGS:** Patricia W. Coll, Ed.M. '75

Joan Anne Porter MacIver: I imagine that hundreds of our class-mates are putting together last-minute entries to the Class Report—I had good intentions and composed many passages while cutting the "lawn" (fif-teen acres) and harvesting the pumpkins, but it was impossible to put pen to paper. The miracle of the Internet makes it feasible to literally make it under the wire.

The most important and critical decision was marrying David MacIver, whom I met in Bahrain in the early 1980s while working with Chemical Bank and he was with Citibank (still is!). Our lives together have brought us many adventures in Bahrain, Puerto Rico, Saudi Arabia, and now England and three great children, David (sixteen), Jamie (fourteen), and Laura (eleven). Of all the things to reflect upon, I must say that the joy of a strong and happy marriage is one to continually feel grateful for—he is a wonder-ful soul mate and father. Coming from a strong and close nuclear family and having an identical twin sister, Barbara Porter, with whom I am in constant contact despite the ocean between us, it is good to pass on this legacy of family to our children.

After leaving Chemical Bank and Bahrain a second time, we moved to Saudi Arabia in 1987, where I started and organized a Harvard Alumni group. This was a huge success and the most wonderful way of getting to know many interesting Saudis and foreigners. Living in Saudi I was also able to expand my knowledge of Arabian archaeology—I had been secretary of the Bahrain Historical and Archaeological Society for a few years in the early 1980s! We still miss the close friends and camping expeditions to the desert and especially to the Empty Quarter. We were living in Riyadh when the Gulf War started—David remained there during the fighting and ducked the scud missiles while I stayed in England at our eighteenth-century Mill House with the children—he had bought it sight-unseen in 1986 and it was well worth it just to have a haven in times of war!

We moved back to the United Kingdom in 1993 and I have found myself feeling very much at home in East Anglia now. I have now lived here over six years—my longest continuous time in one place. The children have attended various private and state schools—we did not want them in boarding school. We live off the land most of the year with extensive vegetable and fruit gar-dens and live a disgustingly healthy existence with endless sessions of jam-ming and preserving. We make our own bread from wheat that we grind—it is a rural idyll—lots of work. Admittedly, I am aided by David's mother, who lives with us in a wonderful extension that we built for her—she is the main vegetable gardener. David is a very fine joiner-carpenter and in his spare time from a demanding job at Citibank, he works to enhance the Mill. I keep us all in order—take on too many volunteer commitments, the Harvard Club of

London of which I am vice president being the most demanding! I continually wonder about the viability of returning to paid employment. Having a large property, which we take care of ourselves, and dealing with long-distance school runs means that I will continue to be close to home until the next Reunion. We live near Cambridge and have the joy of having Oliver Goodenough '75 and Alison Clarkson '77 and their two boys here for the year, while on sabbatical — a great Harvard tie for us all.

HOME: Halstead, Essex, England   OCCUPATION: Volunteer; Smallholder; Mother; Vice President, the Harvard Club of London   BIRTHPLACE: Bonn, Germany   SECONDARY SCHOOL: The American International School, Vienna, Austria; the American Community School, Beirut, Lebanon   YEARS AT COLLEGE: 1972–75   DEGREES: A.B., cum laude, '75   SPOUSE/PARTNER: David MacIver, Dec. 27, 1981 (Hatfield Polytech Univ. '71; M.B.A., Univ. of Birmingham '72)   SPOUSE'S OCCUPATION: Risk Manager; Vice President. The Citibank Private Bank   CHILDREN: David Ritchie, 1983; James Alexander, 1985; Laura Adele, 1988   HARVARD/RADCLIFFE SIBLINGS: Dwight A. Porter '67; Ellen Porter Honnet, Ed.M. '78, Ed.D. '89   COLLEGE ACTIVITIES: Class secretary, Radcliffe College Class of '75 (to date); member, Class Committee, 1975; member, Radcliffe Senior Solicitation Committee; associate ticket manager, Hasty Pudding Theatricals; member, Student Faculty Committee on Undergraduate Education; co-chair, Educational Resources Group; teaching aide, Phillips Brooks House; co-chair, Radcliffe Junior Day Committee; waltz teacher, first Lowell House Ball; night supervisor, Lamont Library

---

Daniel Rob Mackenzie: In 1970 two Harvard admissions interviewers said they found little to distinguish me from dozens of other well-rounded, ambitious, upstate New York WASPs. So for lack of anything more original I told them how the world was going to end before the millennium arrived, and that seemed to focus their minds appropriately. So much for the apocalypse. After Harvard I went to medical school in Albany, where I married Maggie Finery and finished surgical training at the University of Toronto. Maggie and I settled down to raise Christy and Stephen more or less conventionally on an old country farmstead outside a small, liberal college town.

I joined a small general surgical group, put in surgeons' hours, and built a respected practice. I've cut back in recent years to work part-time as medical director for Ithaca's community hospital, and to lead managed care negotiations for our local physician-hospital organization. Maggie tried her hand at a fabric shop, but now likes free time with the kids or a book, more than accounting and store hours.

I've dabbled unsuccessfully at writing medical thrillers, had fun with amateur astronomy, and like to read and discuss natural history. Lately I've been tutored in English horseback riding and computer games by my much more accomplished children. Christy and I had a wonderful week last June exploring one hundred and fifty miles of ancestral Scottish highlands on horseback; Stephen finds trilobites and amazing cults for me on the Web. We're thinking of fencing in some of our sixty-eight acres west of Cayuga Lake for horses next year.

HOME: Trumansburg, NY   OCCUPATION: Vice President for Medical Affairs. Cayuga Medical Center at Ithaca; General Surgeon   BIRTHPLACE: Schenectady, NY
SECONDARY SCHOOL: Niskayuna High School, Schenectady, NY   YEARS AT
COLLEGE: 1971–75   DEGREES: A.B., magna cum laude (highest honors), '75; M.D., Albany Medical Coll. '79   SPOUSE/PARTNER: Margaret Elizabeth Emery, Aug. 21, 1977 (State Univ. of New York, Albany '76)   SPOUSE'S OCCUPATION: Homemaker
CHILDREN: Christina Caitlin, 1982; Stephen David, 1986   COLLEGE ACTIVITIES: Crew, 1971–72; Christian Fellowship

Flora Mary Macquarrie: Upon leaving college, I felt a certain pressure to be a recognized professional, which led me to attend McGill Medical School. After two years, I realized that medicine was not for me. I fell into a career in information systems, which has afforded me many opportunities to truly experience other countries by living and working in: Australia, California, England, Ireland, Scotland, and Norway. My preferred relaxation activity is to experience unspoiled natural beauty, either hiking in the mountains, or cross-country skiing.

At present, my free time is entirely occupied by my two surprisingly young children. My partner stays home with them most of the time, and we feel part of the community. I find the joy of having children unlike anything else in life, watching them grow, rediscovering the world through their eyes, and wondering at their accomplishments.

HOME: Toronto, ON, Canada   OCCUPATION: Life Insurance Software Consultant. SOL-CORP (insurance software provider)   BIRTHPLACE: Canada   SECONDARY
SCHOOL: Ridgemont High School, Ottawa, ON, Canada   YEARS AT COLLEGE: 1971–75
SPOUSE/PARTNER: Eileen MacDougald (McMaster Univ. '75)   SPOUSE'S
OCCUPATION: Teacher; Homemaker   CHILDREN: Isabel, 1993; William, 1995

Ann Marie Madigan: I often say that I've had two lives since graduation. The first eight years, I worked in a family business after marrying a classmate two months after graduation. My first child was born in 1979 — it's hard to believe Glen's a junior at Connecticut College in New London.

By the time I turned thirty, I realized that my secret dream of going to medical school was about to become impossible. So, I returned to Harvard as a postbaccalaureate student to do literally all the pre-med courses I had avoided as an undergraduate. At the same time, we were divorcing and I was learning to manage as a student and single mother of a four-year-old. I graduated from medical school in 1989, one week after marrying a physician I had met as a professor in medical school. My psychiatry residency was completed in 1993 — I delivered my second son the day of graduation.

Private practice has been wonderful and satisfying. I practice psychiatry full-time in my home office, while raising our two young children with a wonderful nanny and my very busy internist husband, who teaches geriatrics and practices at New England Medical Center. We finally had a daughter in 1996.

Life is full and rich with the excitement of two young children and a college student for their older brother. I feel especially fortunate to have had not only a second career but also a second family and a second chance to do a better job parenting, knowing this time how fast children grow and what a brief time they are small — and how very precious they are to me. Being their mother has been the most important and most amazing aspect of my life.

HOME: Milton, MA   OCCUPATION: Physician (psychiatrist)   BIRTHPLACE: Albany, NY
SECONDARY SCHOOL: Cohasset High School   YEARS AT COLLEGE: 1972–75
DEGREES: A.B., cum laude, '75; M.D., Boston Univ. '89   SPOUSE/PARTNER: Glen
Harnish (Harvard '75) Aug. 16, 1975; divorced, 1984; Allen Waltman, May 13, 1989
SPOUSE'S OCCUPATION: Physician (geriatrician)   CHILDREN: Glen Harnish, 1979;
Curtis Waltman, 1993; Elizabeth Waltman, 1996   COLLEGE ACTIVITIES: Harvard-
Radcliffe Chorus

Jeffrey Baldwin Maletta: I have been a lawyer for the past twenty years, and it hasn't been as bad as that would have sounded to us twenty-five years ago. Most of those years have been in private practice representing clients in litigation. While I concentrate on business and securities issues, I have been as much of a generalist as big-firm practice now permits, and it's an entertaining education in many subjects, from helicopters to housing finance. Fame and fortune have spared me, so far. My name graces the contributors' page in a few practice manuals and the counsel line in a number of reports. I have not started and sold any tech businesses. Not even one.

Work does provide satisfactions I had not anticipated, in particular the opportunity to apply experience gained over the years to new situations to get the right result. Call it growing wisdom, maturing judgment, or just plain aging. At least in this respect, moving into the late forties has some benefits.

My wife, Catherine May '75, and I also find increasing enjoyment in the development of our two children into interesting companions. They now join us in our favorite activities, hiking, traveling, and the occasional round of golf, with a stamina, if not always an enthusiasm, that usually surpasses that of their parents. One large regret is that, bowing to the demands of family and work, we have done poorly in keeping up with classmates, and we genuinely look forward to reunions as an opportunity to see people we have not seen in years.

HOME: Washington, DC   **OCCUPATION:** Attorney. Kirkpatrick & Lockhart LLP
BIRTHPLACE: Quincy, MA   **SECONDARY SCHOOL:** St. Albans School   **YEARS AT COLLEGE:** 1971–75   **DEGREES:** A.B., magna cum laude, '75; J.D., Stanford Univ. '79
SPOUSE/PARTNER: Catherine Stuart May, April 30, 1988 (Radcliffe '75)   **SPOUSE'S OCCUPATION:** Psychiatrist   **CHILDREN:** Amalia Elizabeth, 1988; Gabriel David, 1990

Lisa Mann: I can't believe it's been twenty-five years, and yet experience tells me it has. Life has been very full: taking time to journey towards my career as a psychologist; marriage for almost twenty years (!); the fantastic, exhausting and ever-changing world of not only one or two but three children (two came together!); and finally several moves that have brought us from New York City to Westchester to Connecticut. All in all, life has treated us very well. I think back on my Radcliffe/Harvard time as a great moment in a blessed life. The friends I made there and the memories remain very special. I wish for my children the same type of happiness that I have had.

HOME: Ridgefield, CT   OCCUPATION: Psychologist. Trinity School   BIRTHPLACE: New York, NY   SECONDARY SCHOOL: The Dalton School, New York, NY   YEARS AT COLLEGE: 1971–75   DEGREES: A.B., cum laude, '75; Ph.D., New York Univ. '86   SPOUSE/PARTNER: Rocco F. Marotta, Sept. 20, 1980 (Manhattan Coll. '70)   SPOUSE'S OCCUPATION: Medical Director. Intensive Psychiatric Services, Danbury Hospital   CHILDREN: Nicolas, 1988; Alexander, 1992; Lucia, 1992

JoAnn Elisabeth Manson: Since graduation, life has been eventful with several interesting turns and detours. Chris Ames (Harvard '75, Quincy House) and I married in 1979, after my graduation from medical school and Chris's graduation from law school. The high point of our lives was the birth of our children, Jenny (in 1987) and Jeffrey (in 1989). They're truly magical children and become more and more fun every year. Chris and I have also been fairly busy with our work. After I finished my training in internal medicine and endocrinology, I took a detour to study epidemiology and public health. Epidemiology and women's health research really captured my interest, and I've been in the field ever since. After getting master of public health and doctor of public health degrees from the Harvard School of Public Health, I joined an epidemiology research group at Brigham and Women's Hospital. My focus has been women's health and my primary research interests are hormone replacement therapy, micronutrient supplementation, and physical activity in the prevention of heart disease, diabetes, and other chronic diseases in women. I recently became a professor of medicine at Harvard Medical School and chief of the Division of Preventive Medicine at Brigham and Women's Hospital. I continue to have a clinical practice in endocrinology and women's health. Chris has been at Houghton-Mifflin Publishing Company for the past twelve years and is currently a vice president. We live with our children in a two-hundred-year-old antique colonial house on Boston's North Shore, in Beverly (with lots of fireplaces). Our favorite activities are bicycling, hiking, listening to music, or doing almost anything with the children. Life is very full, although admittedly quite hectic and even chaotic at times. Our most recent project is trying to get more sleep.

HOME: Beverly, MA   OCCUPATION: Professor of Medicine. Harvard Medical School; Endocrinologist; Chief of Preventive Medicine. Brigham and Women's Hospital   BIRTHPLACE: Cleveland Heights, OH   SECONDARY SCHOOL: Cleveland Heights High School, Cleveland Heights, OH   YEARS AT COLLEGE: 1971–75   DEGREES: A.B., magna cum laude, '75; M.D., Case Western Reserve Univ. '79; M.P.H., Harvard '84; D.P.H., ibid. '87   SPOUSE/PARTNER: Christopher N. Ames, June 12, 1979 (Harvard '75)   SPOUSE'S OCCUPATION: Lawyer. Houghton-Mifflin Publishing Co.   CHILDREN: Jenn, 1987; Jeffrey, 1989   COLLEGE ACTIVITIES: Phillips Brooks House, 1972–73; *Harvard Independent,* 1972–73; Radcliffe Pottery, 1972; Radcliffe Dance, 1973–74

David Richard Mares: I've had a great time over the past twenty-five years, with a wonderful wife and two great boys. My job as a professor of international politics has enabled me to travel the world over. I'm fortunate that my family accompanies me on the more interesting journeys (the Amazon, Buenos Aires, La Paz, Alaska, China, even Boston!).

HOME: San Diego, CA   **OCCUPATION:** Professor of Political Science. University of California, San Diego   **BIRTHPLACE:** Richmond, CA   **SECONDARY SCHOOL:** Pinole Valley High School, Pinole, CA   **YEARS AT COLLEGE:** 1971–76   **DEGREES:** A.B., cum laude, '75 ('76); A.M. '78; Ph.D. '82   **SPOUSE/PARTNER:** Jane Alma Milner, Sept. 3, 1977 (Radcliffe '74)   **SPOUSE'S OCCUPATION:** Director of Administration. Dept. of Family and Preventive Medicine, University of California, San Diego   **CHILDREN:** Alejandro Cuauhtemoc; Gabriel Pacal   **HARVARD/RADCLIFFE CHILDREN:** Alejandro Cuauhtemoc Mares '03

Robert Franklin Margolskee: Dorothy Jessel (now Margolskee) and I met on my first day at Harvard. In a happy reprise to *Love Story* we courted, played, and studied together during our years at Harvard. From day one we argued about the "right" career path to pursue. We have each continued in medical research, but at opposite ends of the spectrum: Dorothy manages medical research at Merck, I do molecular neurobiology at Mount Sinai.

After college I continued graduate studies in molecular biology at Harvard while Dorothy pursued medicine at Johns Hopkins. The year apart convinced us to get married (in 1977) and motivated me to transfer to the M.D./Ph.D. program at Johns Hopkins. I did my graduate studies with Nobel Laureate Dan Nathans on the molecular genetics of virus replication. After graduation we moved to California (in 1983), where I did post-doctoral studies at Stanford with Nobel Laureate Paul Berg, learning the arcane rites of cDNA expression cloning.

In 1987 we moved back east to New Jersey, where I took a faculty position at the Roche Institute of Molecular Biology. At Roche I started my present research program in sensory transduction, focusing on molecular mechanisms underlying taste. In 1996 I moved to Mount Sinai and, in 1997, I was selected as a Howard Hughes Associate Investigator. My claim to fame, such as it is, is the discovery and study of gustducin, a transducin-like G protein selectively expressed in taste cells. My lab has used molecular biology, biochemistry, transgenic and knockout mice to define taste transduction pathways—it's all covered in the standard molecular neurobiology textbooks.

Along the way we've managed to have three wonderful children Daniel (sixteen) and Alison (thirteen) were born in San Francisco, Andrew (ten) was born in New Jersey. I've even found time to resurrect a Currier House tradition—Friday night poker.

HOME: Upper Montclair, NJ   **OCCUPATION:** Professor; Associate Investigator. Howard Hughes Medical Institute, Dept. of Physiology and Biophysics, Mount Sinai School of Medicine   **BIRTHPLACE:** Boston, MA   **SECONDARY SCHOOL:** Lexington High School, Lexington, MA   **YEARS AT COLLEGE:** 1972–76   **DEGREES:** A.B., magna cum laude, '75 ('76); M.D., Johns Hopkins Univ. '83; Ph.D., ibid. '83)   **SPOUSE/PARTNER:** Dorothy Jessel, June 19, 1977 (Radcliffe '75)   **SPOUSE'S OCCUPATION:** Vice President, Project Planning and Devement. Merck Research Laboratories   **CHILDREN:** Daniel Paul, 1983; Alison Joyce 1986; Andrew John, 1989   **HARVARD/RADCLIFFE SIBLINGS:** Jeanne P. Margolskee '72   **COLLEGE ACTIVITIES:** Currier House poker game, 1972–75; chess team, 1972–75; after dinner backgammon, bridge, and Star Trek at Currier House

---

Guillermo G. Marmol: The years at the college seem far away. Maybe it's too many flight miles. Maybe it's the distance from Boston to Dallas. Maybe twenty-five years is a long time.

After graduation I went on to the business school. Besides training in going without sleep, and other valuable skills, the time there proved important in that I met Gail Marcoux.

I married Gail in 1980, we were both living in Mexico at the time. Once was not enough so we did it again in 1981 this time in Massachusetts, closer to friends and relatives. We have two daughters: Emily, thirteen, and Christina, ten. Emily got her appearance from her mother and her personality from me; Christina the opposite. I'm on the nature side of the nature and nurture debate. Both are still friendly and fun to have around most of the time. Both are good students, have taken up tennis and play the game well. They also speak Spanish; mostly because that is their only choice when they speak to me.

Gail had studied literature, but decided that she too wanted an M.B.A., which she obtained when we were in Chicago. She gave up on a business career when Emily was born and has dedicated herself to our home ever since. Without her the house would literally come apart. Gail is very active in community and church activities, which makes for short interval scheduling and a lot of car-pooling. She has also dedicated herself to improving her tennis game, which has come a long way in the last two years. It is Gail's interest in tennis that motivated the girls to improve their game.

I spent eighteen years with McKinsey and had a productive career there. About five years ago it came time to try something different, so I moved on. I'm in a more entrepreneurial mode today; this September we took a group of Internet professional service companies public under the name Luminant. Hard work given a choppy market and an uneven track record for transactions of this sort. We now have to make this consolidation a success.

Time away from work is in short supply but I make some for soccer, which I play poorly but enthusiastically, and for the Greenhill School where the girls go to school. I still have a lot of energy and look forward to the next, equally eventful, twenty-five years.

HOME: Dallas, TX   **OCCUPATION:** CEO. Luminant Worldwide Corp.   **BIRTHPLACE:** Havana, Cuba   **SECONDARY SCHOOL:** Immaculata-La Salle School, Miami, FL **YEARS AT COLLEGE:** 1971–75   **DEGREES:** A.B., magna cum laude, 75; M.B.A. '78 **SPOUSE/PARTNER:** Gail Ann Marcoux, Sept. 6, 1980 (Assumption Coll. '76)   **SPOUSE'S OCCUPATION:** Homemaker   **CHILDREN:** Emily Elizabeth, 1986; Christina Alicia, 1989 **COLLEGE ACTIVITIES:** AISEC, 1974–75

Barbara Baker Matson: After twenty years away, we moved back home to Boston in 1994. I have been a writer and editor, mostly at newspapers, mostly in sports. The writing has taken me to some interesting events and interesting places; the editing has introduced me to a large cast of characters. I am currently working at the *Boston Globe.*

I have two kids: Lilly is thirteen, Jake is eight. Both are smart, funny, and play their hockey on ice. I still pick up a field hockey stick when I can.

In the summer, we spend as much time as we can on the Vineyard.

I met Didge in the locker room at Dillon—and we have made the journey through the last twenty-five years together. That has made all the difference.

HOME: Dedham, MA   **OCCUPATION:** Writer; Editor. *The Boston Globe*   **BIRTHPLACE:** Boston, MA   **SECONDARY SCHOOL:** Cambridge School of Weston, Weston, MA **YEARS AT COLLEGE:** 1971–75   **DEGREES:** A.B. '75   **SPOUSE/PARTNER:** Steve Dagdigian (Harvard '75)   **SPOUSE'S OCCUPATION:** Teacher; Coach. St. Sebastian's School   **CHILDREN:** Lilly, 1986; Jake, 1991

Catherine Stuart May: Taking but a moment from a busy life to reflect, it is enough to say that I feel blessed. I have a good home, safe neighborhood, healthy children, loving husband, and work that is satisfying. In a profession where office visits are more and more rushed and relationships sometimes tenuous, private practice affords me the luxury of sitting with my patients and understanding their walk through life. Every day I learn from my patients and the resilience of the human spirit never ceases to astonish me.

As the children grow I've become more involved in school and church activities. I am keenly aware of those who are less fortunate and struggle more, and it is a great gift to be able to help.

HOME: Washington, DC **OCCUPATION:** Psychiatrist **BIRTHPLACE:** Northampton, MA **SECONDARY SCHOOL:** Northfield; Mt. Hermon **YEARS AT COLLEGE:** 1971–75 **DEGREES:** A.B., cum laude, '75; M.D., Indiana Univ. '80 **SPOUSE/PARTNER:** Jeffrey Baldwin Maletta, April 30, 1988 (Harvard '75) **SPOUSE'S OCCUPATION:** Attorney. Kirkpatrick & Lockhart **CHILDREN:** Amalia Elizabeth, 1988; Gabriel David, 1990 **HARVARD/RADCLIFFE SIBLINGS:** David William May, M.B.A. '85

John J. McCarthy: When I left Harvard, I wanted to get a Ph.D. and become a professor of linguistics. And that's exactly what happened. I taught first at the University of Texas, Austin, spent two years at Bell Labs in the mid-1980s, and moved to UMass in 1985.

Our department has been very successful—we came out first in the recent national rankings—and I've shared in some of that success—I received a Guggenheim Fellowship in 1992 and an Outstanding Teacher Award in 1995. (I even turned down an offer from Harvard.) Teaching and research are huge sources of pleasure to me; academic politics and administration are not, though I did suffer through three years as department chair. As a native speaker of the Boston dialect, I have a strong professional interest in (and various publications on) the goings and comings of the consonant "r."

I met Ellen while in graduate school. After many years when we worked and lived far apart, she joined the UMass faculty in 1993. She is my most trusted colleague and my best friend.

In recent years, the event that has had the greatest effect on me is the death of my father and what led up to it: four months in an ICU, dependent on a ventilator, as a result of complications after cancer surgery. After almost three years, I am still trying to come to terms with his suffering.

HOME: Amherst, MA **OCCUPATION:** Professor. Dept. of Linguistics, University of Massachusetts **BIRTHPLACE:** Medford, MA **SECONDARY SCHOOL:** Xavier School, Concord, MA **YEARS AT COLLEGE:** 1971–75 **DEGREES:** A.B., summa cum laude, '75; Ph.D., Massachusetts Inst. of Technology '79 **SPOUSE/PARTNER:** Ellen Woolford, Dec. 26, 1981 (Rice Univ. '71; Ph.D., Duke Univ. '77) **SPOUSE'S OCCUPATION:** Professor. Dept. of Linguistics, University of Massachusetts **COLLEGE ACTIVITIES:** Phillips Brooks House

---

James Scott McDonald: Twenty-nine years ago, someone told me that if you could get admitted to Harvard, life thereafter would be simple. That person lacked wisdom.

Building a life—family, friends, community, profession—really has occupied most of the last twenty-five years. Quantitatively: one marriage (wife, Karen); three children—Scott (nineteen) taking a "gap" year after high school; Hunter (fifteen), in his second year at Exeter, and Isabel (six), at the Park School; two parents, age eighty-one, alive, in good health, and resistant to the idea of retirement communities; two dogs; one rabbit; two houses (Dedham, Massachusetts, and Weston, Vermont); two jobs since college (associate and partner at law firm of Choate, Hall & Stewart, Boston; then, last fourteen years with Pell Rudman, an investment firm, now CEO); six books read in the past year—two autobiographies, four novels; at least two hundred hours spent each of the last five years as president of trustees at Fessenden School and in other community activities; average of four hours a week of working out; zero current movies or full-length television programs watched in past year; about one-hundred thousand miles of air travel in past year, including multiple trips to Pell Rudman offices in Denver, Washington, and Baltimore; weight—eight pounds more than 1975 (center of gravity lower); etc.

Would a simpler life be better? No, there will be time for that later.

HOME: Dedham, MA **OCCUPATION:** CEO. Pell Rudman Trust Company, N.A. (investment management organization) **BIRTHPLACE:** Auckland, New Zealand **SECONDARY SCHOOL:** Kingswood-Oxford School, West Hartford, CT **YEARS AT COLLEGE:** 1971–74 **DEGREES:** A.B., cum laude, '75 ('74); J.D., Univ. of Virginia '77 **SPOUSE/PARTNER:** Karen L. **CHILDREN:** J. Scott, Jr., 1980; W. Hunter, 1984; Isabel C., 1993 **COLLEGE ACTIVITIES:** Varsity squash, freshman tennis

Bernie McGarva: Hello Friends and Classmates. I extend my best wishes to you on this important anniversary. The memories of our time together are fresh and full of laughter and bountiful spirit.

I have been blessed with a happy and fulfilling family life. My career has been challenging and rewarding. I have had the good fortune to represent many interesting corporations and individuals over the years of my litigation practice: Canadian Pacific Railways, the Toronto Maple Leaf Hockey Club, Edper Brascan, Lac Minerals, the Ontario Association of Architects, Siemens Electric, Westinghouse (to name a few).

Away from work, we love to ski, bike, and blade. My winters are busy coaching junior hockey.

My thoughts are with you and with Harvard on the path of the new millennium. Keep smiling!! There are new friends to be made and new journeys to begin.

HOME: Toronto, ON, Canada   OCCUPATION: Lawyer; Senior Partner. Aird & Berlis
BIRTHPLACE: Halifax, NS, Canada   SECONDARY SCHOOL: Univ. of Toronto Schools
YEARS AT COLLEGE: 1972–75   DEGREES: A.B., magna cum laude, '75; LL.B., Univ. of
Toronto '78   SPOUSE/PARTNER: Barbara, Dec. 27, 1984   SPOUSE'S OCCUPATION:
Chartered Financial Analyst   CHILDREN: James, 1985; Robert, 1987   COLLEGE
ACTIVITIES: JFK School Fellowship, interviewing congressional leaders in Washington
during Watergate's crisis and resolution, summer 1974; elected Phi Beta Kappa, 1975

Robert Gilmour McIver: Twenty-five years! My how time flies. In some respects I feel as though I have changed very little from the person I was then. Like someone who has walked down a straight road, I can look back and see quite clearly where I have been and where I am; and all the choices, mistakes and successes along the way are plainly connected and visible in my mind.

But enough of that. Where am I now? After two arthroscopies on the same knee, the last about twelve years ago, I got the message and quit playing basketball. At present, it is mostly bike riding, a little tennis now and again, and rough-housing with the kids. I still practice law every work day, having not yet struck it rich and retired to the beach. The work remains enjoyable though, and occasionally lucrative. I have done the associate-to-partner big-firm trip, but am now quite comfortable in the setting of a smaller firm working with my own clients. The further I go in the profession, the more I have come to believe that the highest and best use of an attorney is to help someone, preferably a real person, deal with a real prob-

lem in an honest way. When I can do that the whole experience is most satisfying, and I try to keep that goal in mind as much as I can.

Family life fills much of the rest of my time. There is school, homework, church, camp, sports, Cub Scouts and travel when we can. Given the ages of my children (seven and nine), we constantly fight to resist the inevitable intrusion of the TV-video-mass media culture into their minds and attention spans. It may be a losing battle, but there you go. Like many others, Mary and I try to encourage sports as, we hope, a healthy alternative for the kids. That has been fun, with my greatest pleasure watching in amusement as they transition from daisy chain makers to interested participants. We have a ways to go.

Also, I have to confess I still enjoy drinking a few beers and listening to music of all sorts when the opportunity presents itself. I guess my favorite hobby or personal activity at this point in life is reading. Frankly, I wish I could indulge this interest more than I do. Maybe later.

HOME: Summerfield, NC **OCCUPATION:** Attorney. Clark, Bloss & McIver, PLCC
BIRTHPLACE: Greensboro, NC **SECONDARY SCHOOL:** Woodberry Forest School,
Woodberry Forest, VA **YEARS AT COLLEGE:** 1971–75 **DEGREES:** A.B., cum laude, '75;
J.D., Univ. of Virginia '80 **SPOUSE/PARTNER:** Mary Böhme **SPOUSE'S OCCUPATION:**
President. Piedmont Direct Mail, Inc. **CHILDREN:** Robert B., 1990; Catherine Laird
Gilmour, 1992 **COLLEGE ACTIVITIES:** *Harvard Advocate;* Phillips Brooks House

---

Joel P. McLafferty: I have two wonderful children (Fred, twelve, and Hannah, fourteen) and a beautiful wife (Julia Brownley) of sixteen years.

I received an M.B.A. from Cornell in 1980 and then moved to Los Angeles to work for an oil and gas company. In 1985, I joined some friends in a home building business. My business has changed with the economy. Earlier this decade, I developed affordable housing in the poorest parts of Los Angeles and now I am subdividing vacant land on the city's fringe.

The challenge, work, and rewards of marriage and parenting constantly surprise me. I am having a great time being a dad (family ski trips, little league, boogie boards, etc.). I have good friends and met some of the best of them at Harvard. I enjoy my work. It's challenging and always changing. Although, I would like it to be less stressful and more consistently successful. Maybe I'll change careers after the next boom leaves me flush.

My spiritual life has deepened in the last five years. This has really helped me get through life's bumps and given me a better appreciation for the blessings that I have.

Los Angeles is a weird place. It lacks a strong sense of identity and direction. But, it's fun and I am happy here with family, friends, and plenty of sunshine.

HOME: Santa Monica, CA   **OCCUPATION:** Real Estate Developer. Crescent Bay Co.
BIRTHPLACE: Midland, MI   **SECONDARY SCHOOL:** Ithaca High School   **YEARS AT COLLEGE:** 1971–76   **DEGREES:** A.B.,cum laude, '75 ('76); MB.A., Cornell '80
SPOUSE/PARTNER: Julia Brownley, Oct. 22, 1983   **SPOUSE'S OCCUPATION:** Member. Santa Monica/Malibu Unified School District   **CHILDREN:** Hannah, 1985; Fred, 1987

Susan Kay McLean: Recently, when I was playing a game in which I had to describe myself in one adjective, I was astonished to find myself saying "serene." It seemed almost to be tempting fate to say such a thing, and I did qualify it with "at least for now." I went to grad school in English literature when that was considered very risky. It did take me many difficult years to find a job in my field, and the one I found was over four hundred miles from John, my partner of thirty-two years, but I love teaching, and we have found ways to make a long-distance relationship work.

We both love to travel and get to Europe for about three weeks every summer (I have accompanied student groups abroad twice). We also like to cook and often have company over for dinner. Theatre is still a strong interest of mine, both professionally (it is my main literary specialty) and personally (I get to plays as often as I can, and even acted in one, Ionesco's *Rhinoceros,* during my sabbatical). My youngest sister settled in London, so I get there about once every two years.

My newest interest is in writing poetry. I took it up in 1990, right after finishing my dissertation, and it has filled a need that was not satisfied by the critical articles I have written on Shakespeare, Ursula LeGuin, and Frank Herbert. About twenty of my poems have now appeared in literary magazines, and I am working on getting a book of them published. My poems are autobiographical, feminist, and often based on reinterpretations of myth or fairy tales.

HOME: Marshall, MN   **OCCUPATION:** Professor of English. English Dept., Southwest State University   **BIRTHPLACE:** Washington, DC   **SECONDARY SCHOOL:** Oxon Hill High School, Oxon Hill, MD   **YEARS AT COLLEGE:** 1971–75   **DEGREES:** A.B., cum laude, '75; M.A., Rutgers Univ., New Brunswick '79; Ph.D., ibid. '90   **SPOUSE/PARTNER:** John F. Finamore (Univ. of Maryland '72)   **SPOUSE'S OCCUPATION:** Associate

Professor of Classics. University of Iowa   **COLLEGE ACTIVITIES:** Acted in plays, including: *The Most Happy Fella, A Funny Thing Happened on the Way to the Forum, The Bald Soprano, Dark of the Moon, She Stoops to Conquer;* directed: *It's a Bird! It a Plane! It's Superman!;* costume mistress for *Subject to Fits* and *The Inspector General;* sang in Quincy House Madrigal Society

---

Richard Smith McNamara: Upon reflection, I would have to say that I enjoyed an extended footloose period for most of my first ten years after graduation—living in the Big Apple; thereafter, carving out only a marginally more structured lifestyle as a professional salesman from New York to Boston to Baltimore. It was not until the relatively late age of thirty-nine, having oh-so-happily married Kerry Lynn three years prior, that I began the raising of an "enormous" family of five children in the last seven years: Derek, Keenan, Mitchell, Spencer, and Bridget. We are still recovering, however, from the tragic unexpected loss of what was to be our sixth child: our dearest Leah shared but a sweet, sorrowful six days with us before joining her heavenly Father.

I don't consider this any claim to fame—just rare by almost any days' standards—I am the oldest man I know of fathering five children in as short a space of time, by one wife, where both of us have been married for just the first time! I suspect, classmates, if *any* of you have even had five children they've all filled out Harvard entrance applications by now!

My career remains in the professional sales field—primarily printing and packaging components; but, the most important "move" I ever made, by far, was undertaken three years ago with my commitment to Jesus Christ as Lord and Savior. Once again, my wife and I were relatively late bloomers. In America, the age at which most individuals claim to have made a "decision for Christ" is almost always before exiting their teenage years—with just a small fraction beginning their Christian walk after age forty. In this regard I consider myself truly blessed.

As Thomas Aquinas observed: "In every individual there is a thirst for happiness and meaning." I can genuinely say that I have found my meaning to life in Immanuel; and, since I know I will live forever in His presence, along with the body of believers, how can I help but be happy, indeed joyful!

HOME: Reisterstown, MD   **OCCUPATION:** Sales (printing industry)   **BIRTHPLACE:** Fitchburg, MA   **SECONDARY SCHOOL:** Fitchburg Public High School, Fitchburg, MA

YEARS AT COLLEGE: 1971–76 **DEGREES:** A.B. '75 ('76) **SPOUSE/PARTNER:** Kerry Lynn, May 27, 1990 (Univ. of Massachusetts, Amherst '84) **CHILDREN:** Derek, 1992; Keenan, 1993; Mitchell, 1995; Spencer, 1996; Bridget 1998; Leah, 1999 (died, 1999) **HARVARD/RADCLIFFE SIBLINGS:** Tomas Mark McNamara '73; Jane McNamara '79

Richard Paul Mendelson: Wine, law, and art have been at the core of my professional life since Harvard. Two years at Oxford (1975–77) led me in new directions: wine, food, and France. I met Marilyn, my Australian wife of twenty years, in Burgundy while working for a *négociant.* We moved to California to stay close to the vines and for law school (Stanford J.D. '82). Presently, I am a wine law attorney at Dickinson, Peatman & Fogarty in Napa, where I manage our twenty-lawyer firm; grape grower and producer of Mendelson Pinot Gris and Muscat Canelli Dessert Wines; metal sculptor (welded steel and stainless steel); and Tai Chi devotee. I remain a Francophile and have taught vineyard and wine law at the Universities of Bordeaux and Aix-Marseille and presided over the Paris-based International Wine Law Association (1992–95). I am a director of the Di Rosa Art Preserve and Oxbow Art School, both in Napa. Our daughter, Margot, is a Harvard freshman (Class of '03) and son, Anthony, a high school sophomore. Life after Harvard has been good!

HOME: Napa, CA **OCCUPATION:** Attorney; Managing Partner. Dickenson, Peatman & Fogarty (law firm); Grape Grower and Wine Producer. Mendelson Vineyard; Metal Sculptor. Metal in Motion **BIRTHPLACE:** Jacksonville, FL **SECONDARY SCHOOL:** Bolles School, Jacksonville, FL **YEARS AT COLLEGE:** 1971–75 **DEGREES:** A.B. summa cum laude, '75; M.A., Oxford Univ. '77; J.D., Stanford Univ. '82 **SPOUSE/PARTNER:** Marily Knight, Dec. 15, 1979 (Sydney Univ. '71; M.A., San Francisco State Univ. '83) **SPOUSE'S OCCUPATION:** ESL Department Chair. Napa Valley Adult School **CHILDREN:** Margßot Knight Mendelson, 1981; Anthony Knight Mendelson, 1984 **HARVARD/RADCLIFFE CHILDREN:** Margot Knight Mendelson '03 **COLLEGE ACTIVITIES:** *Harvard Political Review,* 1972–75

Peter Daniel Meyers: After graduation, I went straight to graduate school and almost never came out the other side. At age thirty, fresh out of school, I finally got a job...at a university. Though I had never really tried it, I somehow knew I wanted to teach. And, finally trying it, I loved it. Princeton is a wonderful place to teach, a great place to do physics, and a miserable place to be single. After ten years, an intensive burst of blind dating accomplished two things: gave me a new set of stories of the "dating in New York" genre, and trained me to respond to stories ending with "So, can I introduce you to her?" with a simple "yes." That's how I met Grayson, and life began again at forty.

HOME: Princeton, NJ **OCCUPATION:** Professor of Physics,. Dept of Physics, Princeton University **BIRTHPLACE:** Boston, MA **SECONDARY SCHOOL:** John Marshall High School, Los Angeles, CA **YEARS AT COLLEGE:** 1971–75 **DEGREES:** A.B., magna cum laude, '75; Ph.D., Univ. of California, Berkeley '83 **SPOUSE/PARTNER:** Grayson Barber, April 15, 1995 (Pomona Coll. '78) **SPOUSE'S OCCUPATION:** Attorney **CHILDREN:** Elizabeth, 1997

Richard Hewitt Millington: I have been lucky in my work life. Apart from occasional overdoses of paper grading, I like teaching and enjoy the scholarly work (as in-grown an activity as it sometimes seems) that goes with it. The job still feels inexhaustible, with many things still to read and learn. I was just promoted to full professor, so—barring any spectacular moral lapses—I've at last evaded the evaluated stage of professional life. I've published as I've needed to (on Hawthorne, Willa Cather, Alfred Hitchcock), and still like what I've written—I'm having a successful career, but not an eminent one, I'd say. (Is it a quality of other professional lives to have felt, even as things unfolded smoothly, pretty close to the edge of failure?)

In terms of personal life, the story is more complicated, more bittersweet. After a tough marriage, for both parties, I've had an unusually cordial divorce, though a sequence of hard decisions now finds me, after years of very involved parenting, living with my daughter in Massachusetts for the summers, and getting by on phone calls and visits (to Salt Lake City!) during the school year. While inordinately lucky in who I love, I've had trouble with logistics: my partner Kristie lives in Milwaukee. With all these distances, my domestic life has had a feast or famine quality, fluctuating between a blissfully full house (summers and sabbaticals) to me and the cat.

Major pleasures: playing tennis, music and dance, mountain biking, TV. I still miss and think of my college friends, though I stay in touch as badly as ever.

HOME: Haydenville, MA   **OCCUPATION:** Professor of English. Dept of English. Smith College   **BIRTHPLACE:** Bar Harbor, ME   **SECONDARY SCHOOL:** Wauwatosa East High School, Wauwatosa, WA   **YEARS AT COLLEGE:** 1971–75   **DEGREES:** A.B., magna cum laude, '75; M.A., Yale '77, M. Phil., ibid. '79, Ph.D., ibid. '83)   **SPOUSE/PARTNER:** Stephanie A. Rosenfeld, 1988, divorced, 1997 (Wesleyan Univ. '82); Kristie Hamilton (East Central Univ.; Ph.D., Univ. of Texas, Austin)   **SPOUSE'S OCCUPATION:** Associate Professor of English. Univ. of. Wisconsin, Milwaukee   **CHILDREN:** Callie, 1989   **COLLEGE ACTIVITIES:** Phillips Brooks House

---

Ernest Scott Monrad: After college, I went to McGill University Medical School, where I met my seriously (and still, after twenty-two years of marriage) beautiful wife, Paule Couture. It is hard to imagine how we had time to notice each other, with all the work. A Quebec native, she was learning English and medicine at the same time. (Now she corrects my English.) After training in Boston and a year of study in Zurich, Switzerland, we settled in Connecticut, where, on three acres of land run as a mini-farm, we share the produce evenly with the birds, deer, and ourselves. Our two labor-intensive jobs (cardiology and pediatrics), and overly attentive parenting roles have been demanding. I have spent too much time at work and too few dinners at home with the family. Medicine at a New York City hospital in an academic program feels more like a continuous fight for financial survival than an elegant intellectual pursuit; but the challenge is invigorating. As parents, we are trying hard not to be the worst forms of soccer/skating/hockey mom and dads. We are attempting to raise our three children bilingually, but my version of French is a serious impediment to that goal. Returning to Quebec for family holidays, summer camps, and skiing trips (I snowshoe up the mountains instead, since knee surgery several years ago) we maintain contact with their French roots. We all love the outdoors and fishing, with our annual trip to the Adirondacks becoming a tradition. Although we came from the generation that redefined adolescence, the passage of time becomes undeniable as our own children approach college age. Watching their progress more than makes up for that.

HOME: New Canaan, CT   OCCUPATION: Physician; Interventional Cardiologist; Director. Cardiac Catheterization Laboratory, Albert Einstein College of Medicine Hospital   BIRTHPLACE: Ft. Knox, KY   SECONDARY SCHOOL: St. Paul's School, Concord, NH   YEARS AT COLLEGE: 1971–75   DEGREES: A.B., cum laude, '75; M.D., McGill Univ. '79; C.M., ibid. '79   SPOUSE/PARTNER: Paule Couture, July 30, 1977 (M.D., McGill Univ. '79; C.M., ibid. '79)   SPOUSE'S OCCUPATION: Physician. Pediatric Center   CHILDREN: E. Jean-Marc, 1984; Catherine A. M., 1987; Julie S., 1992   HARVARD/RADCLIFFE SIBLINGS: Bruce H. Monrad '84   COLLEGE ACTIVITIES: Co-chairman, Eliot House "An Evening with Champions"; junior varsity squash

---

Sheri L. Morton: How to write about twenty-five years without making it sound like an excerpt from an obituary? The past twenty-five years were too vibrant, varied, educational, and wonderful to easily condense, so I will just say that I am having a lovely and lively time living in sunny central Florida near DisneyWorld with Chuck Wooley '75. I am still in regular contact with various classmates, including Cora Yamamoto, Jeff Lepon, Seth Riemer, and Bob Egan. Other classmates I see occasionally when they visit DisneyWorld. I send my love and best wishes to all my old friends, and remember you fondly in my heart.

HOME: Lake Buena Vista, FL   YEARS AT COLLEGE: 1971–75   DEGREES: A.B., cum laude, '75   SPOUSE/PARTNER: Chuck Wooley '75

Steven Paul Motenko: When I left Harvard, I still didn't know what I wanted to do when I grew up. I knew I didn't want to learn to think like a lawyer or a CEO, and there was no area of academic study that excited me enough to apply to graduate school. So I spent five years as a newspaper reporter, hoping to learn about the world. I won two California journalism awards, but found that "newspapering" was not in my blood. Music was; so I went back to school at age twenty-eight to get a teaching credential and am now in my thirteenth year teaching elementary general music.

Though my career is rewarding, it is my third love. First is my fiancée, Karen, a.k.a. Moose (who, incestuously enough, is my mother's goddaughter, and therein lies a longer tale). Second love is a cappella music—directing, arranging, singing, recording. I have been involved with a number of semiprofessional a cappella quartets, the most recent of which competed in the regional Harmony Sweepstakes in San Francisco.

After twenty-two years in the Central Valley of California (oh, Lord, stuck in Lodi again), I have recently moved to the Seattle area to be with Moose. Another career change is imminent, and it will likely have something to do with some form of personal coaching in the areas of music and/or education.

HOME: Lynnwood, WA   **OCCUPATION:** Music Teacher   **BIRTHPLACE:** Park Forest, IL **SECONDARY SCHOOL:** Rich Central High School, Olympia Fields, IL   **YEARS AT COLLEGE:** 1971–75   **SPOUSE/PARTNER:** Janet Louise, Sept. 12, 1982, divorced, Dec. 30, 1995; Karen Marie Sciarretta (fiancée)   **SPOUSE'S OCCUPATION:** Stay-at-Home Mom (transitioning to geriatric social work)   **HARVARD/RADCLIFFE SIBLINGS:** Neil Philip Motenko '73; J.D. '73   **COLLEGE ACTIVITIES:** 'Cliffe Notes, a cappella sextet; manager. Publishing Division, Harvard Student Agencies; Glee Club; reporter, newscast anchor, classical D.J. WHRB

Peter Roland Mueser: I left Cambridge in 1977 to attend graduate school in sociology at the University of Chicago, finishing a Ph.D. in 1983. Discovering that I had become an economist (a Chicago economist, at that), I found myself in economics departments, first at Johns Hopkins (1983–85) and then at the University of Missouri (since 1985). I was married in 1983, ultimately solving a joint career problem when my wife and I both got tenure at the University of Missouri in 1991, only to break up in 1994. (We did not have children.).

When I can get out of Missouri — which is not often enough — I still hike, ski, sail, and, when I need an escape in Missouri, I play squash. I canoe. I live in the "country," a twenty-minute drive from my office, and I can watch deer, turkey, and assorted fauna around my house. I enjoy my work. I'm currently looking at the impacts of welfare reform, and developing and testing models of individual behavior.

My politics remain inscrutable to everyone but me. My University of Chicago training convinced me of the importance of protecting property rights and the foolishness of most government intervention. But I still think the justification for redistributing resources is compelling, and I am not convinced that the fall of the Soviet bloc "proved" that free market capitalism is really superior to all imaginable alternatives.

HOME: Columbia, MO   **OCCUPATION:** Associate Professor, Economics. Dept. of Economics, University of Missouri   **BIRTHPLACE:** New York, NY   **SECONDARY SCHOOL:** Mountain Lakes High School, Mountain Lakes, NJ   **YEARS AT COLLEGE:** 1971–77   **DEGREES:** A.B., magna cum laude, '75 ('77); M.A., Univ. of Chicago, '79, Ph.D. ibid. '83

John Michael Murphy: Well, it has been twenty-five years and a lot has happened. Overall, it has been a good ride. Joby and I have four wonderful children who keep us hopping. I have found my niche so to speak. I am a director in the Software Consulting Group at Information Resources, Inc. I really enjoy overseeing the development of custom decision support applications that make information available to our clients. And now, with the Web, it is even more fun.

Of course, life does throw us all some curve balls. I have lost most of my hearing in my right ear. Periodically, Meniere's disease gives me dizzy spells and makes my hearing in my "good" left ear bad for weeks. These attacks are scary and frustrating. The good news is that I can take steps to try to avoid these attacks.

Finally, did anyone think of asking for an "extension" on this assignment to summarize the last twenty-five years by October 15th? I did, but I decided not to.

Here's to the next twenty-five years.

HOME: Monroe, CT   OCCUPATION: Director, Software Consulting Group. Project Management Information Resources, Inc. (provider of consumer packaged goods sales and marketing information)   BIRTHPLACE: Milford, MA   SECONDARY SCHOOL: Medway High School, Medway, MA   YEARS AT COLLEGE: 1971–75   DEGREES: A.B., cum laude, '75; M.B.A., Columbia '77   SPOUSE/PARTNER: Joanne "Joby," Feb. 5, 1983 (Wilkes Coll. '80)   SPOUSE'S OCCUPATION: Homemaker   CHILDREN: Michael, 1986; Colleen, 1987; Karyn, 1990; Brian, 1993   COLLEGE ACTIVITIES: Class treasurer, 1976-1998; football manager, 1971–73; Crimson Key Society, 1971–75

Stephen Dennis Murphy: After leaving Harvard in 1976 (I graduated a year late), I worked in the steamship business for two years managing intermodal container traffic for an agency in Boston. I enjoyed this job! But I really wanted to sail aboard a ship, not just watch them leave port from my office window. So, in 1978, I joined the Navy as an ensign in the Supply Corps.

I served four tours on active duty, two aboard ships, one with the Seabees, and one at a small base outside Washington, D.C. They were some of the best years of my life. I discovered that I was capable and could be successful and could have fun while working very, very hard. I planned to finish my career in the Navy, but other events intervened.

In the early eighties, disturbing reports came to all of us of young men coming down with an odd set of symptoms that eventually and inevitably led to their deaths. We all came to know this syndrome as AIDS, and some of us came to know it better than others. I watched as many of my friends acquired this disease, then in 1986, while serving as the supply officer on the USS *Haleakala*, I tested positive for the HIV virus myself.

Needless to say, these events changed the course of my life. At my own volition, I left active duty; however, I stayed with the Naval Reserve. It was only after leaving the Navy that I discovered my skill as a writer, publishing articles and writing technical documentation on logistics subjects arising out of my Navy Supply Corps background.

Since that time, I have remained healthy (for reasons that no one understands) and have become an expert technical writer. I've done a great deal of volunteer work, some of it with persons with AIDS, plus additional work with my church and community. In January 1999, I was particularly proud to retire as a lieutenant commander from the Naval Reserve. Although I continue to be successful in my profession, it is a bittersweet time in which the "old growth forest" of friends have passed away before their time and the landscape is now filled with shrubs and young saplings.

It would be wonderful to hear from any of my Harvard classmates.

HOME: Alexandria, VA   OCCUPATION: Senior Technical Writer. MURPHUS
BIRTHPLACE: Boston, MA   SECONDARY SCHOOL: Lincoln-Sudbury Regional High
School, Sudbury, MA   YEARS AT COLLEGE: 1971–76   DEGREES: A.B. '75 ('76)

William F. Murphy: By the time I'm actually twenty-five years graduated from Harvard, I will, of course, have: (a) held a national elected office; (b) shot an incredibly large animal on Safari; (c) solved several intractable social problems (poverty; ethnic strife; the lack of good programming content on daytime TV); and (d) written the novel defining our generation for posterity.

I'm a *little* behind schedule, at the moment, but here's the interim report.

Nancy and I have lived in San Francisco since 1979 (following the year I clerked for a federal judge in Los Angeles after law school). We have since been blessed with three great children (Will, now a high school senior; Matt, a high school sophomore; and Anne, a seventh grader), great friends, great colleagues, and a fiercely antisocial Jack Russell terrier. I left a big law firm, Pillsbury, Madison & Sutro, to start my own law firm in 1982 (a potentially super-bad idea made easier to execute by Nancy's temporary confinement with a six-week-old newborn) and — more dumb luck and key life decisions made for me by others, including my spouse, clients, judges, and juries — we're still in business seventeen years later, now with twenty lawyers. The work remains interesting and varied. A million-dollar jury verdict for a disparaged former employee of a large aerospace company (upheld on appeal), the successful defense of a San Quentin prison guard in a five-month jury trial, a five-year battle on behalf of a co-founder of a computer magazine whose start-up was stolen by a (heartless) New York media giant, and walking a civilian employee of the U.S. Navy after he was charged (wrongly) with ordering a munitions train to run over demonstrators at the Concord Naval Weapons Station, are a few of my personal highlights, but every case, every client, matters; I have tried to enjoy them all.

HOME: San Francisco, CA   **OCCUPATION:** Lawyer. Dillingham & Murphy   **BIRTHPLACE:** Aurora, IL   **SECONDARY SCHOOL:** Marmion Military Academy, Aurora, IL   **YEARS AT COLLEGE:** 1971–75   **DEGREES:** A.B., magna cum laude, '75; J.D., Cornell '78 **SPOUSE/PARTNER:** Nancy R. (Wellesley Coll. '76)   **SPOUSE'S OCCUPATION:** Editor. Global Business Network   **CHILDREN:** William R., 1982; Matthew P., 1983; Anne L., 1987 **COLLEGE ACTIVITIES:** *Harvard Lampoon,* 1972–75; Delphic Club, 1972–75; Lowell House Committee, 1974–75; Orator. Class Day Ivy, 1975

Timothy B. Neal: Survived two marriages.

Surviving one teenaged daughter (light of my life).

Twenty-five successful years in a variety of businesses. (Food/beverage manufacturing, distribution.)

Quietly and comfortably pursuing the art of small business in a small town.

I recently had the pleasure to participate in an alumni adventure to Turkey and Greece. Hats off to Roger P. Cheever ('67). Send him money.

HOME: Pacific Grove, CA   **OCCUPATION:** Business Owner. Movie Mart (video and DVD rentals)   **BIRTHPLACE:** San Francisco, CA   **SECONDARY SCHOOL:** Univ. of Chicago Laboratory School   **YEARS AT COLLEGE:** 1971–75   **DEGREES:** A.B. '75 **CHILDREN:** Tara Erin. 1984   **HARVARD/RADCLIFFE SIBLINGS:** Richard C. Neal '69; Stephen C. Neal '70

John H. Noble: I've been spending a lot of time recently with students in their forties talking about career transition and self-assessment. There are a number of exercises I ask them to complete as part of our course that have proven quite intriguing. One asks them to write their own eulogies in an effort to get them thinking about what they have accomplished and what more they'd like to accomplish in life, how they'd like to be remembered, and who have been the most important people in their lives. Accomplishments, attributes, and associations. The exercise seems to provoke thought and discussion. Another exercise asks people to go back in life and list all the major decisions they've made, good or bad, and examine them as they think about the next career move they make. This helps people see their patterns of decision making and suggests to them how to make as good or better decisions in the future. And, there are many other exercises, but the last one, which I find most difficult, asks each student to create a unique personal mission statement. In one paragraph or less, they must identify the core of what they do and who they are and why they're here. I'm still working on mine, but I think I almost have it: something about being a good husband and father, contributing in whatever way I can to help others, and continuing to work on this mission statement. Maybe by the Fiftieth Reunion, I'll have a final draft to share with you. I wonder, in the end, how different each of ours will be.

HOME: Auburndale, MA   **OCCUPATION:** Director of Career Services. John F. Kennedy School of Government   **BIRTHPLACE:** San Francisco, CA   **SECONDARY SCHOOL:** Mt. Hermon School, Mt. Hermon, MA   **YEARS AT CoLLEGE:** 1971–75   **DEGREES:** A.B., cum laude, '75; M.S., Bank Street Coll. of Education '80   **SPOUSE/PARTNER:** Susan E. Hadfield, June 23, 1979 (Mount Holyoke Coll. '73; M.M., New England Conservatory of Music '79)   **SPOUSE'S OCCUPATION:** Self-Employed Piano Teacher   **CHILDREN:** Abigail, 1981; Whit, 1985   **HARVARD/RADCLIFFE SIBLINGS:** William G. Read, '73 (stepbrother); Alisande "Lisa" Citron, '76 (stepsister)   **COLLEGE ACTIVITIES:** Jazz band, 1972–75; concert band, 1971–75; marching band, 1971–75; Hasty Pudding show, 1975; Phillips Brooks House, 1973–75; varsity cross-country team; Dramatic Club, 1973–75

Richard Daniel Packenham: What a long strange trip it's been! It's been a good run with a lot of fun. Knock on wood (as the immortal Eddie Floyd said). Life's been good to me so far. I made my century Deadhead bones. I made the switch to Phish without too much grumbling after Jerry left us. Bob Dylan is back and never sounded better. I saw a freshman named Michael Jordan beat Patrick Ewing and the Georgetown Hoyas in the 1982 NCAAs in New Orleans. I saw Villanova versus Georgetown in Kentucky in the 1985 NCAAs. I saw U2 open their last tour in Vegas. I saw Breeders Cups in Santa Anita, Belmont, and Churchill Downs. I got a doggy bag of Dom Perignon for a beautiful woman in a streetside café on the Champs Elysées. I've been to Sydney, Tahiti, and Memphis. I got married at the tender age of thirty (a babe untimely ripped from my mother's arms) and Susan is still with me. My Mather House roommates, assorted friends, and I celebrated our fortieth birthdays in Bermuda. I practice law, teach continuing legal education (CLE), and roam the highways with my six-CD changer in the trunk. I believe in George Clinton, but not Bill Clinton. I am the last of the bleeding heart liberals. I recently had the thrill of playing a fundraiser golf tournament with my nine-year-old son, Cohn. I help coach or am the coach for Cohn (nine), Olivia (eight), and Luke (five) in hockey and in baseball. Harvard women's hockey rules! It's a thrill to see your daughter check the biggest boys on the ice. Life is also on the go. Get up for the downstroke. Yesterday's history; tomorrow's a mystery; let's work on today. Have fun!

HOME: Walpole, MA   **OCCUPATION:** Attorney; President. Packenham, Schmidt & Federico PC   **BIRTHPLACE:** Newton, MA   **SECONDARY SCHOOL:** St. Sebastian's, Needham, MA   **YEARS AT COLLEGE:** 1971–75   **DEGREES:** A.B., cum laude, '75ß J.D., Boston Coll. '78; LL.M., Boston Univ. '85   **SPOUSE/PARTNER:** Susan Smillie (Boston Coll. '78)   **SPOUSE'S OCCUPATION:** At Home   **CHILDREN:** Cohn R., 1989; Olivia M., 1991; Luke E., 1994   **COLLEGE ACTIVITIES:** Lightweight crew, 1971–73; Mather House Council, 1973–75

Mercedes Barbara Padrino: After leaving Harvard, I became a teacher and married our classmate, Dale Anderson. I taught English in a public high school for four years. Teaching was both exhilarating and exhausting. I took a breather then for a couple of years, but still tried to be a do-gooder and worked on voluntary school desegregation programs in the Boston area. Having confirmed that educational politics are only minimally about education, I cut back to part-time hours and started teaching Spanish to adults and doing translations.

In 1982, Dale and I moved to Pennsylvania to be closer to family. I began teaching English part-time at Trenton State College. Our first son, Daniel, was born in 1983 and our second, Charlie, in 1987. I quit work altogether for a time when each of the boys was little and stayed home reading Dr. Seuss and "Los perritos," playing "shapes bingo," going to Mom and Tot classes, and following the continuing saga of Oscar the Grouch. I also finished writing a novel that nobody wants to publish. In 1992, I went back to teaching, splitting the time between Trenton State and my local community college. The workload was absurd, and two years later I cut back on teaching. Then Dale got me involved editing and translating textbooks. Now I just work on textbooks out of the house and share an office with him. It's really nice.

My biggest concern at this point is helping our boys grow up to be decent human beings. My second is learning enough about soil, pruning, and fertilizing to plant a decent garden. I wish I could make more time for reading, but know it will be there again soon enough. Right now, I'm feeling fortunate to have my family and friends and thankful for the life we have.

HOME: Newtown, PA   **OCCUPATION:** Freelance Writer; Translator; Editor **BIRTHPLACE:** Havana, Cuba   **SECONDARY SCHOOL:** High School of Music and Art, New York City, NY   **YEARS AT COLLEGE:** 1971–75   **DEGREES:** A.B., cum laude, '75; M.A.T., Brown '76   **SPOUSE/PARTNER:** Dale Lynn Anderson, July 24, 1976 (Harvard '75) **SPOUSE'S OCCUPATION:** Freelance Writer; Editor (works from home)   **CHILDREN:** Daniel Sebastian, 1983; Charles Altomare, 1987

Allan Richard Pasch: Twenty-five years have passed quickly. Without question the high point was marriage to Sandy in 1980 — she is my friend/partner/advisor and the best thing that ever happened to me. Following residencies in Rochester and Chicago, we returned to Milwaukee in 1986. Life has been hectic but gratifying. Our three energetic children guarantee few dull moments, particularly now that two are adolescents.

My surgical practice has been relatively insulated from some of the negative changes in medicine. Though Milwaukee has a high penetration of managed care, I have been able to maintain some degree of autonomy and have been able to derive satisfaction from practicing medicine — no small feat in today's atmosphere.

I consider myself fortunate. I have a great family; we are all healthy and I enjoy what I do. I look forward to seeing old friends in June.

HOME: Milwaukee, WI   **OCCUPATION:** Vascular Surgeon   **BIRTHPLACE:** Milwaukee, WI   **SECONDARY SCHOOL:** Whitefish Bay High School, Whitefish Bay, WI   **YEARS AT COLLEGE:** 1971–75   **DEGREES:** A.B., cum laude, '75; M.D., Univ. of Wisconsin '79 **SPOUSE/PARTNER:** Sandra Kawczynski, May 11, 1980 (Univ. of Wisconsin '76; M.S., Univ. of Rochester '81; M.A., Medical Coll. of Wisconsin, '99)   **SPOUSE'S OCCUPATION:** Assistant Professor, Mental Health and Bioethics. Columbia College of Nursing, Milwaukee, WI   **CHILDREN:** Lauren, 1983; Whitney, 1986; Jimmy, 1989

Gregory Pennington: As the world continues on its path of becoming increasingly more diverse, I am pleased to be in a position of helping corporations and organizations create more productive environments by utilizing all of their human resources.

In thinking about the past twenty-five years and the next, there is one fundamental questions to ask: "What have you learned?" It does not matter whether you are evaluating your accomplishments or your failures. In each situation the critical questions include, "What did you learn? What would you do differently next time?" Our lives are full of races to run and mountains to climb. Each day the Lord wakes us up we have a chance to learn something and to make a difference in the lives of others. Then we know we can stand before Him and He will say "Well done!"

For the next twenty-five years, I want to keep my eye on the prize and make a difference.

HOME: Lithonia, GA   **OCCUPATION:** Managing Consultant. J. Howard & Associates (business training and consulting)   **BIRTHPLACE:** Cleveland, OH   **SECONDARY SCHOOL:** Western Reserve Academy, Hudson, OH   **YEARS AT COLLEGE:** 1971–75 **DEGREES:** A.B., cum laude, '75; Ph.D., Univ. of North Carolina, Chapel Hill '84 **SPOUSE/PARTNER:** Kristy L. Woodward, May 27, 1979 (Wellesley Coll. '77)   **SPOUSE'S OCCUPATION:** Associate Broker. ReMax   **CHILDREN:** Kalin, 1986; Kyle, 1987 **COLLEGE ACTIVITIES:** Finalist. Boylston Speaking; founder. Judo Club; cultural affairs coordinator. Afro Society

---

Robert Michael Peppercorn: After finishing years of big city life in Miami, Boston, Baltimore, Salt Lake City, and Palo Alto, I made the unheard of decision to open a medical practice in a small rural community north of Sacramento, California, called Yuba City. Since my second career choice after medicine — being the new Walter Cronkite — wouldn't work out here, I became active in local origination cable TV. In addition to getting my dermatology, cosmetic surgery, and allergy practice off and running, I started a medical information show that has now become the longest-running cable TV show of its kind in the United States, called the *Medical Explorer.* This has made me into a local celebrity as I interview and teach the community about local available medical services and new breakthroughs. After seventeen years of this, I have become a fixture of the community and am proud to be involved in local small town projects such as 4-H, county fairs, etc. Weekend trips, to San Francisco, Lake Tahoe, and beautiful downtown Sacramento always make me appreciate returning to our rural community. Priorities of life changed in 1990 when I married my beloved wife Judy, and now have a wonderful, often stubborn, daughter, Leanna, age seven. Now with twenty employees, another doctor, two physician assistants, and three offices, I'm thinking of running for election to the local school board (instead of my third career choice to become a U.S. senator). Another diversion has been the Internet, where I struggled to learn Web page writing by creating my Web page.

HOME: Yuba City, CA   **OCCUPATION:** Dermatologist; Cosmetic Surgeon; Medical Director. Advanced Skin and Allergy Medical Group   **BIRTHPLACE:** Spartanburg, SC **SECONDARY SCHOOL:** Miami Beach Senior High School, Miami Beach, FL   **YEARS AT COLLEGE:** 1971–73   **DEGREES:** M.D., Johns Hopkins Univ. '78   **SPOUSE/PARTNER:** Judy, June 1990   **CHILDREN:** Leanna, 1992   **COLLEGE ACTIVITIES:** Founder and president, Premedical Society, 1971–73; Freshmen Council, 1971

Winthrop Dunn Perkins: For nearly the last eighteen years New Jersey has been my home and, indirectly, sort of my life's work. I came here because I wanted my own hangar for my newly restored antique airplane, and wound up more or less inventing several different, but related, careers for myself. Morristown Airport was the first major airport in the world to be fully and completely privatized, i.e., long-term control and responsibility for operation and development was conveyed by government to the private sector. I was lucky enough to be in the right place at the right time, and as a real estate developer, I have been allowed to help alter many of the traditional concepts of airport property ownership and use, particularly for corporate aviation.

I also realized there was a large, untapped market for appraisal services that were designed to address the specialized nature of airport and aviation properties and businesses. I go to the airport to "work," and when I fly my plane, other people mostly pick up the tab. If you are a pilot and like to fly, this amounts to basically winning the lottery. When things aren't going so well, as sometimes happens, and I'm feeling put upon, I can usually snap out of it quickly by remembering how lucky I am in this regard. The only downside is that on rare occasions good, able friends and colleagues get killed doing the very thing they (and you) most like to do. Not surprisingly, this also restores lost or obscured appreciation for your life.

I have been very fortunate to have married a woman who provided all kinds of support, and I'm grateful. I still play music as my prime hobby, and am far more serious about it now than I ever was. When every part of me seems deadened by the life described in the first two paragraphs, music brings me back into the land of the living nearly every time. I'm looking forward to the Reunion and seeing people who, though I may not have seen a lot of them in the last twenty-five years, will still be good, close friends, and make me laugh really hard. This is what I believe most people miss most about that time, and as we live our lives downstream from college, this is the main thing that I think is never quite the same as it was back then.

HOME: Summit, NJ   **OCCUPATION:** President. Homedrome Development Corp. and Airport & Aviation Appraisals, Inc. (airport property development and valuation) **BIRTHPLACE:** Concord, MA   **SECONDARY SCHOOL:** Noble and Greenough School, Dedham, MA   **YEARS AT COLLEGE:** 1971–74   **DEGREES:** A.B. '75 ('74) **SPOUSE/PARTNER:** Gloria Susan Lemeske, April 25, 1981 (Florida State Univ. '71) **SPOUSE'S OCCUPATION:** Wife; Mother   **CHILDREN:** Nathan Arizona, 1990; Averill Elaina, 1993   **COLLEGE ACTIVITIES:** Freshman and House football

Daniel Thomas Potts: When I was an undergraduate I became deeply involved at the Peabody Museum, participating in Harvard's archaeological excavations both in the Lower Mississippi Valley (summer 1972) and in Iran (summers of 1973 and 1975). Majoring in anthropology with a specialty in archaeology, I then received a DAAD (German academic exchange service) fellowship and spent the academic year 1975–76 in Berlin, returning to Harvard from 1976–1980, where I did my Ph.D. During this time I met Hildreth Burnett, an amazingly talented artist in many media, got married and then, upon receiving my degree, set off for Cyprus, where I was to take up a job. The job fell through while we were en route. I picked up a one-year appointment in Copenhagen, then a five-year assistant professorship in Berlin, then five more years in Copenhagen, and finally the chair in Near Eastern archaeology at the University of Sydney. I never set out to be an expatriate academic but so it goes. Along the way we've had three fantastic children, Rowena, Morgan and Hallam, and wound up living in a fantastic country and in arguably one of the most livable cities in the world. We are now devout fans of rugby union (go the Wallabies!), cricket, Australian wine, and the Australian way of life. Will we ever come back to the States to live? Who knows. Meanwhile, life keeps on happening and we've just bought a second house in Sydney as a residential property investment. Academia can lead one to some unexpected places and I certainly never expected to live in Australia when I graduated from Harvard. Along the way, my family has given me great love and support as I've written a string of books and excavated a number of sites in the United Arab Emirates. It's been a full, varied life and shows no signs of slowing up. We only wish we weren't so far from friends and family, but we do get back to the States from time to time and more and more people seem to come to Sydney.

HOME: Queen's Park, NSW, Australia   OCCUPATION: Edwin Cuthbert Hall Professor in Middle Eastern Archaeology. School of Archaeology, University of Sydney
BIRTHPLACE: New York, NY   SECONDARY SCHOOL: Verona High School, Verona, NJ
YEARS AT COLLEGE: 1971–75   DEGREES: A.B., magna cum laude, '75; Ph.D. '80; D.Phil. Univ. of Copenhagen '91   SPOUSE/PARTNER: Hildreth Burnett, June 2, 1979 (Harvard Extension School '77)   SPOUSE'S OCCUPATION: Painter; Sculptor   CHILDREN: Rowena, 1983; Morgan, 1985; Hallam, 1994   COLLEGE ACTIVITIES: Captain, Freshman soccer, 1971; varsity soccer, 1972–73

Susan Marie Praeder: I have lived on two coasts and two continents. Six years in the San Francisco Bay Area (1974–80). Gathering of graduate degrees in biblical studies and classics (Greek and Latin). May I help you? Sales clerking in the book and wine departments at Macy's California. Two study trips to Germany and Italy. Will that be cash or charge?

Seven years in Boston (1980–87). Mondays, Wednesdays, and Fridays as Professor SMP at Boston College. An innovative core course on the Bible in art, film, literature, and music. Running around the Chestnut Hill Reservoir, up to the Brookline Reservoir, and out Route 9. The first, the only, and the youngest. Summers and whole semesters in Germany. Thursdays at the Longy School and in Widener Library. Torn to pieces by systematic theologians.

Twelve years in Munich (1987 to the present). Classic Produktion Osnabrück (cpo) Dabringhaus und Grimm (MDG), Koch Classics. Three-hour lunch breaks and walks at Nymphenburg Castle and in my backyard and outdoor think tank, the Old North Cemetery. Trips to Portugal and Spain. Wishing you new musical discoveries and new listening pleasure.

I am not on the career-and-family track. I am too much of a bohemian, clown, dissident exile, and odyssey girl for settled existence. There is not a bourgeois bone in my body. Yes, I am still a vegetarian.

I am currently an editor and translator in the field of classical music. Advertising, CD booklets, opera libretti, songs. I am also a student and teacher at the University of Munich, where my doctoral fields are Portuguese, Spanish, and English literature and my course offerings in 1999–2000 will include Aemilia Lanyer and D. H. Lawrence. In my free time I compose and write.

Harvard is my most frequent U.S. correspondent, and I enjoy meeting candidates for admission in my role as an international interviewer.

HOME: Munich, Germany   **OCCUPATION:** Translator; Writer   **BIRTHPLACE:** San Mateo, CA   **SECONDARY SCHOOL:** Castilleja School, Palo Alto, CA   **YEARS AT COLLEGE:** 1971–74   **DEGREES:** A.B., magna cum laude, '75 ('74); M.A., Univ. of California, Berkeley '79; Ph.D., Graduate Theological Union, Berkeley '80

Janet Collins Prill: While it is pretty sobering to sit down to address this topic, I find myself quite happy at this point in my life. I welcome this stage and the opportunity to remix some of my past accomplishments and interests in the years ahead.

As with many of my female colleagues, I graduated from college with the notion that, if I wanted, there was nothing I couldn't achieve and have in addition to a family. I vigorously pursued this goal in marketing positions with IBM and seemed to be having some success with it. My husband, Dave, moved to Saint Louis with me and our first child in 1989, commuting back to New York to fulfill his responsibilities. He enjoyed calling himself the "trailing spouse" and delighted in my achievement. However, when the twins were born there, the job became too much, causing us to return to the East Coast after just two years. Headquarters proximity would presumably offer greater flexibility to balance a bigger family and dual careers. In addition, I was reluctantly building skills in hiring and managing child-care help, my life-line to a professional life. When our fourth child came along, I felt it was a real badge of honor to have achieved (and survived) in the corporate milieu with a family of this size.

I will never know how long I would have continued on this "I can still have it all" path, because Dave was offered a very interesting opportunity to work in Europe in 1997. Now I am the "trailing spouse" to Paris, a much better deal by all measures. After twenty years at IBM, more than half of this as a working mom, I have had the opportunity to recast my role in the family. It was a difficult adjustment at first, as my value system wasn't calibrated for full-time homework help and lunch-bag packing. How lucky I am, however, at just this time in our children's lives, to have the chance to spend more time with them. It has made me rethink many of the notions that motivated me in my career. I still want our daughter to think she can achieve anything, but — having it all? We'll have to talk.

Living in France continues to be a wonderful experience for our family. The children are in their third year at a French *lycée* and are now bilingual. Beyond that, their exposure to multiple nationalities through school and our community is providing them a rich multicultural experience. My language facility is reasonably good, and I love finally being able to blend in a bit and feel at home. How I wish I had pursued my early interest and majored in language at Harvard! In addition to the language classes, I have indulged in French cooking classes (including at the Cordon Bleu) and am now taken with French antique furniture and decorative arts. This is the area I'm considering when it's time to add work back into the equation.

While the path to this point has not always been smooth, it has been very rich. I can only hope for similarly rewarding years in the next quarter century.

HOME: Fourqueux, France   OCCUPATION: Homemaker   SECONDARY SCHOOL: Bridgewater Raritan High School East, Somerville, NJ   YEARS AT COLLEGE: 1971–75   DEGREES: A.B. '75   SPOUSE/PARTNER: David Andrew Prill (Lafayette Coll. '70; M.B.A., Univ. of Pennsylvania '72)   SPOUSE'S OCCUPATION: Vice President, Industrial Sector Services. IBM Eurocoordination, IBM Global Services   CHILDREN: Derek Collins Prill, 1986; Vanessa Partridge Prill, 1990; Skylar Hyde Prill, 1990; Wyatt Collins Prill, 1995   COLLEGE ACTIVITIES: President, Radcliffe Union of Students, 1973–74; Currier House crew, 1971–72; Radcliffe crew, 1972–73; Harvard cheerleader, 1972–73

Michael Edgar Pulitzer, Jr.: Over these years, I have nurtured a family, a career, and found a sense of place. After graduation, I married Ramelle Cochrane in January 1976 and then headed west to achieve an M.F.A. in film producing at the American Film Institute. Our first daughter, Tia, was born in 1978. Early in her life she was afflicted with Juvenile Rheumatoid Arthritis, a chronic illness that has gone into remission. Then, my namesake, Cael, was born in 1982 and our youngest son Philip was born in 1984. I worked in Los Angeles in the film production area first on the Paramount lot. I headed into sales with a small distribution company and in 1988 moved back east to begin a career in local television management first in national sales and then local sales and now in the operations of a television and radio operation in Winston-Salem, North Carolina. I have hanging in my office a simple saying, "I am not from the South but I got here as quick as I could." I have spent many weekends following my sons across the soccer fields of North Carolina and watching my daughter compete in horse shows. I have joined the Moravian Church and have enjoyed spiritual growth and fellowship with this congregation. The community has appreciated my efforts and I find myself active in the United Way, the Chamber of Commerce, where I chair the film commission, and the Rotary Club. While reflecting on the past twenty-five years, I am grateful for the blessings that I have shared with my spouse, our children, and a career as a broadcasting executive here in Winston-Salem.

HOME: Winston-Salem, NC   OCCUPATION: Television and Radio Executive   BIRTHPLACE: Boston, MA   SECONDARY SCHOOL: St. Mark's School, Southborough, MA   YEARS AT COLLEGE: 1970–75   DEGREES: A.B., cum laude, '75; M.F.A., American Film Inst. '78   SPOUSE/PARTNER: Ramelle Cochrane, Jan. 3, 1976 (Pitzer Coll.)   SPOUSE'S OCCUPATION: Executive Director. Associated Artists of Winston-Salem   CHILDREN: Theodosia "Tia," 1978; Michael "Cael" 3d, 1982; Philip, 1984   COLLEGE ACTIVITIES: Sailing team, 1972–74, NCAA Champion; commodore, Harvard Yacht Club, 1975; Fly Club, 1972–75

Alan H. Rappaport: Life in the twenty-five years since Harvard has been fun and rewarding. My family centers my world; Jill and I have been married nearly twenty years with two great kids—Alex at eleven and Hilary who is eight. Weekends and holidays are happily spent shuttling between events and exploring the world together. The adventures we complete reveal even more that we would like to do.

Following Stanford Business School, I embarked on a career in the financial service industry, where now I am responsible for the asset management business of CIBC Oppenheimer. We invest throughout the world, in developed and developing economies, in both public and private securities. We played a pioneering role in moving capital to emerging markets—not always an easy endeavor—and this global investment activity has proven to be both good business and continually intellectually challenging.

We spend our time between our homes in Bronxville and Martha's Vineyard—communities where Jill and I grew up. In a world where the pace of change has accelerated and lives become increasingly complex, we greatly value our attachment to our communities.

HOME: Bronxville, NY   OCCUPATION: Managing Director. CIBC Oppenheimer (asset management)   BIRTHPLACE: Oak Bluffs, MA   SECONDARY SCHOOL: Middlesex School, Concord, MA   YEARS AT COLLEGE: 1971–75   DEGREES: A.B., magna cum laude, '75; M.B.A., Stanford '78   SPOUSE/PARTNER: Jill Pearson, 1981 (Wesleyan Univ. '78)   CHILDREN: Alex, 1988; Hilary, 1991

Josna Elizabeth Rege: At the time of our Tenth Class Reunion I had just married and had a baby. Now the baby, Nikhil, is in high school, with everything that that implies! In the meantime I went back to school, completed a Ph.D. in English, and am now teaching postcolonial literature at Dartmouth. I discovered postcolonial studies quite by accident in graduate school, but felt immediately that the then-infant field had been dreamed up for me personally. Teaching is a joy, and the undergraduates keep me fresh, although they do seem to get younger every year.

My husband, Andrew Melnechuk, Nikhil, and I now live in Amherst, Massachusetts, where Andrew runs Whetstone Press, his letterpress printing business. Both of our parents have moved here since they retired, so I have my in-laws next door and my parents a couple of miles down the road. Our ten years in Amherst is the longest time I've ever lived in one place, and after a childhood of frequent moves from country to country with all our relatives continents away, it's wonderful to have the support and comfort of extended family close at hand. We lived with relatives in India for half a year when Nikhil was in elementary school, invaluable for him, and the fulfillment of one of my desires. Now, after thirty years in America, I'm finally preparing to take U.S. citizenship, in time for the next elections.

After twenty-five years of going along in a steady state, I am suddenly noticing my age, and find that I must work at staying alert and fit, both mentally and physically. Watching my friends' children leaving for college, I realize that my son, too, will be soon off into the world. I won't get philosophical on you, fellow classmates, but that's only because my three hundred words are up.

HOME: Amherst, MA   **OCCUPATION:** Assistant Professor of English. Dartmouth College   **BIRTHPLACE:** London, England   **SECONDARY SCHOOL:** Mt. Hermon School, Darjeeling, West Bengal, India; Broxbourne School, Broxbourne, Herts, England; Parliament Hill School, London, England; Brookline High School, Brookline, MA   **YEARS AT COLLEGE:** 1971–75   **DEGREES:** A.B., cum laude, '75; M.A., Univ. of Massachusetts, Amherst '89; Ph.D., ibid., '95   **SPOUSE/PARTNER:** Andrew Theodore Melnechuk (Massachusetts Coll. of Art '75)   **SPOUSE'S OCCUPATION:** Owner; Operator. Whetstone Press (works from home)   **CHILDREN:** Nikhil Alexander, 1984

Douglas F. Reid: The time since graduation has gone remarkably fast. I remember many events from Harvard and from business school as if they were yesterday.

The best luck I ever had was meeting my wife, my favorite person in the world, and having our two kids, Jill, age eleven, and Tommy, age six. Tommy was born with a cleft lip and palate, and working through all that, living with his courage and strength, overshadows any other experience I've had.

HOME: Atlanta, GA   **OCCUPATION:** Owner; Executive. United Distributors, Inc. (wholesale beverage business)   **BIRTHPLACE:** Detroit, MI   **SECONDARY SCHOOL:** University-Liggett School, Grosse Pointe, MI   **YEARS AT COLLEGE:** 1971–75   **DEGREES:** A.B., cum laude, '75; M.B.A., Stanford Univ. '77   **SPOUSE/PARTNER:** Patty, November 1987 (Univ. of Virginia '77; M.BA., Tulane Univ. '79)   **SPOUSE'S OCCUPATION:** Community Volunteer   **CHILDREN:** Jill; Tommy   **COLLEGE ACTIVITIES:** Intramurals; *Harvard Independent;* WHRB; Spee Club; Hasty Pudding

Thomas E. Reinert, Jr.: Departed Harvard as a confused psychology major, worked in vocational rehabilitation in New York City for two years, married the love of my life, and, in 1977, returned to Harvard for law school. Law school was a surprising but fortuitous choice for me that proved to be a better path than psychology. In 1980, I moved to Washington, D.C. to practice law with Morgan, Lewis & Bockius, where I became a partner in 1988 and remain today. Professionally, I have spent the last twenty years practicing with a premier, national labor and employment practice, which has used both my legal and psychology training. My practice focuses on employment litigation and labor relations issues, particularly in the airline and railroad industries. I also have become heavily involved in the administrative side of the practice, with special responsibilities for computerization, conflicts, and professional responsibility.

Personally, Chris and I have been busy rearing two great, intellectually alive children. We live comfortably in Fairfax County, Virginia, known nationally for its great school system, high-tech business, and increasingly intolerable traffic. On weekends we escape to Annapolis and the Chesapeake Bay to sail, eat crabs, or work on our boat. Ours is a full and good life.

At twenty-five years out and approaching the millennium, life is becoming more interesting, not less. We have been living through revolutions in information processing and communications, social roles, and business and economics. All of these changes impact the workplace, and my perch as a labor lawyer has given me a great perspective. Harvard did prepare me for life-long learning: over the last several years, I have undertaken to learn computers, legal ethics, parenting teenagers, sailing, and meditation. And I am beginning to believe that amidst this learning, I might be acquiring some wisdom.

HOME: Vienna, VA   **OCCUPATION:** Partner. Morgan, Lewis & Bockius, LLP (law firm)
BIRTHPLACE: Mineola, NY   **SECONDARY SCHOOL:** West Hempstead High School,
West Hempstead, NY   **YEARS AT COLLEGE:** 1971–75   **DEGREES:** A.B., cum laude, '75;
J.D. '80   **SPOUSE/PARTNER:** Christine Anderson, July 17, 1976 (Columbia '75)
SPOUSE'S OCCUPATION: Homemaker   **CHILDREN:** Theodore Andrew, 1983; Anna
Elizabeth, 1986

James R. Repetti: I am composing this letter exactly twenty-eight years after the day I borrowed a car from my aunt, who lived across the street from the South Boston Boys Club, to transport my belongings to Harvard. Having never driven to Harvard Square, I quickly became lost as I crossed the Boston line into Cambridge. Eventually, I found Harvard Square.

I am glad that such an inauspicious beginning for my journey to college did not portend my future journey through life. Life has been much kinder to me than I ever expected or even hoped for in the things that matter the most to me — my family. I am blessed with three wonderful children, who range in age from five to fourteen, and a great wife. We are focused on spending time outdoors and particularly enjoy sailing, skiing, and hiking. As my children have grown, I have also coached every imaginable sport and currently serve as scoutmaster in Dover.

Life has also been kind to me in my career. I am a professor of law at Boston College Law School and counsel to the historic Boston law firm Hill & Barlow. These positions have provided the opportunity for intellectual exploration, spiced with the drama of the real world. After having published several books and articles, however, I am getting "antsy" to try something new.

There are two people who were at Harvard while we were students who I would like to thank for their encouragement and support — Bill Raduchel and the late Coach Bill McCurdy. They guided and provided encouragement to a lost city kid who never would have made it through Harvard without their help. Thank you!

HOME: Dover, MA   **OCCUPATION:** Professor of Law. Boston College Law School
BIRTHPLACE: Boston, MA   **SECONDARY SCHOOL:** Boston Latin School, Boston, MA
YEARS AT COLLEGE: 1971–75   **DEGREES:** A.B., magna cum laude, '75; J.D., Boston Coll.
'80; M.B.A., ibid. '80   **SPOUSE/PARTNER:** Susan L. (Wellesley Coll. '77)   **SPOUSE'S**
OCCUPATION: Counsel. Nutter, McClennen & Fish   **CHILDREN:** Jane, 1986; Tom, 1988;
Caroline, 1995   **COLLEGE ACTIVITIES:** Track, 1971–74; football, 1972–73; House
Committee, 1973–75

Robert Allen Rikoon: As a father, husband, and employer, most of my time is spent trying to communicate with others, although I remain, at heart, a hermit. Santa Fe is a great place to paint outdoors and to train for the assorted summer and winter triathlons in which I participate. I find that of our family's many successes here, the most gratifying is contributing to building a sense of community. As I grow older and more difficult to get along with, I feel grateful and blessed by my friends and colleagues, some from Harvard, but most from the hurly burly of everyday life.

My concerns are many but I retain an optimism that somehow men and women of good intent will see our world through its pressing problems. There is a sense of isolation that I often see and feel around me in my job as an investment advisor, and the publication of my book *Managing Family Trust: Taking Control of Inherited Wealth* (John Wiley, 1999) was written in the hope that the financial world will become a healthier place for our children.

My best wishes go out to all who have the time to read these class notes, though ninety percent of you I probably haven't met or can't remember!

HOME: Santa Fe, NM **OCCUPATION:** President. Rikoon Investment Advisors, Inc. **BIRTHPLACE:** New York, NY **SECONDARY SCHOOL:** New Rochelle High School, New Rochelle, NY **YEARS AT COLLEGE:** 1971–73; 1975–77 **DEGREES:** A.B., cum laude, '75 ('77); M.B.A., Univ. of New Mexico '82 **SPOUSE/PARTNER:** Deborah Kaye, March 9, 1984 (Univ. of Missouri '78) **SPOUSE'S OCCUPATION:** Student of Chinese Medicine. International Institute of Chinese Medicine, Santa Fe, NM **CHILDREN:** Robyn Angela, 1986; Hannah Rose, 1989

Carlo Julian Rizzo: I remained in the Cambridge/Boston area, and immersed myself in two occupations: professional dancer and gymnastics teacher, and later expanded into teaching creative movement and dance. The blend of athletics and performing arts very much agreed with me, making for an exciting, exhausting, hectic, bohemian, grass-roots, workaholic, insomniac career, barely lucrative, but infinitely gratifying. After reaching age forty, I began to phase myself out of performing, to concentrate on teaching. For the last five years I have been flourishing as a teacher in a dynamic and creative small private gym and arts studio for kids in Manhattan's Upper West Side. The school closed in May 1999, freeing me to get bilateral hip replacements in August of 1999. This surgery really munches you. But I'm healing nicely, and rehabbing aggressively. The next few months I'll be traveling, checking out grad-school programs in education and counseling. I hope to make our Reunion and would love to hear from any and all classmates, okay?

HOME: New York, NY   **OCCUPATION:** Teacher   **BIRTHPLACE:** Salisbury, MD
SECONDARY SCHOOL: Concord High School, Wilmington, DE   **YEARS AT COLLEGE:**
1971–75   **DEGREES:** A .B., cum laude, '75

Mont R. Roberts: Since graduation I have had a great life. I went to medical school in my hometown of Chicago. I did a residency in emergency medicine at Denver General Hospital with head honchos Peter Rosen and Vince Markovchick, and am now board certified in both emergency medicine and pediatric emergency medicine. During my first job out of training at Maricopa Medical Center in Phoenix, I went on a scuba diving vacation in the Cayman Islands that resulted in my marrying the dive buddy that I met on the trip. I subsequently moved from Phoenix to East Lansing, home of the Michigan State University Spartans and Gina's tenured position as full professor. Three very excellent children later we are still facing the forces of good and evil and appear to be winning. You know the drill: piano, soccer, swimming, basketball, tennis, and math enrichment....I was involved with the German sport of schutzhund police dog training during my single years, however our family now enjoys a mellow golden retriever. My work stuff: as an associate professor in the section of emergency medicine, I am involved with the training of emergency medicine residents; I co-edited a fifteen-hundred-page text entitled *Pediatric*

Emergency Medicine; and I am the techno-geek and Webmaster of our MSU Emergency Medicine, Lansing Website. My hobby for the last two years has been home brewing — my latest strange brews include Pumpkin Ale, Spruce Ale, Lemon Bavarian Wheat, and a Gulden Draak clone (a Belgian tripel). I am blessed with two parents and two parents-in-law who are all alive and well in their sixties and upper seventies. Sometimes when things seem to get rough, I just think of how lucky the family and I are and count our blessings for our health and happiness.

HOME: East Lansing, MI   OCCUPATION: Physician. Emergency Medical Associates
BIRTHPLACE: Evergreen Park, IL   SECONDARY SCHOOL: Evergreen Park High School, Evergreen Park, IL   YEARS AT COLLEGE: 1971–75   DEGREES: A.B., magna cum laude, '75; M.D., Univ. of Illinois   SPOUSE/PARTNER: Gina Garamone (Univ. of Wisconsin '77, M.A., ibid. '79, Ph.D., ibid. '81)   SPOUSE'S OCCUPATION: Retired Professor. Dept. of Advertising, Michigan State Univ   CHILDREN: Megan, 1988; Monty, 1990; Emma, 1991
COLLEGE ACTIVITIES: Kung-Fu Club, 1971–75; Phillips Brooks House, 1971–73; Harvard Student Agencies, 1971–75

Michael David Robinson: Six years ago, when I applied for staff privileges at my hospital, I was asked to explain to the credentials committee why I had left three previous practice settings before opening my current practice. With the benefit of hindsight, and the motivation to convince them that I was trustworthy and wouldn't skip town, I imposed a logical progression upon my career path since college. However, I knew then (and know better now) that many life decisions, career and personal, sometimes just happen, and conscious planning isn't necessarily a significant part of the process.

I was lucky to get into medical school, receiving the news on the day before Commencement. By the end of my third year, my plan was to pursue training in internal medicine, followed by subspecialty training. These plans did not include falling in love during my fourth year with the woman who is now my wife of nineteen years (not realizing it at the time), nor did they include ending up in Houston for a year in the internship which convinced me to return to the East Coast and psychiatry (which I had also fallen in love with in medical school without realizing it). After three years of residency in Washington, we moved to New York so that I could enter academic psychiatry at Mount Sinai. I learned there that caring for patients was far more gratifying than writing proposals for grants that wouldn't be funded. After one year working for a psychiatrist in practice in central New Jersey, planning to buy into a partnership, I learned that I wanted to have a personal life as well as a practice, and joined the staff of a large private psychiatric hospital near Princeton. I planned to stay there until retirement, but didn't plan on the rise of managed care, which ultimately resulted in the transformation of a gratifying position into one of dysphoria and stress. While there, I was unsuccessfully sued for malpractice, resulting in developing an interest in forensic psychiatry (starting from the wrong end). I interviewed a psychiatrist in Morristown who was selling his practice, planning to learn about the private practice setting with no intention to act quickly, if at all. We came to terms on a purchase contract within two months. I remain in practice to date, and when this goes to press I will have been in one place longer than in any previous position. With no plans to go.

We have three daughters, and our lives rotate around them. Raising them is a venture into wonderful, uncharted territory. I love my practice as well, and have found that caring for people in pain, often helping them, is far more gratifying than I had imagined. It is a privilege to work with them. My practice mixes psychopharmacology, psychotherapy, electroconvulsive therapy (ECT), and forensic psychiatry, and the mix is stimulating and challenging, occurring in the context of a generation of incredible progress in the area of pharmacotherapy (they tell you in medical school that half of the drugs that you learn about will be obsolete in five years, and it's true). I'm also trying to listen to what I tell my patients regarding setting limits — I spend too much time in the office — as well as to my family. My youngest has reminded me that since I'm my own boss, I can fire myself, and that "Daddy, you can't turn back the clock."

HOME: South Orange, NJ   **OCCUPATION:** Psychiatrist (private practice)
BIRTHPLACE: Baltimore, MD   **SECONDARY SCHOOL:** Milford Mill High School, Baltimore, MD   **YEARS AT COLLEGE:** 1971–75   **DEGREES:** A.B., cum laude, '75; M.D., Johns Hopkins Univ. '79   **SPOUSE/PARTNER:** Vicki Kass, Oct. 4, 1980 (City Coll. of New York '76)   **SPOUSE'S OCCUPATION:** Management Consultant; Volunteer
CHILDREN: Alexandra Emily, 1987; Rachel Lauren, 1989; Hannah Rose, 1991   **COLLEGE ACTIVITIES:** *Synthesis* (undergraduate journal of history and philosophy of science); Crimson Key Society; Harvard Band

Owen Lee Robinson: It is difficult to believe that twenty-five years have passed this quickly. After leaving Harvard I went on to a master's degree in biochemistry from Boston University, then an M.D. degree from Northwestern University in Chicago. The day before I started my senior year in medical school I married Linda and this June we celebrate twenty years together. During my residency at Los Angeles County Hospital, Linda and I became the parents of twin boys, Seth and Stuart. Four years later, Kimberly was welcomed into the family. The boys are now fifteen and a half years old and Kimberly is eleven and a half years old. All three are honors students in school, Stuart and Seth are tenth graders and are starters on the junior varsity football team, and Kimberly is, well, a busy sixth grader. Linda went from a busy senior travel agent to a busy mom.

Professionally, I started out working for a large medical group, but after one year of that I went into private solo practice in internal medicine. I have been in the same office for the past fourteen years and love every minute of it. (Well, not every minute.) In 1985, four other doctors and I created the first Independent Physician's Association in the South Bay area. We sold that entity in 1994, and I moved to the board of another similar group which I still serve on. My practice continues to be a busy and active one.

I have tried to keep active in Harvard life. I have been interviewing since 1976 and have served on the board of the Harvard-Radcliffe Club of Southern California in the past. Recently I was asked to serve as a marshal for our Class Reunion. It is difficult to describe the pride that accompanies this honor. I am forever grateful for the opportunity to be a part of Harvard and will continue to be a loyal supporter of the College.

HOME: Los Angeles, CA   OCCUPATION: Medical Doctor   BIRTHPLACE: Los Angeles, CA   SECONDARY SCHOOL: San Marino High School, San Marino, CA   YEARS AT COLLEGE: 1971–75   DEGREES: A.B. '75; M.A., Boston Univ. '76; M.D., Northwestern Univ. '81   SPOUSE/PARTNER: Linda, June 29, 1980   CHILDREN: Seth H. and Stuart J., 1984 (twins); Kimberly S., 1988   HARVARD/RADCLIFFE SIBLINGS: Joanne Robinson '83   COLLEGE ACTIVITIES: Harvard Band, 1971–75 (played Harvard drum 1974–75); stage crew, Hasty Pudding Show, 1973

Marie Louise Roehm: The surprises in a life full of change have been my job and my mate, both of which have been putting up with me for a very long time now (Lillick since January 1980 and Bill since June 1981). I have been working part-time, nonpartnership track in this midsize law firm since 1984 and am beginning to joke about the lack of a set retirement age for associates. Bill and I just celebrated the nineteenth anniversary of the beginning of our relationship, which has seen us through years of sailboat racing (including a quasi-Olympic Tornado campaign that finally gave me burnout in 1996) and into building and running an equestrian boarding and training facility, as well as through years of child raising (I have four stepchildren) and into enjoying grandchildren (three to date). We work harder at loving each other, and are prouder of still doing so, than anything else we do. Having aspired to uniqueness, or at least eccentricity, I am discovering that I am fairly typical of our generation. If you really want to know more, ask. [Yes, I am still an obsessive/compulsive reader, I still have nightmares about sitting an exam in a French class I never attended, and I still avoid responsibility, although with less success.]

HOME: American Canyon, CA   **OCCUPATION:** Lawyer; Associate. Lillick & Charles (law firm)   **BIRTHPLACE:** Nashville, TN   **SECONDARY SCHOOL:** Asociacion Escuelas Lincoln, Buenos Aires, Argentina   **YEARS AT COLLEGE:** 1971–75   **DEGREES:** A.B., magna cum laude, '75; J.D., Stanford Univ. '79   **SPOUSE/PARTNER:** William John Erkelens, Sr., 1989   **SPOUSE'S OCCUPATION:** Entrepreneur (bar owner, contractor, etc.)   **COLLEGE ACTIVITIES:** Sailing team, 1971–75; swimming team, 1973–75; Phillips Brooks House, 1971–73

Arthur W. "Tooey" Rogers II: I've certainly enjoyed myself these past twenty-five years. I've lived in San Francisco, New York City, Boston and Brookline, Massachusetts, and now Concord, Massachusetts. Laura and I have enjoyed travel throughout South and Central America, as well as Canada and the U.S. And we have a hard charging nine-year-old named Luke, who is passionate about soccer, World War II, and Pokémon. I coach his soccer team, "Rogers Rangers" (named after Major Robert Rogers, not me!). I have taught third and fourth grade for the past five years and am now embarking on a year off, during which I plan to keep the home fires alight as well as play and coach soccer, study physics, and work with children on nature education.

Laura is now president of the Massachusetts Audubon Society — their first woman president — and is doing very well. We live in Concord, where

my brother, Bill, sister, Margaret, and cousin, Paul, all live with a collection
of six cousins for Luke to play with.

Harvard, Deerfield, and Bement laid a great foundation for the life I have
led so far. I hope my classmates feel as fortunate as I and give something
back to their favorite institutions and charities... and to those less fortunate
than we have been.

HOME: Concord, MA   OCCUPATION: Teacher   BIRTHPLACE: Greenfield, MA
SECONDARY SCHOOL: Deerfield Academy, Deerfield, MA   YEARS AT COLLEGE:
1971–76   DEGREES: A.B. '75 ('76); M.S., Univ. of New Hampshire, 1982; M.Ed., Lesley Coll.
'93   SPOUSE/PARTNER: Laura A. Johnson, Sept. 5, 1981 (Harvard '76)   SPOUSE'S
OCCUPATION: President. Massachusetts Audubon Society   CHILDREN: Lucian "Luke" J.,
1990   COLLEGE ACTIVITIES: Hasty Pudding; Dunster Film Society; Loeb Drama Center

---

David Edward Rosenberg: For the past twenty years, I've worked
on various aspects of immigration and refugee issues, in community service
organizations, human rights advocacy, state government, consulting, and
the federal government. I'm particularly interested in the complex dynamics of incorporating large and diverse newcomer populations into our society. From 1985–91, I helped create and direct a state agency focused on
these concerns, coordinating a wide range of public and private efforts to
help thousands fleeing war and persecution start new lives in
Massachusetts; for me this was a hugely educational and inspiring experience. Moving on, I consulted for other states, foundations, think tanks and
nonprofits for three and a half years.

In 1995, I came to INS and coordinated a national project that more than
doubled the number of immigrants who became U.S. citizens annually.
Unfortunately, this success became a target of bitter Washington "accusation
and investigation" politics. The resulting unpleasantness continued at
length and has not yet faded entirely. Once again, I've learned lessons they
don't teach in government courses, even at the Kennedy School. Meanwhile,
I've focused on many other efforts to modernize and restructure a massive
bureaucratic organization. But now I'm ready for new challenges.

After twenty-six years, Pat and I continue to enjoy our dance of life
together. Pat has been a local, then national, and now international radio
news anchor. (Even if you're not part of her daily audience in Africa or
Europe or Asia, now you can hear her voice on the Net.) She's always been
a great source of strength, encouragement, and laughter. The great blessing,
joy, and reality check for both of us is our almost-five-year-old daughter

Emily Claire. Becoming parents in our forties, though sometimes exhausting, has somehow tapped new energies and keeps us thinking young.

HOME: Falls Church, VA **OCCUPATION:** Director of Program Initiatives. U.S. Immigration and Naturalization Service **BIRTHPLACE:** Dayton, OH **SECONDARY SCHOOL:** Meadowdale High School, Dayton, OH **YEARS AT COLLEGE:** 1971–75 **DEGREES:** A.B., cum laude, '75; M.P.A. '86 **SPOUSE/PARTNER:** Patricia Ann Bodnar, June 17, 1983 (Boston Coll. '75; M.A., Massachusetts Inst. of Technology '87) **SPOUSE'S OCCUPATION:** International Radio Broadcaster. Voice of America **CHILDREN:** Emily Claire, 1995

Paul Louis Rosenberg: The past quarter century has been a wild ride, with (hopefully) much more to come. At last count, I've had nine different jobs since finishing the J.D./M.B.A. program after graduation. I have had the incredible luck to fall into a number of exciting and interesting situations. The list includes: managing John Kerry's first U.S. Senate campaign; being an entrepreneur in real estate, travel, and financial services for eight years (surviving several financial near-death experiences); being Commerce Secretary Ron Brown's international trade adviser (narrowly missing an actual death experience, having left my position six months before the plane crash that killed him); serving as special counsel to the U.S. Department of State for assistance to Russia; and now being comfortably settled at Bain and Company doing management consulting.

Throughout these years, I have been nourished by the experiences I had at Harvard, and blessed by continuing friendships with classmates like Peter Broer, Dave Hutt, and Dan Small. I have also been extraordinarily lucky (as in "better to be lucky than smart") to have married Sarah Doebler, and to have two wonderful sons, Benjamin and Jacob, with her. The three of them are my greatest teachers.

As time continues to pass, I hope to be able to be open to more and more interesting experiences and challenges to be able to absorb as much as I can for the pure pleasure of it, and to keep some semblance of balance within the swirl of day-to-day living.

HOME: West Newton, MA **OCCUPATION:** Management Consultant. Bain & Company, Inc. **BIRTHPLACE:** Boston, MA **SECONDARY SCHOOL:** Newton High School, Newton, MA **YEARS AT COLLEGE:** 1971–75 **DEGREES:** A.B., magna cum laude, '75; M.B.A. '80; J.D. '80 **SPOUSE/PARTNER:** Sarah Cross Doebler, May 1989 (Boston Univ.; Ed.M., Harvard '92) **CHILDREN:** Benjamin, 1992; Jacob, 1996

Donald Andrew Rosenthal: Our family has grown since the Twentieth Reunion. We now have three terrific kids, and Kristin and I will be celebrating our tenth anniversary the week before the Reunion. I am also in the lucky position of having much more time lately to enjoy them all, including soccer, Little League, and weekend family adventures.

The software company I founded around the time of our last Reunion did quite well and was acquired in 1997. After the acquisition, I continued to run the company as a subsidiary for several years, and have recently moved out of day-to-day operations. I remain on the board of directors and continue in my position of "corporate fellow" with the parent company. Translation: I still get to participate in the excitement of strategic management without the twenty-four-hour workday and near-constant travel. It was an interesting company, based on high performance optimization techniques I originally helped develop for operations of the Hubble Space Telescope. We adapted the technology to advanced planning and scheduling tools for the manufacturing sector. The timing was fortunate, as we appeared on the scene just as the supply chain management industry was taking off.

Kristin, in the meantime has started her own company, and after a year it is a growing, highly successful enterprise that places senior management teams in pre-IPO technology companies.

I personally am hoping to eventually return to the world of "big science," where I spent much of the first fifteen years after graduation. The thrills of the entrepreneurial roller-coaster ride are quite seductive, but it's hard to beat the fulfillment of sitting in the control room of the Arecibo Observatory as signals from pulsars or distant galaxies arrive, aided by systems that you have designed and built yourself. Working at the observatory in the mountains of Puerto Rico in the late 1970s also gave me the opportunity to spend much of my free time sailing the Caribbean. I eventually bought a boat of my own, a 1935 John Alden ketch, left the observatory and moved aboard for a few years. Now, with more time of my own becoming available, I am eagerly looking forward to returning to a life that affords the opportunity for these types of adventures as a family.

HOME: Belmont, CA   **OCCUPATION:** Corporate Fellow. PRI Automation (factory automation and supply chain management)   **BIRTHPLACE:** New York, NY
SECONDARY SCHOOL: Teaneck High School, Teaneck, NJ   **YEARS AT COLLEGE:** 1971–75   **DEGREES:** A.B., cum laude, '75; S.M. '76   **SPOUSE/PARTNER:** Kristin Lee, June 3, 1990 (Stanford Univ. '84)   **SPOUSE'S OCCUPATION:** Executive Vice President. Claria.com   **CHILDREN:** Andrew, 1992; Margot, 1995; Nathan, 1997   **COLLEGE ACTIVITIES:** F-Entry project; Dunster House Drama; Leverett House Drama; Loeb Drama; intramural soccer

Ogden Thorvaldsen Ross: I'm still trying to figure out exactly who I am in life. I have great fear of the destructive power of nuclear war, sorry, Bill, for the Republican Senate. Pinky, please save us from Pakistan. Pay attention to *Looking Backward Bellamy* and *On the Beach.* Of friends come and gone but maybe not forever. That of societal ostracism we would hope to be a lie, but not of the black rhinoceros's fate. Cerinna Mor, a hoped-for survivor. A love affair with Montana's only to become a hapless middle-aged man. Femme Nazis? Whither go our race, the demise of male ego; compromise, please...maybe, below replacement ratio in the West—ask questions. There are no Winston Churchills left. Beware of fascism, isolationism, expansionism. Greenspan and good-bye Clinton. Reagan disdained Mr. Bush. How about Iran, Contra and Kuwait, Kosovo, Vietnam a distant memory. Hippies, now affluent yuppies. Yahoo and Microsoft. I said I was not a day trader but made three hundred trades anyway. Where did the Internet come from anyway? The University of Illinois knew all along. My postgraduate degree in stochastics and Bollinger bands. IINN, TIPS, CHIP, PABN, and then LEAF, ISRI, SBAS, NETSMART, INTASIS and go MVEE. Money made and lost. Please don't put friends in compromising positions. And play, what, earthquakes respond to crustal shrinkage caused by global warming and nuclear subterranean test blasts. Susan Faludi and Charlie Rose, what happened to Quentin. Richard Gere's a Buddhist, what about 711 Boylston Street in '78. Trungpa started it here. Sex is dead. Slipping by and where's the big success? No guarantees for anything. Greener pastures lie ahead or so it would seem. The old boy network became anachronistic, but persists in the form of the Somerset when the Ryder Cup players had dinner but the reporter was refused access. I'd like to think social elitism was dead but the top seven percent hold ninety percent of the wealth. Marx assumed that global capitalism would lead to the end of competition through consolidation and corporate monopoly, creating stagnation and annihilation. To prevent such an outcome, leadership must come from within. Mass media hysteria lead by O.J., Jeanne Benet, and Dershowitz must not lead to the corruption of the judicial system or else if people think if they do it right they can get away with it. Wouldn't it be nice if just once the Yankees didn't have to win over the Red Sox. God save Bucky Dent. Oh yeah, I almost forgot, where's Mr. Mallard anyway?

HOME: Arlington, MA **OCCUPATION:** Analyst; Painter; Etonate.com **SECONDARY SCHOOL:** Milton Academy **YEARS AT COLLEGE:** 1971–75 **DEGREES:** A.B. '75 **SPOUSE/PARTNER:** Sarah Morgan, divorced, Aug. 7, 1998 **SPOUSE'S OCCUPATION:** Qin Ping Tea House **CHILDREN:** Cerinna Mor **COLLEGE ACTIVITIES:** Sailing; skiing: John Finley and Amor and Psyche; J. J. Lingane and Chem 40-A; Newton's search for God and father; Howells and Bro Anthro, E. O. Wilson and pheromones; Oscar Mandlin and a view towards history; visual studies and GSD; Charlie Chan and Elsie's Turkey D and chocolate western JRD and Sundries; Dana and Eliot House and the A.D.

George L. Russell: I compare my Twenty-fifth with my father's in 1973. He died four years ago so I recall what he valued most compared with what I value most.

Like him, I am most privileged to be with my wife during the working day, he and my mother on the ranch, me with Judy at Case. Since she is director of communications, we can commute and travel together, interact professionally and personally during the day, and enjoy significant time and experiences together that most others cannot have in a corporate environment. She is my wife, lover, best friend and co-worker.

Like my father, we enjoy large gatherings with family and friends. He had seven children — we have fourteen nieces and nephews plus children of close friends that give us perspectives on generational evolution and genetic legacy. Consequently, I do not miss not being a father.

Like my father, I enjoy farming. He farmed the land while I work in labs, fields, and dealerships to market farm machinery. We are in a basic business, an honorable, value-added profession that is changing rapidly due to bio- and information technology, globalization, and growing populations and expectations. Case IH has just been acquired by New Holland, a part of Fiat, to become the largest farm equipment company.

Because he was tied to the land, Dad only lived in two places as an adult. We have lived in seven places ranging from California to Vermont. At the Reunion, we will have just moved from Paris, where we spent three wonderful years enjoying Europe, Africa, and the CIS and learning better how Americans are perceived in the world. We are proud of the American virtues of diversity, integration, openness, and big ideas; we are concerned about our country's hubris, budding isolationism, and insensitivity and ignorance about other cultures.

Finally, Harvard. My father convinced me to attend Harvard, citing the life-forming experiences of Harvard and Radcliffe graduates on both sides of my family. He predicted that Harvard College would be the best four years of my life, and that the people that I would meet and the different perspectives I would see would benefit me forever. He was right. Thanks, Dad.

HOME: Paris, France   **OCCUPATION:** Director of Marketing. Case IH Ag, Europe, Africa/Middle East, CIS (farm machinery)   **SECONDARY SCHOOL:** Otter Valley Union High School, Brandon, VT   **YEARS AT COLLEGE:** 1971–75   **DEGREES:** A.B., cum laude, '75; M.B.A., Univ. of Chicago '82   **SPOUSE/PARTNER:** Judith T., June 11, 1977 (Kent State Univ. '74; M.A., State Univ. of New York, Albany '78)   **SPOUSE'S OCCUPATION:** Director of Communications. Case Europe, Africa/Middle East, CIS   **HARVARD/RADCLIFFE SIBLINGS:** Edward S. Russell '78   **COLLEGE ACTIVITIES:** Class marshal, 1975; Harvard Band, 1971–75, manager, 1974–75; manager, varsity baseball, 1972–75; assistant manager, varsity basketball, 1972–74; Harvard-Radcliffe Chorus, 1971–75

Dana Sack: Are we having fun yet? Dating and eventually marrying Misako? Yeah, that was a lot of fun. The formal Japanese wedding at Meiji Kinenken, where the Meiji Constitution was signed, was more fun than I expected. The births of Jason and Mina, a senior and eighth grader by our Twenty-fifth Reunion, are among my happiest memories.

Practicing law? Yeah, that has been more fun than one usually hears about in the press. Closing deals, forming new businesses, and finding the money has been hard work and a lot of fun. Winning trials and cases has been a lot of fun.

Has there been enough playing? Winning sailboat races, even coming in second, has been a lot of fun. Wednesday night sails, watching the sun set behind the fog over the Mann hills and the city lights come on in San Francisco, have been pretty good. Sailing trips in England, France, Portugal, Tonga, Turkey, Mexico, and Greece have been fun. Having four kids along was much more fun than I had expected.

Skiing with children made it fun all over again. Sound effects, races, follow the leader over jumps and through trees. I had just about gotten bored with the sport, when they made it all fresh and fun again, until my teenager started leaving me behind and complaining about how many runs he missed if he had to wait for me. Maybe it is time to take up snowboarding?

Volunteer work? Helping out at the Oakland Zoo, the local soccer league, and a small museum has all been fun. Getting to know a fatherless young man who says he wants to go to college, when no one he knows has ever finished high school, has been a lot more fun than either of us expected.

Misako thinks I have too much fun. If you are not having fun, quit and do something else. We only get to do this once. Don't waste it. Celebrate it, with fun.

HOME: Piedmont, CA   **OCCUPATION:** Attorney. Sack, Miller & Rosendin LLP
BIRTHPLACE: San Francisco, CA   **SECONDARY SCHOOL:** Lowell High School, San Francisco, CA   **YEARS AT COLLEGE:** 1971–76   **DEGREES:** A.B., cum laude, '75; J.D., Univ. of California, San Francisco '79   **SPOUSE/PARTNER:** Misako Maki, Oct. 25, 1980 (Keio Univ. '74)   **SPOUSE'S OCCUPATION:** Senior Legal Assistant; Manager, Business Department Legal Assistants. Morrison and Foerster   **CHILDREN:** Jason, 1983; Mina, 1987   **HARVARD/RADCLIFFE SIBLINGS:** Kirby Sack '78

Stephen A. Sacks: "For I know the plans I have for you," declares the Lord, "plans to prosper you and not to harm you, plans to give you hope and a future" (Jeremiah 29:11). Although I entered Harvard intending to major in religion, I never imagined in September 1971 how true these words would turn out to be. My four years in Cambridge, followed by two years in Paris, helped prepare me for the challenges of the New York City jazz scene. Recording four albums of original Brazilian jazz, performing and recording with David Byrne, Tito Puente, and others, and finally getting my M.A. in music, brought me the satisfaction which sustained me through the vagaries of the commercial music scene. After twenty years, I was sure I would never leave. But the same God who gave me forgiveness and new direction after a painful divorce, new friends in a great New York City church, and new hope for life both here and hereafter, had other ideas: my wonderful new wife Tomoko, and our move to Hong Kong one month before the return to Chinese sovereignty. I resisted Hong Kong at first, but before long discovered unexpected joys: being a big fish in a small musical pond (being solicited to play with the Hong Kong Philharmonic, etc.), discovering God in new ways thanks to my wife and new church friends, and eating authentic Chinese food. We were recently transferred to Tokyo, a city I love, where I'm active on the Brazilian music scene and in music ministry, and working to release my new CD by year's end. I did not deserve any of these good things, and for all of them I am thankful to God, who "will meet all your needs according to his glorious riches in Christ Jesus" (Philippians 4:19).

HOME: Tokyo, Japan   OCCUPATION: Musician   BIRTHPLACE: Washington, DC
SECONDARY SCHOOL: William H. Hall High School, West Hartford, CT   YEARS AT
COLLEGE: 1971–75   DEGREES: A.B., summa cum laude, '75; M.A., City Coll. of New York
'97   SPOUSE/PARTNER: Tomoko Sawada, Nov. 30, 1996 (Osaka Univ. of Foreign
Studies '78; Fordham Univ. '91)   SPOUSE'S OCCUPATION: Senior Market Development
Manager. Japan Comverse Network Systems   HARVARD/RADCLIFFE SIBLINGS: Peter
W. Sacks '79, J.D. '86; Susan Miranda Sacks Green '80   COLLEGE ACTIVITIES: Jazz band,
1971–75; concert and marching bands, 1972

James S. Sadwith: Twenty-seven years ago I was standing in my room in Briggs in a pit of depression, thinking, "If life doesn't get any better than this I will definitely kill myself by the time I'm twenty-one — no, twenty-five — wait — okay, thirty." Who'd've thought life would end up being so much fun, affording me opportunities to: experience four bracing years in veterinary school with summers working on Cape Cod and hitchhiking around the country and to Alaska; work as a vet on Martha's Vineyard for two years; get married and raise children; pursue a midlife career change very early and head to Los Angeles for an education and a career in filmmaking; write TV movies and miniseries and then direct them and create TV series and write for the big screen; experience moving up the domicile ladder from a cockroach-infested Mar Vista one-bedroom apartment to a modest seven hundred and fifty square foot bungalow, to a Topanga Canyon fixer-upper, to a house on the Vineyard (where we had the great good fortune to spend a few idyllic summers), to a wonderful country home in Vermont where we now live full-time raising our family, and where I am still able to write and direct! Does it get any better than this? And twenty-seven years ago I considered checking out?! I have one small regret: rushing through Harvard in two and a half years and not finishing, not investing myself fully enough in my education and friendships and the Loeb. If I could go back and do that part right (but change nothing else that followed) it would make a 9.9 life a 9.99.

HOME: South Woodstock, VT   **OCCUPATION:** Screenwriter; Director; Producer
BIRTHPLACE: New Brunswick, NJ   **SECONDARY SCHOOL:** Hotchkiss School, Lakeville, CT   **YEARS AT COLLEGE:** 1971–73   **DEGREES:** V.M.D., Univ. of Pennsylvania '77; M.A., Univ. Of Southern California '81   **SPOUSE/PARTNER:** Kathleen, May 21, 1983
CHILDREN: Tyler, 1986; Hannah, 1988

John Thomas Sahlberg: Having just returned from the annual October fly-fishing trip in Yellowstone Park, I am in an appropriate reflective mood concerning the last twenty-five years. I can only hope that others are as satisfied with their choices over those years as I am with mine. Following graduation, I worked three years as an economist in the Idaho governor's office, during which time I met and, in 1977, married my wife, Susan. That shows that I am occasionally capable of a very smart decision. In 1978, we moved to Washington, D.C., where I attended Georgetown Law School, graduating in 1981. Early in law school, Susan and I had lunch with Jeff Maletta, who was clerking for a federal judge in Washington, and he mentioned a federal clerkship in Hawaii that was worth looking at. Through Susan's persistence, I was fortunate to end up getting that clerkship, and we spent about eighteen months from 1981 to 1982 living in Hawaii while I worked for one of the finest people I have had the pleasure to know, the Honorable Herbert Y. C. Choy. We remain a part of Judge and Mrs. Choy's "federal family" to this day. Following that clerkship, we moved back to the Northwest and settled in Boise, Idaho, where I went to work for Boise Cascade Corporation and Susan held several jobs, the last one being a special assistant to the governor and head of the Idaho Office for Children. Deciding that she wanted to spend more time with her own children, Susan resigned from that job to become what I call a "sherpa" for our children. Those of you who have soccer, ski racing, or any other such significant commitment know what I mean. We have been fortunate to bring two wonderful daughters into this world: Katrina and Jacqueline. Katrina will be fifteen by Reunion time and, I think, wants to go about anywhere but Harvard because she wonders how any school that failed to educate her father adequately about the 1990s could possibly present any academic challenge. Like most first children, she is a goer and a doer in both academics and athletics. Jacqueline will be nine at Reunion time and has the same drive and ambition as her older sister but manifests it differently, which any parent with more than one child understands. The three women in my life—Susan, Katrina, and Jacqueline—have brought more joy and credit cards to my life than I could ever have imagined. My work as an attorney and as a director of labor relations for a Fortune 500 company has been challenging and interesting, but it has always served, and will continue to serve, as only the means to the family and lifestyle we enjoy. My biggest regrets are that so many friends are so far away and that I have not been better about keeping in touch. I look forward to trying to close that distance in June.

HOME: Boise, ID   OCCUPATION: Associate General Counsel; Director, Labor Relations. Boise Cascade Corp.   BIRTHPLACE: Pocatello, ID   SECONDARY SCHOOL: Pocatello High School   YEARS AT COLLEGE: 1971–75   DEGREES: A.B., magna cum laude, '75; J.D., Georgetown Univ. '81   SPOUSE/PARTNER: Susan Canton, Oct. 20, 1977 (Boise State Univ. '76)   CHILDREN: Katrina Elyse, 1985; Jacqueline Kelsey, 1990   COLLEGE ACTIVITIES: Lowell House athletics; board of directors, Harvard Student Agencies, 1972–74

Paul Nathan Samuels: It's been a wonderful twenty-five years. My parents, brothers and their families, and my close friends and their loved ones are all thriving. My eldest niece Sarah, lo and behold, is applying to colleges and continuing the family traditions of playing on the varsity tennis team and doing whatever she can to help others, and ditto for her sister Stephanie. Adam, Rachel, and Julie also are always a joy to be with. Work has been very rewarding, often I can't believe that I actually get paid to work on public policy and legal issues about which I care deeply. Love and best wishes to all my friends!

HOME: New York, NY   OCCUPATION: Civil Rights Attorney. Legal Action Center
BIRTHPLACE: Cooperstown, NY   SECONDARY SCHOOL: New Hartford High, New
Hartford, NY   YEARS AT COLLEGE: 1971–75   DEGREES: A.B., cum laude, '75; J.D.,
Columbia '79   HARVARD/RADCLIFFE SIBLINGS: David Gordon Samuels '74; Ronald
Charles Samuels '85   COLLEGE ACTIVITIES: Making life-long friends

---

Jo Ana Sanchez: Nothing is as significant as participating in the growth-development of a happy child (now young adult). Stresses in life have come and gone, but each is in perspective with the pending graduation of a young woman who I have learned to genuinely respect, Patricia A. Garcia '00.

HOME: Vernon, TX   OCCUPATION: Psychiatrist (Medical Specialist III)   BIRTHPLACE:
Los Angeles, CA   SECONDARY SCHOOL: Rio Grande High School, Albuquerque, NM
YEARS AT COLLEGE: 1971–75   DEGREES: A.B. '75; M.S., Univ. of California, Berkeley '77;
M.D., Univ. of Texas '79   SPOUSE/PARTNER: Adalberto Garcia, divorced (Harvard '75)
SPOUSE'S OCCUPATION: Chairman. Modern Languages Dept., Midwestern State
University   CHILDREN: Patricia Adriana Garcia, 1978   HARVARD/RADCLIFFE
CHILDREN: Patricia Adriana Garcia '00   COLLEGE ACTIVITIES: Phillips Brooks House;
Radcliffe admissions aide; Raza

Joseph Eric Sandler: When I graduated I figured life was supposed to be a straight line progression. Instead it's a series of changes. The most significant changes for me have been marrying Karen twelve years ago, and the birth of our children, Nora (now in second grade) and Eli (in kindergarten). Every day brings new changes in each of them and new reasons for Karen and me to be thankful for our good fortune.

After graduation I went through Harvard Law School and joined a large D.C. law firm, where I practiced for nearly eight years and pursued politics as an avocation. Then, in about a two-year span, I got separated, divorced, met my current wife, got remarried, and switched careers — to pursue politics as a profession, as staff attorney for the Democratic National Committee (1986–89). I returned to the law firm, became a partner, and then in 1993 rejoined the DNC as its general counsel. I had the pleasure of practicing campaign finance and election law at the cutting edge and of being part of a great team that reelected a Democratic president for the first time in sixty years. That was combined with the intensely unpleasant but enlightening experience of being at the epicenter of one of the never-ending parades of phony "scandals" that have become the principal business of Washington (in place of actually governing the country).

In the spring of 1998 I left the DNC staff and formed a new law firm with my DNC deputy. We continue to represent the DNC but also represent a variety of other clients in the election law/nonprofit areas. Running my own shop is a new and different experience and one I am greatly enjoying.

HOME: Bethesda, MD   **OCCUPATION:** Attorney; Shareholder. Sandler & Reiff, PC (law firm)   **BIRTHPLACE:** Baltimore, MD   **SECONDARY SCHOOL:** Gilman School, Baltimore, MD   **YEARS AT COLLEGE:** 1971–75   **DEGREES:** A.B., summa cum laude, '75; J.D. '78   **SPOUSE/PARTNER:** Karen Yudelson, Jan. 17, 1987 (Emory Univ.)   **SPOUSE'S OCCUPATION:** Self-Employed Consultant, Corporate Training and Development   **CHILDREN:** Nora Lillian, 1992; Eli Michael, 1993   **COLLEGE ACTIVITIES:** Phillips Brooks House

---

Martha A. Sandweiss: Over the past few years I've settled into a new phase of my career. After ten years as curator of photographs at the Amon Carter Museum in Fort Worth, and eight years as director of the Mead Art Museum at Amherst College (where I also earned tenure and taught part-time), I moved into full-time academic life in 1997, becoming a professor of American studies and history at Amherst. While I continue to teach the history of photography, I now teach a broad range of courses in western and southwestern history as well. I can't explain why it took me eighteen years to see the light. I love the challenge of the classroom, where battles are won or lost every day, and now have more time to pursue my own research and writing projects. My work, in general, focuses on photography in the American West in the nineteenth century, and the broader ways in which historians can use visual images as primary sources of evidence.

An academic schedule also leaves more time for family. At the most mundane level, it means more late afternoon driving, transporting Adam (thirteen) and Sarah (nine) from one place to another. But it also means that

summers have become gloriously expansive. Three years ago we purchased a second home in Santa Fe, where we lived before moving to Massachusetts, and we now spend our summers there. The various museums and libraries sustain my work. Adam is plugged into a performing arts group, and Sarah climbs rocks and catches insects. My husband, Bob Horowitz, who works as a family physician at the University of Massachusetts Health Services, is able to get away for much of the summer, and spends his time in Santa Fe hiking and making photographs. At heart, we're all westerners, and we feel grateful, indeed, to have the health, the means, and the good fortune to be able to enjoy our two worlds.

HOME: Pelham, MA   OCCUPATION: Professor of American Studies and History. Dept. of American Studies, Amherst College   BIRTHPLACE: Saint Louis, MO   SECONDARY SCHOOL: University City High School, University City, MO   YEARS AT COLLEGE: 1971–75   DEGREES: A.B., magna cum laude, '75; M.A., Yale '77; M. Phil., ibid. '79; Ph.D., ibid. '85   SPOUSE/PARTNER: Robert Horowitz, 1985 (Kenyon Coll. '73; M.D., New York Medical Coll. '76)   SPOUSE'S OCCUPATION: Physician. University Health Services, University of Massachusetts, Amherst   CHILDREN: Adam Sandweiss Horowitz, 1987; Sarah Sandweiss Horowitz, 1991   HARVARD/RADCLIFFE SIBLINGS: Eric Sandweiss '81

Inger Saphire-Bernstein: Graduate school in Ann Arbor (not the Cambridge of the Midwest as promised) was followed by three exciting years working for the Medicaid Program in Boston while Len suffered through law school. I had always planned to live in Boston, but Len missed something about the Midwest and wanted to be closer to his family. Fast forward twenty years and we are still here. Chicago has grown on me, but each time I travel back to Boston for business or a wedding I have to convince myself to get on the plane back to O'Hare. The Chicago years have been largely consumed with raising kids, working, practicing Judaism, and reading science fiction. I love my husband and children. I even like my job. Watching and trying to influence the development of national health policy is fascinating and disappointing—more politics than policy, and no one seems to care about the uninsured. I guess I'm tired as I write this (having sat on the tarmac for five hours at National Airport last night), but I had hoped for more order, light, and space by this point in my life. The kids are large, articulate, smart, and sloppy. I need a bathroom of my own.

As Donni, our oldest, starts the college application process, those confusing, dazzling fall days of 1971 come rushing back to me. There were so many possibilities around every corner. Many are now foreclosed. I know I will not go to Mars or live in France, and even *Star Trek* is failing me now. But Len and I have built an interesting close family and community of friends, and that is one large possibility made real. It has been a challenging twenty-five years — mostly good mixed with some disappointments. G-d willing, the next twenty-five should be as good, but with fewer soggy towels and boxer shorts on the floor.

HOME: Chicago, IL   **OCCUPATION:** Manager, Health Policy. Blue Cross and Blue Shield Association (trade association for Blue Cross & Blue Shield plans nationwide) **BIRTHPLACE:** New York, NY   **SECONDARY SCHOOL:** Miami Norland Senior High School, Miami, FL   **YEARS AT COLLEGE:** 1971–75   **DEGREES:** A.B., magna cum laude, '75; M.H.S.A., Univ. of Michigan '77   **SPOUSE/PARTNER:** Leonard Bernstein, May 9, 1976 (Harvard '75)   **SPOUSE'S OCCUPATION:** Attorney. Law Offices of Leonard Saphire-Bernstein, Skokie, IL   **CHILDREN:** Daniel Eliah, 1982; Shimon Yitzchak, 1984; Miriam Kayla, 1986; Yocheved Shulamis, 1989   **COLLEGE ACTIVITIES:** Phillips Brooks House, 1974–75, House social chair, 1972–73

Leonard Deitz Saphire-Bernstein: I continue to learn and grow, thank G-d. Marriage and children have created a shower of experiences from which I am still drawing lessons. Work has generated a lesson or two, but mostly, to keep it in its place, and to keep its place as small as possible! Trying to be a good son, a good husband, a good father, and a good man has provided more illumination, and becomes more difficult and rewarding, with every little step of progress. My best wishes to everyone looking forward to the next seventy-five-plus years!

HOME: Chicago, IL   **OCCUPATION:** Attorney (solo practitioner of health insurance and business litigation)   **BIRTHPLACE:** Milwaukee, WI   **SECONDARY SCHOOL:** Nicolet High School, Glendale, WI   **YEARS AT COLLEGE:** 1973–75   **DEGREES:** A.B., magna cum laude, '75; M.A., Univ. of Michigan '77; J.D., Harvard '80 **SPOUSE/PARTNER:** Inger Megan Saphire-Bernstein, May 9, 1976 (Radcliffe '75) **SPOUSE'S OCCUPATION:** Manager. Blue Cross and Blue Shield National Association **CHILDREN:** Donni, 1982; Shimon, 1984; Miriam, 1986; Yocheved, 1989

Clifford Darryl Saron: The world stretches before me since finishing a Ph.D. in neuroscience this September. I'm more worn than at the last graduation, but still rife with potential and resisting definition. I seem to have spent the first fifteen of the last twenty-five years avoiding graduate study, and the past ten regarding it as refuge, while all that time working within essentially the same discipline. The last two years were neither calm nor sheltering — completing a long dissertation with two small kids three thousand miles from my institution while my mentor suffered a major stroke meant dealing with a faculty ill-prepared for the mis-fit between my experience and their expectations of student work, and a family structure stressed and blessed by needs too often unfilled. My future work will likely involve research in human sensory-motor integration using noninvasive electrophysiological and other brain imaging methods of cognitive neuroscience.

The whole enterprise of aspiration and achievement has been recast for me over the past six years as something that needs to emerge from the heart of my family. It's a reprise of the life lessons I learned tending and loving my dying mother thirteen years ago. I find so much fulfillment, challenge, and poignant joy within parenting and marriage that the quest for balance in love and work, openness and purpose, is very much an ongoing concern.

Some highlights: a 1978 trip to the Cook Islands recording sound for a Smithsonian Institution documentation of a never-to-be-repeated dance festival; participating in a dialogue regarding Tibetan Buddhism and western neuroscience with His Holiness the Dalai Lama in 1990 (see www.mindandlife.org), including a field research project in India; a year off doing primary child care — the first of Gabriel's life — while Barb practiced for (and won) the audition for her position in the San Francisco Symphony; holding our children while we listen to their mother play the cello.

HOME: Corte Madera, CA   **OCCUPATION:** Cognitive Neuroscience Researcher; Research Consultant   **SECONDARY SCHOOL:** Ossining High School, Ossining, NY
YEARS AT COLLEGE: 1971–76   **DEGREES:** A.B. '75 ('76); M.S., Yeshiva Univ. '92; Ph.D., ibid. '99   **SPOUSE/PARTNER:** Barbara Bogatin, July 3, 1988 (Juilliard School '74; M.M., ibid. '75)   **SPOUSE'S OCCUPATION:** Cellist. San Francisco Symphony   **CHILDREN:** Gabriel, 1993; Rayna, 1996   **COLLEGE ACTIVITIES:** Loeb, 1971–72; WHRB, 1971

Stephen L. Saudek: Family, etc. A few years out of school, Mark Leib (also of Adams House, '75) introduced me to Janice (J. J.) Durham, and it proved to be a perfect match. Mark, we owe you for everything. J. J. and I were married soon after, and the relationship has brought more joy and comfort than I could have dreamed of. It has also brought Rachel (now eleven) and Peter (eight), who have been magical.

Work, etc. I went down a winding path before homing in on health care. First, I taught high school history for three years. Then, after B-school in public management, I worked in the financial and management areas at the Massachusetts Department of Public Welfare, and later at the University of Massachusetts. After some soul searching, I decided to get into health care and worked at the UMass Medical Center on the management side. I then joined a hospital decision support software and consulting company, where I've been for the past ten years. This has worked out well: I've had a variety of roles at HCm (now Health Management Systems), involving consulting, selling and managing. I've also been at the intersection of a variety of cross-currents: a rapidly-changing health care industry; computer software and technology advances, and the roller coaster of being with a small company as it merges with a larger, public one. It's been interesting and, usually, fun. And it's afforded me a tour of most one-horse towns east of the Mississippi.

Friends, etc. We've lived in Lexington, Massachusetts, for some time now, and have enjoyed it and developed a good group of friends. The best, however, remain the Kicks—the Daves (S. and T.), Mark and Sam—from Adams House, and their wives, Margaret, Michelle, Elizabeth, and Leslie. We don't stay in touch nearly as much as we'd all like to, but they're in my mind often. When we do get together there's a bond that goes far beyond reminiscences of the old days. I can't wait for the Reunion.

HOME: Lexington, MA   OCCUPATION: Vice President. Health Management Systems (health care information systems)   BIRTHPLACE: Bronxville, NY   SECONDARY SCHOOL: Bronxville High School, Bronxville, NY   YEARS AT COLLEGE: 1971–75 DEGREES: A.B., cum laude, '75; M.B.A., Boston Univ. '80   SPOUSE/PARTNER: Janice Durham, 1980   SPOUSE'S OCCUPATION: Health Educator   CHILDREN: Rachel, 1989; Peter, 1991   COLLEGE ACTIVITIES: Sailing team, 1971–75

J. Gordon Scannell, Jr.: I live in North Yarmouth, Maine, with my wife, Amy, son Gordon (age ten) and daughter Emily (age nine). From this vantage point it is obvious that this is where I was headed all along, but there were times when it was less clear.

I have had my share of jobs and adventures. After Harvard, I bicycled from New York to San Francisco promoting bicycle safety and JCPenney products; worked in health care administration in Walla Walla, Washington; led teenagers on bicycle/camping trips through the Canadian Maritimes and Europe; succeeded classmate Gray Holmes as hockey coach for the town of Jaca, Spain; taught cross-country skiing and led canoe trips. There have been other less interesting or fun endeavors.

I had the good fortune to meet Amy Pobst, not surprisingly, on a bicycle ride. We were married in 1980, and moved to Maine two years later when I started law school in Portland. Something of a departure from what I had been doing, I went to law school in the hope of learning a structure to help me make sense of things and solve problems. I also thought it would be nice to have a simple answer to the question of what I did for a living. If not for those reasons, it turned out to be a good decision.

After clerking with a federal judge and several years at a large Portland law firm, I joined a smaller firm in Auburn. Linnell, Choate & Webber is a good fit. My practice requires me to be part lawyer, part social worker, part teacher, and part small business owner. I do mostly real estate, small business, and municipal law, and I enjoy the variety of work, but more, the people. My office is on the first floor of our nineteenth-century brick building, directly behind the receptionist's desk — my clients know where to find me.

I like living in Maine. It is New England, so I feel close to my roots, and there is plenty of space. On a clear day, we can see the faint outline of Mt. Washington from our house, and the ocean is only several miles away. I sometimes miss the energy and affluence of the Boston area, but in balance I prefer Maine's ease of access to the outdoors and friendlier pace.

I still gravitate towards outdoor activity and exercise. I run an occasional road race or marathon (and don't do too badly for an aging mesomorph) and cross-country ski in winter as time allows. My family and I return to the family home in Prince Edward Island, Canada, for a few weeks each summer.

My family is the center of my world and a great joy to me. Having two children so close in age makes me very aware of how quickly they move from one stage to the next. I try to enjoy each as it comes because there is no going back, and try not to become overly focused on my concern for their future or of the world that they will live in. I watch them grow with a mix of pride, anxiety, sorrow and happiness.

As I look to the next twenty-five years and beyond, few words of wisdom and no clear vision. No doubt there will continue to be shifts in the balances of our respective lives. It seems the older we get, the more like ourselves we become. My secondary education, first at Belmont Hill and then at Harvard, remains a strong and positive influence in my life, an integral part. Ironically, that part seemingly increases even as those years become a smaller portion of my life.

HOME: North Yarmouth, ME   OCCUPATION: Partner. Linnell, Choate & Webber (law firm)   BIRTHPLACE: Boston, MA   SECONDARY SCHOOL: Belmont Hill School
YEARS AT COLLEGE: 1971–75   DEGREES: A.B., cum laude, '75; J.D., Univ. of Maine '85
SPOUSE/PARTNER: Amy R. Pobst, 1980   SPOUSE'S OCCUPATION: Homemaker; Nurse
CHILDREN: Gordon Macdonald, 1989; Emily Rice, 1990   HARVARD/RADCLIFFE
SIBLINGS: Charlotte Reischauer '63; Susannah Pomeroy Scannell '80

David John Scheffer: In the past quarter century I have been blessed with good fortune in my family, my professional life, and my health. My proudest moments have been my marriage to Michelle Huhnke and the birth of our two children, Kate and Henry. I have enjoyed my long friendships with classmates Sam Anderson, Mark Leib, and Steve Saudek. Since 1975, my education and work have allowed me to travel much of the world: to stand in awe of the most magnificent landscapes (such as the temples of Pagan and sunrise over the Masi Mara) and to witness the most horrific crimes (such as genocide in Rwanda and mutilated children in Sierra Leone). I remain as optimistic as that first week in Harvard Yard. But I am sobered by the realities of a world at once so beautiful and yet so murderous of the innocent millions. I have had the privilege, since mid-1997, to be U.S. Ambassador at Large for War Crimes Issues, a job that takes me to atrocity sites around the world. Whatever may be our personal travails, I have to believe they pale in comparison to what the victims of sheer evil have had to endure in distant lands on our watch. If, in the next quarter century, we can stop some of the madness before it erupts, we will have met our challenge.

HOME: Ashburn, VA   OCCUPATION: Ambassador at Large for War Crime Issues. U.S. Department of State   BIRTHPLACE: Norman, OK   SECONDARY SCHOOL: Norman High School, Norman, OK   YEARS AT COLLEGE: 1971–75   DEGREES: A.B., magna cum laude, '75; B.A., Oxford Univ. '78; LL.M., Georgetown Univ. '78   SPOUSE/PARTNER: Michelle M. Huhnke, May 27, 1990 (Barnard Coll. '89; J.D., George Washington Univ. '95)
SPOUSE'S OCCUPATION: Associate. Shaw, Pittman, Potts & Trowbridge   CHILDREN: Katherine, 1993; Henry, 1999   COLLEGE ACTIVITIES: *Harvard Crimson; Harvard Political Review;* Bach Society

Cynthia Perrin Schneider: First things first. Harvard gave me something that changed my life irrevocably, and for the better — my husband Tom Schneider (Harvard College '73; Harvard Law '80). We will celebrate our twenty-fifth anniversary in 2000! On the one hand, June 1975 seems long ago, and on the other hand, the time has flown by: from our traveling years while Tom studied for his doctorate at Oxford; to our workaholic years in the 1980s; to our years with children, beginning in 1988; to our political years, beginning in the fall of 1991; to our years in the Netherlands. We are incredibly lucky to have two great children; exciting and stimulating jobs; and lives filled with challenges, adventures, hard work, fun, and love.

My life has taken some surprising turns, but never in a million years did I think I would be coming back to my Twenty-fifth Reunion as the United States ambassador to the Netherlands. Neither did I ever think that a friend would become president. But when Bill Clinton decided to run for president in the fall of 1991, Tom and I plunged in to help him. My involvement in politics and my career as an art historian specializing in seventeenth-century Dutch art (first working at the Museum of Fine Arts, Boston, and then teaching at Georgetown University) came together when the president nominated me as ambassador to the Netherlands.

I truly think that being an ambassador is the greatest job in the world. Life has been very exciting since we arrived in August 1998: the war in Kosovo, the indictment of Milosevic, the trial of the suspects in the Lockerbie bombing all are subjects which affect my work. A typical day might include a run with the Marines, and meetings on war crimes in the former Yugoslavia, biotechnology, military sales, cultural exchanges, and Embassy security. I feel honored to be representing America and to be serving with such a dedicated and talented group of people. (Encourage your children to join the Foreign Service; it is an extraordinary life.)

Tommie and Sam go to the American School in The Hague, and love living here. As I write, I hear peals of laughter as Sam and his friends are playing outside with one of the embassy Marines. Tom has been heroic: commuting between The Hague, Washington, D.C., and Australia (the two home offices of his consulting firm), keeping his consulting firm going, maintaining our house in Maryland, and still making every performance and Cub Scout camp-out in the Netherlands. With a beautiful house filled with great American art, a twenty-four-hour security detail, no household responsibilities, and such an incredible life, I feel a bit like Cinderella. The clock strikes midnight sometime in 2001, but until then, we will continue to make the most of this extraordinary opportunity.

HOME: Sandy Spring, MD **BIRTHPLACE:** Bryn Mawr, PA **SECONDARY SCHOOL:**
Concord Academy **YEARS AT COLLEGE:** 1971–77 **DEGREES:** A.B., magna cum laude,
'75 ('77); Ph.D. '84 **SPOUSE/PARTNER:** Thomas Jay Schneider (Harvard '73; J.D. '80)
SPOUSE'S OCCUPATION: Consultant; President; CEO. Restructuring Associates
CHILDREN: Tommie Perrin Schneider, 1988 Samuel Thomas Schneider, 1990

Jonathan Andrew Schur: How far our thoughts were twenty-five
years ago from the changes that since have swept us along. The world paid no
attention to whatever it was — I can't remember — that we were talking about
under the chandeliers in the dining room in 1975. Perhaps, from here in Paris,
my perspective is different, but college did not prepare me for the three big
movements: chaos, the reduction of character to chemistry, and the death of
the gods.

Chaos theory throws over the certainty that was the hallmark of our undergraduate education. Looking at science and history as a progression towards
disruption, a thin layer of seeming calm while waiting for a discontinuity, this
is not what I recall learning. We were taught to believe in a stable future, or at
least one where change is more or less linear and understandable. Instead, it
turns out that we are just a moment of calm on a hurdling arabesque.

We were also taught that character matters, that our ability to master life's
events depends on our own free will, the inner strength that allows us to gain
control over ourselves and our environment. I remember disdaining Skinner
and his cohorts, with their notions that we were some sort of rat in a box, whose
reactions depended on a built-in mechanism, automatic and unchanging.
There was more to man than that. Our guide was Freud, who was able to show
us the secrets, albeit hidden, for taking control over ourselves. And yet it turns
out that Skinner was right, that our strength of character depends on a chemical feast, with serotonin battling for space with norepinephrine. Who needs
character when there is Prozac? Why battle for character when it is all a question of chemistry?

Which means, unfortunately, that the gods are dead. I do remember that
God died before graduation, or at least I recall reading so in the *New York
Times*. But we took his place — we were the gods. Each of us was a master of
the universe, having learned the rules that control the future, and with the
character to make the great machine work. Look at all the Greek and Roman
temples that litter Cambridge, with us inside them, in the inner sanctuary. It
turns out that we are much less than we were taught to be. We can't control
chaos, and our distinguishing mark, our strength of character, is less important than we thought.

So what should we talk about now, back for a moment under the chandeliers in the dining room? I am still not willing to abandon my old world view and become the animal that I suppose we are. I want to save as much as I can of my old image of man, by learning to live in a chaotic world, creating a new vision of character for the part of life that is ours to control, and finding a moral role that values what we are, while recognizing what we are not. All of this at the risk of missing another unseen trio that will, once again, sweep us along for twenty-five years.

HOME: Paris, France   **OCCUPATION:** Partner. Hughes, Hubbard & Reed (law firm)
BIRTHPLACE: New York, NY   **SECONDARY SCHOOL:** Rye Country Day School, Rye, NY
YEARS AT COLLEGE: 1971–75   **DEGREES:** A.B., cum laude, '75; J.D. '78
SPOUSE/PARTNER: Annie Debbab, December 1986   **SPOUSE'S OCCUPATION:** Nurse
CHILDREN: Solon Emmanuel, 1988; Matthew Lawrence, 1990; Julia Helena, 1994
COLLEGE ACTIVITIES: Writer, *Harvard Independent;* manager, crew team

William Miller Schwartz: I find it harsh to think I graduated from college twenty-five years ago. I am still trying to figure out what I want to be when I grow up.

My life has followed a common and predictable pattern, and I am thankful for the stability it has given me. In law school I met the love of my life. Upon graduation we practiced poverty law. Twenty years later, we find ourselves married and living in the suburbs, with three amazing children, two aging cars, a mortgage, and an irascible cat. What happened? Whatever it was, it snuck up on us slowly and virtually undetected.

Amid all this potentially mind-numbing normalcy, though, my ideals — our ideals — have survived relatively intact. Some of these have continued unimpeded over the years, like helping the needy, serving the community, living simply (or as simply as a 1990s household of teenaged technokids can), and enjoying the outdoors. Others we have rediscovered as our children discovered them for the first time — vegetarianism, for instance, along with our daughter, and music, as each child began to study a musical instrument. (After twenty years, I am singing once again, with a chamber choir that performs music of Spain, Latin America, and the Caribbean.) This is not to say that we always manage our lives in accordance with our principles, but occasionally our reality does succeed in crossing paths with our ideals.

I have chosen my path, and it has given great happiness. My family delights me more than I ever dreamed. My work continues to challenge me intellectually in more ways than my studies prepared me. My commitment to the community keeps me more occupied than I ever imagined. And yet I know that this is merely a temporary stage in my life. I am grateful that I can report that I am contented today; certainly I have faced less happy times and will again. I hope that all of you who read this are leading happy and fulfilling lives, but if you are not, remember that this stage, too, is temporary, and I wish you well.

HOME: Silver Spring, MD   **OCCUPATION:** Senior Attorney. Office of Hearings and Appeals, U.S. Dept of Energy   **BIRTHPLACE:** New Haven, CT   **SECONDARY SCHOOL:** North Haven High School, North Haven, CT   **YEARS AT COLLEGE:** 1971–75   **DEGREES:** A.B., cum laude, '75; J.D., New York Univ. '78   **SPOUSE/PARTNER:** Christine Marie Doyle, Aug. 8, 1982 (Manhattanville Coll. '74; J.D., New York Univ. '78)   **SPOUSE'S OCCUPATION:** Instructional Aide. Montgomery County, Maryland Public Schools   **CHILDREN:** Jane Doyle Schwartz, 1984; Daniel Doyle Schwartz, 1986; Thomas Doyle Schwartz, 1990   **COLLEGE ACTIVITIES:** Gilbert and Sullivan Players, 1972–74; Collegium Musicum, 1974–75

Erik Stephen Schweitzer: After leaving Harvard, I pursued my abiding fascination with the workings of the brain, which sustained me through graduate and medical schools. Although medical school caused my interest in medicine to go into remission, it confirmed my enjoyment of research. I took a post-doctoral position at U.C., San Francisco, where I immersed myself in research on the molecular mechanisms of synaptic neurotransmitter release; I also found time to enjoy white-water kayaking, abalone diving, skiing, sailing, Swedish massage, and flying in my single-place ultralight aircraft. I discovered the rewards of teaching when I met my future wife while instructing beginning kayakers on how to roll over without coming out.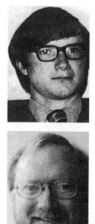

When this life began to seem a bit too hedonistic for someone raised on the Protestant work ethic of the Midwest, I took a faculty position at the University of Wisconsin. Madison is a beautiful place to live, albeit with exceptionally long, cold winters. As the natives say, the cold weather keeps out the riff-raff. After several years of enjoying the dramatic swings of weather, I decided I was part of the riff-raff, and moved to southern California, a faculty position at UCLA, and a rural lifestyle in the Santa Monica mountains immediately adjacent to the sprawling megalopolis that is Los Angeles.

In Topanga Canyon, I have lived a life filled with quiet beauty. I find joy and love in my eight-year-old son, Brendan; satisfaction in working to understand the molecular mechanisms of the brain (currently by establishing and analyzing a cellular model system for Huntington's disease); and unflagging affection and enthusiasm in our golden retriever, Giuliana. My son has introduced me to a whole new realm of life experiences, and I now spend my spare time leading Cub Scouts, discussing Star Wars and Pokémon, and even dancing the Russian dance along with Brendan in the annual Topanga Nutcracker Ballet.

It is a rare treat still to savor the deep bond with old friends from college, and to be able to drop back into earnest discussions about the universe's secrets. Life's marvels continue to be a source of wonder, and if the next half-century of my own life is half as rich as the last, I will feel overwhelmed by the privilege of experiencing it.

HOME: Topanga, CA **OCCUPATION:** Associate Research Neurobiologist. UCLA Medical School **BIRTHPLACE:** Alton, IL **SECONDARY SCHOOL:** Alton Senior High School **YEARS AT COLLEGE:** 1971–75 **DEGREES:** A.B., magna cum laude, '75; Ph.D., Washington Univ. '79; M.D., ibid. '81 **SPOUSE/PARTNER:** Patricia Anne Nolan, May 19, 1985 (New York Univ. '72) **SPOUSE'S OCCUPATION:** Research Scientist. Xoma Corp., Santa Monica, CA **CHILDREN:** Brendan Nolan Schweitzer, 1991 **HARVARD/RADCLIFFE SIBLINGS:** John Nicholas Schweitzer '69

Mark E. Scott: Twenty-five years in three hundred words, where to begin! I returned to the "Burgh" in 1975 and began a career in labor relations in the steel industry. Married Kris in 1978. When the steel industry went on life support (not my fault) I entered night law school (four nights/week, four hours/night, for four years). Needless to say, our social life was nonexistent!

Joined one of the "top three" Pittsburgh law firms immediately after graduation (I actually thought working full-time and going to night law school was a lot of hours!). I formed my own firm in 1987 specializing in management labor law. I still work long hours, but it is a much more enjoyable lifestyle!

I have spent a considerable number of hours coaching soccer and girls' fast-pitch softball. Now my two daughters are old enough and skilled enough to actually have a real coach. Spent eight years as a school board member, two of them as president. Academic results of this effort were good, and we did win the Pennsylvania AAAA football championship in 1993! Now I'm relegated to golf in the never-ending quest to break eighty and attending my daughters' events.

I've been up to Harvard a number of times to see "The Game." Still young at heart, just a little heavier and a lot balder! All told, life has been great since fair Harvard.

HOME: Pittsburgh, PA   **OCCUPATION:** Attorney; President. SG&C Associates, Inc. (labor relations consulting firm)   **BIRTHPLACE:** Pittsburgh, PA   **SECONDARY SCHOOL:** Shaler High School, Glenshaw, PA   **YEARS AT COLLEGE:** 1971–75   **DEGREES:** A.B., cum laude, '75; J.D., Duquesne Univ. '82   **SPOUSE/PARTNER:** Kristin M. (Pennsylvania State '76) **SPOUSE'S OCCUPATION:** High School French Teacher. North Hills School District **CHILDREN:** Erin McGinley Scott, 1984; Courtney McGinley Scott, 1986   **COLLEGE ACTIVITIES:** Freshman football, 1971; varsity football, 1972–74; Varsity Club

---

Thomas Eliot Seder: The past twenty-five years have been filled with good fortune and remarkable stability. I have been married to Sandra Cardone since 1984 (introduced by Harvard roommate David Farneti), and we have lived in the same house since 1985. Sandy has been a wonderful mother and wife and has been the cornerstone of our family life. She shelved her career as a lawyer for twelve years to be a stay-at-home-mom, at the end of which time she returned to school to get an LL.M. degree in taxation.

My kids have brought so much pleasure into my life! Nathan and Kayley are kindhearted, conscientious, respectful, and funny. I love being their father, watching them grow up, and seeing their lives unfold. Both kids are on swim teams and take music lessons (piano for Kayley, bagpipes for Nathan!). They do well in school and know everything about every movie made in the last ten years. Except for occasional fights about whether we listen to Bruce Springsteen or Backstreet Boys in the car, they get along pretty well.

I have been a self-employed manufacturers' rep in the apparel industry for twenty-two years. Woven labels and printed hangtags have been very good to me. The convenience of having my office down the street from my house has fortunately enabled me to stay closely involved with my kids' day-to-day lives.

For relaxation, I still play a fair amount of golf (not as much, though, as fellow club member and Harvard roommate, Larry Bedrosian) and spend many weekends as a "swim parent." Before I was married, I played a lot of duplicate bridge, at which I earned a "Life Master" ranking. I'm hoping my kids will learn how to play bridge.

As our Twenty-fifth approaches, I think about how ancient a forty-seven-year-old seemed to me as an undergraduate. Very scary.

HOME: Belmont, MA   OCCUPATION: Manufacturers Representative. RVL (apparel labels and hangtags)   BIRTHPLACE: Boston, MA   SECONDARY SCHOOL: Belmont High School, Belmont, MA   YEARS AT COLLEGE: 1971–76   DEGREES: A.B., magna cum laude, '75 ('76)   SPOUSE/PARTNER: Sandra L. Cardone, April 1, 1984 (Mount Holyoke Coll. '73; J.D., Univ. of Miami; LL.M., Boston Univ.)   SPOUSE'S OCCUPATION: Attorney (part-time). MassPIRG   CHILDREN: Nathan Edmund, 1986; Kayley Ann, 1987   HARVARD/RADCLIFFE SIBLINGS: Jonathan Davis Seder '74, M.B.A. '78; Eric William Seder '79

Mark Edward Segall: I have now practiced law for over twenty years. While I have had both ups and downs, I have spent the last ten years at the Chase Manhattan Bank and its predecessors and am now a group head in the litigation department. I specialize in workout and bankruptcy litigation and also have an antitrust expertise.

Karen and I have been married for over twenty years. Karen is the administrator of a nonprofit basketball camp. We just completed a significant addition to our house, and we are very pleased. We have two boys. Michael just began his freshman year at the University of Chicago, and Steven is in his sophomore year in high school. Michael has a genuine interest in helping others. Steven is a debater and on the ski team. He also loves the stock market.

I spend much of my free time skiing and playing golf. I still think I ski better than the boys, but they disagree. Steven and I won a golf tournament this fall.

I look back very fondly on my college years. From a long-term perspective I benefited most from my years with the *Harvard Independent*, the classes I took (particularly outside my major) and the very lively debate and dialogue that took place at lunch and dinner at Leverett House. My family accuses me of being the world's slowest eater, a habit I think I developed at college when I so much enjoyed lingering over meals. I hope today's students still appreciate the freedom college provides to learn from each other and discover without too much focus on graduate school or career.

HOME: Scarsdale, NY   OCCUPATION: Senior Vice President; Associate General Counsel. The Chase Manhattan Bank   BIRTHPLACE: New York, NY   SECONDARY SCHOOL: Harrison High School, Harrison, NY   YEARS AT COLLEGE: 1971–75   DEGREES: A.B., magna cum laude, '75; J.D. '78   SPOUSE/PARTNER: Karen Elkin, Aug. 13, 1978 (Wheaton Coll. '73; M.A.T., Columbia '78)   SPOUSE'S OCCUPATION: Consultant. MVP Basketball Camp   CHILDREN: Michael Henry Segall, 1981; Steven Elkin Segall, 1984   HARVARD/RADCLIFFE SIBLINGS: Grant Segall '76   COLLEGE ACTIVITIES: *Harvard Independent*, 1971–75, president

Jonathan Sheffer: When I was at Harvard I wrote a lot of music and met a lot of terribly interesting people. Then, having considered a career in medicine, I left college to continue studying music at Juilliard and Aspen.  Through time and trials I spent my twenties and thirties composing musicals, opera and then, in Los Angeles and New York, film and TV scores. Eventually, I began to conduct orchestras, and that is how I spend my life now. In 1995 I founded the Eos Orchestra in New York, upon which I focus all of my composing and conducting activities, a mix of rediscovery of the riches of American music, the commissioning of new works, and the presentation of uniquely theatrical concerts. This past year has been typical of  the last few: the Eos season in New York, a concert of Gershwin and Copland at the White House, conducting the score of the film *Titus* in London, classical recordings, guest conducting in Japan and elsewhere, and the anticipation of the premiere of my newest opera.

I feel fortunate and, on occasion, fulfilled. I had a belated bar mitzvah at thirty-nine. I've had a few long-term relationships, two scarred by AIDS. As a result, I have been active in gay politics and fund-raising. I have shared my life for the past five years with Christopher Barley, a physician. Yet, with all of this, I have simply not adjusted to the idea that we have come to a time of life that seemed to me as a twenty-one-year-old to represent the pinnacle of adulthood. Perhaps I dimly understood the arc of maturity that lay before us; or perhaps things have gone differently than I could have imagined. Someone said to me recently that at this point in life we have risen about as far as we may expect. That may be true, but I continue to dream of flying higher still.

HOME: New York, NY   OCCUPATION: Musician   BIRTHPLACE: New York, NY
SECONDARY SCHOOL: Staples High School, Westport, CT   YEARS AT COLLEGE:
1971–75   SPOUSE/PARTNER: Christopher Barley (M.D., Syracuse Univ. '89)   SPOUSE'S
OCCUPATION: Physician   COLLEGE ACTIVITIES: Co-composer, Hasty Pudding show,
1974; Collegium Musicum; Bach Society; Loeb Drama Center

Richard Warren Shepro: In the middle of our life's journey I find myself living in a 106-year-old greystone house bursting with books, music, and other treasures near Lincoln Park in Chicago. Lindsay Roberts and I have lived there for fifteen years and seen our children grow to be eleven and eight. Many days, we take our children to school, stop in a café and talk, and then I start my day downtown looking out a post-modern arched window giving legal advice. Papers are everywhere: much of my time I spend returning a cascade of phone calls, voice mails, and emails — like fighting a hydra.

Lindsay and I met in 1978. We're grateful for the rich experiences we had together in our first ten years, living in Cambridge, San Francisco, and Chicago. I finished law school, we traveled a lot, I was law clerk to a federal court of appeals judge. Lindsay worked on two books, worked for the Equal Rights Amendment and then went to law school, and I started at my law firm Mayer, Brown & Platt. Since then, with three and then four of us, we have continued to travel, and spend part of our summers in Seaside, Florida, or in a small house next door to Lindsay's mother in a hilly part of Alabama.

I'm co-head of the corporate and securities law group at Mayer, Brown & Platt, where we have eight hundred and fifty lawyers — six hundred and fifty more than when I started. I've written for the *Financial Times, Harvard Business Review* and other publications, and my book on mergers and acquisitions, *Bidders & Targets,* came out in 1990. While some of my friends have left law and become my clients I've found I like law practice more. I enjoy the problem solving, and helping clients to create something.

My other interests have shifted only gradually over the last thirty years — the arts; foreign travel and culture, particularly relating to France, Italy and England; the workings of the international economy, which is what most of my law practice relates to.

At home, we all play the piano. Claire writes and sings — she is head chorister of the children's choir at our church and has performed in twenty-one opera performances as a member of the children's chorus at Lyric Opera of Chicago. Warren writes and draws: he is working on his *Encyclopedia of Dragons* and a book about transformations, and has his doubts about whether he is really a muggle. They both have musical memories that amaze me.

In my mind's eye, I am still at Harvard, likely still an undergraduate. I feel it when I read books I started in college but never finished — recently *Faust* — and follow the threads through literature, history, music. I feel it when I walk across a college campus. For the last thirteen springs I've taught a seminar at the University of Chicago Law School, where I'm a lecturer in law; the law students look younger and younger, but I can't help but be fooled into thinking I'm still part of the undergraduate life. So many things to explore — it can't be time yet to declare a major. One friend saw my charts of how wine temperatures change over time in the freezer, refrigerator, and in ice and said, "Life is a continual experiment for Rick." How I liked that!

The friends I hold most dear are still those I found while at Harvard. I haven't traveled with you enough yet.

HOME: Chicago, IL   **OCCUPATION:** Partner. Mayer, Brown & Platt (law firm); Lecturer in Law. University of Chicago   **BIRTHPLACE:** Berwyn, IL   **SECONDARY SCHOOL:** Lyons Township High School, LaGrange, IL   **YEARS AT COLLEGE:** 1971–75   **DEGREES:** A.B., magna cum laude, '75; M.Sc., London School of Economics '76; J.D., Harvard '79   **SPOUSE/PARTNER:** Lindsay Ellen Roberts, Sept. 5, 1981 (Wellesley Coll. '78)   **SPOUSE'S OCCUPATION:** Lawyer (not practicing)   **CHILDREN:** Claire Willoughby, 1988; Warren Boyd, 1991   **COLLEGE ACTIVITIES:** *Harvard Crimson*, editorial board, 1972–75, arts editor, 1974–75; Harvard-Yale-Princeton Triangular Debates, 1972 (Kate and Max Greenman Prize)

Terry Earle Shlimbaum: The years since Harvard have been very kind to me. I have been blessed by a twenty-five-year run of positive events and experiences. After graduating I attended New York Medical College, and went on to a family practice residency at Hunterdon Medical Center, in Remington, New Jersey. In my last year of medical school I married Valerie Kelly, whom I had dated exclusively my last two years at Harvard. Our first child, Charlie, born in 1981, has just started his first year at the Univ. of Vermont, and our second, Gus, is a sophomore in high school. They have been the focal point of our existence for most of our married life, but Val and I have continued strengthening our relationship through it all . . . a good thing since the empty nest is much less vacant when experiencing it with such a good partner. After practicing in a three-person private family practice in Califon, New Jersey, for thirteen years, I transitioned to an academic setting as medical director of the outpatient teaching sites for the family practice residency at Hunterdon Medical Center (one in Lambertville and one in Milford, New Jersey). This has proved both rewarding and challenging. Being a hospital employee in the current health care environment after having a private practice is difficult but manageable. Over the years I have maintained close ties with Russ Johnson, Pete Cardellichio, and Joel McLafferty. I look forward to seeing other classmates, reminiscing, and catching up at the Reunion.

HOME: Glen Gardner, NJ   **OCCUPATION:** Family Physician; Medical Director. Phillips-Barber Family Health Center   **BIRTHPLACE:** Bay Shore, NY   **SECONDARY SCHOOL:** Islip High School, Islip, NY   **YEARS AT COLLEGE:** 1971–75   **DEGREES:** A.B., cum laude, '75; MD., New York Medical Coll. '79   **SPOUSE/PARTNER:** Valerie Kelly, 1977 (Emmanuel Coll. '75)   **SPOUSE'S OCCUPATION:** Preschool Director. Happy Face Nursery School, Califon, NJ   **CHILDREN:** Charles W., 1981; August P., 1984   **COLLEGE ACTIVITIES:** Varsity baseball, 1974–75

Tor Adam Shwayder:

Nineteen seventies:
- Harvard, music degree
- Licentiate, Royal Academy of Music, London, England
- Violin teacher
- Medical school, University of Michigan

Nineteen eighties:
- Residency in pediatrics, University of Michigan
- Fatherhood! Ariel Benjamin Ergas Shwayder, born 1981
- Private practice pediatrics
- Career change, residency in dermatology, Strong Memorial Hospital
- Tragedy, father dies in scuba-diving accident, leaves enormous debt
- Fatherhood again! Kobey Adam Ergas Shwayder, born 1985
- Employed: Henry Ford Hospital, dermatology, Detroit
- Begin (long) career as pediatric dermatologist
- Begin saving money like crazy for kids' college tuitions
- Fatherhood again (the last!), Maya Ergas Shwayder, born 1988.

Nineteen nineties:
- Begin midlife crises: Gray, receding hairline, wrinkles, deteriorating body mechanics, seeing colleagues get serious illnesses, wonder why I am still spinning like a top and not enjoying it, health care in America being run by M.B.A.s without compassion
- Antidote to above: Still married to same beautiful, intelligent and wonderful woman; three successful children; first violin with Birmingham Bloomfield Symphony Orchestra; tennis, pie baking, bread baking, rose gardening; regular reunions with Mather House roommates; volunteer time to Camp Discovery (for kids with serious skin conditions) and the Special Olympics; seriously consider other employment options; son, Ariel, enters Harvard. Class of 2003!; Twenty-fifth Reunion, June 2000.

The New Millennium:
- Continue to raise two children at home; get them into good colleges
- Dwindling resources due to college tuitions; embark them into the world with the right foot forward; continue to build on the strong marriage as we age
- Another career change?
- Kids finish college; new-found wealth!

- Anticipate children's marriage and grandchildren. Try not to make the same mistakes with my grandchildren ("What mistakes?!" my wife says.)
- *Oh no,* grandchildren's college tuitions!
- Fiftieth Reunion, June 2025
- Lasting contributions to mankind (well for a few kids at least)
- Obit in the *New York Times Electronic* page, will read in part: "Dr. Shwayder always maintained that one hundred years from now it would not matter what his bank account was, the sort of house he lived in, or the kind of car he drove. . . . But the world may be different because he was important in the life of a child."

HOME: Farmington Hills, MI   OCCUPATION: Pediatric Dermatologist. Henry Ford Dept. of Dermatology   BIRTHPLACE: Detroit, MI   SECONDARY SCHOOL: Cranbrook School, Bloomfield Hills, MI   YEARS AT COLLEGE: 1971–76   DEGREES: A.B., cum laude, '76; M.D., Univ. of Michigan '80   SPOUSE/PARTNER: Aimée Ergas, Dec. 31, 1977 (Wellesley Coll. '75)   SPOUSE'S OCCUPATION: Editor. *Michigan Jewish History Journal* CHILDREN: Ariel, 1981; Kobey, 1985; Maya, 1988   HARVARD/RADCLIFFE CHILDREN: Ariel Shwayder '03   HARVARD/RADCLIFFE SIBLINGS: Michael Shwayder '70; Mark Shwayder '73   COLLEGE ACTIVITIES: Harvard- Radcliffe Orchestra; Saint Lowell in the Fields Orchestra; Mather House Music Society

---

Richard Hung Pong Sia: Lately, I've been pondering the limits of time (and realizing that my mulling this over probably confirms that middle age has set in). There are so many things I've accomplished that give me a sense of fulfillment, but there are many things I still want to do — and I'm afraid there may not be enough time.

I've already realized my career ambitions, at least the ones I had in my earliest days at the *Harvard Crimson.* I've reported on national policy and politics from Washington and covered wars overseas; in various ways I've also affected people's lives in positive ways (except for the bureaucrats, politicians and crooks who provided material for career-ending investigative news stories under my byline). Even after leaving the *Baltimore Sun* in 1994, I've won more national awards than I ever imagined winning; picked up new skills, from guerrilla marketing tactics to Web design; and recently landed at a national magazine dedicated to quality journalism, a rare thing these days.

I've been able to focus more intensely on trying to be the best father I can be to two happy, very intelligent boys, Andrew and Nicholas, both of whom have voracious appetites for learning and yet are quite adept at goofing off and having fun (like me). And I've had time to travel more with

Kathlyn, treating her, for instance, to a wonderful surprise trip to Paris for her fortieth birthday.

Even with a life full of riches, I find myself wanting more time to work, more time with my wife and more time to spend with my children. I want more time for foreign films, jazz, and journeys to favorite destinations and explorations of new ones. I want more moments like the one the other night when I was driving with the family and the Rolling Stones were playing on the tape deck; both boys joined in from the back seat, giving exuberant renditions of "Paint it Black" and "Satisfaction." I know it's a blessing that I derive so much pleasure from my everyday life, but it's also a curse that time well spent now seems much too short.

HOME: Gambrills, MD   **OCCUPATION:** Senior Managing Editor. *National Journal* News Service (journalism)   **BIRTHPLACE:** Cleveland, OH   **SECONDARY SCHOOL:** Punahou School, Honolulu, HI   **YEARS AT COLLEGE:** 1971–75   **DEGREES:** A.B., cum laude, '75
SPOUSE/PARTNER: Kathlyn Louise Amoss, May 18, 1985 (Univ. of Maryland '79; M.L.S., ibid. '83)   **SPOUSE'S OCCUPATION:** Librarian. Anne Arundel County Public Library System
CHILDREN: Andrew Wei Ping, 1990; Nicholas Wei Yin, 1994   **COLLEGE ACTIVITIES:** *Harvard Crimson,* 1972–75; Wireless Club, 1972–75; Winthrop House crew, 1973–75

Rodney Lee Sidley: I love working as an architect and feel that I went to Harvard for my formative years, then to U.C. (University of Cincinnati) for my vocational training. As I reflect, I would have preferred to have had the foresight to reverse the roles of these institutions. However, I would not change anything.

HOME: Wyoming, OH   **OCCUPATION:** Architect. Rod Sidley Architects (sole proprietor architecture firm)   **BIRTHPLACE:** Cleveland, OH   **SECONDARY SCHOOL:** Stanford H. Calhoun High School, Merrick, NY   **YEARS AT COLLEGE:** 1971–75
DEGREES: A.B., cum laude, '75; B.Arch., Univ. of Cincinnati '85   **SPOUSE/PARTNER:** Jacqueline G., Sept. 18, 1982   **SPOUSE'S OCCUPATION:** School Nurse   **CHILDREN:** Addison Wyatt, 1986; Chloe Marina, 1987; Noah Graham, 1995

Louis Grant Silver: We have had the luxury of living in New York, Tel Aviv, Paris, and now London. I have had the luxury of playing professional b-ball prior to earning a "real" living as an attorney and a banker and advisor. We are at home with a few different languages — English, French, Italian, Hebrew... We have found that living amongst different cultures and people has broadened our life perspective and nurtured a greater degree of tolerance toward others. We are comfortable in London, passionate about Paris (and Rome), and at home in Tel Aviv and New York. We have come to realize that there are few things as dear as children, family, and close friendships. We cultivate these relationships relentlessly. I continue to long for life in the country and feel most at peace in nature's surroundings and therefore live a life of contradiction. But alas, we do go down to Erwin's farm...

N.B. trivia question: Who was the last official draft pick of the American Basketball Association in 1975?

HOME: London, England   OCCUPATION: Counseiller Groupe. Discount Bank & Trust Co.   BIRTHPLACE: New York, NY   SECONDARY SCHOOL: Sanford H. Calhoun High School, Merrick, NY   YEARS AT COLLEGE: 1971–75   DEGREES: A.B. '75; LL.B., Tel Aviv Univ. '82; L.L.M., New York Univ. '87   SPOUSE/PARTNER: Michal Eden Silver, Oct. 6, 1976 (M.A., Tel Aviv Univ. '81)   SPOUSE'S OCCUPATION: Director; Designer. Christopher Fan Artweave   CHILDREN: Anntal Rebecca, 1987   COLLEGE ACTIVITIES: Basketball, 1972–75, co-captain

---

Jouni Kalervo Similä: After leaving Harvard, where I graduated in astronomy and physics, I switched promptly to information processing science which is the field I have followed since then, pursuing at the same time both an academic and a business-oriented career. I must tell that I have not regretted that decision; the field has evolved tremendously during the past twenty-five years and it seems that the rate of change is increasing constantly.

Besides the two sons, the family includes presently a Great Dane and a Burmese cat. We live in a big house in the city of Oulu near the border of Lapland, where I was born. My hobbies are related to the memories of my childhood: I go fishing and hunting in Lapland and elsewhere every year — it is a great way to break away from the hectic days at work. My wife is also a nature lover, the boys more urbane perhaps. After spending nearly a year in Greece about ten years ago pursuing some business goals, I and the rest of the family have become infatuated with the Greek islands; we go there once every year.

Life in Oulu revolves very much around the rapid growth in telecommunications. Much of Nokia's key research and development activities are located here and the university is intimately involved in these activities. Oulu has grown quite fast during the last ten years, presently there are about one hundred and fifteen thousand inhabitants, but it still has much of the characteristics of a small town very much suitable for us at this phase of life. After the boys decide what they want to do with their lives — which should happen in a couple of years — we might have a chance for a change in lifestyle, perhaps a year spent abroad.

HOME: Oulu, Finland   OCCUPATION: Professor; Director. Department of Information Processing Science, University of Oulu   BIRTHPLACE: Salla, Finland   SECONDARY SCHOOL: Salla High School, Salla, Finland   YEARS AT COLLEGE: 1971–75   DEGREES: A.B., cum laude, '75; Ph.D., Univ. of Oulu '88   SPOUSE/PARTNER: Teija Marjo-Riitta Manner, 1981 (Univ. of Oulu '84)   SPOUSE'S OCCUPATION: Teacher. Karjasilta High School   CHILDREN: Martti Mikael Kalervo, 1981; Tuomas Juhana Kustaa, 1983

Thomas S. Simons: On the approach of our Twenty-fifth, Harvard doesn't seem like "just yesterday." Quite the contrary. Though I've lived in the Boston area since 1975, and had some interaction with Harvard programming, students, and career guidance, my college experience seems long ago and far away.

Which I am fine with.

Sally and I have had a very full, challenging, and rewarding time — and we feel very fortunate. Two of our three children are in college (University of Chicago and Union) and our third, the caboose, is threatening to follow her sibs to boarding school next year. The empty nest is not far off.

My business has probably consumed too much time and energy, but fortunately, it has been emotionally and financially satisfying, if a drain on my own energy reserve. Check out our site for more info on that.

Could we ever have imagined an Internet (over which I am submitting this) and the extraordinary pace of life that has come of it? My hope is that over the next twenty-five years, Sally and I can lead two lives.

We'd like to enjoy life in Internet time!

But we'd also like to figure out how to dial things back a bit. Play guitar, watch birds, enjoy the family as it evolves and expands. We'd like to pick up where we left off twenty-five years ago, enjoying the company of the great friends we made at Harvard. We look forward to seeing you all this June.

HOME: Boston, MA   OCCUPATION: President. Partners & Simons (marketing communication)   BIRTHPLACE: Oakland, CA   SECONDARY SCHOOL: Kent School, Kent, CT   YEARS AT COLLEGE: 1971–75   DEGREES: A.B., cum laude, '75
SPOUSE/PARTNER: Sally Johnson, June 1974   CHILDREN: Tyler Cunningham, 1978; Emily Hallen, 1981; Molly Hart, 1986   COLLEGE ACTIVITIES: Harvard Student Agencies; VES; Hit The Fan Band; my marriage

---

Daniel I. Small: It has been an extraordinary five years: a chaotic roller coaster, but with much to be thankful for. At the last Reunion, in 1974, I was in Florida where I had gone to be general counsel of a national health care management firm. While I enjoyed the experience (and the Florida winters!), I realized that doing litigation, not just managing it, remained my true passion. I've returned to Boston and joined with friends to open a small litigation and real estate firm. We now have nine lawyers, and my practice is an interesting mix of civil litigation, SEC and other government investigations, white collar crime criminal defense, quit tam, and health care matters. I am now vice chair of the ABA's White Collar Crime Committee.

I have also been doing a great deal of teaching and writing, which I enjoy. In 1998, the ABA published my book *Preparing Witnesses*. This year, they have published a second book, *Going to Trial: A Step by Step Guide to Practical Procedure*. I have also had articles published in a number of newspapers and journals, and am now a regular columnist for the *msnbc.com* news Website. My teaching has included regular involvement with the Harvard Trial Advocacy Workshop. I have not yet written the "Great American Novel" (one of my dreams), but there's still hope!

At home, life has also been chaotic. Our son Bailey is now eight and a joy. In 1996, we added twin baby girls to the family. Unfortunately, my wife Alix had a stroke at their birth, but she is tough, and has had a remarkable recovery. My apologies for having been too overwhelmed during that period to keep friends informed, and my thanks to those who found out anyway and sent their good thoughts. Just in case life was not busy enough, I have also taken up the sport of polo, and am loving it! We are now well and happy, live in Newton, Massachusetts, and would love to hear from classmates!

HOME: Newton, MA   OCCUPATION: Partner. Butters, Brozilian & Small, LLP
BIRTHPLACE: Boston, MA   SECONDARY SCHOOL: Lexington High School, Lexington, MA   YEARS AT COLLEGE: 1971–75   DEGREES: A.B., cum laude, '75; J.D. '79
SPOUSE/PARTNER: Alix deSeite, Sept. 17, 1988   CHILDREN: Bailey, 1991; Schuyler and Gabrielle (twins), 1996   COLLEGE ACTIVITIES: Drama; music; house football

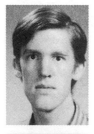

David Alexander Smith: I found a job. In the first four months after leaving college, I worked at about fifteen companies (as a temporary typist); in the twenty-four years since, I worked at two, one of which I started. I found a wife. Met the love of my life in 1979, married in 1982. It was her biggest decision and my best one.

I found a place to live (actually, she found it): rent-controlled apartment until marriage, a condo from 1982–84, this house thereafter.

I found a career. I graduated wanting to be a sportswriter, but through the random draw landed in a particular niche within affordable housing finance: recapitalization of existing properties, an area so obscure that with diligence and energy our company has become its foremost expert and about which we are occasionally invited to confuse or hector Congress and HUD.

I found an avocation. Wrote four published science fiction novels and conceived one mosaic novel (*Future Boston*, in which the Red Sox win six straight World Series, so you know it's science fiction or fantasy). Have written a boatload of specialized articles on obscure topics. In another age I would have been considered an eccentric, but with the Internet, we're all eccentrics.

Today I live less than a mile from my college dorm in Radcliffe Quad and take the subway under Harvard Yard ten times a week. I'll walk to the Reunion, yet I cross the Quad perhaps once a year, always feeling an interloper when I do. Going to work is great entertainment. Coming home is a delight. In between I'm so busy I sometimes forget how enjoyable it all is.

HOME: Cambridge, MA   **OCCUPATION:** President. Recapitalization Advisors, Inc. (transaction consulting in affordable housing finance)   **BIRTHPLACE:** Littleton, NH **SECONDARY SCHOOL:** Marblehead High School   **YEARS AT COLLEGE:** 1971–75 **DEGREES:** A.B., cum laude, '75   **SPOUSE/PARTNER:** Nancy Hiers, 1982 (Oberlin Coll. '77)   **SPOUSE'S OCCUPATION:** President. Middlesex Rental Center   **COLLEGE ACTIVITIES:** Sports editor, *Harvard Independent;* B chess team

Michael J. Smitka: Well...I've been blessed with lots of adventures, including about five years in Tokyo, Japan, and additional time traveling or living elsewhere overseas. Stateside I've lived in New York City (where I met my wife), New Haven (less fun...) and for a dozen years now, the mountains of Virginia. This has meant moving my family to Asia and back three times and Germany once, plus shorter trips to the Philippines and Japan by subsets of the family. Indeed, family itself is an adventure — soon twenty years of marriage, my daughter is now going through her college search as a high school senior, and my son survived middle school to start in fall 1999 as a high school freshman. Lots of work and activities, primarily music (both kids do piano and oboe and handbells) and church-related, and for my son, Boy Scouts. I'm now an assistant scoutmaster, with weekly meetings and roughly one weekend a month on trips. My wife teaches full-time at a school forty miles away, and is involved in various local nursing associations, adding to the family "busy-ness"; I do most of the cooking.

Of course I have work. After a couple years in international banking I headed to grad school, and have been at Washington & Lee since 1986. Here I've taught a large variety of (undergrad) economics courses, and have turned out a modest amount of research (one book on the Japanese auto industry, an edited series on Japanese economic history, academic articles and one of my favorite activities, numerous book reviews). For the past six years I've also been a judge of a management competition for automotive suppliers, which is lots of fun, and am trying to get a new book project underway comparing change in the auto industry in Japan and the U.S. that (grants permitting) will take me back to Japan for a year (with son in tow?!).

Not much contact with Harvard — a couple conferences there (more down the road at MIT) — especially since the only classmate in the area, Steve Hobbs, recently moved from Washington & Lee to the University of Alabama.

HOME: Lexington, VA   **OCCUPATION:** Economist; College Professor. Dept. of Economics, Williams School of Commerce, Washington & Lee University **SECONDARY SCHOOL:** Cass Technical High School, Detroit, MI   **YEARS AT COLLEGE:** 1971–75   **DEGREES:** A.B., cum laude, '75; Ph.D., Yale '89   **SPOUSE/PARTNER:** Gloria A., 1980 (Univ. of the Philippines; M.S., New York Univ.)   **SPOUSE'S OCCUPATION:** Associate Professor of Nursing. Dabney S. Lancaster Community College   **CHILDREN:** Mayumi B., 1982; John M. 3d, 1984   **COLLEGE ACTIVITIES:** Outing Club, 1971–75; Christian Fellowship, 1972–75

Deborah Susan Socolar: In the midst of moving now, I've oscillated along the T's Red Line since college — North Cambridge, Dorchester, Davis Square in Somerville, and now buying a house near the water in Quincy — but tried to hold to the path of working for a more just and equitable world. Since 1985, my jobs have focused on improving access to health care. Our project looks at why Massachusetts has the costliest health care in the nation (and thus the world), and how the ample sums now spent can be "recycled" to gain care for all without higher spending. We've recently examined prescription drug costs, the cost of single-payer health care, how to secure survival of enough hospitals to serve our aging population, and how to increase the share of the health dollar actually spent on care.

Bob and I got to know each other during the 1983 campaign of Mel King, Boston's first serious black mayoral candidate. The mobilization and sense of hope then in many Boston communities — especially communities of color — is like nothing I've seen since. Here and nationally, in too many respects, class, race, and other inequities grew over these twenty-five years.

Other past activities of note: rank-and-file union organizing; traveling to China (where my mother grew up) when Fuzhou opened to westerners (on a trip with family, Steve Carlip '75, and Peter Hogness '76); eight years working in a large hospital; organizing for a few trustworthy candidates and Boston's Rainbow Coalition; surviving ovarian cancer (luckily caught very early) and seeing limits of medical knowledge when Bob was ill; enjoying wonderful nieces and nephews on both my side and his; reading mysteries...I relish conferring on health reform with my father, active on these issues in his "retirement." Now Bob and I are eager to explore our new community.

HOME: Quincy, MA   **OCCUPATION:** Co-principal. Access and Affordability Monitoring Project. Health Services Dept., Boston University School of Public Health
BIRTHPLACE: Chicago, IL   **SECONDARY SCHOOL:** Bronx High School of Science, Bronx, NY   **YEARS AT COLLEGE:** 1971–76   **DEGREES:** A.B., magna cum laude, '75 ('76); M.P.H., Boston Univ. '89   **SPOUSE/PARTNER:** Robert Bamford

Stephanie Sonnabend: When I graduated from Harvard-Radcliffe, my mission was to contribute to people's lives. I headed to Atlanta, where I interned with what was then the Department of Health, Education, and Welfare. I only lasted eight months in the job, but remained working in Atlanta for two years.

I entered MIT's Sloan School in the fall of 1977. Upon graduation, my father did a major recruiting job to get me to join Sonesta Hotels. So, in 1979, I became the first member of the third generation to go into the family business. Twenty years later, seven out of twelve Sonnabends in my generation work for Sonesta. I "worked my way up" and became president of Sonesta in 1996. When I started at Sonesta, we operated eight hotels. There are now twenty Sonesta Hotels on five continents.

In 1985, I married Gregory Ciccolo, a true Renaissance man. His careers and avocations include singing opera; writing, songs and screenplays; real estate development; collecting and selling antique American pottery; photography; and coaching hockey, baseball, and soccer. Our daughter, Antonia, was born in 1987 and our son Nicholas, arrived in 1989. We have a wonderful but hectic life that includes travel to exotic places, such as Egypt, Australia, Chile, and Japan. We live in Brookline, Massachusetts, and spend weekends watching our children play sports and summers boating and relaxing on the New Hampshire seacoast.

I am also very involved in board activities. I am on two corporate boards, Sonesta and Century Bank and Trust. I have been an active member of the Radcliffe Board of Trustees and chaired a number of committees. I continue as one of the founding advisors to Mary Maples Dunn, acting dean of the Radcliffe Institute of Advanced Studies.

Throughout my life, I never lost sight of my mission. I contribute to people's lives by giving them a fabulous experience at one of our hotels. I contribute to our employee's lives by making sure our strong corporate culture of individual respect permeates throughout the organization. I may have lost my idealism, but my purpose and focus remain intact.

HOME: Brookline, MA   OCCUPATION: President. Sonesta Hotels and Resorts
BIRTHPLACE: Boston, MA   SECONDARY SCHOOL: Beaver Country Day School,
Brookline, MA   YEARS AT COLLEGE: 1971–75   DEGREES: A.B., magna cum laude, '75;
M.S.M., Mass. Inst. of Technology '79   SPOUSE/PARTNER: Gregory Martin Ciccolo,
June 30, 1985 (Boston Conservatory '89)   SPOUSE'S OCCUPATION: Self-Employed
CHILDREN: Antonia Rose, 1987; Nicholas Abraham, 1989

Diane Loring Souvaine: Nearly twenty-five years after graduation, I am still learning to be comfortable in my own skin. I am blessed, however, by a husband of twenty-four years, Richard Horn '72, by an eighth-grade daughter, Heather, and a third-grade son, Benjamin. After sixteen years of "exile" in New Jersey, Rich and I moved back to Massachusetts in 1998 to accept positions at Boston University Academy and Tufts University, respectively. Although Ben and Heather were far less clear that we ought to move, they have now settled into new schools and new friendships. Rich and I have experienced a Rip Van Winkle effect in returning to the area, but are beginning to be reacclimated ourselves. We particularly enjoy family trips to Boston cultural events and to northern New England mountains. We look forward to rekindling old friendships and making new ones at the Reunion.

HOME: Lexington, MA   **OCCUPATION:** Computer Science Professor. Dept. of Electrical Engineering and Computer Science, Tufts University   **BIRTHPLACE:** Melrose, MA   **SECONDARY SCHOOL:** The Winsor School, Boston, MA   **YEARS AT COLLEGE:** 1971–75   **DEGREES:** A.B., cum laude, '75; M.A.L.S., Dartmouth '80; M.S.E., Princeton '84; M.A., ibid. '85; Ph.D., ibid. '86   **SPOUSE/PARTNER:** Richard Downing Horn, June 12, 1976 (Harvard '72; M.A.L.S., Dartmouth '80; M.A., Princeton '85; Ph.D., ibid. '97)   **SPOUSE'S OCCUPATION:** Instructor of History; Director of Governance. Boston University Academy   **CHILDREN:** Heather Souvaine Horn, 1987; Benjamin Souvaine Horn, 1991

Amy Alison Spies: Hi. I've had some diverse experiences since college, with the common thread of film/writing focusing on women. I had a
Sheldon Travelling Fellowship, and ran around all over Europe. After that, I
worked at KQED-TV in San Francisco where my then-boyfriend Gary was in
law school. We moved down to Los Angeles when I got a TV development
job (coming up with story ideas, etc.). That led to me writing; one of my
movies got made, and many of my TV shows. In the meantime, Gary and I
got married and had two daughters, Paris and Juliet. After my second
daughter was born, I began learning about interactive media; I wrote a
story/game for kids and an Internet "drama." Recently, we've taken a sabbatical back up in the Bay Area because Gary's law firm opened an office
up here. We're in Ross, a beautiful town in Marin County with one of those
incredible public schools that have almost disappeared. My children are
incredible, and always an amazement to me. I'm still writing, and have a
desire to go back to school in an interdisciplinary graduate area of women's
studies.

HOME: San Anselmo, CA   OCCUPATION: Freelance Writer for Television, Film, and
Interactive Media   SECONDARY SCHOOL: Beverly Hills High School   YEARS AT
COLLEGE: 1971–75   DEGREES: A.B., magna cum laude, '75   SPOUSE/PARTNER: Gary
Gans, Dec. 21, 1981 (Wesleyan Univ. '75; J.D., Univ. of California, Berkeley '79)   SPOUSE'S
OCCUPATION: Attorney; Partner. Richards, Watson, and Gershon (business and
entertainment litigation firm)   CHILDREN: Paris, 1987; Juliet, 1993   COLLEGE
ACTIVITIES: Film activities

John Andrew Stadler: What's important?

Health: So far, so good. I weigh about five pounds more than when I left grad school; I can still swim and bicycle as far and as fast. I have taken up some new sports, like tennis and surf kayaking in the summer, and downhill skiing in winter.

Marriage: Cecile and I have been living together since 1974 and married since 1980. We have recently embarked on a new challenge: working together to start a company. We still talk to each other, although the volume is sometimes elevated a few decibels.

Family: Three kids, all attending the local public school: Russell, fourteen; Lauren, thirteen; and Cara, twelve. We work together a lot on homework, play basketball, go biking together, and all speak at once at dinner. They are all witty, pugnacious, and hopelessly disorganized. And occasionally kind, sensitive, creative, and curious. To quote my son, we put the *fun* back in "dysFUNctional."

Career: I've made enough money to retire, comfortably if not extravagantly. I am fortunate to be able to work on whatever I want. My first company, Clearpoint, was in the computer industry. It grew from zero to seventy million dollars in seven years, at which point I sold it to my partner (who took it to bankruptcy in another three years). I worked on a number of start-ups after that, some successful and some disastrous. In 1991, I became interested in education and mathematics achievement; I began volunteering extensively in the local schools. Two years later I founded the Francis W. Parker Charter School, where I taught mathematics until this June. The school enrolls over three hundred and fifty students and has become a laboratory school for progressive education.

This fall I started working for my wife's company: Traxit Technology. We are developing software and hardware to manage school computers. By the time you read this, we will either be planning an IPO or be long since defunct.

Overall, I am very thankful; life has treated me very well.

HOME: Harvard, MA   **OCCUPATION:** Vice President; CFO. Traxit Technology, Inc. (developer of software for managing school computers)   **BIRTHPLACE:** Chicago, IL **SECONDARY SCHOOL:** Pioneer High School, Ann Arbor, MI   **YEARS AT COLLEGE:** 1971–76   **DEGREES:** A.B., magna cum laude, '75 ('76); M.P.P. '79   **SPOUSE/PARTNER:** Cecile Yew, December 1980 (Univ. of Michigan '77)   **SPOUSE'S OCCUPATION:** President; CEO. Traxit Technology, Inc.   **CHILDREN:** Russell Lewis, 1984; Lauren Beth, 1986; Cara Justine, 1987   **COLLEGE ACTIVITIES:** Beer steward, Dudley Coop House, 1973–76; business staff, *Harvard Crimson,* 1971–72

Paul Robert Staley: This is what I can remember: June 4, 1978: Married my college girlfriend, Cathie Hirshberg. Still married, still in love. August 1978: Packed up the Corolla and moved (back for me, out for Cathie) to San Francisco. Boston's nice and everything, but let's not kid ourselves. October 1978: Began playing football with what evolved into the JPSFL (the Jews and Paul Staley Football League). We still play (albeit sporadically) after over twenty years. August 26, 1983: Birth of our first son, Adam. March 1985: Decided to take the path of least resistance to the big bucks and became an institutional fixed income salesperson at Lehman. September 6, 1985: The biggest surprise of all, the birth of undiagnosed twin sons, Willy and Max. July 1988: Bought the kind of house I always wanted, a Victorian on a hill in San Francisco. February 1999: Opened the Oakland office of Ascend Residential. We buy, remodel, and sell homes in the Bay Area's poorest neighborhoods to first-time buyers. July 1999: Broke eighty.

I didn't leave Harvard with any clear professional ambitions. As a result, my career path has meandered a bit, but I've had a chance to do a variety of things (budget analysis and strategic planning, emerging market debt sales, running a small bank in British Columbia, looking for real estate deals in Mexico). There appears to be a tendency to collect degrees or professional affiliations and then not apply them: a Master of Public Policy followed by eighteen years in the private sector, and a chartered financial analyst (CFA) designation before starting my urban real estate business.

As for keeping in touch with people, well you know how it is. All this work and family stuff takes up a lot of time. I've been lucky that Warren Browner lives a couple foggier blocks away, and Hank Bannister has been a patient mentor on the golf course. There are so many names I haven't heard from in years. Bieser, Burroughs, Rolbein, Rikoon. How are you guys doing?

HOME: San Francisco, CA   **OCCUPATION:** Regional Director. Ascend Residential (real estate)   **BIRTHPLACE:** Boston, MA   **SECONDARY SCHOOL:** Henry M. Gunn High School, Palo Alto, CA   **YEARS AT COLLEGE:** 1971–76   **DEGREES:** A.B., cum laude, '76; M.P.P., Univ. of California, Berkeley '80   **SPOUSE/PARTNER:** Cathie Hirshberg, June 4, 1978 (Jackson State Univ. '75)   **SPOUSE'S OCCUPATION:** Sales and Management Trainer **CHILDREN:** Adam, 1983; Willy and Max, 1985 (twins)   **COLLEGE ACTIVITIES:** Other than dorm crew, nothing that I would want my sons to read about

John Edward Standard: After college, I lived in the Concord area for three years, cutting wood and painting houses. In 1978, we followed friend Des Fitzgerald '74 to midcoast Maine, where Cathy and I settled in to raise our family, work on our old farmhouse, and "live the good life, Maine-style." I became a carpenter, had my own woodworking shop, built spec houses and a schoolhouse for our children's co-operative preschool and child care center. Never really made any money, as Maine was in a deep financial depression, but I sure enjoyed quality woodworking. After our third child was born, we decided to move to the big island, Hawaii, and have been grateful ever since, to embrace the outdoor lifestyle.

Some of my most important personal experiences have been assisting my wife in the birth of our three children — two at home and one a c-section (Wow!), and being able to help with the care of my parents as they became ill. My mother lived with breast cancer for three years, was lovingly cared for, and was able to die at home. My father, a gifted surgeon, got Alzheimer's and was finally institutionalized two years ago. It was an honor for me to give of myself to those I love.

My passion is reading. One of my greatest pleasures has been the creation of our summer house in Maine, having the ability to design and build it all. Being in the trades has given me tremendous satisfaction. I am a semi-hermit, but my marriage is still strong and fun and my children keep coming home. Best to all my friends.

HOME: Hawi, HI   **OCCUPATION:** Carpenter; Woodworker   **BIRTHPLACE:** Brooklyn, NY   **SECONDARY SCHOOL:** Westminster School, Simsbury, CT   **YEARS AT COLLEGE:** 1970–75   **DEGREES:** A.B. '75   **SPOUSE/PARTNER:** Catherine Morgan (School of the Museum of Fine Arts '75)   **SPOUSE'S OCCUPATION:** Artist; Co-operative Gallery Owner   **CHILDREN:** Celina Sophia, 1979; Silas Mason, 1982; Eloise Anne, 1991

Craig Stanley Steele: I rekindled an interest in computers during a stint working as an assistant in the Harvard chemical labs, and followed that thought to Caltech. There I acquired a couple of degrees and enjoyed fighting the good fight for a few righteous causes of "leftish" ilk. In addition to co-founding a graduate-student women's group, I learned something about the student coffeehouse trade, fueling the institute's intellections at the Red Door Cafe. My computer work has covered the hardware and software of high-performance concurrent computing, a fascinating field now somewhat straitened by the reduced military stature of the enemy.

I've found, through varied routes, four fine children and a dear wife. I've recently acquired a small airplane, Cessna '76, to support my somewhat peripatetic existence, balancing family obligations in Nevada, Arizona, and California. Despite the erosions of time, I strive to hold an even course through the updrafts and downdrafts of life. I find I can still write with the finest of points, but struggle to read the same. Best wishes to all my classmates.

HOME: Flagstaff, AZ   OCCUPATION: Computer Scientist. Information Sciences Institute, University of Southern California   BIRTHPLACE: Las Vegas, NV   SECONDARY SCHOOL: Valley High School, Las Vegas, NV   YEARS AT COLLEGE: 1971–74   DEGREES: A.B., cum laude, '75 ('74); M.S., California Inst. of Technology '92; Ph.D., ibid. '92   SPOUSE/PARTNER: Vicky Teague, Sept. 27, 1986, divorced July 7, 1997 (Pitzer Coll.; M.B.A, Cornell); Heidi Wayment, May 24, 1998 (Biola Univ. '77; M.S., Univ. of Southern California '87; Ph.D., Univ. of California, Los Angeles '92)   SPOUSE'S OCCUPATION: Assistant Professor of Psychology. Northern Arizona University   CHILDREN: Benjamin C., 1988; Quinton J., 1991; Hannah K., 1993; Dean A., 1998   COLLEGE ACTIVITIES: SDS, 1972–74

Eric Jon Stenshoel: My formal studies at Harvard were useful in teaching me what it was that I did not want to do with my life (e.g., neoclassical economics). I considered teaching, but as a gay man inching his way out of the closet, I was afraid that Anita Bryant and her crusading friends would not make the profession very hospitable. So I went to law school, which gave me a trade to practice while I figured out what I really wanted to do with my life. In 1980, I took a job with a medium-sized law firm in New York with a European clientele, which paid the student loans and kept me in a multilingual milieu. In 1984, I met theater director William Prosser, my first partner. We did not know then that he was HIV-positive. In the meantime, I satisfied my interest in linguistics by collecting bits of syntactic data from a variety of languages on vacation and business trips. Thoughts of more substantial study were incubating all along, but any considerations of a career change had to be suspended when Bill developed AIDS. Witnessing the passion that Bill brought both to his work in the theater and preparation for his own death made me yearn for the same commitment in my life. Experiencing his death showed me how quickly material concerns melt away in the face of mortality. Soon after Bill's death eight years ago, I met community organizer Michael McKee, my current partner. When Michael told me to stop talking about moving from law to linguistics and start doing it, I needed no further encouragement. After five years of taking graduate courses part-time, I am now taking a sabbatical from the law and devoting my energies to my nascent dissertation at City University of New York.

HOME: New York, NY   **OCCUPATION:** Counsel. Curtis, Mallet-Prevost, Colt & Mosle (law firm)   **BIRTHPLACE:** Cheyenne Wells, CO   **SECONDARY SCHOOL:** Hopkins Lindbergh High School, Hopkins, MN   **YEARS AT COLLEGE:** 1971–75   **DEGREES:** A.B., magna cum laude, '75 ('76); J.D., Univ. of Minnesota '80   **SPOUSE/PARTNER:** William Llewellyn Prosser, Sept. 29, 1984; died, Nov. 22, 1991 (Williams Coll. '64); Michael McKee, Feb. 29, 1992 (Baylor Univ. '62)   **SPOUSE'S OCCUPATION:** Community Organizer. New York State Tenants and Neighbors Coalition   **COLLEGE ACTIVITIES:** Harvard-Radcliffe Orchestra, 1971–74

Charles Louis Stern, Jr.: In many ways my life since college has proceeded along a conventional path — law school, judicial law clerk, private practice, marriage, and children. And yet within that conventional framework, I have tried to find ways to avoid the self-satisfied complacency I too often find among my upper middle class contemporaries in New Orleans, the northernmost of the banana republics (or, as some local T-shirts put it, "Louisiana — Third World and Proud of It"). My wife and five daughters, ranging from fifteen to one, are happy to remind me of my foibles and receding hairline and to puncture the self-importance that seems to be a job hazard for lawyers. My children humble me less directly as well by managing to grow up without the neuroses and anxieties that I still associate with my own childhood and adolescence. For that I thank my wife, who is more skilled with children than anyone I have ever met.

After years of resisting the practice of law, I have found ways to enjoy it, primarily by tapping into my competitive instincts, the same ones that came out during Cabot Hall pickup basketball games (although I hope that I'm a better lawyer than I was a basketball player). I seem to have found my niche with a small commercial practice firm, where I can run my life without worrying about office politics or partnership squabbles. Recent highlights include a Supreme Court argument, at which my older children saw their dad survive thirty minutes of grilling by a politely hostile court, temporarily united, despite their ideological rifts, in rejecting my argument.

Outside of work and family, I've taken up piano, become involved in various nonprofit community groups and, somewhat to my surprise, returned to Jewish roots that I thought had withered and died. Maybe I've finally grown up, even if it is a little late.

HOME: New Orleans, LA   OCCUPATION: Partner. Steeg & O'Connor (private law practice)   BIRTHPLACE: Mobile, AL   SECONDARY SCHOOL: W. F. Dykes High School, Atlanta, GA   YEARS AT COLLEGE: 1971–75   DEGREES: A.B., magna cum laude, '75; J.D., Yale '78   SPOUSE/PARTNER: Jacquelyn Lob, July 24, 1983 (Louisiana State Univ. '76)   SPOUSE'S OCCUPATION: Homemaker   CHILDREN: Erica Rose, 1984; Rebecca Ilene, 1987; Lily Danielle, 1992; Eleanor Margaret, 1996; Emma Winston, 1998   COLLEGE ACTIVITIES: Drama Club, 1971–74; Gilbert and Sullivan Society, 1973–74

Paul Sternberg, Jr.: Although my life since graduation has moved progressively southward from a geographic perspective, my personal growth and satisfaction has experienced definite movement in an upward direction. In 1975, I never would have anticipated settling in Atlanta, marriage to a native of Alabama, and children being educated in a conservative Jewish day school. However, my current status has followed a seemingly logical and quite comfortable progression.

After medical school in Chicago, residency at Johns Hopkins, and fellowship at Duke, I accepted a faculty position at Emory University. Anticipating a brief stint while establishing further my academic credentials, I found Emory to be a school "on the rise" with wonderful resources and a great vision; furthermore, I had the opportunity to play a pivotal role in this institution's growth. Atlanta was the thriving capital of the New South and proved an exciting city in which to live.

I met Gloria, a real treasure; we had two handsome, creative, bright sons and settled down, committed to each other, the Atlanta community, and Emory. During the past few years, I have striven to balance the joys and obligations of family, job, and community service.

I feel very fortunate. I have a wonderful wife, who has brought great sensitivity and love into our home; and two fantastic sons, with all the stimuli of growing up, asking questions, and challenging authority, but also the pleasures of their affection and delight in the world. I love my job, where I am able to combine the rewards of clinical care as a retinal specialist with the challenges of scientific inquiry. Gloria and I remain active outside the home, both participating in Jewish organizations as well as the arts community.

Harvard prepared me well for my life, and I am grateful not only for my education, but for the people I met, the friends I made, and the great times we had.

HOME: Atlanta, GA   **OCCUPATION:** Thomas Aaberg Professor of Ophthalmology. Emory University School of Medicine   **BIRTHPLACE:** Chicago, IL   **SECONDARY SCHOOL:** Phillips Academy, Andover, MA   **YEARS AT COLLEGE:** 1971–75   **DEGREES:** A.B., magna cum laude, '75; M.D., Univ. of Chicago '79   **SPOUSE/PARTNER:** Gloria M., Oct. 17, 1987 (Univ. of Texas '78)   **SPOUSE'S OCCUPATION:** Graduate Student. Georgia School of Professional Psychology, Atlanta, GA   **CHILDREN:** Matthew Gregory, 1989; Zachary Ian, 1992   **COLLEGE ACTIVITIES:** Harvard-Radcliffe Orchestra, 1972–75

Robert H. Stier, Jr.: Nagging questions after twenty-five years: Are there better blues than "The Thrill Is Gone"? Which is more important, creativity or perseverance? What is the most fun you can have standing up? If you could give five more years to a musician who died too soon, who would you pick? When was the last time most of us talked to our best friends? How do you inspire a teenager to clean his/her room? Should our culture provide for a nap time every afternoon? What components make up the greatest vacation? Where do we find intellectual stimulation these days? When will all days be casual dress days, even in the East? Which winery offers the best wines to taste? Should juries decide complex technical cases? Are boys harder to raise than girls? Which public figure should we most admire? Is there anything that improves one's appearance more than a smile? Does tracing your roots contribute to life here and now? How will global climate and population shifts affect our grandchildren? Is it harder to run a marathon or to lose twenty pounds? What would make you consider running for public office? Which actor/actress should be cast to play you? What are your ethical concerns about cloning? How can we be more receptive to the voice of our creator? Do you really want to know what I've been doing for the last twenty-five years? (Short version: two years making Volvos in Sweden, followed by return to Cambridge for law school and marriage to Mary Ellen FitzGerald in 1979; to Baltimore after law school, with Meghan and Erik born in 1980 and 1982; trial practice in Baltimore and Washington, D.C., relocated to Portland, Maine in 1987; Maeve born in 1992; Mary Ellen starts own market research firm in 1993; I change law firms in 1998, joining Pierce Atwood as partner; life is good. Long version: check out this Website: www.concentric.net/insights/reunion.html)
See you in Cambridge. Celebrate life!

HOME: Elizabeth, ME   OCCUPATION: Partner. Pierce Atwood (law firm)
BIRTHPLACE: Berwyn, IL   SECONDARY SCHOOL: Downers Grove High School South,
Downers Grove, IL   YEARS AT COLLEGE: 1971–75   DEGREES: A.B., cum laude, '75; J.D.
'80   SPOUSE/PARTNER: Mary Ellen FitzGerald, Aug. 11, 1979 (Jackson Coll.; Tufts Univ.
'76)   SPOUSE'S OCCUPATION: President. Critical Insights, Inc.   CHILDREN: Meghan,
1980; Erik, 1982; Maeve, 1992   COLLEGE ACTIVITIES: Drama Club; Lowell House Drama
Society; intramural squash

Gregory J. Stone: I was so much older then, I'm younger than that now.
I just inked a three-picture deal with Miramax (which will release the
films under my own label). I will be writing, directing and starring in the
movies, which represent the first three parts of a tetralogy about life in this
century. Ancillary rights to part four are still available.

Meanwhile, my production company went public with great fanfare in
early 1999. I am happy to report that the stock dodecatupled on the first day,
and is currently selling at fifteen hundred times earnings.

It is with great pride that I announce my endowment of the "Stone Chair
of the Incremental Logic of Logical Incrementalism" in a new discipline
called the "Joint Program for Providential Capitalism" sponsored by the
Business and Divinity Schools. We are currently seeking a public relations
representative for this exciting new venture, so qualified applicants are
invited to submit a twenty-five word essay about God, man, and dollar.

After all, it's a global economy these days. Therefore we need to leverage
our core capabilities so that we can grow our ventures synergistically, going
forward to a new millennium of challenges and opportunities. And for God's
sake, let's not beat on against the current, borne ceaselessly back into the past.
Instead, let's sprinkle some pixie dust around some exciting new concepts.

As I sit here in sunny Belmont, not more than three miles from Harvard
Square, I wonder if non-Euclidean geometry is really the key to it all.
Perhaps that which rises doesn't converge after all.

In all seriousness: I owe everything I am to my lovely wife Mary and my
two beautiful children Lauren and Jack.

HOME: Belmont, MA   OCCUPATION: Producer; Writer; Director. Greg Stone
Productions (commercial production and media consulting)   BIRTHPLACE: Elizabeth,
NJ   SECONDARY SCHOOL: Westfield Senior High School, Westfield, NJ   YEARS AT
COLLEGE: 1973–75   DEGREES: A.B., cum laude, '75; M.S., Columbia '80; M.S., ibid. '84
SPOUSE/PARTNER: Mary P.   SPOUSE'S OCCUPATION: Homemaker   CHILDREN:
Lauren A., 1992; John V., 1997

R. Gregg Stone: We are enjoying a brilliant early fall weekend in New England — cloudless skies with the yellow fading sun of the season, touches of early color in the maple and tupelo, and cool temperatures on either end of the day.

On Friday evening I watched our oldest daughter, Gevvie (fourteen), play soccer for her school before carting her and some friends to the movies. On Saturday, after a ritual row in preparation for the Head of the Charles, at the conclusion of which I was lucky enough to hear the Harvard Band banging its way across the river to practice for the day's game, son Robbie (nine) and I participated in the suburban ritual of Saturday soccer. This afternoon I take our second girl, Phoebe (twelve), to ice hockey. Those who know my hockey skills might be amused at my coaching her team. My wife, Lisa, is off today with the Winsor crew, which she coaches, at a regatta in Lowell.

Our life these past five years, or more, joyfully has revolved around children. Primarily our own of course, but Lisa has taken up coaching again, this time at the high school level; I have gained from volunteer activities at the Boys and Girls Clubs of Boston and Camp Pasquaney; and the activities of our children — sports, church, music, schools, etc.— help us enjoy the children of others as well.

Professionally, I have continued to work with young companies through a small venture firm that I co-founded. I must admit that the challenges of growing a small firm have rewarded me with a healthy dose of humility. Most of my activities focus on the life sciences, and I am sorry to report that we did not make the Internet bets that have been rocking our industry and the financial world for the past few years. There can be few regrets, however. These have been generous times for all of us.

Geographically, I have never strayed far from Harvard's shadow. This has led to much enjoyment over the years while we have sampled sports, culture, and even academics. Fortunately, our proximity has not dulled the anticipation of seeing many of you back here again in June.

HOME: Newton, MA   OCCUPATION: General Partner. Kestrel Venture Management (venture capital)   BIRTHPLACE: Greenwich, CT   SECONDARY SCHOOL: St. Paul's School, Concord, NH   YEARS AT COLLEGE: 1971–75   DEGREES: A.B., magna cum laude, '75; J.D., Harvard '79   SPOUSE/PARTNER: Lisa Hansen, 1983 (California State Univ., Long Beach '78)   SPOUSE'S OCCUPATION: Rowing Coach. Winsor School   CHILDREN: Genevra Lea, 1985; Phoebe Barnes, 1987; Robert Godfrey, 1990   HARVARD/RADCLIFFE SIBLINGS: Jennifer Stone '80, M.D. '86   COLLEGE ACTIVITIES: Crew, 1971–75; A.D. Club

Clifton Jairus Stratton, III: My life since graduation has followed a fairly traditional path of graduate school, work, marriage, children, and more work. But along the way, I have also been fortunate to enjoy a good deal of independence and a deep sense of satisfaction. After law school, I worked for several years for large law firms — Perkins Coie in Seattle and Rogers and Wells in Washington, D.C. While I value the discipline and knowledge gained in practicing law, I eventually realized that rather than serving the client, I really wanted to be the client. In 1987, my wife, Winnie, and I moved back to Seattle, where we started a family and plunged into the business of real estate investment and development. The arrival of three children has been a wonderful, life-affirming experience. At the same time, being freed from the time clock of law practice, I have had the opportunity to serve on a variety of community and nonprofit agencies and boards, including terms as chairman of the Seattle Arts Commission and the Pioneer Square Preservation Board, and many years as trustee of the Seattle Art Museum and the Seattle Children's Theatre. The combination of creating my own business and working in the community has been very gratifying. However, at the end of the day, the two things I look forward to most are spending time with my family and salmon fishing off the coast of British Columbia.

HOME: Seattle, WA   OCCUPATION: President. Stratton Interests, Inc. (real estate investment and development)   BIRTHPLACE: Washington, DC   SECONDARY SCHOOL: St. Albans School, Washington, DC   YEARS AT COLLEGE: 1971–75 DEGREES: A.B., cum laude, '75; J.D., Univ. of Pennsylvania '79; M.B.A., ibid. '79 SPOUSE/PARTNER: Winifred Sutton, May 31, 1986 (Univ. of North Carolina, Chapel Hill '75; J.D., Univ. of Virginia '78)   SPOUSE'S OCCUPATION: Attorney (retired); Community Volunteer   CHILDREN: Clifton, 1988; Leland, 1990; Carter, 1993 HARVARD/RADCLIFFE SIBLINGS: Joanna Stratton Roze '76   COLLEGE ACTIVITIES: Phoenix S.K. Club

Michael J. Strauss: Put simply, life right now is very, very good and I feel fortunate to be who I am. I have a professional life I enjoy, and, most importantly, share all with wonderful family and friends. I'd be greedy if I asked for more.

For the Twentieth Reunion I mentioned having "a little more around the middle...a little less on top...and a slightly difficult time reading the fine print on the small ibuprofen bottle..." Five more years has me faring somewhat better, having lost two inches around the waist and stabilized the hair loss. But the ibuprofen bottle and I remain good friends.

My professional life has gone in directions I never anticipated, but it's been an exceptional adventure. I became an internist but never practiced medicine. Instead, after earning a master's in public health and serving as staff to a congressional commission, I caught "Potomac fever" and became a health policy consultant. The firm I started, which dealt with medical product reimbursement, grew fast and I eventually sold it to Corning, Inc. (pots and pans fame). Having stepped down as president and changed to part-time, I have the luxury of spending more time with family and dabbling in other ventures. I serve on boards of two medical device companies and Kaiser Permanente (Mid-Atlantic Medical Group), and a national Medicare advisory committee.

Family and friends keep life in balance. Going through high school for a second time (albeit vicariously through kids) is O.K., and college is next. I just celebrated twenty great years of marriage with a spectacular trip to Australia and New Zealand. For those who haven't been, definitely "put it on the list."

Current strategic plan: Spend even more time with family, read more, think about additional entrepreneurial ventures, and, potentially, write my first whodunit.

HOME: Rockville, MD   **OCCUPATION:** Health Policy Consultant; Executive Vice President. Covance Health Economics and Outcomes Services (consulting and research services firm)   **SPOUSE/PARTNER:** Molly, June 2, 1979 (Pennsylvania State Univ. '75) **SPOUSE'S OCCUPATION:** Psychiatrist. Old Georgetown Mental Health   **CHILDREN:** David, 1983; Rachel, 1987

Andrea Fay Stringos: After several years of a stressful business career, I opted out of work and marriage to raise my two children, do volunteer work (Harvard Club, Junior League, homeless issues), and cultivate friendships and avocations (music and sailing).

I thoroughly enjoyed spending four years getting another bachelor's degree in piano performance, and then went on to work on a master's degree in music theory. One of my highlights was accompanying an opera singer in a training program in Salzburg. I will always remain an amateur musician, but it is great fun to be able to dabble in music. I have also taken up sailing in a big way. I own a Flying Scot (a nineteen-foot sloop) which I race avidly here in Miami, coming in first in the 1999 Miami to Key Largo race, and I frequently crew on various thirty-foot boats. I enjoy the sailing community—there is a camaraderie here that I find deeply satisfying. I use my business background to good effect in volunteer arenas through grant writing and in sailing circles as president of the Women's Yacht Racing Association and as treasurer of the Coconut Grove Sailing Club. For someone who was always terribly shy I find that I am now in the center of a constant storm of activity.

My two children are wonderful kids, both very happy and well-balanced. I feel, in all, that I have been very fortunate and blessed in life.

HOME: Coral Gables, FL   OCCUPATION: Community Volunteer   BIRTHPLACE: LaRochelle, France   SECONDARY SCHOOL: Ursuline Academy, New Orleans, LA   YEARS AT COLLEGE: 1971–75   DEGREES: A.B., cum laude, '75; M.B.A., Univ. of Pennsylvania '78; B.M., Univ. of Miami '93   CHILDREN: Brendan Callahan, 1981; Morgan Callahan, 1984   COLLEGE ACTIVITIES: Varsity swimming team

Thomas S. Summer: Twenty-five years ago, I was winding down a leave of absence, looking forward to returning to Harvard in order to pursue an exciting career in business. I got what I bargained for. I have found the people, emotions, challenges, and victories to be more and more rewarding as my career has progressed. I have also been blessed with a wonderful family: the woman of my dreams, and two beautiful and talented daughters, who serve as an infinite source of support, challenge, and humility. Family and hard work have elevated my spirit while I continue to mature.

HOME: Rochester, NY   OCCUPATION: Chief Financial Officer. Canandaigua Brands (beverage)   BIRTHPLACE: Columbus, OH   SECONDARY SCHOOL: Columbus Academy   YEARS AT COLLEGE: 1971–80   DEGREES: A.B., cum laude, '75 ('80); M.B.A., Univ. of Chicago '82   SPOUSE/PARTNER: Sydney Ann Licht, Aug. 4, 1979 (Smith Coll. '76)   SPOUSE'S OCCUPATION: Artist   CHILDREN: Alexandra P., 1984; Marguerite L., 1988   HARVARD/RADCLIFFE SIBLINGS: Fred A. Summer '68

Daniel George Swistel: I reflect upon the rapid pace of change over the last twenty-five years — how 1984 came and went, the revolution in communications and digital technology and the passing of the millennium. In *Star Wars,* George Lucas has a "robot doctor" attaching a mechanical hand to Luke Skywalker, and I remember thinking how preposterous that seemed. Well, we now have mechanical hearts working in humans and I will soon be one of the first surgeons in this country performing open heart surgery by directing a robot with miniature hands via a computer interface. The future has arrived for me! However, my other research interests revolve around environmental pollution and heart disease and I cannot escape the irony that a great deal of our progress has caused much of our current illnesses. I am, however, gratified by the success of my career and the knowledge that I have directly improved the lives of so many people.

My private life revolves around my family — Alice and our three children, their education and our travels together. I have developed a great love of contemporary art and enjoy accumulating a few choice affordable pieces. Unfortunately, the pace of life in the city doesn't allow for much more than that. We have a vacation home in Santa Fe, New Mexico, and I look forward to restoring my sanity there.

HOME: New York, NY   OCCUPATION: Cardiovascular and Thoracic Surgeon. St.
Luke's/Roosevelt Hospital Center. Associate Clinical Professor of Surgery. College of
Physicians and Surgeons, Columbia University   BIRTHPLACE: Akron, OH
SECONDARY SCHOOL: The Lawrenceville School, Lawrenceville, NJ   YEARS AT
COLLEGE: 1971–75   DEGREES: A.B., cum laude, '75; M.D., Rutgers, The State Univ. of
New Jersey '79   SPOUSE/PARTNER: Alice Katherine Phillips, Nov. 24, 1984 (Tufts Univ.
'76)   SPOUSE'S OCCUPATION: Artist   CHILDREN: Lily Phillips Swistel, 1987; Nina
Gifford Swistel, 1989; Caroline Phillips Swistel, 1991   HARVARD/RADCLIFFE SIBLINGS:
Alexander Julian Swistel '71   COLLEGE ACTIVITIES: Drama Club, 1971–72; Hasty
Pudding Theatricals, 1972–75

S. Tucker Taft: First, a quick summary of the past twenty-five years:
After graduation, I worked four years at the Harvard Science Center as the
first full-time "system mother" for a Unix computer system outside of Bell
Labs. I then went back to Cleveland for a year as a consultant, and there met
my wife-to-be, Phyllis Yale '78, who was heading back to Boston in the fall of
1980 for Harvard Business School. We came to my Harvard Fifth Reunion
together, and by chance found a classmate (Cynthia Perrin) who was vacat-
ing her apartment in the fall. We moved into it in the fall, Phyllis began at
HBS, and I started work for Intermetrics, Inc., where I still work today
(though it has since gone public, then private again, then merged and
changed its name to AverStar, Inc.). Upon graduation from HBS in 1982,
Phyllis and I were married, spent a glorious three weeks in Greece, and then
Phyllis went off to work for Bain & Co., where she still works today (I suspect
we may have earned the "company loyalty" awards in our respective Harvard
classes). In 1983 we moved to Lexington and bought our first house. In 1986
our first child, Rebecca, was born. We moved to our present house, a
"Bauhaus"-style modern house also in Lexington, in 1989. In 1990, our second child, Maia, was born. In the summer of 1998, we made our first foray
into family international travel, with a three-week trip to Italy and England.
In the summer of 1999, we instead decided to rip up our house, and we are
hoping it will be put back together by the time of the Twenty-fifth Reunion.

Family life has been joyous, with our European trip and Rebecca's Bat
Mitzvah this past October being a couple of the recent highlights. Work life
has been challenging, with Phyllis and I alternating between overwork,
major accomplishments, and then occasional downturns and self-doubt. My
work high-point was probably the five-year period between 1990 and 1995,
when I was chief architect for the design of the internationally standardized
programming language, Ada 95. Phyllis is going through a high-point in her

career now, having recently been appointed head of the Boston office of Bain & Co., one of the top management consulting firms in the world. I feel very fortunate to have a family where we can help each other through tougher periods, and celebrate together the major accomplishments.

Phyllis and I both keep in touch with Harvard, through friends who are professors, through Harvard's myriad "development" (a.k.a. fundraising) activities, and more recently, through my teaching a course in computer science as a visiting lecturer. This latter activity was particularly interesting, in that I was reminded of the remarkable level of aptitude of the "average" Harvard student. Perhaps Harvard's greatest asset is its ability to attract the best students and faculty, and bring them together into a vibrant intellectual melting pot. See you all in June 2000 (presuming we all survive January 1, 2000!).

HOME: Lexington, MA   **OCCUPATION:** Technical Director. AverStar, Inc. (software development)   **SECONDARY SCHOOL:** Hawken School, Gates Mills, OH   **YEARS AT COLLEGE:** 1971–75   **DEGREES:** A.B., summa cum laude, '75   **SPOUSE/PARTNER:** Phyllis R. Yale, June 27, 1982 (Harvard '78; M.B.A., ibid. '82)   **SPOUSE'S OCCUPATION:** Vice President and Director, Boston Office. Bain & Co.   **CHILDREN:** Rebecca Yale Taft, 1986; Maia Yale Taft, 1990   **HARVARD/RADCLIFFE SIBLINGS:** Cynthia B. Taft '72   **COLLEGE ACTIVITIES:** Freshman soccer team, 1971

Ruth Eleanor Tait: Twenty-five, or in my case, twenty-six years ago I had no real idea of what I wanted to do with my life beyond something that satisfied my curiosity and generalist dilettantism, probably involving travel, people, writing, variety and change, and a desire to be at the heart of things and to make a difference — possibly the foreign service, publishing, journalism. My plans at this stage did not involve children or business.

I followed in my brother's footsteps to Oxford and then back to Canada to work in government as an advisor to a cabinet minister. In Ottawa I met my future husband, Andrew, an Australian diplomat on his first posting and returned to Australia with him in 1980.

Next followed nine pretty hedonistic years in Sidney working in government and as a management consultant, as Andrew also moved from the Foreign Office to health economics/administration then to management consulting. The undisputed highlight of these years was the life-changing arrival of Alexander in 1989.

In May 1990 we moved to London; Andrew with McKinsey, while I joined Korn/Ferry. It is only because I have found headhunting (particularly long-term relationship building and coaching) to be so rewarding that I have continued to work virtually full-time, except for an eight-month break to write a book on leadership and most importantly to have Nicky in 1994.

My professional and personal interests come together in a general fascination with how to live well, most powerfully as a mother concerned that my boys lead lives that respond to their deepest interests and strengths, but also as a search consultant advising people on their working lives and getting the fit right between company, role, and individual. Probably because of my own early failure to pay attention to my deepest interests, I am intrigued to understand the right path in work and life for others.

Although I feel lucky to love my work, I am passionate about my family. The issue of life/work balance has been the defining one for the last ten years. Two of my brothers have died, one very recently, and the imperative to live and to love well has never been more compelling.

What that will mean, I am only beginning to conceive, but am starting with a sabbatical for the next two months and should have some answers by June!

HOME: London, England   **OCCUPATION:** Partner. Korn/Ferry International (executive search)   **BIRTHPLACE:** Montreal, Canada   **SECONDARY SCHOOL:** Neuchâtel Junior Coll., Neuchâtel, Switzerland; The Study, Montreal, Canada   **YEARS AT COLLEGE:** 1971–74   **DEGREES:** A.B., magna cum laude, '75 ('74); M.A., Oxford Univ. '76 **SPOUSE/PARTNER:** Andrew Doman, 1982 (M.B.B.S., Adelaide Univ.; B.A., Ottawa Univ.; M.B.A., Univ. of New South Wales)   **SPOUSE'S OCCUPATION:** Director. McKinsey & Company   **CHILDREN:** Alexander, 1989; Nicky, 1994

Valorie Taylor: After being retired by genetics from a career in chemistry, I'm now teaching cello, playing in a community symphony, and studying martial arts, Ba Gua and T'ai Chi Chuan. As new interests develop into passions, I actively load them into the modified operating system.

A brazen contrarian dared elicit from gray hopelessness infirmity, jubilee: keen living mindfully, necessitates observing progressive qualities rigorously; shamanic transcendence unveils volition with xenophilic youthful zeal.

HOME: Atlanta, GA   **OCCUPATION:** Cello Teacher   **BIRTHPLACE:** Detroit, MI   **SECONDARY SCHOOL:** Henry M. Gunn School, Palo Alto, CA   **YEARS AT COLLEGE:** 1971–75   **DEGREES:** A.B. '75   **COLLEGE ACTIVITIES:** Bach Society; Radcliffe Track and Field Club; Circolo Italiano

David Aaron Thurm: It's been a fun, exciting, and very fulfilling twenty-five years.

Andrea and I are still happily married, and are about to celebrate our twenty-seventh New Year's together. Our three children are growing rapidly, perhaps too rapidly. Amanda is a high school freshman, Matthew is in sixth grade and James is in kindergarten. Like the rest of you, our lives are crowded with carpools and a whirl of child-centric activities.

I'm still at the *New York Times,* coming up on eighteen years. My career at the *Times* has been a series of challenging assignments across the company that have allowed me to grow professionally and personally. In August, I jumped from the newspaper to our newly formed Internet operation, where I am the chief operating officer. I'm having a great time working with a solid team of people trying to figure out the uncertainties of our increasingly electronic world.

Prior to that I was deep in ink and machinery as the vice president of production at a time when we moved to a multipart paper with later closes and color. The assignment involved everything from building highly automated production facilities to rebuilding relationships with our unionized work force.

I look forward to catching up with friends and acquaintances at the Reunion.

HOME: Bronxville, NY   OCCUPATION: Chief Operating Officer. Times Company Digital (Internet company)   BIRTHPLACE: Winslow, AZ   SECONDARY SCHOOL: Boston Latin School, Boston, MA   YEARS AT COLLEGE: 1971–75   DEGREES: A.B., magna cum laude, '75; J.D., New York Univ. '78   SPOUSE/PARTNER: Andrea Granoff, March 29, 1981 (Harvard '77; M.A., Princeton '82)   CHILDREN: Amanda Margot, 1985; Matthew Charles, 1988; James Richard, 1994

Orrin Eliot Tilevitz: For ten years I taught, Ivy League biases showing, a rather advanced weekly installment in the daily Talmud study program. I'm raising two fellow mountain goats who delight in climbing three thousand feet with me and scampering around a rocky New England summit, and who play the piano too. I live with a wife, the two incessantly squabbling goats, a cat, two rats, and a guinea pig, in a ninety-six-year old house in Brooklyn. In the backyard grow quite acceptable grapes and witch hazels that bloom in mid-winter. I've published half a dozen tax fairy tales including "Little Blue Riding Hood" and a primer on financial derivatives, "The Three Little Pigs." I've achieved my lifelong ambition of working for the world's largest accounting firm. And I've wasted countless hours justifying what any of this has to do with a Harvard biochemistry degree.

HOME: Brooklyn, NY   **OCCUPATION:** Vice President; General Counsel. The Diversified Group, Inc.   **BIRTHPLACE:** Jamaica, NY   **SECONDARY SCHOOL:** Forest Hills High School, Forest Hills, NY   **YEARS AT COLLEGE:** 1971–75   **DEGREES:** A.B., cum laude, '75; J.D., Columbia '79; LL.M., New York Univ. '82   **SPOUSE/PARTNER:** Sarah Laidlaw, Jan. 29, 1984 (Univ. of California, Santa Barbara '75)   **SPOUSE'S OCCUPATION:** Fabric Artist   **CHILDREN:** Yael Zahava, 1986; Chana Aliza, 1989   **COLLEGE ACTIVITIES:** Hillel Society, 1971–75

Barbara Backman Treacy: Well, the accumulation of activities and responsibilities over the past twenty-five years have resulted in a situation where I find it hard to find the time to "reflect," but I welcome this opportunity. In fact, I am really looking forward to the Twenty-fifth Reunion, as I absolutely enjoyed reuniting with classmates I had lost touch with at the Twentieth Reunion.

I had no idea when I graduated where I would be, what I would be doing or who I would be living with, though I suppose it is not entirely unpredictable that I would end up with a husband who I have been married to for over twenty years, three kids, one of whom is a junior at Harvard, a house in a city close to Boston, and a job or two.

Being married and a mother shortly after graduation, I happened into an ideal part-time job teaching basic math to underprepared students at UMass. This turned into a career in education that I stuck with as I raised my children. Several years ago, in part through my involvement as a parent in the local public schools in Peabody, I became fascinated by the potential of technology to impact and improve education, and I found myself applying for a master's degree at the Harvard Ed School in technology in education. I absolutely loved being a student after twenty or more years, and with some new skills, energy, and credentials, I am continuing to teach at UMass while also pursuing opportunities to help schools and teachers learn to use technology in education wisely.

I am looking forward to the Reunion in June! Of course, as usual, we will be juggling attending Reunion activities with making plans for the high school graduation of one of our daughters, which is also scheduled for that weekend.

HOME: Peabody, MA   **OCCUPATION:** Math Instructor. University of Massachusetts; Technology Professional Development Consultant. Boston and Education Development Center (EDC)   **BIRTHPLACE:** Boston, MA   **SECONDARY SCHOOL:** Brookline High School, Brookline, MA   **YEARS AT COLLEGE:** 1971–74   **DEGREES:** A.B., cum laude, '75 ('74); Ed.M. '98   **SPOUSE/PARTNER:** Robert Treacy, Sept. 17, 1978 (Boston Univ.; M.S., ibid.)   **SPOUSE'S OCCUPATION:** Computer Consultant   **CHILDREN:** Erin, 1979; Rebecca, 1982; Denise, 1989   **HARVARD/RADCLIFFE CHILDREN:** Erin Treacy '01
HARVARD/RADCLIFFE SIBLINGS: Steven Backman '72   **COLLEGE ACTIVITIES:** E4A, Phillips Brooks House.

Arthur Chien-Chung Tung: "He Is Like a Refiner's Fire." Twenty-five years ago, rather than submitting these reflections the day before they were due, I would have asked for an extension.

Like most of us, I suppose, I am not only changed, but chastened. But the God of the Lord Jesus Christ has only continued the good work He began while I was at Harvard—where, against some of the odds, I found not only friends, but Him. I am grateful to my Harvard and Park Street Church friends, Yan Chow, Marti Li, Steve Chow, Ingrid Liu, Toby Holleman, David Coleman, Dan Greene, Bo Wood, Jan Porcino; Pastor Dave Steele and Barb Steele; to buddies (Tag Murphy comes to mind) in the Glee Club and in Dunster House—to all, for persisting in getting to know me, who didn't know myself very well at all.

The church speaks of the process of "spiritual formation." That formation continued after Harvard in New York—where, nominally, I went to law school at Columbia; but more significantly, I deepened my view of life as ministry at Broadway Presbyterian Church. Again, friends put up with me, as I insisted on being a sixties fundamentalist—opening a community law practice on the Upper West Side (in a building where my office was flanked by a cleaning service on one side and an incense dealer on the other, and sat above a Spanish movie theater). Finally, I went to seminary.

Being a fundamentalist is the only way to go, because only thus can the ideals that brought some of us to Harvard retain their power to remind us that they are bigger than we are.

Being married does the same thing. Shirley has sustained me during that semi-disastrous first pastorate in Chapel Hill, North Carolina—as, I must confess, I have failed to sustain her during these last eleven and a half years in Upper Darby, Pennsylvania, an inner-ring suburb where people aren't much impressed by where I went to college.

HOME: Upper Darby, PA   OCCUPATION: Pastor. Calvary Presbyterian Church
BIRTHPLACE: New Haven, CT   SECONDARY SCHOOL: St. Paul's School, Concord, NH
YEARS AT COLLEGE: 1971–75   DEGREES: A.B., cum laude, '75; J.D., Columbia '78; M.Div.,
Union Theological Seminary '85   SPOUSE/PARTNER: Shirley Malone, Oct. 17, 1981
(Wichita State Univ. '78)   SPOUSE'S OCCUPATION: Staff Therapist. Life Counseling
Service   CHILDREN: Catherine, 1984; Elizabeth, 1986   HARVARD/RADCLIFFE
SIBLINGS: Paul Chien-Wen Tung '77; James Chien-Ping Tung '81   COLLEGE ACTIVITIES:
Glee Club, 1971–74; Park Street Church Seekers Ministry, 1974–75

Claude M. Tusk: I was always young—youngest kid in my high school class, one of the youngest people in my college and law school classes, youngest lawyer in my firm "class"—so how can it be twenty-five (actually twenty-six) years since I got out of college? If that's true, then by definition I am no longer young.

What really makes me feel old is reading about how conservative attitudes have largely driven liberal ones out of political discourse, and listening to my friends and family explain how growing more conservative is a natural and proper part of maturing. Back in the early 1970s, I was positive that my generation had forever banished the backward views of Goldwater and his ilk, and that Nixon was an aberration. To see and hear on a regular basis the antics of politicians who make Goldwater and Nixon look like "radiclibs" makes me feel like a dinosaur.

At work—which is a wide-ranging litigation practice covering almost every aspect of the law—keeping up with new developments and trying not to fall too far behind the cutting edge helps soothe the feelings of growing obsolescence caused, *inter alia,* by realizing that there are practicing lawyers who had not yet been born when I was graduated from Harvard.

But what really helps is my family: my beloved wife of just over twenty years who is a pinch younger than I and keeps assuring me that I can't be old because she sure isn't; my older boy, who at fourteen is a junior in high school, thinking of maybe trying to come to Harvard, and giving me every opportunity to exercise those calculus and European history muscles I haven't used for twenty-five years; and my younger boy, the seven-year-old, who thinks and acts as if his daddy has all the energy of his friends' thirty-something parents.

I've always loved to read and to travel, and I do a lot of both. Now I even collect rare and antique books (both genuine and facsimile), and spend many happy hours fondling my latest acquisitions. I close by repeating my complaint from previous editions of this Report: I still haven't figured out how to be an ex-president of the U.S. without ever being president. Best to all!

HOME: Briarcliff Manor, NY   **OCCUPATION:** Partner. Swidler, Berlin, Shereff, Friedman, LLP (law firm)   **BIRTHPLACE:** New York, NY   **SECONDARY SCHOOL:** Horace Mann School, Bronx, NY   **YEARS AT COLLEGE:** 1971–74   **DEGREES:** A.B., magna cum laude, '74 ('75); J.D. '77   **SPOUSE/PARTNER:** Joyce M. Perlmutter, May 27, 1979 (Barnard Coll. '77; Columbia '80)   **SPOUSE'S OCCUPATION:** Lawyer (taking time out to raise children)   **CHILDREN:** Warren Meyer Perlmutter Tusk, 1985; Elliot Franklin Perlmutter Tusk, 1992

Kenneth L. Tyler: Following graduation, I went on to Johns Hopkins for medical school before returning home (Boston) for my residency in internal medicine at the Brigham and then in neurology at Massachusetts General Hospital. While at the Brigham I met my future wife, Lisa Tyler. We are coming up to our twentieth anniversary, and have two wonderful children, Max and Eric. Marrying Lisa clearly rates as my most significant accomplishment since graduation! After training I stayed at Harvard until 1991 working in the research quadrangle on Longwood Avenue. Since 1991 I have been a member of the neurology department at the University of Colorado in Denver (currently the vice chairman). We've all enjoyed the quality of life here — I particularly enjoy the chance to go fly-fishing on trophy-level streams a few hours from home. The boys enjoy skiing/snowboarding and we all enjoy the chance to camp.

HOME: Denver, CO   OCCUPATION: Vice Chairman; Professor of Neurology. Health Science Center, University of Colorado   BIRTHPLACE: Boston, MA   SECONDARY SCHOOL: Noble and Greenough School, Dedham, MA   YEARS AT COLLEGE: 1971 74 DEGREES: A.B., magna cum laude, '75 ('74); M.D., Johns Hopkins Univ. '78 SPOUSE/PARTNER: Lisa Johnson, 1979 (Univ. of Massachusetts, Amherst; M.S., Boston Univ.)   SPOUSE'S OCCUPATION: Art Dealer (vintage posters)   CHILDREN: Maxwell Johnson Tyler, 1985; Eric Johnson Tyler, 1987   COLLEGE ACTIVITIES: Spee Club; Hasty Pudding

---

Alexandra Steven Tyng: I had always wanted to be an artist, but my college experience left me without a clear idea of how to pursue that goal. Because I was not sure how art could become a full-time income-producing career, I seriously considered becoming a Jungian psychologist. I was working on the requisite fifty hours of analysis and I completed a graduate degree in counseling psychology (disappointing), then decided I really must follow my "calling" and focus on art. Since I had been continuing to paint all along, the decision was easy, but I had to discover how to earn a living doing what I loved.

The effort has been long and frustrating, but ultimately rewarding. In the last five or six years, my career has really taken off. I have painted portraits of many distinguished and "regular" people — all of them unique and interesting. The process of figuring out the particular look and nuance that is expressive of each individual is, for me, a kind of visual psychology. I'm not really sure how I capture that essence, but I love doing it. I also paint landscapes and buildings — interior and exterior views — and I show these paintings at the Fischbach Gallery in New York.

My husband Steve has been wonderfully supporting and loving. We have two children, Becca and Julian. They are creative, smart, strong-willed, and we feel very lucky to have them. We live in a modest-sized Victorian house that is half-fixed-up and probably won't be completely done until the kids are out of college. How I long for a nice kitchen!

In the summers we spend some time in Maine (where I get the material for lots of my paintings), and we occasionally travel to the West Coast to visit Steve's family. We try to find some time to do volunteer work for our community. A few years ago, I was part of a group of women who designed and made a centennial quilt for the town of Narberth. Steve and I also volunteer our time and talents at our children's schools. It's a busy life, especially since Steve went back to school to complete a degree in biology, but we feel blessed with health, happiness, and wonderful family and friends.

HOME: Narberth, PA **OCCUPATION:** Self-Employed Artist **BIRTHPLACE:** Rome, Italy **SECONDARY SCHOOL:** Friends Select School, Philadelphia, PA **YEARS AT COLLEGE:** 1971–75 **DEGREES:** A.B., magna cum laude, '75; M.S., Univ. of Pennsylvania '77 **SPOUSE/PARTNER:** Steven Brian Kantor, Nov. 26, 1983 (Long Beach City Coll.; St. Joseph's Univ.) **SPOUSE'S OCCUPATION:** Nuclear Medicine Technologist. Dept. of Gastroenterology, Temple University **CHILDREN:** Rebecca Tyng Kantor, 1985; Julian Somes Kantor, 1988 **COLLEGE ACTIVITIES:** Chorus, 1971–72

Lea Beth Vaughn: I transferred (happily) to Princeton University, from which I graduated in 1975 with a major in philosophy. I was fortunate, while at Princeton, to have the guidance and friendship of Mary I. Bunting (for whom I worked one summer) and Adele Simmons, both of whom continued my connection to Radcliffe. After law school, I practiced law for two years, representing unions. In 1984, I was fortunate to return to Seattle and began teaching at the University of Washington. This August, I will assume the duties of secretary of the faculty which will include issues of faculty and university governance, faculty grievance procedures, and oversight of the faculty code.

In the intervening twenty-five years, I have often wondered what has become of friends I made in Whitman and South House. Although I will be "going back" to Princeton for reunions, I hope to get up to Cambridge. I still love children's books and poetry but also, now, garden and play piano. My children are a great source of delight. Although I am a lawyer, I am deeply committed to humane ways to resolve conflict.

HOME: Seattle, WA   OCCUPATION: Professor of Law; Secretary of the Faculty. University of Washington Law School   BIRTHPLACE: Seattle, WA   SECONDARY SCHOOL: Roosevelt High School, Seattle, WA   YEARS AT COLLEGE: 1971-72 DEGREES: J.D., Univ. of Michigan '78   SPOUSE/PARTNER: J. Patrick Dobel, June 3, 1978 (Boston Coll. '70; Ph.D., Princeton '76)   SPOUSE'S OCCUPATION: Associate Dean; Professor. Evans School of Public Affairs, University of Washington   CHILDREN: Hilary Vaughn Dobel, 1986; Matthew Patrick Dobel, 1988   COLLEGE ACTIVITIES: Sailing instructor; vice president, South House

---

Gary C. Vitale: The Lord has blessed me with a very special wife and four great children. I am happy with my work as an educator and surgeon.

HOME: Louisville, KY   OCCUPATION: Professor of Surgery. University of Louisville School of Medicine   YEARS AT COLLEGE: 1971–75   DEGREES: A.B., magna cum laude, '75; M.D., Yale '79   SPOUSE/PARTNER: Melodie A. Borkholder, Sept. 3, 1983 CHILDREN: David Scott, 1984; Emily Anne, 1986; Rebecca Joy, 1988; Mark Andrew, 1990

Lois Benes Voelz: Our first year at Harvard some female classmates advised me to break my engagement and focus on my career instead. After twenty-six years of marriage to my high school sweetheart, I know I made the right choice. In 1975, we returned to Wisconsin, later moved to Texas, and now live on the "Left Coast" and work in Silicon Valley. Everything worked out fine.

When the big family we dreamed of did not materialize, I plunged into the big career instead. Then at about the last moment possible (age forty-two), we were blessed with a daughter. We may be too old to be parents, but at least we can raise her with the perspective and wisdom (I hope) of middle age. Plus, secure careers permit us to give her the long hours that struggling young parents cannot afford. Each of us has spent two years as the primary care-giver, working from home and very part-time. We enjoy the job of teaching her how to be a good human being in this world. Aside from parenthood at last, I am happy that since college I have returned to the active practice of my Catholic faith.

My retirement goal will be to read all of the books I missed on my college reading lists, and just maybe some others too.

HOME: San Francisco, CA   **OCCUPATION:** Partner. Cooley and Godward LLP (law firm)
BIRTHPLACE: Milwaukee, WI   **SECONDARY SCHOOL:** Custer High School, Milwaukee,
WI   **YEARS AT COLLEGE:** 1971–75   **DEGREES:** A.B., cum laude, '75; J.D., Univ. of
California, Berkeley '87   **SPOUSE/PARTNER:** Joel Voelz, Aug. 4, 1973 (Massachusetts
Inst. of Technology '75; M.B.A., Univ. of Chicago '78)   **SPOUSE'S OCCUPATION:** Self-
Employed Software Manager   **CHILDREN:** Joule, 1995

Eric H. Wachtel: University administrator, active member of the
Jewish community, avid sports fan, participant in many Chicago winters.

HOME: Chicago, IL   **OCCUPATION:** Assistant Budget Director. Office of Budget and
Planning, Northwestern University   **BIRTHPLACE:** New York, NY   **SECONDARY
SCHOOL:** Horace Mann School, Riverdale, NY   **YEARS AT COLLEGE:** 1972–75
DEGREES: A.B., cum laude, '75; M.B.A., Northwestern Univ. '82

Richard Ramsey Waite: I hope I haven't peaked, I thought to
myself that sad, rainy graduation day twenty-five years ago. Or had I peaked
four years before when I received my Harvard acceptance in the mail?

I'm still married to my beautiful wife of fifteen years, Jeanne. Got a lucky
break on a blind date arranged by Jeanne's sister Marianne. Our two lovely
and spirited daughters, Catherine and Julianne, bring incredible richness to
our lives. I'm still practicing law with the same wonderful partner I've had
for twenty years, Ludlow Keeney, (a.k.a., Mr. Big) and our younger, also talented partner, Todd Stevens.

As I look back, I realize how it's the little things, the unusual and the
unexpected, that mean so much. I've made my living as a business and real
estate lawyer, but the most gratifying work I've done is representing kids
who've suffered serious personal injuries from foodborne illnesses. I've traveled to exotic places, but nothing compares to waking up with my family in
a tent in the wilderness next to a rushing river or camping on the beach with
one of my lovely daughters on an Indian Princess outing. I've been cheered
on the gridiron in Harvard Stadium, but I get more excited watching one of
my girls score a goal or make a good run down the soccer field.

I learned to surf after I turned thirty and I still get out once or twice a
week. Last week I was out three days in a row on waves that were way over-

head. It wasn't pretty but I made those waves — the speed, power, and exhilaration were, yes, awesome. Last year I broke a board that still sits proudly — in two pieces — in my backyard.

I'm blessed with loving family and friends and supportive colleagues. I'm working too hard and I realize that there are indeed some things I will never accomplish, like write, direct, and star in a classic surf flick. But at least I get out to my Eleventh Street beach break each week. And I did learn to snowboard a few years back.

I hope I haven't peaked, I think to myself. Not yet.

HOME: San Diego, CA   **OCCUPATION:** Attorney; Managing Partner. Keeney, Waite & Stevens   **BIRTHPLACE:** Eugene, OR   **SECONDARY SCHOOL:** Lawrence High School, Lawrenceville, NJ   **YEARS AT COLLEGE:** 1971–75   **DEGREES:** A.B., cum laude, '75; J.D., Univ. of San Diego '81   **SPOUSE/PARTNER:** Jeanne C., Feb. 18, 1984 (Univ. of California, San Diego '73)   **SPOUSE'S OCCUPATION:** Member. Board of Trustees, Del Mar Union School District   **CHILDREN:** Catherine, 1986; Julianne, 1989   **COLLEGE ACTIVITIES:** Phillips Brooks House; freshman football; research, Office of Instructional Research and Evaluation; executive chef, Eliot House Grill; proctor and freshman advisor, 8 Prescott St., 1976

Gary Bruce Walls: The biggest development in our life over the last five years has been the birth of our daughter, Liberty. I was surprised that it was possible for me to fall in love again, but Liberty showed me I could. Francie is doing her clinical psychology internship this year, showing an incredible amount of energy and resourcefulness in being a mother, a student, a psychologist, an occupational therapist, and a wife, in whatever order the situation demands. We had a great trip to the beautiful wilderness of western Montana last summer — Libby saw her first mountains, her first rivers, and her first horses. And we also had a great visit last fall from classmates Dale and Mercy (Padrino) Anderson and their marvelous kids, Daniel and Charlie. I am still practicing psychotherapy, and now also in training as a candidate in psychoanalysis. And while I thought we were supposed to grow more conservative with age, I find myself more and more alarmed by the excesses and cruelties of capitalism, and more and more committed to pursuing radical solutions to the misery of the many caused by the fecklessness of the few. Fortunately, I find my involvement in health care activism as well as psychoanalytic work to be enlivening and fulfilling, rather than dispiriting. I still feel my life to be shaped and enriched by the values imparted to me by our Harvard experience, as trite as that may sound, and I very much look forward to seeing old friends this coming June.

HOME: Chicago, IL   **OCCUPATION:** Clinical Pychologist   **BIRTHPLACE:** Wilmington, DE   **SECONDARY SCHOOL:** Wayland High School   **YEARS AT COLLEGE:** 1971–76   **DEGREES:** A.B., cum laude, '75 ('76); M.A., Miami Univ. of Ohio '87; Ph.D., ibid. '87   **SPOUSE/PARTNER:** Frances K., March 1, 1992 (Univ. of Wisconsin '87; M.A., Chicago School of Professional Psychology '99)   **SPOUSE'S OCCUPATION:** Psychologist. Northwestern Memorial Hospital   **CHILDREN:** Liberty Miriam, 1997   **COLLEGE ACTIVITIES:** Junior varsity wrestling, 1972

Alan Neil Walter: Oy!!!!! Aieee!!!! Oh!!! Ah!! Ha!

HOME: Montclair, NJ   **OCCUPATION:** Vice President; New York State Counsel. Near North National Title of New York   **BIRTHPLACE:** Brooklyn, NY   **SECONDARY SCHOOL:** Herricks Senior High School, New Hyde Park, NY   **YEARS AT COLLEGE:** 1971–75   **DEGREES:** A.B., cum laude, '75; J.D., New York Univ. '78   **SPOUSE/PARTNER:** Tern Benson, June 28, 1981 (Univ. of Minnesota '76)   **SPOUSE'S OCCUPATION:** Architect   **CHILDREN:** Shoshana Eve, 1985; Arielle Helena, 1989 **HARVARD/RADCLIFFE SIBLINGS:** Elisse B. Walter, J.D. '74; Ronald Stern, J.D. '74

Robert H. Waters, Jr.: Since leaving Harvard, I have journeyed to Florida, Kansas, and many other places, earning a law degree in the process. While serving a stint as a local prosecutor in Miami, Florida, fate smacked me in the head! Whether it was fate or the actual blow, I'll never know but, suffice it to say, it resulted in the second most momentous event of my life. I'm talking about meeting and marrying my wife, Zofia, of London, England. Soon thereafter, the most important milestone of my life occurred, the birth and life experience of raising our daughter Dominique, now eleven.

Taking care of these two lovely ladies and working as an assistant U.S. attorney, recently relocated north to the treasure coast, have kept me rather busy. My entire family, including the dog, cat, and bird, along with the few surviving relatives who witnessed my graduation are eagerly anticipating my Twenty-fifth Reunion. I am anxious to see and talk to my friends and classmates who were part of my Harvard experience.

HOME: Hobe Sound, FL   **OCCUPATION:** Assistant United States Attorney   **BIRTHPLACE:** Chicago, IL   **SECONDARY SCHOOL:** Bonner Springs High School, Bonner Springs, KS   **YEARS AT COLLEGE:** 1971–75   **DEGREES:** A.B. '75 ('76); J.D., Univ. of Kansas '81   **SPOUSE/PARTNER:** Zofia, Nov. 20, 1987   **CHILDREN:** Dominique, 1988   **COLLEGE ACTIVITIES:** Band; crew; intramural football

Jonathan Starr Watson: Even getting to graduation was interesting. Was at Harvard one year, dropped out one, spent two at Hampshire College, then two more at Harvard (got unfair deal on transfer credits). First job was in New York City doing computer work for criminal court system research — New York City made me depressed. Only time I lived alone. I got into health foods to control low blood sugar. Soon moved back to Boston to do systems programming — company was unpleasant though. Then I did less music, because it uses same brain parts as programming. Got a girlfriend.

Things got better when I managed clinical computing at Dana-Farber Cancer Institute, 1979–1983 — lot of nice folks there! I got married in 1981. Now I wanted to get into PCs — joined start-up Index Technology in 1983 — exciting, fun, busy. Tried math as a hobby, but it made me nervous. Company slid downhill in late 1980s. We now had two kids, working a four-day week to be with them more.

I moved to Lotus Development in 1989. Also got into yoga, started going to Kripalu Center. For the first time, in 1993, started liking going to work. I joined Unitarian-Universalist church and got back into singing and hiking. Left Lotus in 1997 and tried solo consulting, but moved to Dragon Systems in 1998. Divorced in 1999.

HOME: Belmont, MA   OCCUPATION: Software Engineering Manager. Dragon Systems (speech recognition software products)   SECONDARY SCHOOL: Horace Mann School, New York, NY   YEARS AT COLLEGE: 1969–75   DEGREES: A.B. '75   SPOUSE/PARTNER: Eileen Tell, divorced, 1999   CHILDREN: Julia, 1984; Jacob, 1988   COLLEGE ACTIVITIES: Singing songs in the Dunster courtyard (O.K., some chess team also)

Susan May Weinstein: Life after Harvard continues in a somewhat "smorgasbord" manner. I've been an art therapist; shopping center marketing director; marketing/special events consultant; organizational trainer and psychotherapist — most recently for an employee assistance firm. Either I haven't found my niche or I'm destined to sample life's many offerings. Of them, my greatest satisfaction has been derived from my marriage (in 1990) and from the birth of my daughter, Juliana (December 8, 1996).

At our last Reunion in 1995, I received a lot of support from classmates when I disclosed my desire to finally have a child. Thanks to all who listened, advised, and encouraged me. I recently resigned from my employee assistance position (part-time) so that I may enjoy motherhood without distractions! See you in June 2000.

HOME: Leverett, MA   OCCUPATION: Employee Assistance Counselor   BIRTHPLACE:
Hartford, CT   SECONDARY SCHOOL: Hall High School, West Hartford, CT   YEARS
AT COLLEGE: 1971–75   DEGREES: A.B. '75; M.A., Goddard Coll. '78
SPOUSE/PARTNER: Peter Cinner, Nov. 22, 1990   SPOUSE'S OCCUPATION: Dentist
CHILDREN: Juliana, 1996   STEPCHILDREN: Josh, 1972   HARVARD/RADCLIFFE
SIBLINGS: Sharon R. Weinstein '72

Peter Douglas Weiss: I began life at Harvard as an open-minded,
bright-eyed philosophy major—then drifted into anthropology, biology and
biochemistry, and of course, music...ending up somehow as a philosophical pre-med.

I graduated medical school (CWRU) and furthered my career in internal
medicine at Washington University.

Then life gets good!: I met my wife (Barbara Horn, M.D.) in a true "love
at first sight," which continues to be twenty-twenty! Two children later
(Rachel, fourteen, Nathaniel, eleven) and our life is nonstop.

I specialized in medical oncology and have found a truly challenging
field—academically, intellectually, emotionally, and spiritually. Once again,
I'm back into philosophy (medical), from whence I started.

HOME: Saint Louis, MO   OCCUPATION: Physician. Specialists in
Oncology/Hematology, PC   BIRTHPLACE: Longbranch, NJ   SECONDARY SCHOOL:
South Brunswick High School, Monmouth Junction, NJ   YEARS AT COLLEGE: 1971–75
DEGREES: A.B., cum laude, '75; M.D., Case Western Reserve Univ. '80
SPOUSE/PARTNER: Barbara A. Horn, April 25, 1982 (Clark Univ. '75; M.D., Washington
Univ. '82)   SPOUSE'S OCCUPATION: Physician. Specialists in Oncology/Hematology,
PC   CHILDREN: Rachel, 1985; Nathaniel, 1988   COLLEGE ACTIVITIES: Oboist, Harvard-
Radcliffe Orchestra; Bach Society Orchestra; Lowell House musicians; intramural sports

Joe Ramon Whatley, Jr.: How do you describe twenty-five years in three hundred words or less? The years went by much too quickly. I have been very fortunate. Starting with family: for more than twenty years, I have had a wonderful wife, Susan. We have two great sons: Beau, who will be completing his senior year in high school as we have our Twenty-fifth Reunion; and Alec, who will be finishing the seventh grade. No one goes through the teenage years without some problems, but they are doing well. Beau has no interest in going to Harvard, but will probably go to college in New York or Los Angeles. My greatest achievement was being named the first "father of the year" by the Alabama NOW chapter. In terms of my career, immediately after college, I returned to law school at the University of Alabama. I clerked for a year with the chief federal judge in north Alabama, and I have been trying lawsuits throughout the Southeast since that time. Our practice is exclusively litigation, primarily on behalf of plaintiffs, with an emphasis on class actions, other complex litigation, personal injury, civil rights, and representation of unions. We also represent the democratic side in most of the political litigation in the state. I still enjoy and feel good about what I do. Birmingham, Alabama, has become a good place to live and raise a family, but we travel a great deal, especially to New York so that we can keep up with how most of the rest of you folks are living.

The best thing that I can say about the past twenty-five years is that if I had to do it over again, I would not change very much, but I sure would like to do it again.

HOME: Birmingham, AL   OCCUPATION: Attorney. Whatley & Drake, LLC
BIRTHPLACE: Selma, AL   SECONDARY SCHOOL: Monroe County High School, Monroeville, AL   YEARS AT COLLEGE: 1971–75   DEGREES: A.B., cum laude, '75; J.D., Univ. of Alabama '78   SPOUSE/PARTNER: Susan Colvin, Dec. 30, 1978 (Univ. of Alabama '79)   SPOUSE'S OCCUPATION: Volunteer   CHILDREN: Braxton Beauregarde, 1982; Charles Alexander, 1986   COLLEGE ACTIVITIES: Getting to know other students was probably most important, otherwise, rugby; Kennedy Institute of Politics; and Philips Brooks House

Daniel R. White: The bad news: Waited till I was thirty-nine to get married.

The good news: The wait was worth it. In any event, it's not as if I had any choice. Commitment phobia dies hard.

The bad news: Delay in getting married didn't allow much time to sit around just being married, before going for kids.

The good news: Ally, our five-year-old, curly-haired wonder, takes her parents' love as her due — which is as it is and should be.

The bad news: Spent two years, eleven months, and four days practicing law.

The good news: Made some lasting friendships. Actually enjoyed law school. Also, picked up loads of good comic material.

The bad news: Now live in Dallas. (We take summer vacations in hell, for the cooler climate.) My wife got a job offer here she couldn't refuse.

The good news: We have a nice house, with a yard that Ally enjoys, and she's in a good school that has a pond with ducks.

The bad news: A struggle with real, clinical depression (long before the move to Dallas).

The good news: A great shrink, modern pharmacology, and vastly enhanced understanding of self and others.

The bad news: Didn't accept a position as a screenwriting fellow at the American Film Institute in Los Angeles a number of years ago.

The good news: All I can say here is, I guess I've still got my health.

The good news: I am Mr. Mom, supported by my wife.

The better news: I am Mr. Mom, supported by my wife.

HOME: Dallas, TX   OCCUPATION: Freelance Writer; Dad   SECONDARY SCHOOL: Westminster Schools, Atlanta, GA   BIRTHPLACE: Atlanta, GA   YEARS AT COLLEGE: 1971–75   DEGREES: A.B., magna cum laude, '75; J.D., Columbia '79
SPOUSE/PARTNER: Flory Bramnick, Oct. 10, 1992 (Yale '77)   SPOUSE'S OCCUPATION: Vice President of Business Development. Belo Interactive   CHILDREN: Alyssa, 1999
HARVARD/RADCLIFFE SIBLINGS: Benjamin T. White, J.D. '73   COLLEGE ACTIVITIES: Marching band

Jeffrey Wescott White: After Harvard, I spent six years on a Ph.D. in botany at U.C. Berkeley looking at growth of bean plants. This included a two-year return to Colombia for field work at the International Center for Tropical Agriculture (CIAT). In 1981, I moved to Lima, Peru, to work on producing potatoes from seed at the International Potato Center. I married Teresa in 1983, and we moved to Colombia for a twelve-year stint as a crop physiologist back at CIAT. We adopted twins in 1994 and liked the parenting business so much we added Mateo in 1995. Deteriorating financial conditions at CIAT and security concerns lead to a move to International Center for Maize and Wheat Improvement (CIMMYT) in Mexico, where I am currently working in Geographic Information Systems and databases for maize and wheat systems.

HOME: Mexico City, Mexico   BIRTHPLACE: Los Alamos, NM   SECONDARY SCHOOL: Los Alamos High School   YEARS AT COLLEGE: 1971–75   DEGREES: AB., magna cum laude, '75; Ph.D., Univ. of California, Berkeley '81   SPOUSE/PARTNER: Teresa Gutierrez, Jan. 21, 1983 (Univ. Agraria La Molina; M.Sc., Univ. of Florida)   SPOUSE'S OCCUPATION: Homemaker   CHILDREN: Gabriel and Teresita, 1993 (twins); Mateo, 1995 HARVARD/RADCLIFFE SIBLINGS: George N. White 3d '72

S. Thomas Wienner: My wife, Jane, and I will celebrate our twenty-fifth wedding anniversary shortly after each of our twenty-fifth college reunions. Jane received a degree in early childhood education from B.U., and then put me through law school. She recently resumed her teaching career after spending many years at home with our children.

We have a son, Adam, who is seventeen, and a daughter, Carly, who is fourteen. They attend the same high school, where Adam is a senior and Carly is a freshman. They are the greatest kids in the world.

I have specialized in civil litigation ever since graduating from law school. I started at a large law firm in Detroit, and made the difficult decision to leave after fourteen years. At that point, I joined a practice with two other lawyers who also had started at the same firm. Our new firm, where we primarily focus on commercial litigation and product liability defense work, now has nineteen lawyers.

As our Reunion approaches and my son goes through the process of applying to college, I have spent a lot of time reflecting on my own college experience. I remember with great fondness the days we spent together in Cambridge.

HOME: Bloomfield Hills, MI   OCCUPATION: Lawyer. Feeney, Kellett, Wienner & Bush, PC   BIRTHPLACE: Detroit, MI   SECONDARY SCHOOL: Seaholm High School, Birmingham, MI   YEARS AT COLLEGE: 1971–75   DEGREES: A.B., cum laude, '75; J.D., Univ. of Michigan '78   SPOUSE/PARTNER: Jane S., July 26, 1975 (Boston Univ. '75)   SPOUSE'S OCCUPATION: Teacher. Way Elementary School, Bloomfield Hills, MI   CHILDREN: Adam, 1982; Carly, 1985   COLLEGE ACTIVITIES: WHRB

Stephen John Williams: Thus far, I have maximized most effectively my undergraduate training in history in a twelve-year stint as history editor/essayist at the *City Sun,* a Brooklyn-based community weekly newspaper the content of which, at times, has had national implications. Otherwise, I have used the best of my native and acquired skills at the Scrabble crossword game board. From my leave of absence from the college (1973–74), I have been a card-carrying Scrabble player (a member in good standing of what today is known as the National Scrabble Association), playing in many sanctioned clubs and tournaments and many unofficiated head-to-head sessions. To date, I have captured the top prize in two promotional tournaments held in Manhattan, but the high point of my crossword game endeavors thus far has been my winning the New York City Tournament, then the most sought after distinction in the game, in 1977. At present, I am known universally for a defense-based style of play that can serve to baffle even an unsuspecting high-rated opponent. To support the "Scrabble Jones," I have worked at intervals as a clerk, a messenger, a "printer's devil" and a tutor. Currently, I am collecting disability insurance until I can realize a gainful career in adult education.

Sorry to say, but as a Harvard history concentrator, I was oriented in "white studies." Finally, at the *City Sun,* the managing editor, Utrice C. Leid, changed my world view perspective from eurocentric to afrocentric; to this day, I can appreciate this conversion. If I do anything more with my historiographic skills, it will be from a strictly afrocentric perspective. It has been this mindset, predictably enough, that has precipitated my tacit rejection of mainstream values in large part. In the future, I see myself traveling on the mainstream superhighway only at intervals; other times, I seek to blaze new trails in life that may lead me to pinnacles more meaningful to me than destinations reached by traveling on the beaten path. At present, I have not fathered a family, nor even taken on a significant other. The only way the latter will take place will be if the would-be significant other is expressly willing to travel the long, winding, rocky road upon which I must embark if I am to realize success I have not desired except on my own terms. Otherwise, I will remain content strictly to "go it alone."

HOME: Saint Albans, NY   OCCUPATION: Writer   BIRTHPLACE: New York, NY
SECONDARY SCHOOL: Andrew Jackson High School, Cambria Heights, NY   YEARS
AT COLLEGE: 1971–76   DEGREES: A.B. '75 ('76)   COLLEGE ACTIVITIES: WHRB news
and traffic, 1971–73; Kuumba Singers (tenor), 1972–74; Harvard-Radcliffe Afro, 1971–76;
Scrabble Club director, Rack Seven, 1974–75; Students for a Democratic Society, 1971–72

Karen Grace Wilson: As I write, I'm in the midst of several major
transitions. Ironically, pursuing the life plan I put together a quarter century
ago has brought me almost full circle to where I was in 1975 — independent,
contemplating a new career in a distant city, and full of hope and anticipation for whatever lies ahead. Like most in our generation, I expected to
"have it all," which, for me, included a family, a satisfying vocation and an
opportunity to make a meaningful contribution to society. To date, these
goals have been surprisingly elusive and I am still largely a work in progress.
Through a difficult eighteen-year marriage, a suspended financial career, and
the discovery of talent and interest in creative fields, I have come to better
understand my strengths and limitations and to appreciate and accept life's
imperfections. While effort in some areas has brought disappointment, over
the past decade I've derived tremendous satisfaction from renovating my
home in the Connecticut countryside northeast of New York City. An avid
do-it-yourselfer, along the way I've acquired knowledge and skills in architecture, site planning, the building trades and interior design and I'm exploring ways to parlay this experience into a possible new career. With the
renovation now completed and the property soon to be sold, I am planning
to relocate to a major urban center, most likely Chicago, and to rediscover
the pleasures of big-city living. Blessed with abundant energy, good health
and the wisdom of experience, I am eagerly anticipating new life directions
and the inevitable challenges that will bring opportunities for growth and
fulfillment.

HOME: New Canaan, CT   OCCUPATION: Homemaker   BIRTHPLACE: Buffalo, NY
SECONDARY SCHOOL: The Buffalo Seminary, Buffalo, NY   YEARS AT COLLEGE:
1970–75   DEGREES: A.B., cum laude, '75; M.S., New York Univ. '77; C.P.A., ibid. '79
SPOUSE/PARTNER: Brian A. P. Mooij, 1978, divorced, 1997 (Harvard '76)

James Clayton Wimberly: My views of life since graduation — has it really been twenty-five years? — are shaped by my marriage to a wonderful person. Peggy has taught me to give of myself, to be a compassionate person, and to realize that together we are truly one. We are very proud of our three children and all of their accomplishments. Most of all, we pray that they continue to trust in God for their inspiration.

I am a telecommunications instructor, traveling to my business on a weekly basis. I have enjoyed trying to bring some insight to my students, many of whom have been professional programmers and analysts for years. It is a pleasure to see them grasp some concept, or understand why they do what they do to insure that the world's information systems operate smoothly and efficiently. To my customers, Y2K is just one of our daily challenges!

On those occasions when I can stay at home we are involved with our church and missions, as well as our extended families. Our faith has sustained us through many trials, and our Christian service is a source of much of our happiness.

HOME: Randallstown, MD   **OCCUPATION:** Network Consultant. WNC Consulting (telecommunications education)   **BIRTHPLACE:** Tulsa, OK   **SECONDARY SCHOOL:** South Kent School, South Kent, CT   **YEARS AT COLLEGE:** 1971–76   **DEGREES:** A.B. '75 ('76)   **SPOUSE/PARTNER:** Peggy Ann (Virginia State Univ. '75; M.Ed., Univ. of North Carolina, Greensboro '81)   **SPOUSE'S OCCUPATION:** Teacher (learning-disabled children)   **CHILDREN:** Aia, 1975; Langston, 1989; Sydnee, 1992

Michael Martin Wiseman: Since leaving Cambridge, I have practiced law at Sullivan & Cromwell in New York, focusing on financial institutions. My practice has been fairly varied — capital markets, regulatory, legislative, mergers and acquisitions, joint ventures, and white collar work. The virtue and challenge of my practice is that, as I arrive each morning, there is considerable uncertainty as to what I will end up doing that day. Most importantly, I married Helen Garten. We live in Connecticut with both a suburban home and a "farm" in the Litchfield hills. We have become quite active in environmental issues in northwestern Connecticut. My great escape, however, remains being under sail. Helen and I have cruised most of New England waters, and began our marriage with a honeymoon in a nor'easter.

HOME: Westport, CT   OCCUPATION: Attorney; Partner. Sullivan & Cromwell
BIRTHPLACE: New York, NY   SECONDARY SCHOOL: Fairfield Coll. Preparatory
School   YEARS AT COLLEGE: 1971–75   DEGREES: A.B., magna cum laude, '75; J.D. '78
SPOUSE/PARTNER: Helen Ann Garten (Princeton '75; J.D., Harvard '78)   SPOUSE'S
OCCUPATION: Professor. Rutgers Law School, Newark, NJ

James B. Witkin: My life, like the lives of most people I know, revolves around work and family. At work, I am a lawyer focusing on issues at the intersection of environmental and real estate law; at home, I am dad to Danny (nine) and Matthew (six), and husband to Nancy, who is an attorney with the Justice Department, enforcing environmental laws.

For the past two decades, I have practiced commercial real estate law, focusing on environmentally challenged properties. Many of the transactions I work on involve "brownfields," former industrial or commercial sites that are being cleaned up. I enjoy the mixture of law, policy, and environmental science, a bit ironic for someone who fulfilled his natural science requirement with the softest course imaginable.

I still write, but for a more narrow audience than at the *Harvard Crimson*, or *Let's Go* — my writing is primarily for attorneys. The second edition of a book I edited, *Environmental Aspects of Real Estate Transactions*, was just published by the American Bar Association.

At home, in Takoma Park, a closed-in suburb of D.C., Nancy and I are constantly amazed and challenged by our two boys. How did I end up with sons who are good at sports? I'm grateful to them and to Nancy for the joys of family life, especially in the midst of these hectic times.

HOME: Takoma Park, MD   OCCUPATION: Partner. Linowes & Blocher (law firm)
BIRTHPLACE: Philadelphia, PA   SECONDARY SCHOOL: Germantown Friends School,
Philadelphia, PA   YEARS AT COLLEGE: 1971–76   DEGREES: A.B., cum laude, '75 ('76);
M.Sc., Univ. of London '77; J.D., Harvard '80   SPOUSE/PARTNER: Nancy A. Flickinger,
Nov. 19, 1988 (Swarthmore Coll. '77; J.D., New York Univ. '81)   SPOUSE'S OCCUPATION:
Attorney. U.S. Dept. of Justice, Washington, DC   CHILDREN: Daniel Zachary, 1990;
Matthew Jonathan, 1993

Edward Pearce Wobber: I spent the better part of last weekend in a referee suit, chasing young people around a soccer pitch. How much has changed in the twenty-five years since my days at Harvard!

California sunshine has replaced the rain and snow of Boston. I now curse the Giants rather than the Red Sox when they blow a lead in the ninth. I spend more time on the soccer field than the bridge table. Brahms and Chopin are now better represented in my music library than the Grateful Dead. My piano gets frequent attention, while my guitar gathers dust. The cupboard now holds porcini mushrooms and truffle oil rather than Kraft Macaroni and Cheese.

However, in all this change, some things remain constant. My wife and lifelong companion, Linda DeMelis (Radcliffe '75), remains as young and as vibrant as she was in Currier House. Our joint love of travel has given us, and we hope will continue to give us, memories that can't be adequately captured in a photo album. Our daughter Tory has grown from a brash and assertive infant into a strong, confident, and radiant teenager, eager to get on with the challenges of life. Last, but not least, the search for understanding is still as compelling as it was when we sat around the Currier dining room sketching ill-formed theories on napkins. Although computer science has changed dramatically over the last two decades, it remains a stimulating and challenging profession. After all, I'm paid to play with computers!

I have a loving family, a fun job, a home in the most beautiful place on earth, and a daughter who seems destined to exceed her parents in every possible dimension. This must be the definition of happiness.

HOME: Menlo Park, CA   **OCCUPATION:** Computer Scientist. Compaq Systems Research Center   **BIRTHPLACE:** New York, NY   **SECONDARY SCHOOL:** The Lawrenceville School, Lawrenceville, NJ   **YEARS AT COLLEGE:** 1971–75   **DEGREES:** A.B. '75   **SPOUSE/PARTNER:** Linda Marie DeMelis, Sept. 24, 1977 (Radcliffe '75)   **SPOUSE'S OCCUPATION:** Attorney. Venture Law Group   **CHILDREN:** Victoria Elizabeth, 1983   **COLLEGE ACTIVITIES:** Bridge Club

Anthony F. Wolf: Happily married to the same woman for fifteen years. Our daughters are both in graduate school. The oldest is finishing her Ph.D. in government at SUNY, Stony Brook. The youngest is finishing a masters in education prior to returning to teaching and is getting married in March. Our spare time at home is taken up with gardening; enjoying the fine Texas weather, hopefully at the pool; and meeting the demands of our large brood of dog and cat companions. We vacation a lot and just returned from a week on a houseboat on Lake Powell.

I've been doing strategy consulting and corporate turnarounds for the past several years, primarily in oil and gas, aerospace, computers and software, and telecommunications. Three of us formed Wolf & Wolfe several years ago to try to build a brand name and grow beyond the limitations and egocentrism so common to one-man practices. We've done well for our clients, ourselves, and still remain friends and partners.

Recently became a Freemason and find the fraternity and work stimulating and a reinvigorating moral work in process. Still remain friends with my college roommate David Harris. Looking forward to the Reunion of 2000 — it will also be my father's Fiftieth Reunion.

HOME: Arlington, TX   **OCCUPATION:** Managing Director. Wolf & Wolfe LLP (consultants)   **BIRTHPLACE:** New Rochelle, NY   **SECONDARY SCHOOL:** Sonora High School, La Habra, CA   **YEARS AT COLLEGE:** 1971–76   **DEGREES:** A.B., magna cum laude, '75 ('76); M.B.A., Univ. of Chicago '81; M.A., Univ. of Southern California '77
SPOUSE/PARTNER: Paula Catherine, Nov. 30, 1984   **CHILDREN:** Julie Anne Lazarus; Ellen Lee Lazarus   **COLLEGE ACTIVITIES:** None seem that significant in hindsight

Dorming Wong: After being kicked out of Harvard with a magna in bio-chemistry, I sojourned to Baltimore, where I was to meet some of Karl Popper's followers at Johns Hopkins Medical School. I was all set to join the brotherhood of neuroscientists, when through some incredible shortcoming on my part I forfeited what others have described as a brilliant career in molecular neuropsychiatry. I bitterly accept exile to UCLA, where, while cursing the fates, I find my wife slogging out an internship in a dingy emergency room in some dingy county hospital where UCLA farms out its residents. I was so smitten that I wound up doing her scut work so that she could finish her day's work early enough to date me.

For those of you who don't know her, my wife, Kathleen Beatrice Sullivan, Harvard Class of 1976, was on the first Radcliffe crew in 1971, which was also the first U.S. women's crew. On one of our first trips together, my hips give out on me halfway up the Benson plateau on the Columbia Gorge. My then-girlfriend not only carries my pack to the bivouac site, but also comes back and carries me up too. I made up my mind then that this was the woman for me. Some time later, while we were sheltering from a freak summer snowstorm in a cabin by Jenny Lake in Wyoming, I propose to her while reading *Moby Dick,* with our counterpane all tucked up around us. We get married in a Park Avenue church with some twenty or thirty Harvard and Radcliffe friends in attendance as well as about three hundred Chinese. A week later, we get married again, by the episcopal bishop of Portland, Oregon, in his cathedral church.

During this time, we were sequentially training in anesthesiology at Stanford and UCLA. Stanford and UCLA have been like second families to us, and for that I am grateful. Both my wife and I tried research for a while, but we gave it up and never looked back. We finished our stints as assistant professors of anesthesiology at UCLA and moved to Orange County.

We entered private practice just as the HMO wars started to get into high gear in southern California. The group which we helped form spent the next decade fighting what seemed to be an interminable series of skirmishes and battles. Our group is now maybe the fourth or fifth largest single specialty group in southern California, allied to an even larger network of providers. I am not sure that we have accomplished anything other than size and survival.

My marriage has blessed me with four wonderful children. I am extremely lucky in that they are all gifted in some way. I hold forth nightly on quantum mechanics, music theory, and military history. I inflict cuisine on them every chance I get. My thirteen-year-old says that having tasted Brie de Meaux, all other cheeses taste somewhat insipid. My wife, the jock, insists that everybody know how to trot, butterfly, and hockey-stop. Somehow, my children are still smiling, and say, at least, that they still love me.

It is funny how life turns out. You learn to make do and to do the best you can. I have learned to stop cursing the fates, and to look towards the future.

HOME: Laguna Hills, CA   **OCCUPATION:** Consultant Anesthesiologist. California Anesthesia Associates Medical Group, Inc.   **BIRTHPLACE:** Taipa, Macao, China **SECONDARY SCHOOL:** Stuyvesant High School, New York, NY   **YEARS AT COLLEGE:** 1971–75   **DEGREES:** A.B., magna cum laude, '75; M.D., Johns Hopkins Univ. '79; M.P.H., ibid. '79   **SPOUSE/PARTNER:** Kathleen Beatrice Sullivan, Oct. 20, 1984 (Harvard '76) **SPOUSE'S OCCUPATION:** Consultant Anesthesiologist. California Anesthesia Associates Medical Group, Inc.   **CHILDREN:** Alexander Sullivan Wong, 1986; Andrew Sullivan Wong, 1989; Augusta Sullivan Wong, 1992; Adam Sullivan Wong, 1994

Edward James Woodhouse, Jr.: If I had my way, I'd still go down to Newell Boat House every day and row for Harry Parker. That hasn't changed. Most everything else has.

HOME: Apex, NC   **OCCUPATION:** Division Counsel. BASF Corp. (chemical manufacturer)   **BIRTHPLACE:** Durham, NC   **SECONDARY SCHOOL:** Kent School, Kent, CT   **YEARS AT COLLEGE:** 1971–75   **DEGREES:** A.B., magna cum laude, '75; J.D., Univ. of Virginia '78   **SPOUSE/PARTNER:** Cynthia Ellen Dodge, Nov. 28, 1980, divorced, December 1992 (Radcliffe '75); Susan Tatum Vass Gal, April 15, 1994 (Radford Univ. '80) **SPOUSE'S OCCUPATION:** Writer   **CHILDREN:** Victoria Hapeman, 1983; Edward James 3d, 1990   **COLLEGE ACTIVITIES:** Heavyweight crew, 1972–75

Anna Wu Work: Twenties. Despite graduating in 1975, the rest of my twenties were occupied completing my education and training. First stop, New Haven, where in addition to obtaining a Ph.D. in biochemistry, I met the man I was to marry. The remainder of that decade we hopscotched across the country to California, trying to coordinate postdocs, residency, and fellowships.

Thirties. Jeff and I finally both landed in the Los Angeles area and married in 1985. The decade was spent acquiring the obligatory careers (in biomedical research and cardiology), house, vehicles (this is Los Angeles, after all), assorted pets, and best of all, three children. Lizzie, the queen, brilliant splashes of pink and purple, birds, music and math interwoven. Kelsey, grounded, centered, organized and steady, and obsessed with horses. Jeremy, on one hand the typical boy (T-ball and soccer, Pokémon and chess), on the other hand, watch out, he remembers everything. Into this business, a brush with a life-threatening illness forced a long pause and a

time for reflection. Slowly at first, then faster and faster, we are in a whirl-wind of activity again, but with a more acute sense of the preciousness of ordinary events and everyday life.

Forties. We are no less busy, just the details are different. There is a hint that things are settling down; I find time to squeeze in piano lessons and Jeff takes early morning mountain bike rides. Work provides a means to meld basic science with realworld issues, and also opportunities to travel to Germany, Greece, and Australia. We find it hard to believe that twenty-five years have passed, but can't ignore the creeping gray hairs and presbyopia. Life is full, too full! But I wouldn't want it any other way.

HOME: Sherman Oaks, CA   **OCCUPATION:** Associate Research Scientist. Beckman Research Institute of the City of Hope (biomedical research)   **BIRTHPLACE:** Waynesboro, VA   **SECONDARY SCHOOL:** Waterford-Halfmoon High School, Waterford, NY   **YEARS AT COLLEGE:** 1971–75   **DEGREES:** A.B., cum laude, '75; M.Phil., Yale '77; Ph.D., ibid. '79   **SPOUSE/PARTNER:** Jeffrey William Work, May 11, 1985 (Stanford Univ. '75; M.D., Yale '79)   **SPOUSE'S OCCUPATION:** Physician. Cardiology Consultants Medical Group   **CHILDREN:** Elizabeth Anne, 1986; Kelsey Lynne, 1990; Jeremy Julian, 1993   **COLLEGE ACTIVITIES:** Harvard-Radcliffe Chorus, 1971–72; Collegium Musicum, 1972–73; Leverett House Arts Society, 1972–75

Victoria Elizabeth Wells Wulsin: Spiritually, I try to "Do the loving thing," which isn't always the right thing or the easiest thing. Intellectually, Harvard/Radcliffe authors are among my favorite: George Colt, Anne Fadiman, Lani Guinier, Nick Lemann (*The Promised Land* should be required reading for every American high school student), Mark O'Donnell, Katha Pollitt, Patricia Williams. Best book in twenty-five years: *Long Walk to Freedom,* by Nelson Mandela, a true hero.

Physically, I walk most days with Laws, a friend, or a colleague. I play tennis with Lawson or the boys occasionally.

Politically, I read more than I act. My work for the National Institute for Occupational Safety and Health (1986–89), Cincinnati Health Department (1989–95), American Red Cross (1995–98), and Cincinnati's Free Clinic (1998 to now) is a bit political, as I am ever trying to improve the health of the less powerful: the worker, the poor, the African with HIV, the homeless.

Emotionally, I was happiest during our family's residence in Kenya (1995–97). Singing, dancing, dinner parties, and e-mails from Ada (Fan), Kaffee (Kang), and Sarah (Webster Goodwin) buoy my spirits. My favorite times are being with the boys, playing charades or Ultimate, traveling/camping, or just listening to music, talking, and laughing. Wells is disciplined and guileless; Reed fearless and artistic; Stuart political and passionate; John happy and irresistible. Lawson "looks on tempests and is never shaken."

Practically, I remain a lazy (lousy?) cook; shop at Goodwill; drive the speed limit; taught myself Spanish during a period of insomnia (late 1980s); spend more money on bicycle equipment than clothing (including boots!); pay someone to grocery shop; enjoy *New York Times* crossword puzzles; have graying hair that I wash once a week (don't worry — I *shower* nightly with Laws); love the ease with which e-mail makes communicating with old friends. So write! I promise to write back.

HOME: Cincinnati, OH **OCCUPATION:** Epidemiologist. Univ. of Cincinnati
BIRTHPLACE: Elyria, OH **SECONDARY SCHOOL:** Shaw High School, East Cleveland,
OH **YEARS AT COLLEGE:** 1971–75 **DEGREES:** A.B., magna cum laude, '75; M.D., Case
Western Reserve Univ. '80; M.P.H., Harvard '82; D.P.H., ibid. '85 **SPOUSE/PARTNER:**
Lawson Reed Wulsin, July 2, 1978 (Harvard '74) **SPOUSE'S OCCUPATION:** Psychiatrist.
University of Cincinnati **CHILDREN:** H. Wells, 1979; L. Reed, Jr., 1982; Stuart C., 1983;
John C., 1986 **HARVARD/RADCLIFFE CHILDREN:** H. Wells Wulsin '01
HARVARD/RADCLIFFE SIBLINGS: Jefferson Wells '74 **COLLEGE ACTIVITIES:** Gilbert
and Sullivan Society; marching band; Phillips Brooks House; Radcliffe Union of Students

---

Geraldine A. Wyle: It can't be twenty-five years — I don't feel older — just a bit wiser, happier, and more disciplined. After my departure to UCLA to finish undergraduate and then law school, I stayed to raise my children while they were tiny. I entered the work force late, which has been a difficult but ultimately rewarding odyssey. I now spend my days being a trust and estate litigator with a great group of people, and spend my nights and weekends as wife and mom, playing as much as possible. My new husband is my greatest friend, Lauren is a sophomore studying at Brandeis while she ponders selecting her major, and Ben, who is in tenth grade, excels at Greek and Latin, as well as the sciences. He has discovered competitive outrigger canoeing in ocean-going, six-man boats, and loves it. Note to Harry Parker: he's also a life-long early riser!

HOME: Los Angeles, CA **OCCUPATION:** Attorney. Ross, Sacks & Glazier LLP
BIRTHPLACE: New York, NY **SECONDARY SCHOOL:** Andrew Warde High School,
Fairfield, CT **YEARS AT COLLEGE:** 1971–73 **DEGREES:** B.A., magna cum laude, Univ.
of California, Los Angeles '76; J.D., ibid. '79 **SPOUSE/PARTNER:** Jay Warner,
divorced, February 1994; Carl Oven, November 1995 (M.A., Otis Arts Inst. '63)
SPOUSE'S OCCUPATION: Artist **CHILDREN:** Lauren Wyle Warner, 1980; Benjamin
Wyle Warner, 1983

Robin French Wynne: In June of 1975, I was looking down Mt. Auburn Street from my Quincy House window and knew that I would soon be gone. Now, twenty-five years later, I'm anxious to look down Mt. Auburn Street again and reflect on my past twenty-five years.

After law school and a year of seminary, I moved back to my town of Fordyce, Arkansas, to carry on the family law practice (est. 1905) with my brother, Tom, Class of '69. The world view from Fordyce is quite different from the view from Boston, Dallas, or any other city that exceeds five thousand population. What happens in Fordyce rarely makes the news, except when Keith Richards of the Rolling Stones was arrested and held in the town jail in the early 1970s or when propane gas backed up into our water lines and commodes started exploding. Fordyce hasn't changed much in my lifetime. It is a secure place to raise a family.

In Fordyce everything revolves around the triangle of the home, school, and church. So naturally that is where my interests are. I met my wife, Margo, nineteen years ago when I was in seminary. Four sons and 231 Little League baseball games later, we now have a full-blown family. All of our boys are being educated in the Fordyce public schools. Margo and I are co-chairpersons of the Fordyce "Redbug" Booster Club and attend almost every athletic event that the school offers. The schools are less than one mile away or three minutes from home and office. (The golf course is five minutes from the office.) The United Methodist Church takes up the remainder of our time. Margo and I help coordinate youth activities in the church and I teach Sunday school.

Politics has always been in the Wynne blood. But after serving in the Arkansas State Legislature for four years under Governor Bill Clinton, my thirst for politics was quenched. I chose to return to the more traditional role of a family man.

My wife and I are active in everything our children do. We are committed to our community and, more often than not, find satisfaction in this way of life. There are times we yearn for more, yet hope that in the meantime, we are doing enough. Time will tell.

HOME: Fordyce, AR   OCCUPATION: Attorney; Partner. Wynne & Wynne (law firm)
BIRTHPLACE: Warren, AR   SECONDARY SCHOOL: Fordyce High School, Fordyce, AR
YEARS AT COLLEGE: 1971–75   DEGREES: A.B., cum laude, '75; J.D., Univ. of Arkansas '78
SPOUSE/PARTNER: Margaret Louise Sanders, Aug. 16, 1980 (Univ. of Arkansas)
SPOUSE'S OCCUPATION: Homemaker   CHILDREN: Robin French Wynne, Jr., 1982;
Christopher Wade Wynne, 1985; Grant Thomas Wynne, 1989; Hayden Sanders Wynne,
1993   HARVARD/RADCLIFFE SIBLINGS: Thomas D. Wynne 3d '69; Terry Frank Wynne '72
COLLEGE ACTIVITIES: Golf team, 1971–75; football, two years; president, Sigma Alpha
Epsilon fraternity; athletic director, Quincy House; member, Big Brother Association; fifth
and sixth grade Sunday school teacher, Harvard Epworth United Methodist Church

Tom Yellin: As I write this I am planning ABC News' twenty-four-hour coverage from December 31, 1999 through January 1, 2000 and sending producers and correspondents from Times Square to Timbuktu. So next June seems a long way off, but twenty-five years doesn't seem long at all.

As for me, in those twenty-five years I've been pretty lucky. I've got two great kids and a wonderful wife. I work at things I care about, my golf game is still much better than it was in college, there are lots of people in the world I really care about, and I have become respectable at Zydeco dancing (a long story there is no space for here).

So no complaints so far.

HOME: New York, NY   OCCUPATION: Executive Producer. ABC News   BIRTHPLACE: New York, NY   SECONDARY SCHOOL: White Station High School, Memphis, TN   YEARS AT COLLEGE: 1971–75   DEGREES: A.B., cum laude, '75   SPOUSE/PARTNER: Shari Finkelstein, June 15, 1998 (Harvard '87)   SPOUSE'S OCCUPATION: Producer. CBS News, *60 Minutes*   CHILDREN: Chloe, 1985; Isabel, 1987   COLLEGE ACTIVITIES: Captain, golf team, 1975

Robin Tsu-Wang Yuan: I'd have thought another quarter century of living would bring me wings of great wisdom, but only within a vastly expanded universe. Medical school, surgical residencies, a private practice of plastic surgery in Beverly Hills, an assistant clinical professorship at UCLA, ten reconstructive missions overseas performing plastic surgery on children, a beachside wedding in Jamaica, a wife of six years and now two adorable children, Ryan Christian, four, and Robyn Nicole "Nikki," ten months, along with multiple attempts at screen- and playwriting, a published book of vignettes, *Cheer Up... You're Only Half Dead (Reflections at Mid-Life)*, and a current novel in progress have taught me that I don't know half of the things I thought I knew before going to Harvard. And much more than half of the things I did learn at Harvard, I've forgotten.

I've learned that rejuvenation of the human soul, spirit, and purpose is more important than rejuvenation of the body or face, but you can earn a decent living doing the latter. Much of life is spent with my much-too-rapidly-developing kids, reliving the joys and challenges of a childhood I so quickly spent preparing for a place like Harvard, not knowing you can never quite prepare yourself for such an extraordinary environment.

I've laid down my squash racquet that I still treasure from my "glory days" at Adams House and picked up an underachieving three-wood, seen my

Bancroft tennis racquet evolve into graphite, and continued to look for time to take up my ill-tuned violin...maybe when my son learns to listen better.

I would never trade my undergraduate experience at Harvard in the 1970s for any other in the world. But I also wouldn't trade life as it has been for life as it might have been.

HOME: Beverly Hills, CA **OCCUPATION:** Plastic Surgeon (private practice)
BIRTHPLACE: Boston, MA **SECONDARY SCHOOL:** Newton High School, Newtonville, MA **YEARS AT COLLEGE:** 1971–74 **DEGREES:** A.B., cum laude, '75 ('74); M.D. '78
SPOUSE/PARTNER: Joanne Patricia, July 10, 1993 (Florida Atlantic Univ. '82; M.B.A., ibid. '84) **SPOUSE'S OCCUPATION:** Flight Attendant. Delta Airlines **CHILDREN:** Ryan Christian, 1995; Robyn Nicole, 1998 **COLLEGE ACTIVITIES:** President, Chinese Students Association; intramural squash and tennis, Adams House 1971–74; Intercollegiate Chinese Students Association, 1974

Mark Asher Zatzkis: Since graduating Harvard, I have moved to New York, Los Angeles, San Francisco, and subsequently settled in Santa Monica. I am a member of an eight-physician cardiology group (seven of my partners either went to Harvard College or to Harvard Medical School). By both living in and working in Santa Monica, I have been able to avoid some of the hassles of living in Los Angeles (such as freeway commuting), and despite the stereotypes, I drive less than four thousand miles per year.

Nevertheless, life is extremely busy. We have three children who collectively mirror the strengths and weaknesses of their parents. They are each smart and creative, but are struggling in different ways with their own life issues. Melissa and I are doing well, and I honestly regret that I haven't kept in better touch with my classmates. My recreational hobbies include running, reading, and following sports. I would to hear from some old friends.

HOME: Santa Monica, CA **OCCUPATION:** Cardiologist. Pacific Heart Institute
BIRTHPLACE: Newark, NJ **YEARS AT COLLEGE:** 1971–75 **DEGREES:** A.B., magna cum laude, '75; M.D., Columbia '79 **SPOUSE/PARTNER:** Melissa Harris, Aug. 25, 1984 (Univ. of California, Berkeley '75) **SPOUSE'S OCCUPATION:** Registered Nurse **CHILDREN:** Elliot David, 1987; Hayley Michelle, 1990; Gregory Ethan, 1994 **HARVARD/RADCLIFFE SIBLINGS:** David Zatzkis '83 **COLLEGE ACTIVITIES:** Room 13 (phone help line)

Steven Eftyhios Zeimbekakis: Life after Harvard is never the same. After acquiring higher level skills in technology and business (M.S. and M.B.A.) I set out to carve my own career path in a unique way.

First at CitiBank working for the chairman's chief of staff (John Reed) I managed to complete my entire corporate career in five years, having done all I could in finance, marketing, and management and rising to a vice president. Then continued with Kidder, Peabody and Oppenheimer in senior positions trading for the firms in options and derivatives arbitrage and equities. Continued as market maker in options, I was a wealthy private client manager at one point winning the U.S. Investment Championship in 1988. Having caught the attention of famous hedge fund manager George Soros, I became a senior fund manager for Soros Fund Management. Returned to Kidder, Peabody as a senior portfolio manager on large institutional accounts and development of new equity products in asset management.

Since 1991, I have developed my own money management business through a combination of products. A hedge fund with high growth/stable earnings companies targeting twenty-six annually (Zephyr Capital). An off-shore fund (Zephyr Hedge). A market neutral alternative investment fund (Phoenix). A broker dealer money management business and an allocation fund of funds. Also registered as a C.T.A. with business in financial commodities mostly institutional. I have evolved as a money manager seeing all aspects and trying to build something better than anything out there (risk/reward). Hoping to be the next Soros by the retirement Reunion.

On a personal basis I am close to starting a family, but have not done it yet. In our business (money management) people normally live an extra twenty-five years since they are independent, working without bosses, so I am working on that timetable. And we never retire since work is also a hobby. I have traveled extensively and sit on the board of the endowment fund for the University of Crete and am in line to be chairman. One fund is donating millions over time to publish high quality original or translated science and other college and graduate school texts in Greek.

I invested extensively in real estate during the 1980s, prior to expanding to the financial markets.

Have had the time to become a prolific reader with interests in investments, science, politics, and history. I intend to spend future years traveling and exploring the world. Growing my money management business and growing a family. Any classmates that feel like chatting about anything are encouraged to contact me.

HOME: New York, NY   **OCCUPATION:** General Partner. Zephyr Capital Partners LP (investment management)   **BIRTHPLACE:** Chania, Crete, Greece   **SECONDARY SCHOOL:** Second Gymnasium, Chania, Greece   **YEARS AT COLLEGE:** 1971–75 **DEGREES:** A.B., cum laude, '75; S.M., Harvard '76; M.S.I.A., Carnegie Mellon Univ. '77 **COLLEGE ACTIVITIES:** Soccer team, Chess Club, Greek Students Association of Harvard/MIT

Steve Zelditch: When I entered Harvard, my goal was to become a novelist. All I did in high school was read novels and write short stories. Now, twenty-five years later, I am a math professor at Johns Hopkins specializing in mathematical physics. Nothing against literature at Harvard, but the math professors and students at Harvard made such an overwhelming impression that I just had to switch. Moreover, the philosophy professors kept professing that there was no truth outside of scientific truth. That did it. The transition to math made my time at Harvard rather difficult, but I am glad I made the change. If you're curious about what I do, take a look at my page at mathnt.mat.jhu.edu/zelditch.

The other big change is that I am now married with two small children, Bennie and Phillip, who might read this one day. They and their mother, Ursula Porod, are the center of my life. Ursula is Austrian and we spend a month or two each year in Austria, in either Graz or Vienna.

We travel to a lot of other places too. So far, the kids like traveling (the streetcars of Vienna and Graz made a particularly good impression), and I hope that we will become a family of cheery globe-trotters instead of settling in to American suburbanism.

HOME: Lutherville, MD   **OCCUPATION:** Professor of Mathematics. Johns Hopkins University   **BIRTHPLACE:** Gallup, NM   **SECONDARY SCHOOL:** Gunn High School, Palo Alto, CA   **YEARS AT COLLEGE:** 1971–75   **DEGREES:** A.B., cum laude, '75; Ph.D., Univ. of California, Berkeley '81   **SPOUSE/PARTNER:** Ursula Porod (Ph.D., Johns Hopkins Univ. '94)   **CHILDREN:** Benjamin, 1996; Phillip, 1998

Andrew Caldwell Zimmermann: The primary focus of my work has been sculpture. I've been working with welded steel and bronze for about eight years now, and have exhibited large-scale outdoor sculptures at the DeCordova Museum, Chesterwood Museum, and other sculpture parks and sculpture exhibits in Massachusetts, New York, Illinois, and Pennsylvania. I've sold some pieces to museums and collectors. I've exhibited indoor works and installations in galleries in Boston, Chicago, and lots of other places, and last year I had a solo show in New York City.

This past year I've been working with photographs that I enlarge, manipulate, and distort using a computer, then have printed out in large scale. I then build these into three-dimensional sculptures with welded metal frameworks. Three of my sculptures in this series were exhibited at the Boston Science Museum as part of the first Boston CyberArts Festival.

Certainly my greatest joy is my family. My two children, Leo and Martha, turned out and continue to be bright, creative, and witty. And I am happy and lucky to still be married to the lovely and talented Rosamond Pappenheimer Zimmermann, published poet and mother extraordinaire.

I have in the last two years been acting as an alumni interviewer of students from Lexington who are applying to Harvard. I enjoy having this contact with these bright young people, and getting to have a little influence on Harvard's future. We also continue to be a host family for Harvard grad students from other countries.

I've been playing music all this time, and for the last couple of years now I've been playing electric guitar and cello with a group consisting of a poet, another guitar player, and a drummer. We play a generally raucous, spoken-word, poetry music that I enjoy enormously, and have been performing at Passim's and other clubs in Cambridge and Boston once or twice a month.

HOME: Lexington, MA   OCCUPATION: Sculptor   BIRTHPLACE: St. Paul, MN
SECONDARY SCHOOL: Morgantown High School   YEARS AT COLLEGE: 1971–76
DEGREES: A.B., cum laude, '75 ('76)   SPOUSE/PARTNER: Rosamond Pappenheimer
(Univ. of York '80)   SPOUSE'S OCCUPATION: Writer (works from home)   CHILDREN:
Leo Pappenheimer Zimmermann, 1987; Martha Pappenheimer Zimmerman, 1990
HARVARD/RADCLIFFE SIBLINGS: Bernard Zimmermann 3d '74

Peter Zurkow: Having migrated around from mergers and acquisitions lawyer to risk arbitrageur to distressed investor to venture capital/principal investor, I've most recently settled into an investment banking role focusing primarily on the explosive growth of the Internet and Web-based solutions for consumer and business communities. My many shifts in professional focus (which after a drink or two I can argue are simply variations on a theme) would probably have given me by now a severe case of vertigo, but for Erica's loving support and the constant wonder of our three small boys. At the risk of repeating myself from the Twentieth Reunion book, I'm still amazed at the adventure hidden in the simplest of daily activities and the overall feeling of getting younger every day.

HOME: Scarsdale, NY   **OCCUPATION:** Investment Banking (technology). Paine Webber, Inc.   **BIRTHPLACE:** Wilmington, DE   **SECONDARY SCHOOL:** Tatnall School, Wilmington, DE   **YEARS AT COLLEGE:** 1971–75   **DEGREES:** A.B., cum laude, '75; J.D., Syracuse Univ. '78   **SPOUSE/PARTNER:** Erica Gross, July 3, 1996 (George Washington Univ. '82)   **SPOUSE'S OCCUPATION:** Commercial Real Estate Broker. New Spectrum Realty Services, Inc.   **CHILDREN:** Benjamin Eli, 1993; Jacob Andrew, 1997; Henry Michael, 1998   **COLLEGE ACTIVITIES:** Sports: soccer, golf, rugby; Hasty Pudding Theatricals; Delphic Club

Steven C. Zweig: Thanks to the generosity of the financial aid office and my parents, I was able to attend Harvard. There I learned from people smarter than me — and discovered that nothing was impossible. When I moved back to Missouri to attend medical school, I learned about family medicine. Being a physician is a great opportunity; patients share their lives and we strive to help them. I have learned a great deal from those relationships. Family medicine led me to geriatrics which has shown me the need to fix systems of caring for older people and to improve end-of-life care. I am going to be working on these projects for a while!

My wife Susan has been a true life partner — and we have been blessed with two sons. I share a love of movies with Ben and baseball with Alex. I strive to teach them the reality of the mystical relationship, to work hard at what they love the most, and to not worry about the consequences. Our children are fortunate to have known and learned from our parents. I have wonderful friends and colleagues here in Missouri, but regret being such a poor correspondent with my former mates at Harvard. I love nothing more than standing in cold, running water casting flies to wild trout. Life is a great adventure! While I have probably learned enough stuff, I am working on gaining wisdom.

HOME: Columbia, MO   **OCCUPATION:** Professor; Associate Chair, Family and Community Medicine; Medical Director, Care in Aging. Dept. of Family and Community Medicine, School of Medicine, University of Missouri   **BIRTHPLACE:** Saint Louis, MO **SECONDARY SCHOOL:** Kirkwood High School, Kirkwood, MO   **YEARS AT COLLEGE:** 1971–75   **DEGREES:** A.B., magna cum laude, '75; M.D., Univ. of Missouri, Columbia '79; M.S.P.H., ibid. '84   **SPOUSE/PARTNER:** Susan E. Even, Jan. 2, 1982 (Cornell Univ. '74; M.D., Univ. of Missouri '80)   **SPOUSE'S OCCUPATION:** Director. Student Health Center, University of Missouri   **CHILDREN:** Benjamin F. E., 1983; Alexander P. E., 1985 **COLLEGE ACTIVITIES:** WHRB, 1971–72; *Synthesis,* the undergraduate journal for the history and philosophy of science, 1972–75

You may also enjoy from The New Press:

42 Up: "Give Me the Child Until He Is Seven and I Will Show You the Man"

Edited by Bennett Singer
Introduction by Michael Apted
PB, $16.95, 1-56584-465-3, 160 pp. with 100 black-and-white
    photographs.

A richly illustrated companion to Michael Apted's award-winning "7Up" documentary series — the longitudinal study critics have been calling "utterly fascinating," "groundbreaking," and "unparalleled"— tracks the maturation of fourteen seven-year-olds from all walks of British life, revisiting them at seven-year intervals, and chronicling their successes and failures, fears and dreams, convictions and compromises.